Malthus

MALTHUS

The Life and Legacies of an Untimely Prophet

ROBERT J. MAYHEW

The Belknap Press of
Harvard University Press

Cambridge, Massachusetts, and London, England   2014

Library of Congress Cataloging-in-Publication Data

Mayhew, Robert J. (Robert John), 1971–
Malthus : the life and legacies of an untimely prophet / Robert J. Mayhew.
  pages cm
Includes bibliographical references and index.
ISBN 978-0-674-72871-4 (alk. paper)
1. Malthus, T. R. (Thomas Robert), 1766–1834. 2. Demographers—Great
Britain—Biography. 3. Economists—Great Britain—Biography. I. Title.
HB863.M29 2014
304.6092—dc23
[B]

2013037774

For my family

Contents

Malthus

Prologue

Opening the Door on Malthus's Roller Coaster

HIDDEN BEHIND THE LEFT-HAND DOOR in the West Front to Bath Abbey lies one of those many wordy, slightly dull funereal monuments of which our ancestors were so fond. Its epitaph is hardly racy in its evocation of "one of the best of men and truest philosophers" whose qualities are said to be his "spotless integrity" and "sweetness of temper[,] urbanity of manners and tenderness of heart."[1] As a schoolboy, I must have passed this tablet on my way to my school's annual Founder's Day service, unaware of its existence because when the doors to the Abbey are open to admit visitors, it is obscured from view, hidden behind the hinges. But I doubt that these words, had I actually noticed them, would have done much to fire my youthful imagination: "native dignity of mind" and "a serene and happy life" hardly set the pulse racing.

A quarter of a century and more later, my views about this epitaph's subject and the subject of this book, Thomas Robert Malthus, are passionate. Malthus's life was indeed as plain as the tablet suggests, and we will touch on it only briefly in Chapters 3 and 5.[2] But with the passage of time I increasingly view a "serene and happy life" as a remarkable achievement at the core of social, political, and economic reasoning about "eudaemonia"—the good life—from Plato to the present. While one may enjoy reading biographies such as Rosemary Hill's marvelous account of the Gothic Revival architect Augustus Pugin, who, "by the time he was twenty-one . . . had been shipwrecked, imprisoned for debt and widowed," few readers would either want to live such a life or wish it on another.[3] Intellectually, Malthus's achievement is as momentous and the responses to his work as varied, exciting, and impassioned as was Pugin's life. These form the subject of *Malthus*, partly because of their intrinsic historical importance, but also because they seem of pressing relevance to the political, economic, and environmental context in which we find ourselves today.

In terms of achievement, Malthus not only analyzed the socioeconomic dynamics of all advanced societies up to his own age but also formulated a problem that all societies from the age of industrialization down to the present day would confront. As the Nobel Prize–winning economist Paul Krugman wrote in the *New York Times,* "Malthus was right about *the whole of human history up until his own era.*"[4] This might be dismissed as journalistic hyperbole but for the fact that it is firmly grounded in the best recent long-range analyses of global economic history by Sir Tony Wrigley, Gregory Clark, Edward Barbier, Oded Galor, and others, who discern that societies before the eighteenth century exhibited an oscillatory system of negative feedbacks in which any increase in resources led population to rise, which in turn reduced per capita income and resource availability. This would lead to smaller families and the cessation of population growth. As such, over the long run preindustrial societies saw all but static population sizes and per capita resource availability. It was this system that Malthus was the first to excavate and explain.[5] Malthus, then, did not restrictively analyze "population" as a freestanding category; on the contrary, he looked to the interconnections between population and resource levels, and to the political imperatives that managing their interconnection would generate for states and societies. The questions that Malthus posed for his own society and ours were simple. Will we hit the buffers of a negative feedback loop by too great a population growth leading to the exhaustion of available resources? If so, what sorts of policy response are demanded to stave off such an eventuality? By bringing into one analytical framework population size, resource limitations, and political response, Malthus opened up what we would now call an environmental-economic discourse whose significance only appears greater as our societies grow ever bigger and ever more resource hungry. These elements of Malthus's achievement will be canvassed in Chapters 3 and 5.

In terms of responses, one of the most passionate modern supporters of Malthus, Garrett Hardin, once wrote that "if ever someone constructs a carefully documented graph of the public attitude toward population after Malthus, it surely would look like a roller-coaster ride."[6] Whatever the truth of this assertion, it clearly applies to attitudes toward Malthus himself: Marx and the romantics despised him and attacked him with extraordinary vitriol, while Darwin and Wallace both credited him as being the friction that sparked the evolutionary match. As we shall see, each era has seen this bifurcation of responses to Malthus, a roller coaster of ups and downs, and the results have never been the dullness one might anticipate from his epitaph. In fact, wherever one turns in Anglophone intellectual history, Malthusian links are to be found.[7] It is a core contention of *Malthus,* then, that Anglophone debates about the nexus of economics, public policy, and the environment over the past two centuries cannot be properly comprehended without reference to Malthus and his interlocutors and that these debates form the context out of which present-day discussion has emerged and in which it is framed.

Finally, why return to Malthus now? Even if one admits the penetrating quality of his ideas and that they have been debated with passion for two centuries, why do we need to canvass all of this in the twenty-first century? Simply put, if Malthus staked out for modern intellectual life the first great analysis of the interconnectedness of population, environment, and the economy, current trends in each of these arenas are drawing us back to an engagement with his insights. This will be addressed in greater detail in Chapter 9, but in terms of population, the United Nations' "median" projection for global population now predicts that it will peak at around 10 billion. This has attracted a fair amount of commentary, both optimistic and pessimistic, much of it less than helpful, and all of it invoking Malthus.[8] Demography, that of both increasing and declining population sizes, remains a fundamental political and environmental issue, and concerns arising from both absolute population sizes and their structural composition mean that Malthus is a key interlocutor for present-day analysts. It is not, of course, purely the size or composition of global populations that demand attention today, but also the question of their consumption of scarce environmental resources. As the ensuing chapters will chronicle, Malthus saw resources restrictedly in terms of food and land, while succeeding generations attended to coal and then the broader category of fossil fuels, before turning to the biotic limits of ecosystems after World War II. Today, it is possible limits and threshold effects in our global climatic systems that arouse concern, but that concern is still, mutatis mutandis, fundamentally Malthusian; the concern is that population will, via its patterns of resource usage, create a negative feedback loop that impacts the numbers who can extract a living from the earth. And finally, the economic downturn created by global austerity since 2008 also seems to make this an auspicious time at which to return to Malthus's insights, his mature work as an economist being forged in the depths of recession during the Napoleonic Wars, and attending as it did to scenarios where the economy faced a lack of demand. Keynes turned to Malthus as he constructed his blueprint for state responses to unemployment and low demand in the Depression of the 1930s, and eighty years later it seems important to revisit Malthus in similar economic times. Malthus was the untimely prophet of how population, economy, and the environment interact; from each of these directions, our present global predicaments seem to demand that we attend to his insights and to the responses they have garnered as we plot our path in troubled times.

Returning to Malthus's tombstone, there is something symbolically appropriate about its location and content. In terms of its content, many people have heard of Malthus, but few, I fear, read him because of a general sense that, true to the epitaph, he is worthy and important, but also likely to be rather dull to wade through. I hope that the Malthus I introduce in Chapters 3 and 5 will scotch that sense. And in terms of location, Malthus's tablet is damned awkward: to read it, the kind guardians of the Abbey have to close the door on one of Bath's major attractions, leading to queues of frustrated tourists. In like fashion, Malthus's works form an obstruction to the smooth ascent of consumption, suggesting we may hit the buffers. Truly, his was the "first" inconvenient truth posed to mass capitalism at the very moment of its birth. A quarter of a century after first walking past Malthus's gravestone, I now feel it vitally important to open the door on Malthus's arguments and then to trace their roller-coaster ride down to the present. Herein, perhaps, lies the potential to give historical depth to our present planetary concerns. To do so, however, we first need to get a sense of the mental stage onto which Malthus's work erupted. It is to this that we now turn.

CHAPTER ONE

Before Malthus

A Shandean Opening: Hatches, Matches, and Dispatches

It is hard to imagine two more contrasting characters than those of Thomas Robert Malthus, the subject of this book, and his most famous eighteenth-century predecessor at Jesus College, Cambridge, the novelist Laurence Sterne. Where Malthus is the great progenitor of the "dismal science" of classical economics, Sterne possesses irreverent Rabelaisian wit; sex is a realm of reproduction for the one, of double entendre for the other. While Malthus was a good family man and a diligent Anglican clergyman, quite the Dr. Primrose from Oliver Goldsmith's *Vicar of Wakefield* (1766), Sterne the cleric spiraled out of control as he became enmeshed in the libertine society of midcentury London and in anticlerical circles in Paris, his wife leaving him when she could no longer bear the burden of his dalliances with other women.[1] And yet, for all the differences between their characters and their lifestyles, Sterne and Malthus in fact shared one preoccupation: vital events. Their very differing contributions to eighteenth-century culture were both shot through with an attention to births, marriages, and deaths, or, in a more Shandean vein, to hatches, matches, and dispatches.

Laurence Sterne's masterpiece, *The Life and Opinions of Tristram Shandy* (1760–1767), opens with Tristram's conception, and the woes that ensue from Mrs. Shandy's otherwise innocent question as to whether Mr. Shandy has remembered to wind up a long case clock: "it was a very unseasonable question at least,—because it scattered and dispersed the animal spirits, whose business it was to have escorted and gone hand-in-hand with the HOMUNCULUS, and conducted him safe to the place destined for his reception." To this event Tristram ascribes the eccentricity of his character that the rest of the novel exemplifies and that spawned the eighteenth-century adjective "Shandean." In doing so, Tristram also argues that character is determined by (Shandean) genetics, not by environmental conditions: "he derived the singularity of his temper more from blood, than either wind or water, or any modifications or combinations of them whatever."[2]

And yet the Shandean analysis of the centrality of "hatching" to character is by no means concluded by this opening sally as might be the case in a conventional autobiography. On the contrary, well over half the book is digressively preoccupied with Tristram's birth as we meet the local midwife, mired in myth and muddle about childbirth, and then Dr. Slop, the local man-midwife, whose bag of obstetrical tricks looks set fair to kill Tristram before he is born and whose forceps leave Tristram with a mangled nose that his father sees as wholly unpropitious to greatness. Sterne depicts the experts on childbirth as ignorant and barbarous, their combined incompetence making it a miracle that anyone successfully arrives in this world. And when Tristram is finally delivered, "almost into the middle of my fourth volume—and no farther than to my first day's life," all foretell his immediate death as he is born in a fit. The haste to baptize the newborn before his death (thereby allowing him a Christian burial under Anglican rites) leads to the bungle whereby he is named "Tristram," the one name his father thinks it impossible to bear and make any mark in the world.[3]

All the traumas Tristram endures—his botched name, his squashed nose, his ruffled animal spirits—take place in Shandy Hall in Sterne's native Yorkshire. And yet the first two of these events in the mock epic that is Tristram's birth would have been located in London but for Mr. Shandy's marriage contract, which is laid before the reader in volume 1, chapter 15 of *Tristram Shandy*. Fearful of the barbaric ignorance of rural midwifery, Mrs. Elizabeth Shandy is allowed by her marriage settlement to go to London for childbirth, as she had done with Tristram's elder brother Bobby, except, as an additional clause states, on such an occasion as when she has previously had a phantom pregnancy and gone up to London for no purpose. "The fact was this, That in the latter end of September, 1717, which was the year before I was born, my mother having carried my father up to town much against the grain,—he peremptorily insisted upon the clause;—so that I was doomed, by marriage articles, to have my nose squeezed as flat to my face, as if the destinies had actually spun me without one." The terms of Mr. Shandy's matching, then, lead to the catalogue of catastrophes stretched over four volumes that is Tristram's hatching at Shandy Hall.[4]

Tristram Shandy's lightheartedness about hatches and matches does not conceal the central reality of death either. One of the most fêted moments in the novel, the opening to volume 7, sees an encounter between Tristram Shandy and the Grim Reaper that was immortalized by the artist Thomas Patch in a picture that hangs in Malthus and Sterne's alma mater. Praising his animal spirits for endowing him with good humor, Tristram recalls the encounter that led to his hasty decision to travel to France:

> when DEATH himself knocked at my door—ye bad him come again; and in so gay a tone of careless indifference did ye do it, that he doubted of his commission—
> "—There must certainly be some mistake in this matter," quoth he.
> "—Did ever so grave a personage get into so vile a scrape?" quoth Death.

Celebrated as this moment is, the specter of death punctuates Sterne's tale more generally. We have already seen that Tristram himself nearly meets his maker at birth, but before this we have already encountered his midwife, whose career was determined by her being widowed, and also within the first volume is narrated the mock sentimental death of Parson Yorick. Toward the close of volume 4, and shortly after Tristram's birth, Mr. Shandy hears of the death of his eldest son, Bobby, a fact he is still taking in at the opening of volume 5. If the Grim Reaper is bamboozled by Tristram's eccentric humor, he takes his toll on others in the course of the novel.[5]

Thomas Patch's picture of the encounter with the Grim Reaper actually substitutes Laurence Sterne himself for Tristram Shandy in imaging that moment. The intertwinings of Sterne and his comic creation, Tristram Shandy, are many and have been the fodder of Sterne's biographers for two-and-a-half centuries. Certainly with regard to the vital events that amount to obsessive mooring points in the digressive structure of *Tristram Shandy,* we can say that they reflect Sterne's own unavoidable preoccupation with disease, death, and life. Like Tristram, Sterne had repeated encounters with the Grim Reaper, and attempted to find in comedy his way out of the situation. As he wrote to his fellow humorist, the actor David Garrick, about his removal to Paris in 1761, "I Shandy it more than ever, and verily do believe, that by mere Shandeism sublimated by a laughter-loving people, I fence as much against infirmities, as I do by the benefit of air and climate." Sterne was to die in 1768, two years after Malthus's birth, at the age of fifty-three, but in a letter of 1762 penned in

Paris, where he, like Tristram, had fled to improve his health, he reports that he had nearly died while up at Jesus College, "of breaking a vessel in my lungs. It happen'd in the night, and I bled the bed full." In the end it would be the consumption—pulmonary tuberculosis—of which this student experience was the first sign, that would kill Sterne. In the meantime, Sterne's eventual dispatcher also led to his matching, in that he was, as his biographer notes, drawn into marriage to Elizabeth Lumley when she was on death's door with consumption in 1741.[6]

Within two years, Sterne's marriage was "in a downward spiral" and he was repeatedly drawn into sentimental amours with other women who were wracked by illness, most notably Elizabeth Draper, the subject of Sterne's late masterpiece, the *Journal to Eliza* (1767). One of the reasons for the unraveling of Sterne's marriage was undoubtedly his anxiety about the failure of his matching to lead to hatching; while the evidence is scant, it appears that Elizabeth Sterne had several stillborn children, for which Sterne may have blamed himself on the grounds of his syphilis. With certainty we know that Sterne's first daughter, Lydia, was born on October 1, 1745. She, like Tristram Shandy, was baptized on the same day, but unlike him did not escape an immediate return to her maker, being recorded by Sterne in his capacity as parish priest as buried on the next day. For all the humor that characterizes Tristram's naming debacle, it was in fact the transmutation of Sterne's personal pain into literary creativity. The Sternes did eventually have another daughter, also named Lydia, who would survive into adulthood. She, like her father, suffered from chronic poor health, most probably due to epilepsy.[7]

Simply put, if hatches, matches, and dispatches were at the heart of the Shandean success of Sterne's literary masterpiece, this was not simply literary gamesmanship, a comic parlor game produced by an insouciant genius, but is more accurately seen as an expression of Sterne's anxieties about the unceasing round of illness, loss, and pain that he felt in his personal life.

Diarists of the Eighteenth Century

If Sterne's genius was in good part the sublimation of the pain that lies behind the exterior of vital statistics, the sheer centrality of births, marriages, and deaths, of disease and the struggle to negotiate a niggardly environment are also at the core of those more prosaic windows onto life in the age of Malthus provided by contemporary diarists. There is a tendency to domesticate many of the great diaries of the eighteenth century with such mildly demeaning epithets as "charming" and "delightful."

Both things they may be, but they are also windows onto the struggle for existence visited upon individuals on all rungs of the social ladder.

We can make good this claim by looking to three diarists whose work marks out the arc of Malthus's own life from his birth in 1766, through the great breakthrough of his *Essay* at the middle point in his life in 1798, to his death in 1834. In the decade before Malthus was born, and tailing off in the year before his birth, the Sussex shopkeeper, undertaker, schoolmaster, churchwarden, and overseer of the poor Thomas Turner (1729–1793) was writing his diary, a private document never intended for publication. Turner's diary only saw the light of day in 1859, and it owes its modern popularity to an edition that came out in 1984. Turner is an ideal representative of the "middling sort" whose virtues of prudential calculation Malthus was to champion in his *Essay*. Turner's calculations are littered through his diaries, pages of entries being devoted to his expenditures, debts, and receipts. In 1754 alone, the first year of Turner's diary, we are told of his losing money at cards (tuppence), the cost of his hiring of a live-in servant (30 shillings for the year), the price he had paid for pipes to sell in his shop, and so on. Turner also notes that he has helped friends to call in their debts in his village of East Hoathly. And alongside this litany of prices, of financial incomings and outgoings, is a roll call of births, marriages, deaths, and illnesses. Again for 1754, Turner records in March the death of the local dignitary and former prime minister Henry Pelham "on Wednesday the 6th instant about 6 o'clock in the morn." Eight days after Pelham's funeral, Turner recorded the burial of Thomas Butler's wife. Whereas Pelham was reported to have died from immoderate eating, Butler's wife may well have been a victim of the bitterly cold weather Turner records at this time, the snow being sixteen inches deep by his reckoning at the time of Pelham's funeral, with even more snow having fallen in the interim. If the Henry Pelhams of Turner's world had the wealth to overcome an exceptionally harsh winter, those lower down the social spectrum like Thomas Butler's wife struggled to make ends meet even at the best of times, a tough winter sometimes quite literally making the difference between life and death. And yet as the seasons turned and the harsh winter of 1753–1754 became a mere memory, happier events visited Turner, his wife, Margaret, being pregnant. Ever the calculator, Turner noted that he had paid "Dame Smith to nurse my wife at 2s 6d per week." Whether Dame Smith was more effectual than Sterne's midwife in *Tristram Shandy* is hard to tell; all we can say is that Margaret Turner was safely delivered of a son, Peter, on August 19, but that she was "very bad" such that Thomas "Sent for Dr. Stone to her" within a week of Peter's birth. Turner's diary breaks off in this climacteric, only to resume in January 1755 with both his wife and son "very bad." Peter died on January 16, and Turner's entry for that day and the following sum up the interweaving of the economic and the demographic that the diary more generally performs:

> *Thurs. 16 Jan.* This morning about 1 o'clock I had the misfortune to lose my little boy Peter, aged 21 weeks, 3 days. Paid for flour and other small things 16d. . . . *Fri. 17 Jan.* Went to Framfield concerning the burying of little Peter. Met at Framfield Messrs. Grant, Barlow and Wigginton's man. My mother paid him £30 in full to September last. This day balanced accounts with John Dulake and paid him for the carriage of 2½ tuns salt, 2 bushels sand and 2 cwt. Cheser cheese: 18 s., which with 6s.6d. received of him was in full to this day.[8]

If Turner's ability to conjoin deaths and accounting seems callous to the modern eye, we need to remember the sheer frequency of childhood death at this time, something that may have inured God-fearing men like Turner to its sting and that this was a private diary of short memos and jottings, never aimed at posterity. Furthermore, at the next great moment of loss in Turner's life, his pain is palpable. In 1761, Turner records the death of his wife, Margaret: "About 1.50 it pleased Almighty God to take from me my beloved wife, who, poor creature, has laboured under a severe though lingering illness for these 38 weeks past, which she bore with the greatest resignation to the Divine will. In her I have lost a sincere friend and virtuous wife, a prudent and good economist in her family and a very valuable companion." Margaret was only twenty-seven at the time of her death, something that in advanced modern societies would be a terrible and anomalous tragedy, but that was a far more routine part of life expectations in Turner's time. Turner's diary finally breaks off in 1765, just a year before Malthus's birth, and this not because of Turner's death but a very different and far happier vital event, his remarriage to Mary Hicks, who would outlive him and indeed see in the new century. And yet, while we do not have Turner's words to trace the details, the twining of economy and vital events clearly continued to set the pattern of his life, Turner accruing substantial capital in later life and investing in some land, while also having some seven children with Mary, only three of whom outlived him.[9]

Thomas Turner died in 1793, some five years before the publication of Malthus's epochal *Essay* and thirty since he had laid down his diarist's pen. Yet still going strong at that time was another of the great diarists of the eighteenth century, Parson James Woodforde. Like Tristram Shandy, Woodforde had nearly died at birth, being baptized by his father at three days old in 1740. By 1758, Woodforde had begun to write a diary that would extend over the better part of a half century until his death in 1803. As his father's profession suggests, Woodforde was born into the comfortable clerical classes, a rung up the social ladder from Thomas Turner but at very much the same stratum in which Malthus was born and in which he would live out his days. Woodforde likewise remained in this part of the social spectrum, going to Winchester and Oxford before taking holy orders as rector of Weston Longeville in Norfolk. Woodforde's diary is beloved of coffeetable consumers of history for his obsession with food and drink; he seems to personify our stereotype of the worldly clergyman in a secular eighteenth century. And yet if we look at his diary for 1798, the year of Malthus's *Essay,* there is much of interest beyond Woodforde's detailing of "rost Beef, Tripe &c," much that links to the worlds of Thomas Turner and Robert Malthus. As with Turner, there is the punctuation of daily life by the specter of death: as the rector, Woodforde was called to send his curate to perform the last rites for a Mrs. Mann in February. Likewise in December Woodforde's clerk, Thomas Thurston, died "by a sudden & rapid Swelling in his Throat which suffocated him" and hard on the heels of this, within the same week, he learned of the death of "my dear Sister Pounsett." This latter was of particular concern to him as Pounsett's daughter had in the same year married one Frederick Grove under a settlement that Woodforde considered in shades of Mr. Shandy's additional clauses to be "a very bad one & a very cunning one." Woodforde himself was by this time in poor health, complaining in November of a fainting fit. And meshed with these events that marked out Woodforde's year as a cleric were the concerns he shared as a landowner with his rural parishioners about weather and harvests, about yields and taxes, about the economic conditions that helped or hindered human flourishing. In this particular year, Woodforde noted that January was "hazy & unpleasant," but by springtime he was encouraged as two of his sows had large litters and his cow had a bull-calf. By late summer, he was positively rejoicing: "Never was known scarce ever so fine a Harvest Season. Lord! make us truly thankful & grateful for the same." All this at least counteracted Woodforde's gripes about the heavy new taxes on the clergy and his repeated concerns about a potential Napoleonic invasion via Ireland. Rather like Thomas Turner, Woodforde was keenly aware of the ways in which economic balance sheets and the rhythm of vital events interacted, and of the complex connections that both of these had with political and environmental conditions. In that same year of 1798, a clergyman of the next generation, Robert Malthus, would pen perhaps the most important treatise ever written on this most essential of conjunctions.[10]

Around the time of Malthus's death in 1834, Samuel Bamford, some-time radical agitator, weaver, and journalist, abandoned his other activities to become a full-time writer, mainly of autobiographical works. Just as early Victorian England started to express concern about the conditions in the great industrial cities that were mushrooming in Malthus's declining years, Bamford was able to depict the horrors of the lives led in these environments with an intensity that neither the bien-pensant novels of Elizabeth Gaskell and Benjamin Disraeli nor the social reportage of the wealthy industrialist Friedrich Engels could muster, for the simple reason that Bamford had been born and had lived out his years as a laborer in this environment. If Turner's diary epitomizes the frugal middle classes whom Malthus praised and Woodforde's encapsulated the social stratum in which Malthus himself traveled, Bamford's writings bring vividly to life the lot of the poor that was to preoccupy Malthus in the various editions of his *Essay*. Bamford was born in 1788 and would live to the ripe old age of eighty-four, but this was most unusual for one from Bamford's background, the laboring classes in industrializing Lancashire. As volume 1 of Bamford's autobiography, *Early Days* (1849), chronicled, life was nasty, brutish, and frequently short in this milieu at the time when Malthus wrote his *Essay*, far more so than for the social worlds depicted by Turner and Woodforde. Recollecting his early life, Bamford pointed to the palpable hardships visited upon the laboring poor by the same revolutionary turmoils that were mere rumors to Woodforde in Weston Longeville: "Woe to the poor weaver then, with his loom without work, the provision shop without credit, and his wife and weans, foodless, and looking at each other, and at him, as if saying—Husband! father! Hast thou neither bread nor hope for us?" Bamford recalls his father as old before his time, as worn down by the diurnal struggle to feed his family in this context, a struggle that was only eased in the context of tragedy, an outbreak of smallpox that killed Bamford's younger siblings Hannah (four) and James (two). The same outbreak would also kill his uncle and finally his mother. Bamford himself was pushed from family to workhouse, never living with his father after he remarried. Before his tenth birthday, Bamford was running errands and winding bobbins in Middleton near Manchester, while his elder brother was already working a loom to make ends meet. Both children had inherited the lot of backbreaking toil from a father whose health had in its turn been ruined by a life that described the same course. However much Samuel Bamford dignified this course of events for his readership, his own life would never securely escape from penury either: he was imprisoned for his radicalism in 1817 and was kept from destitution by public subscriptions in the 1840s and

1860s. Unlike his siblings Hannah and James, Samuel Bamford's life was a long one, but despite some literary success, it was never one that, his industry and intelligence notwithstanding, would escape from the mesh of familial poverty.[11]

Life, Economy, and Environment in Malthus's England

So far, we have attended to social and literary reportage about the nexus of ideas that Malthus was to revolutionize in 1798, the interweaving of life, economy, and environment. As such, we have seen the patterns and pitfalls that denizens of England in the age of Malthus had to negotiate as individuals and family members. But what of the broader picture? Fortunately, we are possessed of a vast and fairly robust set of data about the composite realities of life, land, and labor in eighteenth-century England that can be juxtaposed with the individual anecdotes canvassed to date.

For a half century now, the Cambridge Group for the History of Population and Social Structure has been using parish records of births, marriages, and deaths to reconstruct life chances in early modern England. The origins of this type of inquiry go back to the age of Malthus and before, but the Cambridge Group has used rigorous sampling to render their results robust. What do they tell us as we move from the individual and the anecdotal to the social and statistical analysis of life chances in the age of Malthus?

As Thomas Turner started to pen his diaries and as Malthus was born in the mid-eighteenth century, the population of England and Wales was just under 6 million. This was an increase of fewer than 1 million souls from the English population a century previously, the later seventeenth century having seen a small dip in total population before a revival in the early eighteenth century. But such simple totals mask the question of how many souls had to be born and how long they lived to create the overall population of the nation. In 1751, life expectancy at birth was just over forty-two years, just over half the figure we enjoy in the present day. And yet this was the high point in life expectancy at birth in the two centuries before 1800, the low being thirty-one years in the 1680s. We need to know, however, how this life expectancy was constituted in the eighteenth century to have a better handle on living and dying in Malthus's world. Our anecdotal opening to this chapter gives us a sense of why; as Tristram Shandy and James Woodforde nearly died in the first week of life, and as neither Thomas Turner's son nor Laurence Sterne's daughter reached their first birthday, so aggregate statistics show us that birth itself and the first year of life posed a risk of staggering proportions in the eighteenth century. In the decade of Malthus's birth, the 1760s, it is estimated that some 166 children per 1,000 live births died in the first year of life and a further 113 died in the first four years of life. Simply put, well over one in every four children did not live to see their fifth birthday. And yet this was, in fact, a significant amelioration in the chances of infant survival from the generations of Malthus's parents. To gain some perspective on this from our vantage point in the early twenty-first century, in England and Wales in 2011, only 5 boys per 1,000 and 3.7 girls per 1,000 died in their first year of life, with only a further 0.2 per 1,000 dying by the age of four. Where the death of a young child is a tragic divergence from the normal course of life for us, it was understandably woven into the warp and weft of existence in the eighteenth century. Thomas Turner's world was at the very least thirty-three times more likely to see a child die in the first year of life than is our own and more than fifty times as likely to see a child die in their first four years (even assuming they were live births, a category incalculably more precarious then than now but the only one that parish records allow us to scrutinize); his ability to juxtapose burial arrangements with business was not callous, but a sociopsychological necessity, a capacity of endurance from the world we have lost. To clear the hurdle of the first five years was to have very different life chances. Thus, if expectation of life at birth was around forty-two years in 1750, it is equally the case that a twenty-five-year-old in 1750 could expect to live a further thirty-seven years on average, having successfully negotiated the vast tithe the Grim Reaper took in the infant years. When Thomas Turner's first wife, Margaret, died at the age of twenty-seven, then, the palpably different level of distress from that he recorded at the death of his first son again reflected the impress of demographic realities on social and emotional expectations, this vital event being far more contrary to the course of nature as his contemporaries routinely experienced it. If Margaret had died in childbirth or the ensuing months, Thomas may have been equally distraught, but he may have been less surprised; adjusted for deaths after a stillbirth or no live birth as best as proxy data from Sweden will allow, just under 10 women died per 1,000 births in the 1760s, when Malthus was born, a rate more than one hundred times greater than that for England and Wales today.[12]

One of the Cambridge Group's key findings is that marriage and fertility were the key determinants of changes in England's population size and character over the three centuries to 1837, far more so than mortality. As Peter Laslett pointed out many years ago, our image of the world we have lost tends to assume that couples in early modern England married very young and then had extremely large families. The aggregate data whose analysis Laslett's Cambridge Group initiated has shown us that realities were very different. Average age at marriage in the mid-eighteenth century was around twenty-seven or twenty-eight for men and twenty-six for women. Marriage was only possible once a couple was economically established, and this delayed it considerably. While anecdotal evidence suggests that some individuals used contraception and other means to limit conception—perhaps most famously the diarist James Boswell with his frequent recourse to "armour" (condoms) when meeting prostitutes—in aggregate, natural fertility in marriage was the norm. As such, the key determinants of family size were age at marriage and the spacing between births. The age at marriage fell over the course of the later eighteenth century, increasing the number of fertile years in marriage to the order of eighteen years on average. But this was nowhere near a maximal fertility regime, as women would have been able to bear children from around fifteen years old at this time (menarche came later in the eighteenth century than today due to inferior nutrition), but on average delayed marriage by the order of a decade. Once a couple married, the spacing between births seems to have been on average around thirty months, meaning parents averaged six to seven children, but of course the average family might expect one or two of those children to die in the vulnerable early years.[13]

Thus far we have deliberately painted a fairly static picture of vital statistics at midcentury, the time of Malthus's birth. But it is worth adding the element of temporal change to the picture to discern what the demographic trends were in the decades up to 1800. Such trends set the factual context under which Malthus matured, and may have helped to shape his perceptions as they crystallized in 1798. The most important change in the half century to 1800 seems to have been a secular fall in the age at marriage. Far from increasing over time, the marriage age in fact decreased over the later part of the century by between two and three years on average for both sexes, to twenty-five years old for men and twenty-three and one-half for women. Moreover, teenage marriages doubled in the same period. Given that the key determinant of fertility was age at marriage in an age prior to (statistically significant) contraception, this was of great importance. While a change of two or three years in average age at marriage does not sound much, it has been calculated to result in a 20 to 25 percent increase in fertility. This in turn almost entirely explains the increase in total population estimates for England and Wales in the half century after 1751 from 5.9 million to 8.7 million, although expectations of life at birth were also moderately higher for the half century after 1751 than they had been for the half century before. Statistically speaking, Malthus grew up in an England where couples were marrying younger and, as a consequence, having larger families. Tied with a less dramatic but nonetheless important decline in mortality rates, population was increasing at a rate that, while modest compared to that witnessed globally in the nineteenth and twentieth centuries, was unprecedented.[14]

As well as setting our figures in motion over time, it is also worth scrutinizing them over space too, and that in two senses. First, when the experience of England and Wales is looked at on a broader scale, it is clear that it shares certain features with Europe that made that continent different from the rest of the world but also that, demographically speaking, England and Wales were exceptional even within Europe. Scholars have detected in European demographic history three long-term cycles of population rise and fall in the ancient, medieval, and early modern periods, the last of these seeing population stagnate for one-and-a-half centuries to 1650 before growing slowly until 1800. Moreover, Europe was unusual in that, taken as a whole, it exhibited a pattern of delayed marriage determined by economic viability, and this in turn led to a lower fertility regime than that found anywhere else in the early modern world. England and Wales took this uniquely European demographic regime to its furthest extreme, having some of the latest ages at marriage, and lower than average death rates that in combination produced faster population growth than any other European nation. Taken together, whereas Germany, Spain, Italy, and France saw population growth of between 50 and 80 percent over the era 1550–1820, English population rose in the same era by some 280 percent. Statistically speaking, then, Malthus was right to discern, contrary to many of his contemporaries, that English population was increasing at a historically unprecedented rate in his lifetime, but was equally wrong to think that the response needed to be a newfound moral restraint; on the contrary, England was already the land of delayed, prudential, and economically determined marriage par excellence.[15]

Second, it is worth breaking down the English demographic experience to the subnational scale. The main focus of historical demography for England and Wales has been the national scale; however, more recent work has recognized that there were significant geographical variations in demographic regimes. In some arenas—notably fertility trends—there was a shared national experience, but mortality was a very different story. Two environmental regimes led to notably higher mortality rates: the marshlands of lowland England, wherein the "ague" (malaria) reduced

life expectancies by three or more years; and the great cities, whose un-
sanitary conditions produced an annual excess of deaths over births, which
was only compensated for by large flows of migrants from the countryside.
Both of these high mortality regimes attracted the attention of contemporaries, the Grim Reaper's scythe being palpably so much sharper there,
but more generally mortality data reveals that child mortality went up
dramatically in the industrializing towns over time, while it fell with
almost equal rapidity in the market towns and remained static in agricultural areas. The different sense of the proximity of death one gets reading
Samuel Bamford and James Woodforde, then, corresponds to statistical
realities.[16]

Demography was so tied to environment because the daily realities of
making a living, the business of economic survival for each household,
were tied to the soil and the land with an immediacy it is hard for us to
feel intuitively in advanced, postmodern societies. As historians have
made clear, Malthus was born in the dying embers of a system they label
as the "advanced organic economy." During Malthus's lifetime, this would
be superseded by a "mineral-based economy" ultimately resting on the
release of energy stored in the form of coal (and later oil and natural gas)
over geological time. But until this new system came to dominate, European economies were determined (and limited) in their productivity by the
amount of energy from the sun that could be harnessed directly in the
form of agrarian production, together with the utilization of power produced by wind and water. In terms of energy efficiency this is a massively
flawed system as even the most efficient of plants capture only 3 percent
of the sun's radiant energy and the human body can convert only 20 percent of that calorific intake into usable energy. As such, organic economics
"condemned the majority of the population to poverty." Such unceasing
dependency on the returns of the soil for clothing, energy, and food explain
why rural diarists such as Woodforde were, as we have seen, so attentive
to weather conditions and so (to modern eyes, comically) proud of their
sows' litters; they were the quotidian guarantors of affluence for those
higher up the social spectrum and were literally matters of life and death
for the poor.[17]

Britain possessed perhaps the most efficient of the advanced organic
economies in Europe. Without it, the population increases charted in earlier paragraphs would have been quite simply impossible. Economic historians tell a story that dovetails neatly with what we have heard from
demographers. Given the foundational nature of agriculture to survival,
population increase was facilitated by incremental improvements in agricultural productivity per acre, coupled with an expansion in the cultivated

arable acres in Britain from 11 to 14.6 million, 1700–1850. Such increments appear to have been able to absorb modest rises in population size in the early eighteenth century, but the acceleration in population growth rates noted by demographers appears to have outstripped increases in productivity in the later eighteenth century and right on to the end of the Napoleonic Wars. Average food consumption did not increase prior to 1840 (although recent studies suggest it was more calorifically enriched than was thought previously), something gauged by the fact that the average mature height for Englishmen of the eighteenth century was at least 10 centimeters shorter than it is today throughout the period, and real wages seem not to have increased prior to 1815. As such, through most of Malthus's lifetime and quite possibly for its entirety, population was outstripping the capacities of the British to feed that population and to employ it gainfully, resulting in periodic food crises and the need to import in ever-increasing quantities.[18]

If one tries to paint the picture as it might appear looking from 1750 or even 1815, then, rather than relying on what we know "came next," the best quantitative data suggests that population and resources were in a tense balance throughout Malthus's life and that of his parents before him. The population increases charted by the reconstructions of the Cambridge Group were not easily absorbed but left the economy permanently struggling to provide food and gainful employment for them. To the extent that this struggle was an even contest rather than an abject failure, it was due to massive projects of environmental manipulation and landscape change as well. First, there was the process of enclosure whereby small strips of arable land were consolidated into the checkerboard of fields separated by hedges that we (mistakenly) see as quintessentially and timelessly "English" today. Consolidation of fields started in good earnest by local agreements in the seventeenth century and continued into the eighteenth century before legal compulsion via parliamentary act completed the process in the later eighteenth and early nineteenth centuries.[19] Second, and commencing only slightly later than enclosure, was the great work to drain the marshlands of lowland England, especially in East Anglia, Essex, and Kent, work that transformed massive areas from miasmatic zones of shortened lives into the most productive parts of the nation, albeit with considerable social dislocation. There was also the continuing depletion of forests for fuel, building resources, and shipbuilding, leaving lowland England predominantly deforested by Malthus's time. Yet for fuel at least, rapid increases in coal mining came to the rescue, coal production increasing sevenfold in the period 1650–1800, this process also demanding massive transformations in the landscape.[20] In addition to all these specific changes to the English environment, there was also the need to coordinate these changes: with the emergence of an increasingly integrated market economy, arable and pastoral landscapes became ever more segregated, and both were orientated around London. And as areas specialized in specific goods, so they became reliant on other areas for other products, the inevitable result being a massive expansion in the need for roads and landscapes of transportation; docks, warehouses, and the like mushroomed to allow the English organic economy to sustain its increasing population. If, then, demographers have pointed to a major increase in population in the second half of the eighteenth century and economic historians have shown how this was sustained by incipient capitalist structures, all of this was also predicated on unprecedented achievements in the manipulation of the physical environment: "the lands of the British Isles were among the most intensively managed of any society during the early modern period."[21]

In sum, modern historians can show us with startling precision and reliability that massive transformations took place in English population dynamics, these changes starting around the time of Malthus's birth. It is clear that demographic change was predicated on and in turn necessitated major advances in the efficiency with which a still essentially agrarian economy functioned. That efficiency was engendered by expansion and improvement in the manipulation of the physical environments of the British Isles. Population, economy, and environment—Malthus's great trilogy—functioned in a complex interconnection that (by and large) proved capable of absorbing change. Denizens of the eighteenth century did not have access to the historically robust picture drawn here, but that does not mean they did not try to piece together the interconnections between population, economy, and environment. It is to these efforts of Malthus's predecessors that we now turn. How did they try to pan out from the individual experiences recorded by diarists to the social whole?

Understanding the Social World before Malthus

If, as has often been claimed, "modern" social science can be traced back to the efforts of the eighteenth century, at the core of that suite of work was a desire to trace the connections between population, economy, and environment. One of the most immediately visible outgrowths of this interest was a debate about whether the population of Europe was increasing or declining in the period, a debate that drew in some of the greatest minds of the Age of Enlightenment. That the denizens of Europe in the era of Malthus's birth did not even know in which direction population numbers were trending has often been seen as proof of their ignorance or of the neophyte status of social inquiry at this time. On closer inspection, however, the lines down which the debate ran will be seen to have opened up quite sophisticated ideas about causation and counting, lines that Malthus would both draw on and upend as the century drew to its close.[22]

The population debate started with Montesquieu's *Persian Letters* of 1721, a set of epistles purportedly written by two Islamic travelers touring through Europe and offering an outsider's view of the continent, its social structure and mores. Letter 112 began a series of eleven that addressed the question of population change, the premise being that population had clearly decayed dramatically since the time of the ancients. In line with many thinkers of the age, and not inappropriately in the mental world framed by an advanced organic economy, Montesquieu saw a direct link between population size and the fertility of the soil: "Why is it that the world is so thinly populated in comparison with former times? How is it that nature has managed to lose the prodigious fertility that she had originally?" Montesquieu's "Persian" offers the claim, "after making as exact a calculation as possible," that "there is scarcely a fiftieth of the number of men on earth that there was in Caesar's time." In fact, of course, Montesquieu had made no calculations whatsoever, there being no suitably extensive quantitative data available on which to make such a claim, and there is no evidence that he was even aware of the early quantitative work being conducted in his native France or his beloved England. The capricious nature of Montesquieu's numbers is made plain by their dramatic adjustment in posthumous editions after 1758 to suggest global population was one-tenth, not one-fiftieth, of its ancient tally.[23]

If Montesquieu's quantification is (and was seen in its own age as) self-evidently spurious, the lines of causal reasoning he used to explain population change and to depict its social significance were both representative of their age and enduringly significant. Montesquieu's claims and the debates they fostered were one of the crucibles in which modern social science was forged. Montesquieu not only wished to tie population to the fertility of nature, he also investigated "moral," or, as we would term them, "social," causes of population change. In particular, Montesquieu's Persian correspondents focused on the baleful effects of modern religions— Christianity and Islam—upon population growth. In Islam it was polygamy and the culture of the eunuch that depressed population while Christianity had its own eunuchs, the celibate Catholic clergy whose vows of chastity had "annihilated more men than plagues or the most savage wars." Why did a declining population matter? The answer for Montesquieu lay in the realm of what Adam Smith would call the "science of the legislator," or, in our terms, it was a political and economic issue: "the more men there are in a state, the more trade flourishes." And the wealth that trade generated was the "sinews of power" for any government, bankrolling its military activities. Yet for Montesquieu this was not simply one-way traffic; on the contrary, there was a complex mutual causation, population strengthening the state, but the form of government reciprocally determining population dynamics. The final letter concerning population (number 122) expanded on this theme, arguing around a binary between despotic governments that depress reproduction and "gentle methods of government [that] have a wonderful effect on the propagation of the species." Montesquieu, then, both here and in his celebrated *Spirit of the Laws,* made population size the outcome of a complex amalgam of natural and environmental factors on the one hand, and of social, economic, and political structures on the other. As a result of his efforts, population would be at the heart of reasoning about economy, society, and nature in the three-quarters of a century prior to Malthus's epochal intervention.[24]

Looking at society and economy first, those who came in Montesquieu's wake developed two main lines of discussion. First, there was a growing awareness that population dynamics varied with the nature of the society under investigation, something that Montesquieu had first gleaned between the composition of the *Persian Letters* and the *Spirit of the Laws.* In particular, Enlightenment literati detected very different contexts for population growth in more "primitive" societies and in the vast expanses of the underpopulated colonies of North America. In such societies, where nature's resources had scarcely been tapped, population could grow rapidly: as the French economist Mirabeau put it in 1758, "people multiply like rats in a barn if they have the means to subsist." On the ground amid Mirabeau's rats in the underutilized lands of colonial British America, Benjamin Franklin penned his highly influential "Observations Concerning the Increase of Mankind" in 1751, which suggested "our People must at least be doubled every 20 Years," a calculation that would echo down the decades and be recycled by Malthus at the century's end. Second, and implicit in the comments of Mirabeau and Franklin, was an awareness that matters were arranged differently in the advanced economies of Europe, wherein space and agricultural land were already at a premium. Here, population dynamics would be different, and it was for such societies that the specter of "limits to growth" and declining population was debated. The most cogent rejection of Montesquieu's thesis of declining population in modern societies came from the genteel pen of David Hume, whom we remember as a philosopher, but who in his own era was most famed as an essayist, in which capacity he wrote a lengthy tract, "Of the Populousness of Ancient Nations," published in 1752. Despite rejecting his conclusions, Hume's mode of reasoning about the question was very much in accord with Montesquieu's, looking for causal arguments from society and economy to explain population dynamics. For Hume, if the small states and the equality fostered in ancient societies encouraged population more than did contemporary arrangements, this was in all likelihood more than counterbalanced by the ubiquity of slavery, almost perpetual war, and far inferior commercial vibrancy. And yet with his normal skeptical *apatheia*, Hume recognized that there was evidence on the other side of the question, in particular that the great commercial metropolises of modern Europe were killers: "LONDON, at present, without much encreasing, needs a yearly recruit from the country, of 5000 people." Others carried this analysis forward and, fusing the moral with the economic, suggested that cities both fueled and embodied a decadent luxury that enervated society and led to a declining and enfeebled population. This was the argument of John Brown's wildly successful *Estimate of the Manners and Principles of the Times* (1757) and Robert Wallace's Montesquieuian *Dissertation on the Numbers of Mankind in Ancient and Modern Times, in which the superior populousness of Antiquity is maintained* (1753). Both of these authors took some of the only reasonably reliable quantitative data available at the time—the London Bills of Mortality, whose utility to demographic analysis had been well understood since the work of John Graunt in the 1660s—and extrapolated from its message of an excess of births over deaths to paint a (factually false) picture of decaying population.[25]

Hume's essay in the main canvassed social and political arguments to weigh the population question, but toward its close he made a speculative link with environmental factors. He suggested that modern Europe was warmer than it had been in antiquity and that this was favorable to population. True to the massive manipulations of the landscape that were necessitated to support a growing population in an organic economy, Hume suggested this greater warmth was a consequence of the fact that "the land is at present much better cultivated, and . . . the woods are cleared, which formerly threw a shade upon the earth." This was something of a sidebar in Hume's argument, but it does draw our attention to the fact that a broader body of arguments existed at the time linking the dynamics of population and economy to the physical environment, something that was hardly surprising in an age when, like our own age of environmental economics but not that of the two centuries intervening, "wealth was essentially [seen as] a property of the physical world." As Keith Thomas sketched in his study of English attitudes to nature, the mid-eighteenth century on saw an important move away from the "breathtakingly anthropocentric" way of viewing the natural world. As he charts, this was in part thanks to a new aesthetic of untouched nature as "pure," encouraged at exactly the time when, as we saw earlier, millions of acres were being incorporated into agrarian regimes for the first time. It was also in good part thanks to pioneering inquiries showing the extent to which the natural environment could vary in its impact on human health.[26] Of course, the suggestion that health is determined by the environment is as old as Hippocrates, but in the eighteenth century there were the first sustained attempts to put empirical flesh on these ancient conceptual bones: "environmental pathology offered a means to experiment with alternative approaches to individual and general health." Most notable in the English context was the work of Thomas Short, who in the 1740s compiled tables of mortality to show that the countryside was more salubrious than the towns. But Short did not rest content with a quantified version of Cowper's binary that "God made the country, and man made the town," but instead argued for the manipulation of physical environments to improve properties for human health. Noticing also a correlation between marshy areas and high mortality, for example, Short argued for drainage as a way to improve human longevity and therefore to improve demographic regimes. Short was by no means alone in suggesting that landscapes should be manipulated not only in order to maximize productivity, but also to procure human health, with Richard Price, Joseph Priestley, and others concurring. While such suggestions would really take root in the Victorian programs, there were also campaigns to improve sanitation as the importance of ventilation, street widening, and drain building came to be increasingly recognized in the later eighteenth century. Regardless of whether population was rising or falling, scholars began to realize that the environment was not simply a fixed backdrop for human affairs but was instead an active and variable determinant of life chances that could itself be manipulated in ways that aided or retarded those chances. Viewing nature as manipulable and not always best arranged for human needs also led as an unavoidable corollary to an increasing recognition that human inventiveness could be called into play by environmental limits: as Hume put it, "It may seem an odd position that the poverty of the common people in France, Italy and Spain is in some measure owing to the superior riches of the soil and happiness of the climate; and yet there may not want many reasons to justify this paradox. . . . Necessity is the great spur to industry and invention."[27]

And yet for all the conceptual sophistication of the causal links Enlightened scholars proposed between population, economy, and environment in the wake of Montesquieu's initial speculations, they were also well aware that such links needed to be demonstrated by solid quantitative evidence not merely proposed. Hume recognized this in his essay "Of the Populousness of Ancient Nations." As he put it with characteristic diffidence: "This I readily own: All our preceding reasonings, I acknowledge to be mere trifling, or, at least, small skirmishes and frivolous reencounters, which decide nothing. But unluckily the main combat, where we compare facts, cannot be rendered much more decisive" as no such facts exist. Or, as someone not best known for mathematical reasoning, Jean-Jacques Rousseau, put it: "Calculators, this is your problem: count, measure, compare." Rousseau made his injunction in 1762, by which time in fact there had been at least a century of efforts to respond to this call to calculative arms. For as the greatest quantitative demographer in the generation before Malthus, Johann Süssmilch, put it in 1741, it was John Graunt in the 1660s, "a Columbus . . . in the registers of deaths and diseases," who had first counted, measured, compared. Graunt's work had been promoted by the Royal Society and was further popularized by William Petty's pioneering statistical efforts at a science he called "political arithmetic," the quantitative study of society. Edmund Halley had furthered this type of work by his construction of the first life tables based on mortality data for the German city of Breslau in the 1690s, these being published in the Royal Society's *Philosophical Transactions*. From these modest beginnings, the eighteenth century would see an explosion in such inquiries, such that in the decades after Malthus's birth a range of local scholars all but forgotten to posterity such as John Fothergill, William Black, John Howlett, and John Heysham were producing mortality returns for major English towns and cities. And yet these inquiries remained scattered and patchy in their coverage; only a state-sponsored census could lead to more representative figures. Calls for a census were made repeatedly in England, starting well before Malthus's birth. An act was drafted in 1753 to be put before Parliament under the prime-ministership of Henry Pelham, whose burial was one of the first matters recorded in Thomas Turner's diary, but proposals for a census ran into opposition on the grounds that it would merely be used to levy further taxes, that it infringed on the liberty of freeborn Englishman, and that the Old Testament enjoined kings not to count their subjects on pain of divine retribution. It would be another half century before, hard on the heels of Malthus's revolutionary tract, a census was finally empowered by parliamentary act on December 31, 1800.[28]

If we take a step back, it becomes readily apparent that behind the complex surface of claims and counterclaims about counting and causation, there were three key assumptions that acted as the fixed points around which the debates canvassed here revolved. First, there was the belief that a large population was a desideratum for a healthy and powerful state. To be able to measure a population was to find an objective proxy for whether a government and/or an economy was doing its business effectively. Rousseau encapsulated this belief in his clarion call to quantification: "What is the object of any political association? It is the protection and prosperity of its members. And what is the surest evidence that they are so protected and prosperous? The numbers of their population. Then do not look beyond this much debated evidence. All other things being equal, the government under which . . . the citizens increase and multiply most, is infallibly the best government. That under which the people diminishes and wastes away is the worst." Second, there was a shared belief that the current population in England, in Europe, and in the world more generally, whether rising or falling, was less than that which the physical environment of our earth could sustain. While an awareness of compound numbers allowed the more mathematically minded to understand that if humans multiplied like Mirabeau's rats they would soon eat the barn empty, that remained a purely theoretical and mathematical speculation to most inquirers. There were actual limits to growth imposed by poor government, large cities, and adverse environments such as marshlands, but these were local difficulties. The perception of the global state of play in the generation before Malthus was best summed up by an author Malthus would himself cite approvingly, Johann Süssmilch, who estimated that the earth was home to 1 billion people at midcentury (a number not far off the estimates of modern historical demographers), but its full habitable surface, used with maximal efficiency, could sustain 4 to 5 billion. Depending on assumptions about doubling rates, Süssmilch concluded that even not allowing for human innovation, this meant environmental limits would not be felt for between two hundred and five hundred years. Finally, there was a clear sense that this mutual adjustment between population dynamics, economic innovations, and environmental resources was God-given, was proof that a wise Creator had made the whole with a plan as a welcoming home for mankind. Again, the mathematically inclined Süssmilch lays these presumptions bare for us. He took as his text the divine injunction from Genesis, "be fruitful and multiply," arguing that God had so arranged the interrelationship between births, marriages, and deaths to allow for the realization of this injunction, but that this escapes our limited human attention unless we approach it through number:

This divine order is as elusive as it is impressive. It seems bent on escaping our notice, and the concealment is the easier because there is nothing suggesting to the outward eye any kind of order in births and deaths. . . . It fell to Graunt to be the first to perceive an Order in the registers of deaths and diseases . . . by which he has laid the foundations of this science, which . . . stirs us up to know better and reverence more the all-wise framer of this order of nature; which science, too, displays to the gods of the earth set over me as their rulers, and teaches them that they can only make themselves and their State happy and powerful by following the rules of that Order which the Supreme Ruler has chosen and established for the populating of the earth.

Süssmilch in this extract in fact reveals the mutual interconnection of the three guiding assumptions that framed discussions of population, economy, and environment in the age before Malthus. It is into this intellectual context that Malthus was born, and his *Essay* would wholly upend each of the assumptions under which work to date had functioned, bringing in presumptions more familiar to us, more redolent of the economic and environmental concerns of the modern world order. He would reject the equation between a large population and a good government, arguing that populations can become too large. He would deny that overpopulation, or the experience of environmental limits to growth, was only a hypothetical concern to be postponed to an all-but-uncharted futurity; nature was immediately niggardly, not unceasingly generous. And he would deny that God's ordinances only allowed for happiness in this world; in Malthus's vision, pain, poverty, and harsh choices about resource allocation became the lot of society and its legislators. But before we can fully understand Malthus's revolution in the *Essay* of 1798, we need to see the impact of a more proximate revolution, the French Revolution of 1789, which spawned the ideas about the interconnections between population, economy, and environment that were the immediate cause of Malthus's decision to put pen to paper.[29]

Prophets of Perfection

A Revolutionary Triptych

O N THE EVENING of November 4, 1789, a tall, gaunt man in his mid-sixties rose slowly to his feet to speak to a hushed audience in the heart of London at the Old Jewry meeting house, a long-standing home of radical thinking. The gentle remains of a childhood spent in the South Wales valleys still faintly discernible in the lilt and rhythm of his voice, he broached a subject that had always aroused patriotic pride in Britain, the so-called "Glorious Revolution" of 1688. By the time he sat down almost an hour later, he had galvanized his audience with revolutionary fervor, waxing lyrical about the news wafting across the Channel of events in France. The speaker had—appropriately enough on the evening before Guy Fawkes Night—laid a political and patriotic powder keg that would soon explode into one of the most vitriolic contretemps British political life has ever witnessed.

French schoolchildren up and down the nation still have the date of "Le Quatorze Juillet" etched into their patriotic consciousnesses as a symbol of national identity. On the English side of the Channel, however, children ought perhaps to learn the dates November 4 and 5, 1789, not that of the storming of the Bastille. British critics and advocates of the French Revolution alike looked on uncomprehendingly at the events taking place in the summer of 1789. Like Christopher Columbus, who lived and died believing he had reached the Far East, who died ignorant of the meaning of his great voyage of 1492, scholars, commentators, and village politicians did not yet know what to make of the new world of politics that the events of Le Quatorze Juillet had ushered in. It was too early. But as summer faded and winter took hold (as it did far earlier and far more vigorously in the eighteenth century than in our own age), battle lines in Britain began to crystallize, a "left" and a "right" wing began to form, the terms themselves deriving from the seating plan of the revolutionary National Assembly. It was, however, our Welsh speaker's dignified call to revolutionary arms that would make the situation erupt. His life having been spent as an advocate of a radical Christianity, his final great act—he would die two years later, in April 1791—was to deliver a very militant *nunc dimittis*. This particular servant would depart not in peace, but in the eye of a furious maelstrom of political controversy.[1]

If our Welsh orator, Dr. Richard Price by name, laid a political powder keg on November 4, 1789, it was Edmund Burke, sparked by Price's speech, who lit the fuse in his furious denunciation of the French Revolution, *Reflections on the Revolution in France* (1790). In one of the rhetorical gems of the English language, Burke would wax both eloquent and nostalgic about the passing glories of the French ancien règime, most notably its last queen, Marie Antoinette. This led Burke's most effective critic, Tom Paine, in his best-selling *Rights of Man* (1791), to charge that Burke "pities the plumage and forgets the dying bird"; to mourn the loss of French courtly decadence was obscene given the mass poverty on which it had been predicated. Burke also harangued at those on both sides of the Channel who were so excited by what he saw as butchery, both literal and metaphorical, infamously castigating those who precipitated the events of Le Quatorze Juillet as "a swinish multitude" and denouncing as well the mild-mannered Richard Price. Burke's master image of a swinish multitude—evidence of his neuroses if critics contemporary and modern are to be believed—sprang from his belief that the French Revolution marked the advent of popular politics. And down the two centuries from those fateful summer days in 1789, the French Revolution has borne a weighty burden as the event that ushered in democracy, popular participation, the divisions of left- and-right wing thinking, in short, modern political life itself. Modern scholarship has complicated this stereotype of the French Revolution considerably. We now know the extent to which the Revolution was not a "national event" but was predicated on the micropolitics of Paris only. We are now aware that the storming of the Bastille was a middle-class moment, rather than a populist upswelling of the masses. It is clear that a clandestine world of radical print paved the intellectual path toward the momentous events of 1789 for decades beforehand: the Revolution did not emerge out of nowhere like a summer hailstorm in the Scottish Highlands. Finally, we know that economic and environmental breakdown guided all, not an abstract political indignation; poor harvests and the problems of how best to feed the vast Parisian metropolis left people enraged and fearing for their daily bread.[2]

But if scholars have considerably qualified our image of the events of July 1789 as a *popular revolution,* they have neglected all but completely the extent to which the events on the other side of the Channel a few months later, the events of November 1789, were intertwined with a *population revolution.* Students of geography, history, and politics are familiar with the idea of societies passing through a *demographic revolution,* this having begun in France and Britain in the age of Price and Burke, and being a process of transition from a regime of high births and deaths to low births and deaths that is still unfolding in the less-developed nations of the globe. They are far less aware of a population revolution that occurred at the same time as the demographic revolution of the age of Price and Burke, of a revolution in how people thought about the relationships between population, resources, and the economic well-being of societies. How this particular revolution has slipped off the scholarly radar is unclear, for its key protagonists, the men who transformed our understanding of this set of relationships, have at least as good a claim to having ushered in modernity through the invention of social scientific analysis as has the French Revolution itself. And it is ironic that this population revolution has gone undetected for its leaders were none other than three of the most celebrated participants in and defenders of the French Revolution. Furthermore, each of these three men had a part to play in laying the political powder keg at the Old Jewry meeting house on November 4, 1789. The three men were Richard Price, who delivered the address that aroused Burke's ire; Jean-Antoine Nicolas de Caritat, Marquis de Condorcet, who received the formal congratulations of Price's audience as a member of the French National Assembly; and William Godwin, who in a flush of youthful enthusiasm attended the November 5 follow-up meeting the evening after Price's address and scribbled in his ever-present notebook our only remaining knowledge of those congratulations that Condorcet received. To paint a triptych of these three men's work on population, economy, and resources is to limn a picture of modern social science in its birth pangs. That we no longer remember much of their achievement is thanks to Malthus, who was to overpaint their portrait of society in very different colors before the revolutionary decade of the 1790s was out.[3]

Richard Price: Mathematics, Morality, Mortality

For the first panel of our triptych, let us start with Dr. Richard Price, who, as his astute modern biographer points out, tends to be labeled as "the unfortunate Dr. Price" on the basis of his intellectual mauling late in life at the tip of Edmund Burke's quill, an instrument of unparalleled ferocity and elegance. Price's biographer is right to note just how misleading this epithet is, not simply because his political ideas have shaped "our political traditions" down to the present day, but also because, viewed from the perspective of the moment he mounted the platform to give his speech in the Old Jewry meeting house on November 4, 1789, he was one of British society's most revered polymaths. For by this time, Price had conquered a number of different fields of inquiry and was lionized by different sectors of London society, being simultaneously a grandee of the "radical establishment" (if one is allowed that oxymoron), a revered preacher, a penetrating philosopher of questions of free will and determinism, an eloquent apostle of liberty, a leading mathematician and Fellow of the Royal Society, and a pioneer of social insurance schemes. And lest this makes Richard Price sound like a "jack of all trades and master of none," there was in fact an Ariadnian thread that ran through this diverse array of achievements in the form of a deeply held Christian belief in the necessity of promoting liberty and self-reliance in order for all to achieve individual self-realization before God. If one of Edmund Burke's most insightful biographers detects in his subject a "great melody," a set of core convictions that make sense of the whole, the target of Burke's antirevolutionary ire, Richard Price, also possessed a refrain that ran through his work every bit as tuneful, albeit to a very different key signature.[4]

When Richard Price stood on the podium on November 4, 1789, he was one of the most respected and revered scholars of his age, that reputation the result of four decades of patient inquiry. The full range of his achievement has been well analyzed and is beyond my scope here, but one key element of that achievement, one motif in his great melody, was his work on population and insurance. In many ways, Price's core concern—to quantify mortality rates to allow for successful life insurance schemes based on mathematically robust tables of life expectancy—sounds prosaic enough, but it in fact fitted into a far more grandiose socioreligious vision of revolutionary and utopian progress. Price had already made a considerable name for himself as a preacher, educationalist, philosopher, and mathematician when he turned his attention to the question of the British population in the early 1760s. Price's interest in population was piqued by the question of whether the British population was rising or falling in his own era. Price consolidated the results of his researches in the book that made his name, the rather cumbersomely titled *Observations on Reversionary Payments* of 1771. All but unknown today, Price's *Observations* was in its own age a roaring success, lauded by Benjamin Franklin as "the foremost Production of Human Understanding that this Century has afforded us."[5]

In *Observations*, Price approached the question of the British population through the traditional lens described in the previous chapter: "Everyone knows that the strength of a state consists in the number of people. The encouragement of population, therefore, ought to be one of the first objects of policy in every state." Good statecraft, therefore, would lead to an increasing population; Price was convinced that British population was declining precipitously. A range of data lifted from parish registers was used to support Price's contention, and his correspondence includes letters to and from that most effective of eighteenth-century data-collecting devices, the network of parish clergymen. Thus, for example, when, on March 18, 1773, John Disney, an important dissenting clergyman, wrote to Price with details from the parish records of Swinderby in Lincolnshire, where he was the incumbent, Price hungrily snapped up such mathematically reliable data, which became fodder for his narrative of population decline. For reasons that will become clear, Price paid particular attention in his *Observations* to the state of his adopted home, London, concluding from mortality and natality data for the era 1716–1736 with a very plausible show of (somewhat spurious) precision that "calculating from hence on all the same suppositions with those which made 651,580 to be the present number of inhabitants in London, it will be found that the number then was 735,840, or 84,260 greater than the number in the present year 1769. London, therefore, for the last 30 years, has been decreasing." Scaling this picture up to the entire country, and using data from the Hearth and Window Tax Returns in conjunction with parish registers, Price asserted that the nation as a whole had "since the year 1690, decreased near a *million and a half.*"[6]

If it was Richard Price the mathematician who constructed these figures, it was Richard Price the moralist and political activist who both diagnosed the causes of this (to his mind) fateful decline in the British population and projected remedies for both individuals and society at large. In terms of causes, Price detected three major socioenvironmental reasons for the pattern of decline that the hard logic of mathematics had identified. In a quantified and politicized version of Cowper's famous poetic injunction that "God made the country, and man made the town,"

Price identified a destructive interrelation between changes in the countryside and the town, each of them driving down population. The key
motor in the countryside was "engrossing," the taking of agricultural land
formerly tenanted by a hardy yeomanry (who were, in Price's eyes, "the
chief strength and security of every state") by a restricted, grasping, self-
serving squirarchy who built ever-larger parcels of property. Engrossing
was hardly new, Thomas More's *Utopia* (1516) having, in a celebrated
image, called this the devouring of men by sheep some 250 years earlier.
Yet for Price the pace and the scope of this process had increased alarm-
ingly in his own age. Undoubtedly the suite of farming changes that historians sometimes label retrospectively as the "agricultural revolution"
meant that the land could produce ever-greater quantities of food with
ever-fewer farmers, but for Price the economics of such a transition were
not compensation for the moral rent they made in the fabric of English
social life: "it is, indeed, erecting *private* benefit on *public* calamity; and,
for the sake of a temporary advantage, giving up the nation to depopulation and distress." The result was to force a formerly self-sufficient,
hardy, moral body of working men to pack their bags and head for the
towns in search of gainful employment. And the state of England's towns
was the second great cause of dramatic depopulation that Price's quantitative work revealed. For both environmental and moral reasons, Price
saw towns as precipitating depopulation: "In general; there seems reason
to think that in towns . . . the excess of burials above the births, and the
proportion of inhabitants dying annually, are more or less as the towns
are greater or smaller." The environmental reason why towns were a
drain on population was the insalubrious conditions present in overcrowded houses that did not enjoy the benefits of the Victorian sanitation
movement. Price's observations in this regard lacked any detail. That
said, his basic point about the insalubrious nature of the eighteenth-
century town wholly chimes with modern demographic studies of urban
life expectancies in this era. Price waxed rather more lyrically on the
moral reason why towns shortened life expectancy and checked population increase under the catch-all category of the evils of "luxury," a fashionable term of social analysis in the mid-eighteenth century thanks to
John Brown's best-selling *Estimate* (1757), a furious denunciation of
English consumerism at the point of its birth. Price believed that "luxury" left people selfish and debased, unhinged the Christian principle of
neighborliness, and led to the wealthy looking on with cold indifference
as the rural poor they themselves had dislodged from the countryside by
their engrossing of the land succumbed to disease in the unhealthy towns:
"we [the British] are far advanced in that last and worst state of society,

in which false refinement and luxury multiply wants, and debauch, enslave and depopulate." The only exception to his simple binary of healthy countryside and corrupted town, and the third cause of declining population, was constituted by those rural locations that were also insalubrious and therefore led to an excess of deaths over births. Again drawing on parish data, Price acknowledged, for example, that the malarial marshlands of England and the Alps dramatically shortened life expectancy and called for more work on "what influence different airs and different situations have on the duration of life." If God had made the country, then, some parts were more Godly than others.[7]

Perhaps unsurprisingly, Price's solutions to the problems that the quantitative evidence of population decline proved to be real, not merely the product of a moralist's imagination, lay in reversing the trends in engrossing and the flight of displaced rustics to urban centers. The ideal society would be one that had advanced beyond barbarism, wherein life would indeed be nasty, brutish, and short, but that had not tipped over into the commercialized excesses that Price anatomized as a moralist and that, in the same decade, Adam Smith would analyze as a political economist in his celebrated *Wealth of Nations* (1776). The key to realizing this societal balance for Price lay in allowing for self determination. This is why Price became a consultant to numerous fledgling life insurance schemes. Many such schemes had floundered earlier in the century for want of adequate information about life expectancies. Combining his mathematical and demographic knowledge, Price advised on sensible weekly contribution rates that would ensure such funds would not fold by accruing excess liabilities through underestimating likely death rates. Price's aim here was to support schemes that would allow the poorer strata of society to support themselves in later life, notably if they lost their major breadwinner. Self-determination for the hardy, industrious laboring class, which Price, as we have seen, valued as the backbone of a stable, virtuous society, demanded that such individuals, by thrift and foresight, be enabled to cater for their futures. But self-determination also depended on building a form of government that fostered it: "let there be entire liberty; and maintain public peace by a government founded, not in *constraint,* but in the *respect* and the *hearts* of the people." This argument was not new to the Price of *Observations* in 1771; on the contrary, for more than a decade he had been arguing in his political work that Britons needed to protect their much-vaunted liberties as granted through the Magna Carta and renewed by the Glorious Revolution of 1688. The argument only grew more pertinent in the context first of the American War of Independence (1776–1783) and then of that crowning moment in

Price's intellectual life, the French Revolution. Even before the American revolution against the imperial yoke of Britain, Price had argued that America was in that ideal balanced position between barbarity on the one side and commercial excess on the other: they were "in the first and the happiest of states" "a very striking proof" of which was the evidence of their rapid population increase. Yet this did not apply evenly to the British colonies on the other side of the Atlantic; on the contrary, population was increasing in "the back settlements" of the interior, where a hardy yeomanry could farm their own land and grow their families apace. By contrast, debauchery and luxury had begun to show themselves in Boston and other cities, where as a result the population was static.[8]

For all this ambivalence about urban America, when the fledgling United States of America's independence was acknowledged in Britain, Price, the champion of "entire liberty," welcomed it in a 1785 pamphlet, *Observations on the Importance of the American Revolution and the Means of Making It a Benefit to the World,* which earned him brickbats from many in his own country but led to an offer of citizenship across the Atlantic. For Price, America was populated by "plain and honest farmers," not "opulent and splendid merchants." The vast lands of the Americas had ideal soils for producing all that a virtuous society could need. As such, American independence was not merely an idyll in and of itself (Price declined to emigrate by virtue of his age), but pointed toward a utopian futurity for mankind: "Perhaps I do not go too far when I say that, next to the introduction of Christianity among mankind, the American revolution may prove the most important step in the progressive course of improvement. It is an event which may produce a general diffusion of the principles of humanity, and become the means of setting free mankind from the shackles of superstition and tyranny." It seems a long way to the modern mind from combing the archives in Swinderby parish church for death rates to freeing mankind from the shackles of superstition and "the steps ordained by Providence to introduce these times," but to Price there was an unbroken and fairly short chain tying these things together. Population was the proof of good (or bad) government; government was the facilitator of human happiness on this earth; the whole was part of God's plan to lead humans toward self-realization.[9]

And so, when in the twilight of his years Price witnessed the events of the French Revolution, it is unsurprising that he fitted them into the same providential and demographic schema. Even before Le Quatorze Juillet, Price was enthusing in a private letter to Mirabeau that "a revolution so important brought about in a period of time so short by the spirit and unanimity of a great Kingdom without violence or bloodshed, has scarcely a parallel in the Annals of the world." Four months later, Price's oration at the Old Jewry, published as *A Discourse on the Love of Our Country,* welcomed the French Revolution in terms long familiar to readers of his demographic and political writing. Most governments were "usurpations on the rights of men and little better than contrivances for enabling the *few* to oppress the *many*." This condemnation was extended to explicitly encompass his own nation, which had an unrepresentative government: "it wants . . . the grand security of public liberty. Increasing luxury has multiplied abuses in it." As we have seen, in his 1771 *Observations on Reversionary Payments,* Price had made good these rather vague claims by attending to hard, quantitative evidence about putative population decline in England during his lifetime. While in his most notorious publication, the *Discourse,* Price did not rehearse the same arguments, overly sterile as they would have been, as he reached his feverish exordium, he did, for one last time, resort to linking population, liberty, and providence in a summa of his life's work as a mathematical scholar and of his life's creed as a radical Christian:

> I have lived to see a diffusion of knowledge which has undermined superstition and error. I have lived to see the rights of men better understood than ever, and nations panting for liberty, which seemed to have lost the idea of it. I have lived to see thirty millions of people, indignant and resolute, spurning at slavery, and demanding liberty with an irresistible voice, their king led in triumph, and an arbitrary monarch surrendering himself to his subjects. After sharing in the benefits of one Revolution, I have been spared to be a witness to two other Revolutions, both glorious. And now, methinks, I see the ardor for liberty catching and spreading, a general amendment beginning in human affairs, the dominion of kings changed for the dominion of laws, and the dominion of priests giving way to the dominion of reason and conscience.

Here, then, Price's "great melody" played one last, triumphant strain.[10]

Condorcet: Reason and Revolution, Progress and Population

Four months before Price's famous speech at the Old Jewry, in a letter of July 4, 1789, addressed to Count Mirabeau, Price predicted the influence of the French Revolution would "spread till it has overthrown every where the obstacles to human improvement and made the world free virtuous and happy" and asked the count to pass on his "congratulations on this occasion" to "the Marquis Condorcet" for "the presents . . . sent him of . . . valuable publications." Price had been corresponding with Condorcet for a number of years by the time of the momentous events of 1789 about shared interests in what we might, as a shorthand, call "radical demography," the quintessentially enlightened idea that the application of mathematical reasoning to the amelioration of social problems was the key to unlocking the door to utopian progress. Demography, the counting of vital statistics and their utilization for government planning and for the emancipation of the poor via social insurance, was the great proof of the worth of this radical platform. But if Price and Condorcet shared an extraordinary affinity, their life paths would diverge wildly in the months and years following Price's enthusiastic eulogy on events across the Channel. Price would die peacefully in his bed in April 1791, his loss lamented in newspaper obituaries and his funeral a public occasion; Condorcet would die only three years later (despite being twenty years Price's junior), an imprisoned fugitive from the Revolutionary government he had espoused. And there could be no public celebration for Condorcet at this time; dying in somewhat suspicious circumstances in a state jail (he probably, in fact, had a heart attack, but the timing of the event lent it the air of scandal and none-too-judicial murder) in March 1794, his death was hushed up until it leaked to newspapers some nine months later. Price, then, died a scion of the radical establishment; Condorcet died, like Hamlet's father, "unhousel'd, disappointed, unanel'd."[11]

The Marquis de Condorcet, Jean-Antoine Nicolas de Caritat, had been born to a minor noble family from Picardy, who had generation on generation made their way by distinguished military careers. Condorcet's father died a few weeks after his son's birth, leaving him to be brought up by a doting, protective mother who kept him attired in girls' white dresses until the age of eight. And yet, for all the mockery that this rather peculiar petri dish of an upbringing may have brought down upon Condorcet's young shoulders, he flourished academically, disclosing a unique gift in the mathematical sciences. His first academic article—about integral calculus—appeared in 1765 when he was still only twenty-one and led to his being eulogized by the Academy of Sciences as one of the ten finest mathematical minds in Europe. In the age of French reverence for Newton's achievements, math was à la mode; Condorcet was singled out for lionization and thereby saved from a military career, for which he was singularly poorly suited. It also led Condorcet into the salon society of the French Enlightenment, where, initially provincial and bearing all the marks of the stereotype of the socially gauche mathematician, he soon found his feet and lost his heart to the savant hostess Julie Lespinasse (herself lover of one of the great moving spirits of the French Enlightenment, Jean D'Alembert).[12]

Condorcet drafted deeply from the cup of the radical Enlightenment that Voltaire and the contributors to the *Encyclopédie* were filling with the hope of social reform. The strange blend of calculus and the salon could only lead Condorcet in one direction; toward the application of mathematics to the analysis and amelioration of "real-world" problems. And for this rather new blend, Condorcet coined a term that has stuck in lexicons on both sides of the Channel: "social science." The first outing for Condorcet's "social science" came at a uniquely congenial moment in the history of French policy making, under the tutelage of that most rare of beasts, a scholarly politician, in the shape of Anne-Robert Jacques Turgot. Turgot argued for root-and-branch reform of the economic and social policy of the French ancien règime in the mid-1770s, suggesting that free trade would alleviate the problems of food scarcity and seeking other improvements to the infrastructure of the nation. Turgot had taken Condorcet under his wing; in return, Condorcet continued to champion Turgot after his rapid fall from power in 1776. For Condorcet, Turgot had mastered "the science of the legislator"; he was the rational legislator that the radical intelligentsia had sought. His fall from grace only showed just how far France still had to go to achieve enlightened governance; Condorcet would become enmeshed in the radical democratization of French government in the 1790s, indeed, he was the architect of much of its machinery of voting and representation, but he was never wholly sanguine about the merits of democracy after Turgot's demise. After 1776, a year that marked a watershed in Condorcet's career, he consistently applied himself to the question of how mathematics could create enlightened public administration.[13]

It was this question that led Condorcet to address demography as one of the core components of his vision of a science of society. For, as a realm, vital statistics were quantifiable and, as noted, there had already been decades' worth of studies in this field. For Condorcet, what was needed were more precise and widespread data harvests—he, like Price, advocated the instigation of national censuses long before they came into being—and a greater effort to correlate demographic data with social and environmental factors as causal variables. Condorcet espoused this creed most transparently at a moment of personal triumph, his successful if bitterly contested election to the French Academy in 1782. His "reception speech" was blunt: "in every science the ultimate goal is to arrive at quantitative results." For a government to be able to "evaluate accurately the increases or decreases in population or wealth produced by different causes . . . depends on all kinds of physical information." Notable was the need for information about the climate and physical environment of the governed country, the "things held in common (such as the water of rivers)," to ensure that usage by one person or group did not infringe upon the equal rights of others. Like Richard Price's in England then, Condorcet's intellectual trajectory had followed a predictable course for a mathematician with a social conscience; from math to applied math; and from applied math to questions of good governance. And the population-environment nexus was at the nub of all this: to count vital statistics and correlate them to climatic and environmental conditions was to enhance the understanding of legislators and allow them to improve the lot of common humanity, setting mankind on the path to progress. The flowery opening to Condorcet's 1782 speech laid all this bare: "And now at last we can exclaim: truth has conquered; the human race is saved! Each century will add new enlightenment to that of the century that has preceded it, and this progress, which nothing can henceforth halt or delay, will have no other limits than that of the duration of the universe." There is tragic irony in the disjunction between his sanguine hopes for social reason and his own fate in 1794, when he wrote of "the consoling certainty that we will never again see those leagues of factious men still more fatal to the happiness of citizens than to the tranquillity of princes, nor those massacres, *those proscriptions of peoples,* that have sullied the annals of the human race."[14]

And yet, at the outset of the revolutionary tumults in the summer of 1789, Condorcet clearly felt that events were fulfilling his Panglossian predictions of 1782. Torn between excitement and his quintessentially enlightened pacifism, Condorcet took to the streets and joined the revolutionary militia, but, as story has it, he refused to carry anything more threatening than an umbrella! It has also become enshrined in revolutionary folklore that Condorcet's only child, Eliza, was conceived on the night of the Fall of the Bastille. Picaresque anecdotes aside, by the autumn of 1789, Condorcet and the like-minded members of the "Society of 1789" were hard at work advocating social reform. In particular, Condorcet advocated social insurance schemes backed by Price's work as a cost-effective way of alleviating and finally eradicating the ills of poverty. More generally, Condorcet threw himself into the aftermath of 1789, seeing it as the opportune moment when social science might at last rationally pull the levers of government: "to bring together so many scattered and inconsistent elements, to seek the integrating principles of the economic sciences and especially their common link with the general science of civilization, such is the object of the *social art.*" If Condorcet had been touting his ideas of a social science of rational governmental calculation for the fifteen years since Turgot's demise, he saw an opportunity to actually be heard in 1789.[15]

The transition from policy advisor to political participant came for Condorcet in the wake of Louis XVI's abortive attempt to flee the clutches of the revolutionary government in 1791, an event that radicalized him into one whom Burke would vilify in print as "the most furious of the extravagant Republicans" in 1791 and privately as one of "the whole flight of the magpies and Jays of philosophy" best ignored. On his own side of the Channel, by contrast, Condorcet rode the wave of popular sentiment, elected a member of the Legislative Assembly in August 1791, and becoming one of its most bellicose advocates of war. Obviously the time had come to cast aside the philosopher's umbrella. And yet not quite. The most contentious issue Condorcet was called to cast judgment upon in the Assembly was whether the king should face the death penalty for his flight from revolutionary justice, that defining moment in Condorcet's own political conversion. Condorcet voted that the king had plotted against the people and was thereby a threat to the security of the state, but he refused to sanction the death penalty, being among those who advocated the severest penalty short of death for the deposed monarch. When the king's head did roll, severed by the guillotine on January 21, 1793, it also marked the beginnings of Condorcet's own descent into a not dissimilar fate a mere fourteen months later.[16]

Condorcet's refusal to sanction the execution of Louis XVI was one of a set of positions he adopted that set Danton and Robespierre against him as 1792 waned and 1793 waxed. Above all, Condorcet saw in the mob violence of Robespierre's Paris Commune an irrational form of government that would extinguish his hopes for an enlightened politics as the science of statecraft. As such, Condorcet drafted new systems for representative government founded on universal (male) suffrage. He also founded a journal of social mathematics that he hoped would teach the populace rational decision making. In this journal, written amid the bloodshed and frenzy of the king's execution, Condorcet calmly called for a government that would conduct scientific censuses of its population and correlate the findings with environmental and climatic data, the project of his 1782 reception speech reborn in unrecognizably different circumstances. An umbrella, actual or intellectual, is of little use in a hurricane, meteorological or sociological. Condorcet would be blown away by the sheer ferocity of Robespierre's malevolence as it peaked in the so-called "second phase" of the Terror. A warrant for Condorcet's arrest was promulgated on October 3, 1793. He fled the capital, initially reprising his childhood attire by escaping in women's clothing before traveling under the alias of Pierre Simon. It was an innkeeper in Clamart-le-Vignoble who alerted the authorities on March 27, 1794, to a suspicious man who, despite his poor appearance, had lodged an incongruously "aristocratic request for a twelve-egg omelette." Condorcet died the following day in prison, most probably of a heart attack despite rumors that he had taken a vial of poison he had secreted in his clothing.[17]

And yet Condorcet was to have the last laugh in some ways against his revolutionary oppressors, his victory coming not by the sword, nor the umbrella, but by his pen. For years (going back to the heady days of his 1782 reception speech) he had been composing a philosophical testament, a credo that brought together the beliefs that had driven him on the remarkable odyssey from his own (literal and intellectual) apron strings to political and intellectual celebrity. That testament, the *Equisse d'un tableau historique des progrès de l'esprit humain (Outlines of an Historical View of the Progress of the Human Mind)*, was published in 1795 by his devoted wife with the blessing of the Convention. It became the rational manual of the later years of the Revolution after Robespierre's demise in 1794. It was also the sacred cow of progressive thought that Malthus would seek to butcher at the peak of England's revolutionary fears in 1798. The *Outline* was Condorcet's last and greatest rumination on the themes of reason, progress, and population. Condorcet saw in human history a great arc that described a course of progress in ten epochs, the last of which would impel us toward human perfectibility, both individual and social. Much of this was commonplace to Enlightenment thought: settled agriculture was the origin of human progress and population growth; science was the key driver for social progress, Francis Bacon having first revealed the way to study nature—"observation, experiment and calculation"; conversely, the reign of priestcraft in the form of medieval Christianity had been a "disastrous epoch."[18] But what really excited Condorcet's readers and ensured that his voice lived on from the grave was his vision of futurity as a realm of infinite progress and perfectibility. If Condorcet has become uniquely identified with the utopian speculations of his tenth epoch, he himself gave credit to others: "while the fabric of prejudice was tottering to its foundations, a fatal blow was given to it by a doctrine, of which Turgot, Price and Priestley were the first and most illustrious advocates; it was the doctrine of the infinite perfectibility of the human mind." What distinguished Condorcet from his predecessors was the passion and the conviction of the image he had painted of a perfectible future, completed even as he fled furtively from the bloodthirsty emissaries of Robespierre's far from progressive reign of terror. Condorcet foresaw a future in which inequality between individuals and between nations would be eliminated. Advance would be not merely in the technologies the nascent industrial revolution was creating, but in our human capacities, bodily and mental, in "our natural organization itself." Taken together, technological and human advances would allow forever-smaller portions of ground to support ever-larger populations. While medical and sanitary advances would not secure human immortality, Condorcet could envisage a time when "the interval between the birth of man and this decay, will itself have no assignable limit." Acknowledging that "it is equally impossible to pronounce on either side respecting" whether there might be a "limit" to these apparently unceasing processes of advance and progress, Condorcet clearly erred in his answer toward the negative. Progress—political, personal, and demographic—could continue unabated for as long as the universe itself. No wonder the literati on both sides of the Channel were so seduced by this splendid vision, spawned triumphantly in defiance of the circumstances of suspicion, squalor, and slaughter that had engulfed their noble author.[19]

William Godwin: "No War, No Administration of Justice, No Government"

The momentous events of 1789 also stirred an East Anglian man, younger than Price or Condorcet, but hardly youthful at the age of thirty-three given the life expectancy of the era. Unlike Price, the scion of Dissent, or Condorcet, Voltaire's intellectual son, our East Anglian, William Godwin, was as yet all but unknown. But 1789 sparked his already radical consciousness, his passion for liberty and self-determination, the secularized version of the Calvinism he had imbibed so deeply as a child. As he penned (presumably retrospectively) in his private diary: "This was the year of the French Revolution. My heart beat high with great swelling sentiments of Liberty." If not yet known to the general public, Godwin was nonetheless known in radical and dissenting coteries. While Godwin had not been at the Old Jewry on November 4 to hear Richard Price's electrifying speech, he was among those who reconvened the following evening in Price's company, still feeding off the energy of that great moment in radical oratory, to construct a message of support for the revolutionary government in France from the "Revolution Society of London." Godwin recorded this event in his diary; the attendees were no less than a who's who of English radicalism, with Andrew Kippis, Theophilus Lindsay, and Horne Tooke present, among others. And it was Godwin who carefully recorded in draft the message of support and kinship sent by the assembled company to their revolutionary brothers across the Channel: "the proceedings of the people of France will secure tranquillity, and all the virtues of patriotism to themselves, and a dawn of justice and moderation to surrounding nations. The inhabitants of Great Britain in particular may expect to derive the most essential benefit from the Revolution in France; and united as we are to you by congeniality of sentiment, by the cultivation of science and truth, and by the love of that freedom for which our ancestors bled, we trust it is scarcely possible for any occasion to offer that can lead two such nations to engage in mutual hostilities."[20]

From being "one in the crowd," the diarist of revolution, Godwin would be catapulted into being its superstar on the British side of the Channel. This elevation from bit-part player to the lead would happen with startling rapidity; Richard Price would not live to see it, but before Condorcet's demise, Godwin secured his fame with the publication of his momentous work, *An Enquiry Concerning Political Justice* in 1793. Traveling to Warwickshire in the following year, Godwin recorded in his diary this strange, philosophical moment of celebrity: "There was not a person almost in town or village who had any acquaintance with modern publications that had not heard of the 'Enquiry Concerning Political Justice.' . . . I was nowhere a stranger. . . . If temporary fame ever was an object worthy to be coveted by the human mind, I certainly obtained it in a degree that has seldom been exceeded." The conservative establishment was equally attuned to the notoriety of author of the *Enquiry:* he came to be regarded as "one of the most dangerous enemies of established society." For in many ways the timing of its publication came accidentally at one of the high-water marks of English fear and frenzy about matters French. Published on February 14, 1793, the *Enquiry* breathed a universal love, but its critics saw it as more the manual of a Valentine's Day Massacre, appearing as it did not a month after Louis XVI's execution and only two weeks after Condorcet and the revolutionary government of the French National Assembly had declared war on Britain.[21]

Like Condorcet's, Godwin's talents were recognized young; if Condorcet was only emerging from dresses at the age of eight, Godwin at the same age was beginning to preach to his neighbors. If a staunchly Calvinist upbringing might have led Godwin to a career in the ambit of radical dissent and thus made him a natural successor to Richard Price, that became impossible when Godwin lost his faith completely and crushingly. The rest of his life would be spent triangulating an earnest sense of moral probity already evidenced in his childhood preaching with a secular sense of social advance. That life would be long—Godwin died in 1836—and would take in a breathtaking array of interests. If his youth had pointed to a career in the church and his fame in the mid-1790s suggested the life of a political savant, thereafter Godwin took different paths. For a start, he unexpectedly turned to literature, writing a series of novels that, while hard to pigeonhole generically, can only be described as on the cusp of gothic and historical fiction. For Godwin, fiction and politics were of a piece; he noted in his diary that his first (and best) novel, *Caleb Williams* (1794), was "the offspring of that temper of mind in which the composition of my 'Political Justice' left me." Whatever the merits of this view, critics still regard *Caleb Williams* as "easily the most impressive English novel of the 1790s."[22] And if Godwin had started to turn to fiction to promulgate his message and in the hope of more adequate remuneration, his life also started to play out like the most extravagant of gothic novels after 1796, once he met and fell in love with the radical writer and feminist Mary Wollstonecraft. Within five months of the kindling of their relationship, Mary was pregnant, Godwin's "chance-medley" (rhythm) system of contraception having failed. To inevitable satirical pillorying from the conservative establishment, the ardent feminist and Godwin, who had famously pronounced in his *Enquiry* that marriage was "a system of fraud," tied the knot in St. Pancras Church on March 29, 1797. Taunts aside, Mary and William were happy together, but they were torn asunder when Mary died in the month following the birth of their daughter in August 1797, the scene being a brutal reminder of the perils of childbirth that Laurence Sterne had transmuted so humorously into fiction in *Tristram Shandy*. Mortified, bereft, Godwin—in common with most widowed fathers in the era—remarried promptly in 1802. But even this was not the end of Godwin's domestic travails; on the contrary, while his second marriage, if somewhat loveless, was at least stable, his growing daughter Mary was to throw his life into turmoil again in the summer of 1814 when, not yet seventeen, she eloped with the married poet Percy Bysshe Shelley. The young Shelley had been much impressed by the radicalism of Godwin's *Enquiry*, writing to Godwin in 1812 that this single work had "opened to my mind fresh & more extensive views, it materially influenced my character, and I rose from its perusal a wiser and a better man." Thus it was a delicious irony (to adversaries) that the great critic of marriage and domesticity, Godwin, had reaped his own bitter harvest, his disciple Percy Shelley having shattered his own domestic tranquility by the elopement. Shelley's first wife, while hardly impartial, put his actions down "entirely" to the influence of Godwin's ideas. Matters were patched up, but the sense of Godwin as the absurd visionary whose own actions proved the vacuousness of his radical pronouncements stuck in the public consciousness. It became too easy to mock Godwin. The most feared critic of the establishment in the mid-1790s, he became, by the first decade of the new century, the butt of jokes, easy prey to the well-turned put-down. Even those like the romantics who had once been entranced by the rhapsody of his vision turned coat: for Robert Southey, Godwin was "like a Close Stool pan, most often empty, & better empty than full," while Hazlitt found him anything but rhapsodic in person, castigating his conversation for being "as flat as a pancake," his wit for being as quickfire as a grandfather clock that "had to be wound up long before it could strike." Thus, where the *Outline* saw Condorcet's fame and reputation rise defiantly from the bloodshed of the Terror, his life transformed into an icon of hope, Godwin's trajectory was quite otherwise, the fame of his *Enquiry* being long outlived by its author, who having been feared and then ridiculed was—in a fate more ignominious still—forgotten.[23]

What was it, then, about that landmark book of 1793, the *Enquiry*, that made Godwin's resplendent but short-lived fame? What made that work, in the words of William Hazlitt, "a sun in the firmament of reputation"? Why was "no one more talked of, more looked up to, more sought after" than Godwin? Like Condorcet's, Godwin's career was enwrapped in what one of his biographers deftly terms "a fantasy of reason": the *Enquiry*, the acme of his intellectual achievement, would tread a course through the same enthralling patterns of prophecy, progress, and population as Condorcet's *Outline*. And yet, the *Enquiry* in fact *opposed* revolution. The work that made Godwin public enemy number one of the English establishment—the tract whose radicalism only escaped prosecution by Pitt's government on account of its expense, which meant that it (unlike Tom Paine's *Rights of Man*, which sold forty thousand copies in a year) was beyond the reach of the poor—in fact saw revolution as delaying the progress of civilization. Believing, as did Condorcet, that "politics is a science," Godwin saw revolution as "disturbing the harmony of intellectual nature" and therefore retarding the rational progress of human social and political change. And yet, Godwin's ideas, though anathema to revolution, were hugely subversive to the establishment. Progress in human capacities should lead to the withering of unnecessary fetters on human liberty, be they religious or political. For his core conviction that "all supererogatory co-operation is carefully to be avoided," Godwin has been hailed as the intellectual progenitor of anarchist politics. It led Godwin to some positions that seem more absurd than threatening, notably his prediction that societal advance would lead to the abandonment of music concerts and the production of plays: "It may be doubted whether men will hereafter come forward in any mode formally to repeat words and ideas that are not their own? It may be doubted whether any musical performer will habitually execute the compositions of others? . . . All formal repetition of other men's ideas seems to be a scheme for imprisoning, for so long a time, the operations of our own mind." For all its quirks, however, the same message of absolute liberty, of progress as self-determination, had far more bite when it came to the realms of property and would affright the establishment with its potential consequences. Property was the use of resources by one person or group "by a permanent or temporary exclusion of the rest of the species," which could only be justified in a scientific politics where this exclusion resulted in "a greater sum of benefit or pleasure than could have arisen from its being otherwise appropriated." While Godwin eschewed rabble-rousing, the consequences of this position were made clear in a condemnation of luxury that had strong affinities with Richard Price's critique: "in what manner are . . . seeming superfluities usually procured? By abridging multitudes of men to a deplorable degree in points of essential moment, that one man may be accommodated, with sumptuous yet, strictly considered, insignificant luxuries." The progress of the human mind would demand the elimination of these injustices, not by the force of arms but of reason.[24]

And how did population fit into this schema? Having already argued that the limits of our physical environment in terms of climate could not interrupt the march of progress—"physical causes [only] appeared to be powerful till moral ones can be brought into operation"—at the close of the third, 1797, edition of the *Enquiry*, Godwin turned to population on the grounds that "several writers upon these topics have treated it in a way calculated to produce a very gloomy impression" about the prospects for social and political advance. Though arguing that, left to its own devices, nature tended to create an equilibrium between population and resources, and also acknowledging that "there are various methods by the practice of which population may be checked," Godwin foresaw in the longer run a way out of any gloomy interrelation between population, politics, and progress. In an argument closely paralleling Condorcet's, Godwin provided technological and human reasons why population could not impede the smooth march to a self-determining future. In technological terms, three-quarters of the globe was not currently cultivated and, more importantly, improvements in agricultural techniques "as yet cannot be reduced to any limits of calculation." On this basis alone, Godwin concluded that "myriads of centuries of still increasing population may pass away, and the earth be yet found sufficient for the support of its inhabitants." At the same time, medical advances would allow us "to

prolong our vigour, if not to immortalize it." For Godwin, human progress was a story of the triumph of mind over matter; and one of the tri-
umphs that would soon unfold was "to diminish our eagerness for the
gratification of the senses." As a consequence, if agriculture could see us
through myriads of centuries, by the time that this physical resource
reached its limits, the entire motor for population as a threat to rational
governance would have disappeared as humans "will probably cease to
propagate. The whole will be a people of men, and not of children. Generation will not succeed generation, nor truth have, in a certain degree,
to recommence her career every thirty years." The upshot of this longevity would be wisdom, personal, social, political. In a remarkable closing exordium, Godwin summoned up what this golden future would look
like: "There will be no war, no administration of justice . . . no government. Beside this there will be neither disease, anguish, melancholy, nor
resentment." Godwin had seen the future; for one brief moment, English
society looked set fair to be swept away by his vision.[25]

Multitudes and Millions: Challenging Revolutionary Demography

Retrospectively, it is all too easy to dismiss my revolutionary triptych:
Richard Price, an old man trounced by Burke and ignorant of what was
about to happen; Condorcet, the umbrella-carrying prophet of a blood-
less advance to perfection whose otherworldly speculations were cut down
by the realities of Robespierre's Terror; and Godwin, the opponent of
marriage who was twice married, the novelist who thought it slavish to
read the words of others, and the father of two who had expected the urge
to propagate to wither, in sum, a self-deluded prophet of self-realization
who was rightly ridiculed and cast aside in his own lifetime. It is easy
to underestimate Price's *Discourse,* Condorcet's *Outline,* and Godwin's
Enquiry as irrational products of heady times, as books that are rightly
forgotten. And yet that is to ignore just how seriously these three men
and their emancipatory messages were taken in the maelstrom of debate
that the French Revolution sparked. In their own era, Price, Condorcet,
and Godwin formed a powerful phalanx that, conjoining mathematics
and social concern, seemed to be plotting a scientific path toward political perfection for a rational populace.

Just how seriously the prophets of perfection were taken can be gauged
from Edmund Burke's attempt to respond to their arguments about population in his celebrated *Reflections on the Revolution in France* (1790).
Burke attracted notoriety in his own age and ever since for only one comment he made about population in the *Reflections,* the reference to the

common people of France as "a swinish multitude." Later in his *Reflec-tions*, however, in a rather neglected passage, Burke turned to the ques-tion of population in good earnest. Drawing on the traditional political-demographic argument that a nation is made strong by having a large populace, he protested that France's massive population of 30 million could not have been sustained but for the fact that its government was not wicked: "Among the standards upon which the effects of government on any country are to be estimated, I must consider the state of its popu-lation as not the least certain. No country in which population flourishes, and is in progressive improvement, can be under a *very* mischievous gov-ernment." Burke then utilized the reports of the French intendants to suggest her population had been 18 million as the eighteenth century began and 24,670,000 by the year 1780, according to Turgot and Con-dorcet's nemesis, Jacques Necker. For his terminal figure for the popula-tion of France on the eve of the French Revolution, Burke happily relied on Richard Price's estimate of 30 million in his *Observations on Rever-sionary Payments*. Thus, in an essay provoked by Price's eulogy of the French Revolution, Burke daringly used Price's own work to diffuse the picture Price had helped to paint of a corrupt regime, noting in passing that on the matter of population, "I certainly defer to Dr. Price's author-ity a good deal more in these speculations, than I do in his general poli-tics." Burke concluded his demographic excursus moderately and in Christian fashion:

> I do not attribute this population to the deposed government; because I do not like to compliment the contrivances of men, with what is due in a great degree to the bounty of Providence. But that decried government could not have obstructed, most probably it favoured, the operation of those causes (whatever they were) whether of nature in the soil, or in habits of industry among the people, which has produced so large a number of the species throughout that whole kingdom, and exhibited in some particular places such prodigies of population.

For Burke, then, the sheer size of the population of France refuted the radical demographers' attacks on French government.[26]

And yet it would not be Burke who turned the radical demographers to ridicule. For, if the French government had spawned a vast, impover-ished peasantry, how was the mere number of people who eked a living from the soil a proof of the merit of the ancien règime? Within two years of the *Reflections*, Arthur Young's *Travels in France* (1792) made the daily realities of life for the 30 million in France painfully apparent: "she presents in every quarter such spectacles of wretchedness." The obscene disjunction between the decadence of Versailles and the wretchedness of the common people, too malnourished to have the energy to be swinish, pointed up the critique of luxury ventured by Price and Godwin. It would take a different line of argument to refute the radical demographers, with their enticing prophecy of progress for all the population. It would take someone with the courage to challenge them in their own area of expertise, the realm of mathematicized social science. That would be Malthus.[27]

CHAPTER THREE

Malthus's *Essay* and the Quiet Revolution of 1798

Parallel Lives: Bob and Jane, in Youth and Revolution

Amid the revolutionary fervor and utopian enthusiasms of the decade following the French Revolution as chronicled in Chapter 2, the concerns of the young Thomas Robert Malthus (known to friends and family as Robert or Bob) can come across as a somewhat less than intoxicating blend of the quotidian and the genteel. If, for Wordsworth in *The Prelude,* "Bliss was it in that dawn to be alive,/But to be young was very heaven," the twenty-three-year-old Malthus's ardor was clearly not thus ignited by matters across the Channel. The only documentary traces for Malthus in 1789 are twofold. First, two letters written to him by his father, Daniel, discussing the state of his mother's health, which was, he was doubtless delighted to hear, the tale of "an uninterrupted progress in recovery," although "the swelling of the ancles [*sic*]" remained as "the only symptom of consequence." Daniel's letters also discussed one other matter, his attempts to secure for his recently ordained son the stipendiary curacy of Okewood in Surrey as his first paid employment since leaving Cambridge University the previous year. Daniel was duly successful in having Sir Frederick Evelyn, the rather less distinguished descendant of the diarist John Evelyn, nominate his son to this living in June 1789. And it was in this capacity that we receive our only other trace of Malthus's life and thought as revolutionary events began to unfold across the Channel in the form of two rather bland sermons first preached at Okewood in July and November of that year. A parishioner arriving late to the sermon Malthus first delivered in Okewood on July 19, 1789 (he would, like most in the cloth, recycle his sermons numerous times), just five days after the Storming of the Bastille, might be forgiven for imagining the young curate was carried away by the excitement of the moment: "We shoud [sic] then see no injustice & hear no complaining in our streets. Injuries & oppressions woud not then invade the quiet of private life; nor would ambitious power violate the rights of nations, & extend desolation thro the world." But Malthus was in fact expatiating on how society would look if we all obeyed Christ's injunction in Matthew 7.12, which he rendered for his congregation as "All things whatsoever ye would that me shoud do unto you, do ye even so to them." Thus, for Malthus it was the Gospels, not political change or human progress, that would build the sort of ideal societies Condorcet and Godwin were trying to fashion. So, for Malthus, the iconic year of 1789 was when his mother recovered, when he received his first paid job courtesy of his father's family connections in Surrey, and when he first trotted out some rather conventional homiletics.[1]

The information we can glean about Malthus in the 1790s prior to the publication of his groundbreaking *Essay* in 1798 at first glance scarcely changes this picture of modest domestic comfort and staid conventionalism. For example, the two sermons Malthus had fashioned on his first appointment at Okewood were delivered again, both here and in the neighboring parish churches of Cranley and Ockley, with some regularity, Malthus duly recording nine uses of them by 1795. And in 1795, Malthus went off on a tour of the Lake District, picturesque guidebooks in hand, scrambling to find the best viewing stations. Thus, as Condorcet's posthumous masterwork the *Outline* was appearing in English translation for the first time, and as Godwin was reworking his *succès de scandale*, the *Enquiry*, for its second edition, we find Malthus assessing the relative merits of different views of Langdale Pike as advocated in Thomas West's *Guide to the Lakes* (1778) and in Arthur Young's *Six Months' Tour through the North of England* (1770): "Sail'd down the lake & visited all the celebrated stations—prefer upon the whole the first that is mentioned in the guide. The rocky hill immediately on the left gives it an advantage, but Mr. Youngs takes in Langdale Pikes, which has a finer shape than any of the other mountains. Dined upon cold veal pye & oat cakes at the Ferry house." All here seems genteel and tame in the vein of James Woodforde; nothing presages the fact that within three years Malthus would emerge as the reviled scourge of the revolutionary establishment, upending their verities by discussing nature's niggardliness, not its beauties.[2]

Malthus's drowsy sermons and aesthetic ramblings all seem to belong to the world modern readers know most affectionately through their satirical depiction in the novels of Jane Austen; his picturesque strictures may remind one of Catherine Morland's earnest rejection of "the whole city of Bath, as unworthy to make part of a landscape," but one hopes the curate did not present himself to his parishioners in the same unflattering light as Mr. Collins and Mr. Elton appear to us. And in the seeming disjuncture between the mundane facts recorded and the intellect that was growing in Malthus in the 1790s, it is hard to resist the parallel to Jane Austen, a woman nine years Malthus's junior, growing up in a rather similar social environment in rural Hampshire. Malthus was twenty-three as the events of 1789 unfolded; Austen reached the same age at what was perhaps an even more incendiary date in British history, 1798, the year in which Malthus would publish his *Essay*. As late as 1969, the avowedly "vehement Socialist journalist" Raymond Postgate was palpably excited by the revolutionary potential of that year in his *Story of a Year: 1798*, suggesting that Britain "was in graver danger than it had been since 1588" and that "the war that was in progress in 1798 was a world war as truly as either of the later wars [of the twentieth century]." This assessment, muted by scholarly caution, is one that more sober historians still endorse today. And yet 1798 looks rather different when viewed through the lens of the twenty-three-year-old Jane Austen's letters. Writing from the family home in Steventon to her beloved sister Cassandra, who was staying in Kent, Jane filled her letters with details about health, clothing, and the social whirl of balls and tea parties. The correspondence throughout the second half of 1798 is a litany of Jane's mother's valetudinarian complaints, including a "gouty swelling & sensation about the ancles" with which, as we have seen, Henrietta Malthus might have sympathized. Likewise, in the tumult of the Irish Rebellion of 1798, Jane's only reference to "the Irish" is to the Irish linen she bought which was "not so fine as I should like it."[3]

And yet we should see another parallel between the twenty-three-year-old Robert of 1789 and the twenty-three-year-old Jane of 1798; amid the gentle round of family life, social observation, and middle-class commentary, both were in fact fomenting acute, precise, and antirevolutionary responses to the events of that most tumultuous of decades that followed the French Revolution. In her consistent debunking of sentimentalism and the excesses of gothic fiction, Austen has been shown to be an antirevolutionary novelist. Indeed, what we know of Austen in 1798 shows her to be not quite as indifferent to the revolutionary events of that year as is often suggested. For a start, she was acutely aware of the flourishing of her brother Frank's naval career in an atmosphere in which Britons were neurotically expectant of an attempted Bonapartist invasion via

Ireland throughout the summer and looked to the wooden walls of the navy as their only salvation. But also, the novel Jane began in that year, which would only see the light of day in 1818 as *Northanger Abbey*, makes some play with revolutionary fears. Just after Catherine Morland has dismissed Bath as unworthy, her conversation shifts to "something very shocking indeed, [which] will soon come out in London. . . . It is to be uncommonly dreadful. I shall expect murder and every thing of the kind." As Malthus's rather supercilious brother in the cloth, Henry Tilney, clarifies, Catherine, obsessed with the excesses of fashionable gothic novels, is referring to a new book, where Eleanor Tilney takes her to be discussing real murder and insurrection: "You [Catherine] talked of expected horrors in London—and instead of instantly conceiving, as any rational creature would have done, that such words could relate only to a circulating library, she [Eleanor] immediately pictured to herself a mob of three thousand men assembling in St George's Fields; the Bank attacked, the Tower threatened, the streets of London flowing with blood." Austen in 1798, then, uses mockery and reason in the form of Henry Tilney to criticize sentimental excess, seeing in that excess something that in Catherine Morland's case leads to the merely harmless, nay hapless misunderstandings that plague her and provide the comic backbone to *Northanger Abbey*, but that in other hands and less genteel circumstances could lead to the real riots and insurrections that Eleanor fears and that were constantly experienced in that most turbulent of years.[4]

If Austen was not as insulated from or indifferent to the revolutionary tumults as she appears at first sight, the same observation applies to Malthus. His extraordinary *Essay* of 1798 did not appear ex nihilo. Literary scholars have quite rightly scotched the twee, simpering, and sanitized image of Jane Austen that still beguiles tourists and film executives alike, but in Malthus's case the mud thrown at his reputation, most notably by Karl Marx, depicting him as a shallow lackey of the wealthy, an unthinking supporter of privilege, has stuck rather more persistently. This has made it hard to see not only how profound and humane is Malthus's *Essay*, but also how perceptive and radical Malthus was in his own age, precisely how little he was a comforter of the establishment because of his ambivalent relationship with it. And yet, even within the texture of the genteel material we have discussed thus far, there are signs, tokens of a Malthus very different from that of Marxist caricature. While the authorial position Malthus was to adopt in the *Essay* was clearly on the wealthy side of a rich-poor binary—"I cannot by means of money raise a poor man . . . without proportionably depressing others in the same class"— his own position was in fact more ambiguous. On his tour to the Lakes, he reported an encounter with someone in Sedbergh who "mistook me for a fine gentleman" but later "deserted me as one of the swinish multitude." Evoking Burke's notorious depiction of the poor in his *Reflections,* Malthus places himself squarely on the other side of the rich-poor binary he was to discuss in the *Essay.* As we will see, it was perhaps Malthus's ambivalent position in the social hierarchies of the late eighteenth century that allowed him this twofold vision. And why was Malthus thus deserted in Sedbergh? It was because he asked "some question about the market place." In fact, alongside Malthus's flirtations with picturesque views, his 1795 tour reveals him as anything but a male version of the deluded Catherine Morland. On the contrary, the journal is peppered with discussions of agriculture, prices, markets, and the conditions of the poor. For example, while ascending the Old Man of Coniston, the highest point of Coniston Fell above the lake, Malthus took in the view and suggested it "answers very exactly Thomsons description" in *The Seasons* in aesthetic mode, but then also stopped at the slate quarries, looking at how the slate was "rived" (split into slices) and finding out the rates of pay of the slate miners. It is every bit the journal of the budding student of economics, agriculture, and public policy who would shoot to fame three years later.[5]

If one is willing to look beyond the superficial appearance of things, to reject simple stereotypes in favor of closer examination, one will find great profundity and a unique voice in Robert Malthus. In Austen's and Malthus's parallel lives, brilliance emerged from and commented on the mundane and the everyday; indeed, that was the nature of their shared gift. Where this is well accepted for Austen, it is all but unknown for Malthus. Where did Malthus's unique voice come from, why did that voice come to find its muse in the events of 1798, and what did that voice actually say in response to those events in the *Essay on the Principle of Population?* Those are the questions we will address in this chapter.

The Making of Malthus—Early Life

Robert Malthus was born on February 13, 1766, to Daniel and Henrietta Malthus in Surrey. His family background was one that both historians and contemporaries would have labeled as that of the "middling sort," a rank or class Malthus was to eulogize in his *Essay* for its diligence and mental exertion. There were, of course, gradations of wealth within this sort, and Daniel Malthus was clearly more comfortably off than was Jane Austen's father, George. Daniel Malthus came from an affluent family whose wealth had been garnered through the law, and he had been prosperous enough to go to university, entering as a student at the Queen's College, Oxford, in 1747 and leaving—as gentlemen of distinction tended to—without taking a degree. (George Austen, who also went to Oxford, stayed on to take a degree and become a Fellow.) Quite how Daniel made a living is hard to discern, but one might venture to suggest that life would always be harder for a younger son like Robert Malthus than it had been for his father as the firstborn. This may well account for why Robert, like George, did take a degree when he went up to Cambridge in the 1780s. Daniel's family soon transplanted to near Bath before finally settling back close to where Malthus was born, in Albury, in the picturesque heart of the Surrey part of the Weald. Akin to the more impoverished George and Cassandra Austen, Daniel and Henrietta Malthus created a warm, loving, and educationally advanced environment for their children, being eulogized in print by Malthus's soon-to-be teacher Richard Graves for "having happily united in their domestic oeconomy, the elegant simplicity of the pastoral ages with the refinements of modern life." It was exactly this model that Malthus would endorse as productive of a progressive, rational society in the *Essay*.[6]

Daniel was a man of considerable intellect, which tended in the direction of educational experimentation and freethinking. He was a warm admirer of the work of Jean-Jacques Rousseau, to the point of indulging in craven hero-worship, pestering Rousseau to stay with him during his trip to England in the 1760s. Some of this would be visited upon his discernibly bright second son, Robert. Robert's first formal education came in the period 1776–1782 under the guidance of the Reverend Richard Graves. Graves was a poet and wit, one of Samuel Johnson's "nest of singing birds" at Pembroke College, Oxford, in the 1730s. Graves had gone on to a fellowship at All Souls before being forced to leave his academic career in 1749 for having eloped with and married one Lucy Bartholomew. Left without a reliable income, Graves had been rescued after being offered the rectorship of the small parish of Claverton, a picturesque village of honey-colored limestone buildings, set on the slopes of the winding River Avon some two miles upstream of Bath. Two miles can matter a lot: while Charles Wesley memorably depicted Bath as "that Sodom of our land" in 1741, on the other side of the splendidly named Brassknocker Hill, Graves formed the picture of the virtuous country cleric, supplementing his meager income with revenue from a school he founded in 1750, which he would run for nearly forty years. It was into this school that Malthus was enrolled in 1776. The ten-year-old Robert clearly enjoyed himself, flourishing in his studies and also enjoying the rough-and-tumble of "fighting for fighting's sake," according to Graves, for which he was affectionately know as "Don Roberto."[7]

Robert seems to have taken away two key lessons beyond those of construing his Latin from the experience at Claverton, both of which would be shot through the texture of both his *Essay* of 1798 and of his life's work more generally. First, the pleasures of wit, of satire, of lively repartee in social and scholarly life. For in Richard Graves, Malthus encountered one of the finest satirical wits of his age. Where we only tend to commemorate the caustic satire of a Pope or a Swift, we have forgotten the more gentle modes of mockery that Malthus's own age valued and of which Graves's poetry and in particular his novel ridiculing the excesses of Wesleyan Methodism, *The Spiritual Quixote* (1773), were supreme examples. For denizens of the Enlightenment like Graves, mockery could unravel the pretensions of loose and irrational fears and superstitions, enforcing rationality in religion, in society, and in life generally. Malthus had a lifelong connection with Graves, and would administer the last rites to him on his deathbed in 1804. The nature of that connection is impossible to discern from surviving archival evidence, but Malthus clearly found something congenial in the gentle raillery in which Graves indulged, for he would, as we shall see, use similar tools of satire and mockery to unravel the pretensions of a very different form of unreason (as he saw it), political unreason, in his *Essay*. And yet, as Graves's biographer notes, for all his friendly disposition toward his charges and his domestic happiness with his wife, there was in Graves something "a little frenetic . . . the autobiographical disclosures . . . have a despairing tone." It is suggested that this tone emanated from Graves's painful awareness that he had impoverished the woman he loved, perhaps leading her to an early grave after she had borne him five children they could but marginally sustain through his combined incomes as a clergyman, a teacher, and an author. And it is here that Malthus took from Graves the second lesson that would have an impact on the texture of his argument in the *Essay* and beyond. Love, morality, and integrity could not make for a happy life, social or individual, unless they were coupled with economic prudence and foresight. Where Daniel Malthus as a firstborn could sustain his large family with relative ease, an impoverished clergyman such as Graves (or indeed George Austen who, to sustain his plentiful progeny also ran a school), could not. His was a constant battle to retain status in the middling sorts. As Malthus, himself a younger son who was destined to earn his keep rather than inherit it, put it with feeling as a thirty-two-year-old: "A man of liberal education, but with an income only just sufficient to enable him to associate in the rank of gentlemen, must feel absolutely certain, that if he marries and has a family, he shall be obliged if he mixes at all in society, to rank himself with moderate farmers, and the lower class of tradesmen. . . . Two or three steps of descent in society, particularly at this round of the ladder, where education ends, and ignorance begins, will not be considered by the generality of people, as a fancied and chimerical, but a real and essential evil."[8]

Daniel Malthus may have been dissatisfied with the education his son was receiving under Graves at Claverton. For all his wit and literary skill, Graves followed a fairly traditional course of instruction, centered on Greek and Latin, and his response to the pedagogic theories of Daniel's hero, Rousseau—"he is verbose, pedantick, and chimerical"—would not have endeared him. Whatever the reason, in 1782 Malthus was dispatched to Warrington, to study at the Dissenting Academy under the tutelage of Gilbert Wakefield. Despite Wakefield's reminiscence that a third of the pupils in the Academy were members of "the establishment," this was a brave (or self-indulgent) move on Daniel's part. In an age in which many public offices still required formal subscription to the established, Anglican Church, to place Robert in a dissenting academy was, ipso facto, to place him at the margins of institutional power even if instruction there was reasonably conventional. Why did Daniel make this move? If Richard Graves was one of the finest of the "second rung" of literary talents in the later eighteenth century, Gilbert Wakefield was one of the very finest biblical scholars and religious controversialists of his age, purveyor of a "rational religion" that would have been far more congenial to Daniel's blend of Christianity and Rousseauian fervor. On the very cusp of the Industrial Revolution (historically, not geographically) in Warrington, Malthus noted the price of coal in a letter to his father and acquired a lifelong aversion to the social consequences of industrialization. More clearly, Malthus took two additional things from the two years he spent with Gilbert Wakefield, first in Warrington and then as the only pupil at Wakefield's abortive school at Bramcote: first, a typically enlightened sense of the value and dignity of reason; and second, a willingness to think unflinchingly about God and religion through the dictates of reasoned inquiry about nature and society, not trammeled unduly by the dictates of orthodoxy, or, as he would later put it, to "reason from nature up to nature's God, and not presume to reason from God to nature."[9]

Even as Wakefield's career as an educator was fizzling to its ignominious conclusion, he furnished Malthus with one last service, making suitable introductions to allow for Malthus's admission as a student at his alma mater, Jesus College, Cambridge, where Malthus matriculated in

1784. In the later eighteenth century, Cambridge was not the academic powerhouse we take for granted today. On the contrary, a Cambridge education was often little better than that received at a rather poor finishing school. The wealthy "fellow commoners" of the period frequently ran amok, not needing a degree and therefore not obliged to conform to the rigors of intellectual life: "Intoxication was the 'besetting sin of the university' . . . rioting and disorder were frequent. Occasionally, moreover, there were something like pitched battles in the streets." And yet modern scholarship has shown a more serious side to Cambridge life in the period, one more in line with our modern expectations of a research university, in the culture of Newtonian mathematics and the diligence with which many tutors and students approached instruction. Malthus's university life as manifested in his letters to his father bespeaks the more serious Cambridge. Malthus comes across as a diligent young student preparing to take a degree as a passport into professional life while reading widely to cultivate his mind. The family's finances were severely stretched by the decision to send their second son to university, and, as his first term comes to a close, Malthus anxiously writes to his father offering up some rough-and-ready accounts of his bill of £44, "16 of which is the income of my rooms, & 7, tuition & other articles for the 2 quarters Midsummer, & Michelmas," concluding, "you will see that I have not spent more than was absolutely necessary." In fact, there was some considerable tension with Daniel Malthus over this question as Malthus's university career progressed: Malthus, surrounded by the frolicking dissipation of the well-heeled, was himself constantly watching his expenses, but also clearly felt under the constant disapproval of his father for failing to achieve the impossible, that is, failing to keep within the budget Daniel recalled from his student days in 1740s Oxford: "It might be otherwise when you were in Oxford, but from the little knowledge I have gained since I have been here at Cambridge I could almost affirm it to be absolutely impossible for a person to live here . . . upon 60£ a year." In an age when the concept of inflation had not been fully fleshed out—and even if it had been, Daniel would have been precious little interested in it—his son's protestations clearly fell on unreceptive ears: "I am sorry you feel a desire of convincing me that nobody can go to our universities without spending 100£ a yr for you are not likely to succeed. I don't rest the matter upon one time or another . . . but upon the nature of things." This contretemps, however minor and polite in its expression, is perhaps the first documentary trace we have of the familial tension that would express itself more fully in the later 1790s, when

Malthus was forced by economic necessity to live once more under his father's roof.[10]

Financial issues notwithstanding, Malthus clearly worked hard during his four years in Cambridge. In addition to his prescribed studies, we find him toward the end of his university career "endeavouring to get some little knowledge of general history & geography," for example, knowledge that would come in handy when he came to exemplify his arguments in the *Essay* a decade later. But Malthus recognized, as later scholars have also attested, that in eighteenth-century Cambridge one's reputation and academic attainment came predominantly through one's proficiency in pure mathematics, the university still working as it did in the shadow of its greatest alumnus of the preceding century, Isaac Newton. As Malthus put it in 1784, soon after his arrival in the Fens, "the chief study is mathematics, for all honour in taking a degree depends upon that science." And here Malthus and his father found a point of considerable agreement, an agreement that would drive the entirety of Malthus's life's work: to focus on pure mathematics was stultifying; math was only noble inasmuch as, true to the principles of the Enlightenment, it was applied to the amelioration of human life in the real world. It was Daniel who opened up this question in a letter of 1785, as he spoke of his hopes for his son's career on completing his studies: "There is scarcely any part of learning which I esteem more [than mathematics] . . . [but] I cou'd always wish to see it applied, & that I desir'd to see you a surveyor, a mechanick, a navigator, a financier, a natural philosopher, an astronomer, & [not] a meer speculative *algebraist*." Malthus responded enthusiastically to this comment by his father, adding that "the plan of Mathematical & Philosophical reading pursued at Cambridge is perhaps too much confind to speculation." He also went on to reveal that his extracurricular reading had earned him a reputation as someone interested in applied mathematics, being "rather remark'd in College for talking of what actually exists in nature, or may be put to real practical use." Such interests placed Malthus squarely in the ambit of the most influential moral philosopher to emerge from mid-eighteenth-century Cambridge, William Paley, whose Christian utilitarianism Malthus would echo throughout his career and whose fearless willingness to engage with sensitive political and moral issues despite social opprobrium Malthus would emulate when he tackled the Poor Laws.[11]

Malthus, then, was plowing a rather lonely furrow for himself in the Cambridge of 1786, eschewing that which would lead to academic plaudits in the university culture of his day in favor of applied, practical, and socially engaged studies. This furrow led along a suitably straight path to the achievement of his *Essay* twelve years later, with its use of mathematical logic in the service of a political and economic argument of radical import. And yet we should not underestimate the fortitude it took for a poor second son in his early twenties to cope with paternal disapproval over his finances and to ignore the glittering rewards on offer for those who toed the Cambridge line in favor of pure mathematics, preferring instead to set his own course guided by quietly held, deeply seated convictions about what really mattered. It was the same fortitude that had allowed Malthus to overcome the impairment of a cleft palette and the resultant impediment to his speech to succeed regardless in a scholarly sphere where oral skills were pivotal in a way that no longer holds good today. In truth, of course, Malthus also had a precious resource that allowed him both to overcome his disability and to square the particular circle he faced in the pure-mathematical basis of undergraduate success at Cambridge: intelligence. While pursuing his extracurricular interests in applied mathematical studies, in navigation, political arithmetic, and geography, Malthus also attained the rank of "ninth wrangler" in his degree examinations; in other words, he placed ninth overall in his year group. Not bad for someone whose intellectual passions and interests were increasingly directed elsewhere. On this basis, Malthus was elected to the Fellowship at Jesus College in 1793, but, as we have seen, by this time he was living back in Surrey, having taken up his clerical position at Okewood in 1789 after completing his degree.

In Malthus's early career, in his emergence from a loving, educationally motivated family, in his passage through the seminaries of Richard Graves and Gilbert Wakefield, and in his devotion to his studies at Cambridge, we find the seeds that would flower in the patterns of belief, interest, and argument that would catapult him to fame. Malthus believed in personal diligence and prudence, in the family as a unit that conjoined affection and sober economics, in reason and in the power of wit and satire to enforce that reason, and in thinking both freely and with a mathematically inspired rigor about the social and moral world. Many in the world of late-eighteenth-century England had a classical education in wit, satire, and rhetoric, and many others had a solid grounding in mathematics and natural philosophy, but Malthus was highly unusual in being so comfortable in both of these worlds. In this sense, Daniel Malthus's bold, Rousseauian willingness to experiment with his son's education was an unqualified success. He would come to feel, however, that his trust had been betrayed.

Locating the *Essay:* Albury, Surrey, and 1798

If on examination the biographical and educational career of Robert
Malthus up to his departure from Cambridge in 1788 can uncover for us
many of the components that would be arrayed in his *Essay* a decade
later, what it cannot account for is why Malthus chose to put pen to
paper. Many of his university-educated contemporaries were happy to
retreat into clerical obscurity, to spend a life serving up the sort of indifferent sermon Malthus himself delivered to his parishioners in 1789.
What made Malthus want to forego the easy route? Some of the answer
to this must lie within the psychology of a driven intellect, something
common perhaps to all authors, but we can at least identify three *catalysts* that help us to situate the writing of the *Essay* before it came to the
attention of an astonished public in the dying embers of the eighteenth
century.

First, there is Malthus's position in the mid- to late 1790s. Life at Cambridge was exciting. Yes, he had worked hard, but he also played hard,
writing to his father of skating to Ely in January 1786, and walking home
"the last seven miles in the dark." A few months later he was denying a
suggestion from his valetudinarian mother that he may have "caught my
Rheumatism by shooting in the fens," while acknowledging his pleasure
in shooting in an area that, according to one historian of Cambridge
University, was "a cheap paradise" for those like Malthus who were
devotees of the sport. If shooting was not to blame for Malthus's illness
in March 1786, he did acknowledge an incident where "in a Canoe [I]
got myself overturned" as the likely cause of a cold in June. If Malthus
later acquired a reputation as a dour progenitor of the "dismal science"
of economics, a reputation that belied the genial wit and personal charm
acknowledged by all who met him, his youthful exertions suggest he was
as fun-loving as the next twenty-something gentleman during his university career. But when that career terminated in 1788, Malthus landed
with a depressing thump back in his family home in Albury, Surrey, his
clerical income not yet sufficient to allow him to set up home. After his
election to the fellowship at Jesus College in 1793, he could enjoy the
odd jaunt up to his alma mater to relive the fun of his early twenties, but
such trips probably only exacerbated by way of contrast his frustrations
and sense of stagnation at still being dependent on familial assistance as
he moved toward and then into his thirties. We have already seen the tensions that existed between Malthus and his father over his income when
he was at Cambridge, and such tensions, though lacking documentary
traces, must have grown with each passing year.[12]

In this context, it is easy to imagine why Malthus hoped that a writing career could provide a way out of his dilemma. Malthus's first and unsuccessful effort in this direction was a pamphlet he wrote on political affairs in 1796 entitled *The Crisis*. The London publisher John Debrett turned down the pamphlet, and it finally only reached the printers in extracts published with Malthus's obituaries in the 1830s. Daniel Malthus commented in a letter encouragingly on his son's first literary effort, but added, "I am very glad, my dear Bob, that your next week's dinners did not depend on your pamphlet." They did not, because Bob's dinners were still being provided by his mother in Albury, the address to which this letter was sent by Daniel, who was sojourning at that time in Bath. And despite Daniel's kindness, herein was the implicit snub Malthus sought to overcome, that of the dependency of a grown man upon his parents.[13]

In 1798, the *Essay* would enable the independence that Malthus had failed to gain two years earlier with *The Crisis*. The catalyst for the *Essay*, appropriately enough, was, as its preface described, "a conversation with a friend, on the subject of Mr. Godwin's essay on avarice and profusion, in his *Enquirer*." Malthus family lore confirms that the friend in question was Daniel Malthus, whose bien-pensant support for the revolutionary optimism of William Godwin provoked his son to pick up his pen. And yet this itself raises a question: why, when Daniel Malthus was such a supportive father, did his advocacy of schemes of radical optimism à la Godwin so irritate his son? Granted that one catalyst for Malthus's writing the *Essay* was a need to find his own way in the world, why was this realized in an argument (albeit a very polite one) with his father? To answer this question, we need to look at the second catalyst that helps us locate the production of the *Essay*, which in turn demands that we step beyond the walls of the Malthus household at Albury to inspect the conditions that Malthus encountered in his travels in rural Surrey.[14]

Today, the British tend to associate rural Surrey with wealth; it is the epitome of the so-called "Stockbroker Belt," where executives seek rural refreshment from the rigors of life in the square mile of the City of London. Houses in Malthus's curacy of Okewood are advertised by real estate agents as in an "idyllic rural situation" and yet "not isolated" thanks to a wealth of transport options, the "journey times to Waterloo [being] from around 53 minutes." One also gains a measure of the place by the fact that "recreational opportunities" in the Okewood area include horse riding and polo. And such a location does not attract only investment bankers, but also the famous; the late actor Oliver Reed, true to his Surrey roots, owned Pinkhurst Farm on Okewood Hill, which, as the *Times* of London reported in 2009, had its "own heliport, stables, paddocks and . . . a private cinema." There is nothing new about this; Okewood's location, its combination of picturesque beauty, extended views from its location on the scarp of the Weald, and proximity to London have long since attracted the smart set. The first train line to London opened just four years after Malthus's death in 1838, and in 1911 the *Victoria County History* opined that the area was "the favourite resort of all lovers of the picturesque near London." And indeed, this combination was noted long before transport links were intensified and accelerated by the innovations of the age of industrialization, John Evelyn saying of his birthplace, Wotton, the parish wherein Okewood is situated, in the mid-seventeenth century that "the distance from London [is] little more than twenty miles, and yet so securely placed, as if it were one hundred."[15]

But if today we associate Malthus's locale with wealth, we must be cautious about projecting our assumptions onto the age in which Malthus traveled Surrey's byways. The rural beauties we associate with this area were considerably compromised for contemporaries in the seventeenth and eighteenth centuries by blast furnaces that manufactured iron ordinance, using and depleting the forests of the Weald in the process. This industry's last embers were dwindling in the early decades of Malthus's life, but their loss only highlighted something else he would have noted in Okewood, the preponderance of individuals engaged in the hard grind of subsistence farming, barely able to make ends meet. Rural Surrey was not the well-connected hub of a metrocentric transport network in Malthus's time; on the contrary, travelers such as Arthur Young in the 1760s noted the peculiarly dreadful nature of the Surrey roads, which left communities isolated and self-reliant. And in that isolation was unending labor and the persistent specter of poverty. Taking the modern census district of the Mole Valley in which Okewood is located, and looking at the data for 1840, the first year for which we can analyze census data in detail, some 21 percent of the population were engaged in agriculture (the figure was under 2 percent in 2000), and 33 percent of people were still engaged in mining and allied activities. Likewise, in 1855, the infant mortality rate for the area was around 157 per 1,000, nearly twice the national average, where the fertility rate was 162 per 1,000, very much at the national average. As late as 1880, 36 percent of the population were aged fifteen or less, around twice the present-day figure, while those aged sixty-five or older amounted to only 4 percent, a quarter of the current tally. Simply put, life in rural Surrey was short for the vast majority who were engaged in industry and agriculture. The line between independence and poverty was one on which many teetered: in 1802–1803, more than 13 percent of the Surrey population saw its hardships eased by Poor Relief, the figure rising to upward of 40 percent in some parishes. If most of these figures necessarily come from the mid-nineteenth century (when the accumulated pressure for national statistics to be gathered via the census which Malthus and others advocated finally yielded results), projecting back a half century to Malthus's age, we can assume the figures are likely to have been more depressing still in the picture they would paint of agrarian poverty, of high birth rates and short life spans. What we see as the playground of the rich and famous was, in Malthus's age, the graveyard of the poor and industrious.[16]

And that is why the things Malthus saw as a country clergyman in rural Surrey catalyzed him to write the *Essay*. Bien-pensant visions of unending social and personal improvement could be projected by William Godwin and ardently advocated in affluent parlors by the likes of Daniel Malthus, but they jarred disconcertingly with the realities Malthus saw on his travels. Malthus was interested in "what actually exists in nature," and the daily poverty he saw put the lie to utopianism. The following lines from the *Essay*, while fusing the satirical wit of Richard Graves with the attention to truth of Gilbert Wakefield, crystallize the disjunction he must have felt in 1798 between experience and abstract theories of social improvement: "The sons and daughters of peasants will not be found such rosy cherubs in real life, as they are described to be in romances. It cannot fail to be remarked by those who live in the country, that the sons of labourers are very apt to be stunted in their growth, and are a long while arriving at maturity . . . a circumstance, which can only be attributed to a want either of proper, or of sufficient nutrition." The *Essay* would also discuss the dietary patterns of laborers in the south of England and compare them with those in the north and Scotland, drawing together Malthus's observations from Surrey with those recorded in his 1795 tour of the Lakes. Malthus, the close, empirical observer of social realities, had been confronted throughout the 1790s by the harsh realities of rural poverty in Britain, both north and south, and the disjunction between these facts and the genteel discourse of his parental household in Albury was the second great catalyst to the production of the *Essay*.[17]

And if we have spoken thus far of two spaces, two geographical locations, Albury and Surrey, as the catalysts to Malthus's great work, the third and final factor to mention turns our attention to time, to the historical context in which he was living, to the events that confronted Malthus in the 1790s, and in particular to the historical moment that was their culmination, 1798. The preface to the *Essay* is dated June 7, 1798. This was in fact a Thursday, and it came sandwiched amid some of the most troubled days in British history. For it was in the last days of May and the first week of June that the Irish Rebellion reached its murderous climax, June 7 itself being the day of the Battle of Antrim and at the peak of the Wexford Rebellion. As Thomas Packenham notes, this was "the long dreaded day, when the French Revolution would spread to Ireland." If, on the other side of the Irish Sea, Malthus could not know of these events and their uncanny simultaneity with the completion of his counterblast against the radical excesses spawned by the French Revolution, he would have been aware of and embroiled in the climate of fear and paranoia of that summer, as were all of his class and intelligence (even, as we have seen, Jane Austen, as she penned *Northanger Abbey*). For a start, the English remained unclear where a French fleet under Napoleon's charge had sailed to; they knew it had sailed from Toulon on May 19, but were not to know that Napoleon was uninterested in the Irish question, preferring instead to concentrate on his Egyptian campaign. Their fears were exacerbated by the knowledge that their traditionally reliable wooden walls, the Royal Navy, had seen serious mutinies the previous year, "spectacular events" whose consequences were still reverberating the following year. More generally, the wheels seemed to be coming off the wagon of British success: they had been repulsed from Haiti by the island's liberator, Toussaint L'Ouverture, in February, and were facing serious insurrection in India, masterminded by the Sultan of Mysore. Under the pressure of events, the British prime minister, William Pitt the Younger, seemed to have been thrown into a slough of alcohol-fueled despond, from which he had emerged only briefly to fight a duel in late May. As a response to this, and in an unprecedented show of loyalty, some 150,000 Englishmen had signed up as volunteers to defend their nation from Franco-Irish incursions. We get a vivid window onto the concerns of the summer of 1798 through the diaries of the painter Joseph Farington. The fifty-one-year-old Farington was one of those who joined the volunteers, in his case the St. Pancras division in London, and took part in drills and musters to improve the nation's readiness. All this was provoked by a conversation with the American painter John Trumbull, who had recently returned from Paris, and reported to Farington in lurid detail that "despotism marked everything—Woemen [*sic*] profligate—Children no respect to parents—Society dissociated—No education—no religion—return to nation of ferocious Goths." His fears were only confirmed when news of the events in Wexford reached London on June 8, and when three days later he heard of thousands of deaths in Ross.[18]

And the events of the summer of 1798 came in the context of a decade of unrest, tumult, and fear. Food riots had crippled the nation successively in the years 1794–1796, the efforts of the poor to remain independent and self-sufficient defeated by a series of poor harvests and resultant high food prices. There were also widespread and related labor disputes as those reliant for their income on industrial work saw machinery replacing them: in particular, the 1790s witnessed acts of machine breaking, threatening letters sent to factory owners, and labor riots spreading through the countryside surrounding Bath that relied on the woolen industry, an area that Malthus knew well. Using as a point of reference the River Avon at Claverton, where Malthus was taught by Richard Graves, there were attacks on machinery upstream at Bradford-on-Avon in 1791 and a riot downstream at Twerton, on the Bristol side of Bath, in 1797. More generally the area saw sporadic violence and unrest in all the key local towns such as Westbury, Trowbridge, and Chippenham; in these towns discontent erupted in good earnest in the 1790s, and would peak in the so-called "Wiltshire Outrages" of 1802. The country more generally was gripped by such unrest, all of which pivoted around the scarcity of food and the low wages offered to the laboring classes.[19]

The summer of 1798, then, saw the confluence of medium-term fears with a short-term crisis. The fears of the ruling orders had been raised by the persistent rioting around issues of food and labor. While such protest was customary and mostly within the bounds of the normal expectations of early modern England, it had been experienced with greater intensity in the 1790s and was viewed with greater fear in the context of evolving events across the English Channel in the years after the Revolution of 1789. And then events in the summer of 1798 seemed ready to ignite the regular round of protest and riot in food-strapped England into something more catastrophic: with Napoleon at sea, his destination unknown, with 340,000 well-trained soldiers at France's command and "much of western Europe under her control," and with a rebellion sweeping like wildfire through Ireland, it seemed quite likely that England's ragbag of volunteers, the all-too-deserving fodder of satirical engravings by James Gillray, would be all that stood between the nation and a rerun of the events of the summer of 1789 on the English side of the Channel. Catalyzed by fear, some, like Joseph Farington, joined the volunteers; others, like Robert Malthus, joined the fray pen in hand.[20]

The First Inconvenient Truth: An Essay on the Principle of Population

In terms of the three catalysts that provoked Malthus to pick up his pen, we have seen that he commented obliquely on the conditions of the poor in Surrey when he dismissed romantic delusions about them as "rosy cherubs." We've also seen Malthus make rather more direct, albeit respectful, reference to the tensions he experienced under his father's roof at Albury in the preface to his famous work. And yet, it was the third catalyst—the events of 1798 and the decade of radicalism that had sown their seeds— that is at the heart of his *Essay*, starting with its very subtitle: "with remarks on the speculations of Mr. Godwin, M. Condorcet and other writers." While "remarks" can of course be positive or negative, Malthus's depiction of France in the age of Condorcet left the reader in no doubt of his view, chiming as it did with Joseph Farington's high-flown depiction of societal breakdown. For Malthus, the scene in France was of "the human mind in one of the most enlightened nations of the world, and after a lapse of some thousand years, debased by such a fermentation of disgusting passions, of fear, cruelty, malice, revenge, ambition, madness and folly, as would have disgraced the most savage nation in the most barbarous age." Thus the French Revolution, which Malthus likened to "a blazing comet," was more likely to "scorch up and destroy the shrinking inhabitants of the earth" than "inspire [them] with fresh life and vigour." But why had the French Revolution and the incendiary optimism it had inspired in England failed? The answer to this question lay in reading the book of nature aright.[21]

Faithful to his Newtonian training in Cambridge, Malthus maintained nature was a set of law-like regularities that were amenable to detection by human scrutiny. The "quantifying spirit" of the age saw Newton's achievement as paradigmatic: he had reduced the complexities of the heavens to the operation of simple laws about attraction at distance. The universe really was as simple as one of the orreries that increasingly adorned the studies of the wealthy. The task for students of the natural and social history of our earth was to uncover similar simple, quantifiable laws underlying the world in which we live. This ambition defined what it was to be enlightened, and it was an ambition shared, as we have seen, as much by Condorcet and Price, as it was by Malthus, who expressed something all of them might have agreed on when he opined that "the constancy of the laws of nature, and of effects and causes, is the foundation of all human knowledge." The point at issue, however, was what such an analysis revealed about nature both in itself and as the home of human societies. And it was here that Malthus detected the "first" inconvenient truth, a reality nature disclosed to those willing to inquire without fear or favor, which would undo the radical, utopian, progressive ambitions of the radicals canvassed in Chapter 2. The truth in question, perhaps startlingly obvious in the present day, something that is a taken-for-granted reality for policy makers, environmental analysts, and economists alike, would derail much radical rhetoric in Malthus's age and, as we will see, would inspire praise, revulsion, and argument in an unbroken succession for the next two centuries.[22]

Malthus's "quiet revolution" is easy to encapsulate: enlightened, quantitative analysis of causal relations shows that nature is a niggardly bundle of limited resources and that societies, both human and animal, always tend to overstep the limits set by those resources. Of course, an image of nature as niggardly was not new; on the contrary, Christian scholars had for centuries seen the earth after Adam and Eve's Fall from Eden as a place filled with thorns, wherein we their fallen inheritors had to work by the sweat of our brows to make ends meet. Malthus's great originality was in arguing for the empirical rather than theological truth of this vision (although he never denied the theological version of the argument either), taking the tools of Enlightenment reason and using them to invert its normal stories of human progress in favor of a narrative of human society as "condemned to a perpetual oscillation between happiness and misery." This was the realization of his personal determination in Cambridge to devote himself to what we would call applied mathematics, or, as he said, "for talking of what actually exists in nature." Malthus framed the issue with Euclidean precision, arguing it was fair to "make two postulata. First, that food is necessary to the existence of man. Secondly, that the passion between the sexes is necessary, and will remain nearly in its present state." As a mathematical matter, Malthus argued that population could increase in a geometric ratio, whereas agricultural productivity could increase only in a smaller, arithmetic ratio. As an empirical matter, as something Malthus's general reading in history and geography at Cambridge could have illuminated, he argued that "the power of population is indefinitely greater than the power in the earth to produce subsistence for man," such that human societies always faced resource scarcity issues and that these were the drivers of social change and collapse as witnessed throughout history.[23]

Malthus's postulates could be put forth in a matter of a few sentences; that they actually led to the real-world outcomes of scarcity and competition for limited resources, however, was something that required rather more exemplification. Thus Malthus spent the next six chapters of the *Essay* (around one-third of the book) taking his readers on an excursion through the animal kingdoms, where he saw the same dynamic at work, then onto a whirlwind historical tour of human societies from savage to civilized ones, and thereafter on a geographical circuit that took in Europe, China, India, and North America to make his point, upsetting the optimism that Condorcet's equally sweeping account in the *Outline* had offered. For plants and animals, where reason was not to be found, procreation led to a superabundance of individuals that would be "repressed afterwards by want of room and nourishment . . . and among animals by becoming the prey of others," what Malthus would dub "positive checks." For human societies, endowed with reason, this check was "more complicated" but no less forceful. Malthus, true to the Enlightenment belief in progress, traced the advances of human society, but depicted modern society as unable to escape the shackles of resource scarcity. Starting with hunter-gatherer societies, they were not (contrary to his father's hero Rousseau) noble and innocent, but, as a cursory inspection of "North America Indians . . . [and] the Hottentots near the Cape" would show, oppressive to women, destructive to the weak, and at constant war: "the picture will not appear very free from the blot of misery." Shepherd societies as "the next state of mankind," under pressure of subsistence, "set in motion" the "clouds of barbarians" Malthus and his contemporaries knew of through Edward Gibbon's *Decline and Fall of the Roman Empire*. Civilized, modern societies saw a great shift away from "positive" to "preventive" checks, to the use of reason and forethought to limit population and thereby alleviate the direct pressure of resource scarcity. But this changed only how the principle of population expressed itself, not its aegis. This narrative gleaned from Malthus's general reading in history and geography reinforced his opening contention: "Necessity, that imperious all-pervading law of nature, restrains them within the prescribed bounds. The race of plants and the race of animals shrink under this great restrictive law. And the race of man cannot, by any efforts of reason, escape from it." But why had this great truth of biology and social science, of history and geography, escaped detection by previous inquirers? For Malthus, the "principal reason is, that the histories of mankind that we possess, are histories only of the higher classes," where the pressure of scarce resources predominantly expresses itself in the lives of the poor and the weak, of children and their mothers. Implicit in Malthus's argument, then, was a powerful demand for a more inclusive history.[24]

How did all of this speak to the core question Malthus had posed at the outset: the reason for the failure of the French Revolution and its descent into barbarity? If, in the enlightened arc of history that the *Essay* describes, society had indeed progressed in its treatment of women and the poor and in its ability to use reason to restrain the passion between the sexes, Malthus had no doubt, however, that no amount of progress would allow us to escape the pressure of the principle of population: "this necessary oscillation, this constantly subsisting cause of periodical misery, has existed ever since we have had any histories of mankind, does exist at present, and will for ever continue to exist, unless some decided change take place, in the physical constitution of our nature." But for Malthus this was exactly what the great theorists of revolutionary optimism— Condorcet and Godwin—ignored. Despite their professed reverence for reason, theorists of radical social and personal advancement lived in a delusion, in a "fantasy of reason," and Malthus would level all of the satirical artillery he had acquired from Richard Graves to blow up their position, seeing it as pernicious, encouraging as it did fanaticism and the unhinging of society. The primary delusions that possessed Godwin and Condorcet were first, that any pressure for space, food, and resources that our earth might pose lay in the far distant future, and second that changes in human nature, individual or societal, might act to relieve such pressures. Malthus's potted global tour seemed to answer the first point. It was at the second that Malthus aimed his caustic wit. Of Condorcet's closing speculation in his *Outline* concerning the perfectibility of mankind, Malthus pointed out there was no empirical evidence to support it, and that to advocate an argument without evidence was "a kind of mental intoxication":

> A writer may tell me that he thinks man will ultimately become an ostrich. I cannot properly contradict him. But before he can expect to bring any reasonable person over to his opinion, he ought to show, that the necks of mankind have been gradually elongating; that the lips have grown harder, and more prominent; that the legs and feet are daily altering their shape; and that the hair is beginning to change into stubs of feathers. And till the probability of so wonderful a conversion can be shown, it is surely lost time and lost eloquence to expatiate on the happiness of man in such a state, to describe his powers, both of running and flying.[25]

But it was William Godwin who was Malthus's chief target, writing as he did in the context of the revolutionary fears of England in the summer of 1798, for, unlike Condorcet, Godwin was English, alive, and still at the peak of his influence as a writer. Malthus debunked the extraordinary closing rhapsody of Godwin's *Enquiry* with the same kind of ridicule he deployed against Condorcet: "there are no more genuine indications that man will become immortal upon earth, than that he will have four eyes and four hands, or that trees will grow horizontally instead of perpendicularly." Further, there was no empirical evidence to support Godwin's claim that the advance in human intellect will lead to the prolongation of life. In a memorable reductio ad absurdum, Malthus pointed out that "the citizen who has retired, and whose ideas, perhaps, scarcely soar above, or extend beyond his little garden, puddling all the morning about his borders of box, will, perhaps, live as long as the philosopher whose range of intellect is the most extensive." More generally, Godwin ignored the actual nature of human beings in favor of fantasies about reason's empire. Human beings are in reality "creatures compounded of a rational faculty and corporeal propensities," and the passion between the sexes that led to the making of marital bonds was not to be despised merely because it was such an amalgam. Malthus wished, however, to show just how fantastical Godwin was. To that end he engaged in a thought experiment to demonstrate how, if one created a new society based on Godwin's "most beautiful" system of equality, the pressure of population against limited resources would ultimately lead to the institution of private property and to inequalities of income and opportunity. Above all, Godwin was wrong to ascribe such social phenomena to human intentions: human causes are "mere feathers that float on the surface" in comparison with the moving force of nature in the form of the disparity between population and resources. To ascribe all the misery and inequality in society to human institutions, political and religious, was to foment a potentially revolutionary discontent that served no good purpose, as any recast society, still operating under the pressure of nature's limited resources and our plentiful capacity to procreate, would suffer the return of the same structures of inequality (even if they expressed themselves differently) as all history and geography showed. And in the revolutionary overthrow of one society to create those self-same, natural pressures anew, multitudes of individuals would suffer unnecessarily, for the sake of "a beautiful phantom of the imagination": "An experiment with the human race is not like an experiment upon inanimate objects. . . . [T]he bursting of the bonds of society is such a separation of parts as cannot take place without giving the most acute pain to thousands: and a long time may elapse, and much misery may be endured, before the wound grows up again."[26]

The nub of Malthus's critique of the revolutionary accounts of Godwin and Condorcet is, then, that they misread nature and fantasize about the untrammeled powers of human reason. Read aright, nature is a bundle of limited resources that the procreative power of human, animal, and plant communities tends to overwhelm. Because human beings are a compound of reason and the passions, and show no signs as individuals or social groups of becoming purely rational entities, they cannot escape from the empire of nature's limitations over human improvement. This empire also means that it is not human beings who create, enforce, and perpetuate misery and inequality; these are the inevitable outcome of forces more powerful and profound than our governmental structures. Thus, to wish to overthrow our government is to mistake a consequence of inequality and misery for its cause. Any such overthrow, as the experience of France in the decade after 1789 shows, cannot remove the structural problems that nature's niggardliness creates, but can exacerbate them by unhinging established patterns of charity and neighborliness in favor of social experimentation. But if, for Malthus, revolutionary calls to insurrection are ultimately futile, grounded as they are in false reasoning about how societies work, that does not mean that the alternative is to do nothing, that there is no need to try to improve our lot as individuals and societies. On the contrary, understanding the principle of population has three major sets of consequences for our approach to social and economic policy.

First, the principle of population means that it is incumbent upon societies to maximize the impact of "preventive" checks, individual controls on population growth of prudence and reason, and to minimize the empire of "positive checks" of famine, war, pestilence. Malthus's enlightened history of social progress is itself the narrative of the changing power of these two checks, of the growth of preventive checks and the diminution of the immediate power of positive checks. This is viewed in an affirmative light by Malthus as it is the real story of the growing power of reason over nature through the ages, as opposed to the fantastical one sketched by Godwin and Condorcet. It follows for Malthus that government policies and social sanctions should encourage the power of the preventive check. It is as a consequence of this that Malthus was fiercely critical of the English social security system of his own era, the Poor Laws, and strongly inclined to eulogize the virtues and prudence of the "middling sorts" from which, as we have seen, he himself hailed. Malthus was infamous in his own day, reviled by Marx, and is remembered today for his critique of the Poor Laws. His name has been hijacked by neoconservatives with whom he would have had little truck for the same reason. But his hostility to the Poor Laws followed logically from his opposition to any policy that made a disconnection between reason and procreation. The Poor Laws "create the poor which they maintain" in two ways. First, poor relief allowed people to have children they had no means to support. But second, by diverting food and other scarce resources through relief, the Poor Laws also effectively increased prices, the result being that many of the laboring poor would be priced out of self-sufficiency and would become, therefore, stuck in a vicious cycle of increasing dependency on state assistance. As a consequence, Malthus famously (or infamously) asserted "dependent poverty ought to be held disgraceful" in the hope that social sanction would help to prevent its spread. If the old Christian proverb "the poor are always with us" tended to encourage apathy and acceptance of poverty, the important point is that social policies can exacerbate or alleviate their numbers, and that the Poor Laws as currently construed misguidedly did the former. He advocated instead the "total abolition of all the present parish laws" and their replacement with a system of county workhouses with compulsory labor for the dependent poor. The aim of these proposed changes to social welfare was to enforce the prudential necessity among the laboring classes to abstain (financially and sexually) and save money for a time when they wanted to support a family. And in advocating these changes, Malthus would be trying to visit on the less wealthy sector of society a pattern of behavior he already discerned in the middling sorts, where "the sons of tradesmen and farmers are exhorted not to marry . . . till they are settled in some business, or farm, that may enable them to support a family."[27]

Second, an awareness of the power of the principle of population led Malthus to advocate that policy makers think not only about what might be called the "demand" side of the equation, about ways to discourage people from having children they could not afford, and who would consequently demand resources, but also that they address the "supply" side, the ways in which natural—predominantly agricultural—resources could be maximized. Where agricultural land was abundant and fertile, there was no problem, as was the case in the early decades of the British colonies in North America. It was this abundance that permitted rapid population growth, not, as Richard Price had suggested, virtue and the absence of corrupting luxuries. But where this was not the case, where a territory was full and its lands already in tillage, it was incumbent upon politicians and policy makers to encourage agriculture rather than other modes of production. Malthus thought that modern Europe saw "this natural order of things . . . inverted": commerce and manufactures were encouraged at the expense of agriculture and paid higher wages. Taking a polite distance from the strictures of Adam Smith's *Wealth of Nations* (1776), Malthus argued that such a system of incentivizations might create profit for individuals, but it could not be productive for society as a whole, as manufactures could not increase the total natural endowment on which was predicated the number of people and their average true wealth: "Every accession to the food of a country, tends to the immediate benefit of the whole society; but the fortunes made in trade, tend, but in a remote and uncertain manner, to the same end, and in some respects have even a contrary tendency. The home trade of consumption, is by far the most important trade of every country." This argument was driven again by Malthus's concern for the poor. Smith's conception of the "wealth of nations" might advantage those in higher stations of life, but augmentations to profit in trade and exports would not help the poor: Smith's definition of the wealth of the nation ran counter to the wealth of the lower classes. In accord with Richard Price, then, for Malthus (perhaps reflecting back on his observations in Warrington) the increase in trade and manufactures that had profited the rich had left the poorer classes "employed in manufactures, and crowded together in close and unwholesome rooms."[28]

Finally, for Malthus the ordained minister of the Anglican Church, the principle of population enforced the necessity of the Christian dispensation to a viable social life. Taking another swipe at the radical atheists, Condorcet and Godwin, Malthus noted that it was paradoxical that, having abandoned belief in a future state, they had then transferred their hopes of immortality to our present lives on earth through their speculations about the indefinite extension of the human life span: "After all their fastidious scepticisms concerning the only probable mode of immortality, they introduce a species of immortality of their own . . . completely contradictory to every law of philosophical probability." Amid the scene of poverty, of famine, of war and illness that he had sketched as the inevitable consequence of the laws of nature undergirding his principle of population, Malthus detected a higher, Christian plan. In this, of course, he echoed the Christian utilitarianism he had imbibed in William Paley's Cambridge; he also perpetuated the connection of demography and divinity, which went back to the earliest aggregate analyses of population in the English language by the likes of William Petty and which we have also seen Süssmilch deploy. And yet despite these continuities with his predecessors, Malthus's religious views in the *Essay* were bold and would be attacked by the clerical establishment immediately on publication. They were by no means the hackneyed, conservative apologia radical critics would suggest in later decades. On the contrary, we should note that Malthus's *Essay* was published by Joseph Johnson, the leading radical publisher of the age (who also published Condorcet's *Outline*), and that its religious content, the product of his schooling in the concept of "rational religion" at the feet of the heterodox Gilbert Wakefield in Warrington some fifteen years previously, immediately raised the hackles of conservatives, who demanded that Malthus recant his apparent heterodoxy. Malthus argued we need to "reason from nature up to nature's God, and not presume to reason from God to nature." The pressures the principle of population imposed on individuals and on societies in the aggregate were "the first great awakeners of the mind": "Necessity has been with great truth called the mother of invention. . . . Had population and food increased in the same ratio, it is probable that man might never have emerged from the savage state." However dismal the consequences of the principle of population were for individuals, their impact in sum was to fuel societal progress. God, then, worked via the principle of population for the greater good, but he did so through laws that could produce temporary or partial ills: "if God were frequently to change his purpose . . . a general and fatal torpor of the human faculties would probably ensue. . . . [It is] to the constancy of the laws of nature . . . we owe all the greatest, and noblest efforts of intellect. To this constancy, we owe the immortal mind of a Newton." Malthus's argument, then, was not at all gloomy; he would not see himself as the progenitor of a dismal science. Taken in the round, he was a rational Christian and an enlightened optimist. Further, taken on his own terms, Malthus would have seen his achievement as the empirical demonstration of how nature's laws functioned and how those laws led to societal progress in contradistinction to the delusive rationalist arguments about social advance that had led to the social incendiarism into which France had been plunged in 1789 and on whose brink Britain appeared to teeter as he put pen to paper in 1798.[29]

Malthus's early life right up to the production of his epochal *Essay* may seem as mundane as his picture of a man "puddling in his border of box." Amid the quotidian round of Surrey life and picturesque tours, however, an intellect of vast and unusual comprehension was being formed. Malthus's *Essay* was an immediate *succès de scandale* and has never been out of the public consciousness for the two hundred years since it was written. And yet the *Essay* has never been properly understood for what it really is. In its own age and since, it has been misprisioned as conservative due to the antirevolutionary ambitions with which it was penned in 1798, but in fact the *Essay* reveals the mind of a man who had been educated in ways scornful of any simplistic binary between "conservatism" and "radicalism," as the closing religious chapters demonstrate. The *Essay* has also tended to be retrospectively pigeonholed as an "economic" or a "demographic" treatise; in truth, it is so much more besides, taking in as it does geography, history, environmental studies, and theology among other interests to construct an extraordinarily ambitious enlightened, clerical, bourgeois rebuttal of radicalism, an inconvenient truth with which to diffuse the tensions of 1798. Of course, to the historian, misunderstandings of Malthus are at least as important as the complex brilliance of his arguments as it is those misunderstandings that have kept his name alive decade on decade down to the present day. In many ways, to begin tracing these misunderstandings leads us back to 1798 and to Malthus's old stomping ground, Cambridge.[30]

CHAPTER FOUR

Malthus as the Malign Muse of Romanticism

1798: A Very Different Revolution

Some thirty-six days after the June day when Malthus signed off the preface to his epochal *Essay,* came another, more famous manifesto about the relationship between nature, economy, and society that its author dated July 13, 1798. The manifesto in question was penned by an author who shared with Malthus a middle-class background (albeit one that had been dislocated by the death of the author's father) and a Cambridge education. The two authors shared further commonalities; they were witnesses of the great events and developments of the era: the French Revolution, the Napoleonic Wars, the Industrial Revolution, and the birth of modern economic thought. Despite these confluences of upbringings, times, and places, however, intellectually their two visions of nature's relationship with society were poles apart and were set on a collision course whose dialectic would mold intellectual debate for the next half century and still echoes down to our own age. The manifesto of July 13, 1798, feverishly written on the author's return to Bristol after a tour up the Wye Valley, was, of course, William Wordsworth's "Lines Written a Few Miles above Tintern Abbey," one of the most critically acclaimed of the poems Wordsworth collected for publication with Samuel Taylor Coleridge in their *Lyrical Ballads,* a work that has (however problematically) come to be seen as the foundation on which the romantic movement was built.[1]

"Tintern Abbey" is not, of course, a direct rebuttal of Malthus's vision—that would come later. Instead, it acts in juxtaposition to reveal a completely different understanding of what nature is, of how humans live in connection with nature and, resultantly, of what the moral life, both individual and collective, looks like. As the poet contemplates the landscape, he is filled

> not only with the sense
> Of present pleasure, but with pleasing thoughts
> That in this moment there is life and food
> For future years.

This is, of course, a rather different conception of sustenance from that we have seen in Malthus's work the month previously. And what is this metaphorical nutrition, the poetic fecundity the Wye Valley offers to Wordsworth? What such an "unremembered pleasure" feeds is the moral spirit:

> A good man's life;
> His little, nameless, unremembered acts
> Of kindness and of love.

In short, the sustenance that nature and the landscape offer is the moral cement that binds a society through generosity of spirit and action. A society is fed by Christian virtues of humility and charity, and it is the "life and food" offered by our interaction with nature that generates those virtues. Nature, then, leads to

> A presence that disturbs me with the joy
> Of elevated thoughts; a sense sublime
> Of something far more deeply interfused,
> Whose dwelling is the light of setting suns,
> And the round ocean, and the living air,
> And the blue sky, and in the mind of man,
> A motion and a spirit, that impels
> All thinking things, all objects of all thought,
> And rolls through all things.

For the Wordsworth of "Tintern Abbey," then, nature is numinous, not niggardly: "Nature never did betray/The heart that loved her—." Toward the close of the poem, Wordsworth takes on the voices who will mock this vision of nature, saying that "neither evil tongues,/Rash judgements, nor the sneers of selfish men" will undercut this understanding of the interrelationship between nature and society. It is hard not to see the "selfish men" in question as the political economists of whom Malthus would soon become the most notorious representative in Wordsworth's generation, especially in the context of the other poems in the *Lyrical Ballads* that address rural poverty and the decay of social bonds in a countryside increasingly transformed by towns, manufactures, and agrarian rapacity: poems such as "Last of the Flock," "Michael," and "The Old Cumberland Beggar."[2]

Taking "Tintern Abbey" as a leitmotiv for English romanticism, we see, then, a little over a month after Malthus's *Essay*, the appearance of another completely different understanding of nature and its relationship to individuals and societies. If romanticism is defined in historical terms as the attempt to reassert the centrality of the imagination to human beings in the face of reason's empire as constructed in the Enlightenment, this would put it on a collision course with the project on which Malthus had embarked. For Wordsworth, nature acts as food for the soul. This moral nutriment is not unconnected, however, to the more material needs for food with which Malthus and the political economists were concerned; on the contrary, labor and livelihood are secured by the social cement of the moral imagination that nature feeds, and charity toward those in need is the sort of unremembered act that nature engenders in the soul willing to hear her message. Nature, then, is bountiful, not mean, and leads inevitably upward toward its creator, not down into misery and penury. Those who cannot feel the numinous in nature, those enmired in the selfishness of calculation, are precisely those who create the world in which charity is undermined, social bonds are broken, urban manufactures thrive, and poverty blights the countryside. The selfish sneers create this world; they do not merely analyze it. In 1795, Wordsworth's coauthor, Samuel Taylor Coleridge, had neatly captured much of this vision, writing in a letter to George Dyer that:

> the best of us are liable to be shaped & coloured by surrounding Objects— and a demonstrative proof, that Man was not made to live in Great Cities! Almost all the physical Evil in the World depends on the existence of moral Evil. . . . The pleasures, which we receive from rural beauties, are of little Consequence compared with the Moral Effect of these pleasures—beholding constantly the Best possible we at last become ourselves the best possible. In the country, all around us smile Good and Beauty—and the images of this . . . are miniature on the mind of the beholder, as a Landscape on a Convex Mirror.[3]

Clearly, we have here the lineaments of a very different understanding of the relationship between man and nature as mediated by social and economic relations from that mapped by Malthus and the political economists.

The romantic vision is one that has threaded through the annals of Western modernity, and has most recently been advanced as an "ecological"
imperative for our imperiled societies as we negotiate the fraught relationship between a global population of 7 billion and the changes this is
visiting on natural systems. We need, it is suggested, to be attentive to the
"song of the earth" to regain our moral bearings, our sense of the numinous, and of values beyond those of commercial self-aggrandizement.[4]
Obviously, this image of romanticism as "ecology" is a contemporary
appropriation of the project forged in the *Lyrical Ballads* and beyond,
indeed, undisguisedly so, but it does plausibly point up the extent to
which romanticism for all its diversities and differences in fact possesses
a sense of the role of nature, acting via the creative imagination, in building flourishing societies. Romanticism has been seen to center on natural
supernaturalism, on the cult of the author, around revolution and optimism, or as, in fact, not a singular movement at all but our retrospective
construction. And yet, romanticism's many dimensions notwithstanding,
those we label as "romantics" shared, almost without exception, a hostility toward the dictates of calculation and political economy. That hostility
manifested itself most persistently, trenchantly, and aggressively in vilify-
ing the person and ideas of Malthus, in attacking in every way and from
every angle imaginable for a half century his vision of society, of the individual, and of nature. It is to this trajectory of critique that the present
chapter is devoted.[5]

Wordsworth and Coleridge: Forging the Malign Muse

If the *Lyrical Ballads* is taken as the fountainhead of English Romanticism, for all the interpretive limitations of this supposition, that landmark
publication was not, of course, pitched directly against Malthus and his
Essay; chronology rules out this possibility. Coleridge was an early reader
of the *Essay,* noting he received Malthus's work from its publisher, his
friend the radical Joseph Johnson, and that he read it before setting off
with Wordsworth for Germany in September 1798. But by this time "Tintern Abbey" and *Lyrical Ballads* were already completed, the table of
contents established in late May, and the volume ready for binding in
August before its appearance in October. And yet both the poem and the
collection were aimed at the habits of mind that Malthus shared with
those who were forging early forms of utilitarianism by fusing English
and Scottish currents of enlightened thought. And it was in Coleridge's
writings in particular that the direct confrontation between Malthus and
romantic thought was first staged explicitly. Before attending to this, how-

ever, we should look to Wordsworth's response to Malthus, which, suitable to his self-fashioning, was oblique, poetic, and autobiographical.[6]

Wordsworth's greatest single poetic achievement is, perhaps, *The Prelude,* his recasting of his life's story in verse. As *The Prelude* is thousands of lines in length and exists in three distinct versions, any reading of it is bound to be partial. Here, we can only attend to the poem with a view to unveiling the intersections and antipathies between Malthus's ideas and Wordsworth's account of the formation of his creative vocation.[7] Like Malthus, Wordsworth went up to Cambridge and, though strongly critical of the learning on offer at the university in book 6 *of The Prelude,* he acknowledges:

> The Pleasure gathered from the elements
> Of geometric science.—

This fascination with mathematics, which bears kinship with Malthus's interest in the subject, continued after Wordsworth left Cambridge in 1791, with Euclid still being essential reading for him in 1796. Between these two dates, Wordsworth had been drawn into a complete fascination with the French Revolution, a fascination that led him to cross the Channel and participate in the unfolding drama. A goodly part of his enthusiasm was galvanized by falling under the spell of Godwin's *Enquiry* of 1793, the work Malthus set out to refute. Some of Wordsworth's enthusiasm must also be ascribed to the rejection of his family's pressure for him to take holy orders having completed his education, a route Malthus took, but that Wordsworth could not countenance. By the time Malthus penned his *Essay,* Wordsworth had also rejected Godwin's system, a rejection that he narrates in book 10 of the 1805 *Prelude:*

> This was the time when, all things tending fast
> To depravation, the philosophy
> That promised to abstract the hopes of man
> Out of his feelings, to be fixed thenceforth
> or ever in a purer element,
> Found ready welcome.—

It was precisely Wordsworth's rejection of Godwin's schema, it "did not lie in nature," that led him back to mathematics for its "clear/And solid evidence." Like Malthus in Okewood, Wordsworth was at this time living surrounded by rural poverty, in his case in Racedown, Dorset, where he noted that the "country people are wretchedly poor; ignorant and overwhelmed with every vice that usually attends ignorance." Where Malthus's quest for a response to the failings of revolutionary fervor and the lot of the poor came to a rest with mathematics, "geometry was Wordsworth's intellectual bridge from Godwin to One Life, a further redefinition of revolutionary possibility in the relation of mind to nature." For what Wordsworth valued in geometry's "proportions and relations" is their correspondence "with the frame/And laws of Nature":

> Yet from this source more frequently I drew
> A pleasure calm and deeper, a still sense
> Of permanent and universal sway
> And paramount endowment in the mind,
> An image not unworthy of the one
> Surpassing life—

That correspondence suggests a "sense/Of permanent and universal sway" presided over by God. Moreover, "the paramount endowment in the mind"—of which man's mastery of geometry is but one example—instills confidence that the numinous may be perceived directly in nature by the poet, unmediated by the Newtonian Laws of Nature upon which Malthus and the intelligentsia of the Enlightenment relied.[8]

Wordsworth steered an intellectual course that intersected with Malthus's in the early 1790s, but in his case Cambridge had not been pivotal, a clerical career had been his aversion, and mathematics had merely been a staging post on the way to a very different response to nature, society, and rural poverty. It is in book 12 of the 1805 *Prelude* that Wordsworth rehearsed his encounter with political economists of the day, Malthus included. In an obvious reference to Adam Smith, Wordsworth famously suggested in book 12 that the "test/Of solid life" showed "The utter hollowness of what we name/The wealth of nations." To actually experience nature, to see it and its peoples directly as did the poet of "Tintern Abbey," was to refute the sophistries of political economy. Later in the same book comes what may well be a more direct allusion to Malthus himself rather than political economy in general. Here, Wordsworth attacks those who

> think that strong affections, love
> Known by whatever name, is falsely deemed
> A gift (to use a term which they would use)
> Of vulgar Nature

Here Wordsworth deploys a move many romantics would follow (as we shall see), criticizing those—of whom Malthus was by some margin the most notorious—who reduced the Christian conception of love and marriage to a utilitarian calculation of imprudence. As he continued the thought on love in book 12, Wordsworth granted something to Malthus's analysis only to take it away in a powerful critique of the self-centeredness of the putative science of political economy. What Wordsworth granted, reflecting doubtless on the rural poverty he had first witnessed a decade earlier in Racedown, was that

> True it is, where oppression worse than death
> Salutes the being at his birth. . . .
> And labour in excess and poverty
> From day to day pre-occupy the ground
> Of the affections, and to Nature's self
> Oppose a deeper nature—there indeed
> Love cannot be

And yet the word "oppression" tells us where Wordsworth found Malthus's argument wholly wanting. For Wordsworth, "oppression" was not the product of nature as it was for Malthus, but was instead the consequence of how:

> Society has parted man from man,
> Neglectful of the universal heart

Indeed, not only did the work of Malthus and the political economists misunderstand the cause of poverty, ascribing to nature what was the work of mankind, they by their very forms of argumentation created the breeding grounds of that poverty by justifying this parting of man from man:

> How we mislead each other, above all
> How books mislead us—looking for their fame
> To the judgements of the wealthy few, who see
> By artificial lights—how they debase
> The many for the pleasure of the few[9]

If the 1805 *Prelude* was a product of Wordsworth's early poetic maturity, in 1831, with his radicalism a dim-distant memory, Wordsworth still vilified Malthus, albeit more directly. Writing to Lady Beaumont, he declared "it is monstrous to affirm with Mr. Malthus that the World is overpeopled." He added his disagreement with "Mr. M" that the poor "should not marry at all." And yet Wordsworth by this stage in his life was more evenhanded, granting with Malthus that "they err grievously on the other side who talk as if there were no obligations upon people to reflect before marriage how their children are to be maintained." This was Wordsworth's only direct engagement with Malthus (although his 1835 "Postscript" to his poems is far more forthright in its condemnation of the New Poor Law, which was widely associated with Malthus and Malthusian reasoning), and it came long after younger romantics—to whom we will turn later—had penned powerful attacks on Malthus.[10]

Wordsworth's life and thought, then, traced an arc from curious proximity with Malthus to a well-defined, entrenched opposition. Samuel Taylor Coleridge, however, was the first romantic to stage a direct attack on Malthus: where Wordsworth had been poetic and allusive, Coleridge would be direct and vituperative. And yet Coleridge, like Wordsworth, would never in fact publish a word against Malthus; all his comments would come in notebooks, in posthumously published table talk, and in scrawled marginalia.

Coleridge was born the son of a clerical schoolteacher in Devon; portrayals of this childhood environment have strong resonances with the world of Richard Graves's school in Claverton, where first we traced Malthus's life and thought. Like Wordsworth, Coleridge is very much Malthus's contemporary, born only six years after him (and two years Wordsworth's junior). Wordsworth's middle-class family had been torn asunder by the death of his father, leading to an anxious, peripatetic, and impersonal childhood compared with that of Malthus, and the same observation applies to Coleridge, whose father died before he was nine, leading to his schooling at Christ's Hospital in London. Coleridge went up to Malthus's alma mater, Jesus College, Cambridge, in 1791, shortly before Malthus was made a fellow. Thus their paths intersected, although there is no evidence that they knew one another personally. The lack of any direct connection makes sense, for Malthus and Coleridge inhabited two very different Cambridges. Where Malthus sought to excel in mathematical studies leading to the tripos examinations, Coleridge put in for prizes in Greek and Latin poetry. Where Malthus actually lived within his means as a sober scholar, Coleridge was the model of that which Daniel Malthus feared; protesting to his family that he was a frugal "economist," he was, in the words of his biographer, "dabbling in university politics, running up disastrous debts, flirting with drink, whores, and suicide." Indeed, by Coleridge's own acknowledgment in later life, "I became a proverb to the University for Idleness." Coleridge's "dabblings" in politics were more serious than this phrase implies, closely tied as he was to the radical religious calls for reform of Cambridge University and of British political life channeled through William Frend, a Fellow at Jesus College. Upon leaving Cambridge without a degree, Coleridge knew he could not "return to the small existence of college honours . . . or the narrow prospect of a clergyman's career." In the mid-1790s, then, Coleridge, strongly influenced by the ideas of Rousseau (of which Daniel Malthus might have approved), threw himself into a round of radical lecturing in Bristol and, together with Robert Southey, devised a utopian scheme for a commune in the backwoods of the United States of America, to be founded on the principles of Pantisocracy (government by all) and aspheterism (common ownership of property).[11]

By 1797/1798, Coleridge's ardor for communes and the radical rostrum were cooling. The same events that led to Malthus's composition of his *Essay* prompted Coleridge to write some of his finest poetry up to and including his contributions to the *Lyrical Ballads*. There were axes of fascination and fear that Coleridge shared with Malthus, but his ultimate response was very different. For Coleridge remained true to his hostility to the British establishment, his 1797 poem "Fear, Famine and Slaughter" conflating "Pitt" (the prime minister) with the "pit of Hell" and containing a personification of Famine, delighted by the current prospect of an Ireland in flames, cackling that "Wisdom comes with lack of food," a view Coleridge detested and that he and other Lake Poets would often impute to Malthus in later years. Coleridge's most complete response to the events of these two years, to the events that were also the catalyst for Malthus's *Essay*, came in his poem of April 1798, "Fears in Solitude." Here, the poet's contemplation of the Somerset hills, where he has found "religious meanings in the forms of nature," is quickly displaced by dissonant sounds of war and possible invasion from France. Coleridge suggests that the long absence of warfare on the ground in Britain has left her people:

> ignorant of all
> Its ghastlier workings, (famine or blue plague,
> Battle, or siege, or flight through wintry-snows,)
> We, this whole people, have been clamorous
> For war and bloodshed.

The hysteria around a possible French invasion was rife in the Quantocks, where Coleridge was living at this time; in fact, it was so intense that Coleridge's and Wordsworth's rambles into the countryside were believed by Pitt's government to be likely spying missions for the French. For Coleridge, this hysteria was the wages of the sin of England having willingly engaged in warfare. His bracketed list of the consequences of war was, of course, a startlingly accurate anticipation of what Malthus would call "positive checks" to population growth. For Coleridge, these checks were:

> dainty terms for fratricide;
> Terms which we trundle smoothly o'er our tongues
> Like mere abstractions, empty sounds to which
> We join no feeling and attach no form!

Where lay redemption? The answer for Coleridge was clear and was the same as that articulated by Wordsworth in "Tintern Abbey": in nature and family. In nature, the poet has

> drunk in all my intellectual life,
> All sweet sensations, all ennobling thoughts,
> All adoration of the God in nature

The poem concludes as Coleridge's vision of invasion subsides, the poet given unction by the calming truth of God's landscape, and descending to a view of "beloved Stowey," "the mansion of my friend" (Wordsworth) and "my own lowly cottage, where my babe/And my babe's mother dwell in peace!"[12]

Coleridge first read Malthus some five months after penning "Fears in Solitude," in September 1798, as *The Rime of the Ancyent Marinere,* sometimes called his "green parable," was about to appear in print. For all the obvious differences between the two men, Coleridge did not at first react negatively to Malthus. It was only in 1803, on reading the second edition of Malthus's *Essay,* that Coleridge was led to stage the first direct opposition between the romantic way of seeing nature and society and that which Malthus had forged. That opposition was vituperative and explosive. First, Malthus's recourse to mathematics in the form of his arithmetic and geometric progressions was bogus: "all the silly Pomp of Numerals & Ratios ‹might have been› cashiered" with no loss of sense. Indeed, Coleridge could not resist his own arithmetic riposte: "the whole work is written in the same ratio, viz.—8 lines of Sense & substance to $8 \times 30 = 240$ Lines of Verbiage and senseless repetition." Second, it was contrary to reason to depict the passion between the sexes as an equally tyrannical necessity as physical sustenance, and as such its empire over us was not as Malthus claimed:

The whole Question is this: Are Lust & Hunger both alike Passions of physical Necessity, and the one equally with the other independent of the Reason,

& the Will? Shame upon our Race, that there lives the Individual who dares even ask the Question!

Third, and the point that was to undergird Coleridge's fervid dislike and impassioned denunciation of Malthus for the next three decades, Malthus's system was contrary to the Christian dispensation that he as an Anglican clergyman professed to believe. For Coleridge was abidingly Christian to the core of his being, and it was this sensibility that Malthus's arguments provoked. Malthus's contention that it was wrong "in a moral view" to invade parts of the globe that were thinly inhabited, irked Coleridge in ways which chime poorly in a postcolonial world:

> The stupid Ignorance of the Man! a moral view! . . . If it be immoral to kill a few Savages in order to get possession of a country capable of sustaining a 1000 times as many enlightened and happy Men is it not immoral to kill millions . . . by crowded Cities, by Hunger, & by the Pox?

For Coleridge, then, Malthus was immoral and unchristian. Immoral, as in his system all vicious means of keeping population down, "whether Abortion, or the Exposure of Children, or artificial Sterility on the part of the Male . . . would become Virtues." Unchristian, as Malthus's schema ignored "the Almighty himself, when he pronounced the awful command 'Increase and multiply—.'"[13]

Coleridge's denunciation of Malthus, for his style, his substance, and the moral and religious consequences of his argument, never developed beyond this first set of notes scribbled on the margins of a copy of the second edition of the *Essay*. And yet it is interesting just how frequent and how vitriolic were Coleridge's attacks on Malthus, which pepper his notebooks and his recorded table talk. Malthus was "so contemptible a wretch" and his work was a "monstrous sophism" that bolstered the "contemptible democratical oligarchy of glib economists." In sum, and as his affidavit on Malthus, Coleridge averred in 1832:

> I declare solemnly that I do not believe all the heresies and sects and factions which the ignorance and the weakness and the wickedness of man have ever given birth to, were altogether so disgraceful to man as a Christian, a philosopher, a statesman, or citizen as this abominable tenet.

This was not, however, quite Coleridge's last pronouncement on Malthus. The scholarly edition of Coleridge's notebooks contains some 6,918 entries. Only days before his death on July 25, 1834 (and only six months before Malthus was also to die), in note 6,915, Coleridge was still fulminating against the "plans & particular measures of our Malthuses. . . . From the inmost Soul I abhor them—with all the energies of my Heart,

Mind and Spirit I *defy* them." For Coleridge, the good fight of faith had been a duel to the death with Thomas Robert Malthus.[14]

The Lake Poets: Southey, Hazlitt, and De Quincey Rebut the Malign Muse

As we have seen, Wordsworth only attacked Malthus obliquely via his poetry, while Coleridge's vitriol was exclusively expressed in private. The task of rebutting Malthus in print fell to the group of poets and critics whom Wordsworth and Coleridge inspired, on those who gathered round them in the Lake District and were known, pejoratively at first by Francis Jeffrey in the *Edinburgh Review* (and subsequently by Byron) and by now as a term in the literary-critical lexicon, as the "Lake Poets."

If we return for a moment to Coleridge's scribblings in the margins of Malthus's *Essay,* we should not imagine this as a solitary and silent activity of sober scholarship. On the contrary, the notes emanated from reading the *Essay* aloud to a group, somewhere early in January 1804, the intoxication of alcohol and opium making for raucous reading and rancorous rebuttal. Interleaved with Coleridge's comments were those of his old friend from the radical scene in the Bristol of the 1790s, Robert Southey, who had recently moved from Bristol to share Coleridge's home in Keswick. In the same spirit as Coleridge but more tersely, Southey marked with his pencil that Malthus was a "fool," an "Ass," and a "booby." In fact, the whole project of reading the *Essay* did not originate with Coleridge, but has as its genesis Southey's agreeing to review the book for the *Annual Review,* one of the innumerable such tasks Southey undertook to make ends meet. The review that emerged from this evening of riot and radicalism, from this throwback to the heady radicalism of a decade earlier, was the first public, printed clash between romanticism and its malign muse, Malthus.[15]

Robert Southey would go on to be the poet laureate, his name synonymous for later romantics such as Hazlitt, Byron, and Shelley with apostasy from the radical cause of truth, love, and poetry. And yet his early career was infused with the same radicalism as Coleridge's; Southey's own education in Bath, just downstream from Malthus's in Claverton, had been an equally mixed, experimental project fusing dissent and Anglicanism. This had ultimately been derailed when, sent to Westminster School, he was expelled for a fairly innocuous display of schoolboy dissent in a newspaper he founded. He went on to Oxford, but opined in later life that he had learned only how to row and swim at university. It was on departure from Oxford that Southey's life became entwined with Coleridge's for the first time as their mutual youthful ardor projected a commune fueled by Christianity, the embers of the optimism engendered by the French Revolution, and a good dose of Godwinian rationalism: "When Coleridge and I are sawing down a tree we shall discuss metaphysics; criticise poetry when hunting a buffalo, and write sonnets while following the plough." It was exactly the sort of cocktail of enthusiasm, unworldliness, and Enlightenment that Malthus was to poke fun at and puncture in the more irreverent parts of his *Essay* four years later. By this time, Southey himself had dispensed with ideas of the commune, had broken with Coleridge (despite their interrelation by marriage), and distanced himself from his youthful radicalism. But through this journey of the mind, Southey remained staunchly Christian and hostile to what he perceived as the impiety of political economy. It was this that led him to accept the invitation to assess Malthus's *Essay* in the pages of the *Annual Review*.[16]

A couple of weeks after their raucous reading and impassioned annotation of Southey's review copy of the *Essay*, Coleridge appears to have had a change of heart. Writing on January 25, 1804, Coleridge advised Southey "in your Review of Malthus be exceedingly temperate & courteous & guarded in your language." Too late! Southey was a prodigious writer, producing thirty-three reviews for the second edition of the *Annual Review* alone. He saw himself "as a good reviewer" but also admitted "it is dull work." Southey seems to have enlivened the job by adding more than a dash of authorial vitriol: of another book he reviewed in the same year as Malthus's *Essay*, he concluded that it was "a national disgrace." But toward no other author was Robert Southey so extremely and ongoingly aggressive, contemptuous, and enraged as he was toward Malthus. The lines of this hostility, which like Coleridge's would continue unabated for three decades, were laid down in their entirety in 1804. Much of the review was taken verbatim from Coleridge's notes; what was not was a set of vituperative variations on the same theme. Malthus's discussion of checks to population was meaningless and self contradictory: "he has played off his positive check and his preventive check, but they have not saved him from this check-mate." Malthus's success was a pure outcome of having written "the political bible of the rich, the selfish, and the sensual." And his bible comforted those who were heartless to the poor in the name of the principle of population: Malthus would encourage the rich to see the laboring poor "as cattle," a herd to be managed. And what better way to manage them than by castration? There would be the ultimate positive check: "The proceedings of government would be wonderfully facilitated, for John Bull has been at times a refractory animal, but John Ox would certainly be tractable." For Southey, then, as for Coleridge, Malthus made of virtues vice and of vices virtue. And yet as Southey pushed beyond Coleridge to record his contempt in print, he also gave expression to the central romantic contention about the falsity of Malthus's argument with unsurpassed clarity; poverty is not the product of nature, but of social arrangements: "All checks to population, till the power of production can be pushed no farther, and actual room for farther increase be wanting, must be attributed to error and ignorance in man, not to unerring nature and omniscient goodness." Here Southey presages the key anti-Malthusian arguments that have ramified down to the present day via writers such as Marx and, in a very different idiom, Julian Simon. Where Southey's argument differs from these later authors is in its trenchant Christian foundation.[17]

In his private correspondence, Southey suggested that the distinguished demographer and statistician John Rickman should follow his lead and demolish Malthus: "set your foot upon such a mischievous reptile and crush him." To the same correspondent in 1804 he thundered that if Malthus replied to his review, "I will gibbet him in a pamphlet, and draw and quarter him." In fact, when Malthus did reply in 1807, Southey refrained from responding to Malthus and his allies, those he characterized as "voiders of menstrual pollution," for another five years anyway, whereupon he returned to the fray with an even more spectacularly abusive attack in the influential *Quarterly Review* of 1812, which he was happy to reprint in his collected essays twenty years later. Much of Southey's 1812 essay recycles material from eight years previously either verbatim or conceptually, and the heady ether of Coleridgian fellowship still hangs thick over it. And yet the essay is even more aggressive and does make some new points. In terms of personal vituperation, Malthus is cast as a "philosophicide" advocating death and, taking up on his epistolary image of Malthus as menstrual pollution but changing the angle of bodily attack, Southey dismissed his work as "a colliquative diarrhoea of the intellect." The core point remains unaltered from 1804 to 1812 and on to 1832: Malthus's system is "rubbish" because our problems of poverty are caused by "man . . . not his maker." The one area where the *Quarterly Review* essay does move Southey's opposition forward, and does so in ways prescient of two very different currents in later-nineteenth-century thought, is in its analysis of what would happen if Malthus's ideas were adopted and how Britain should respond. If Malthus's ideas were taken up, Southey warns, the poor would be left to starve. Where the social compact of a community is broken, the poor and the dispossessed will have "resort to the right of the strongest." In their very different ways, both Marx and Darwin would recur to this thought decades later. And, having shown his readers this abyss into which Malthus's reasoning would lead us, Southey paints a very different picture of the solution to the problem, one that is a rhapsodic reworking of the thoughts of that heady night when Coleridge and he had first "tossed and gored" Malthus. The Christian injunction was that we should "Replenish the earth and subdue it." Malthus was mistaken because there were numerous lands that lay empty, or nearly empty, where this injunction could be obeyed with due humility and reverence, and thus there was in the foreseeable future no real "population problem": "Let the reader cast a thought over the map, and see what elbow-room there is for England. We have Canada with all its territory, we have Surinam, the Cape Colony, Australasia. . . . It is time that Britain should become the hive of nations, and cast her swarms; and here are the lands to receive them." For Southey, this was an injunction consonant with "the laws and institutions with which Providence has favoured us above all others." Prefiguring the rhetoric of the age of high empire in mid-Victorian Britain, Southey portrayed the British as having a civilizing mission that would simultaneously short-circuit the incipient class, Darwinian, or Hobbesian revolution toward which the logic of Malthus's argument would lead us. To the modern mind, Southey's argument seems an odd mishmash of the radical and the conservative, of empire and indignation, a place where prefigurations of Darwin, Marx, and Victorian self-satisfaction meet incongruously. For him, however, Christian faith was the Ariadnian thread through all of his responses to what he perceived as Malthus's impiety. Truly mighty contests had arisen from the trivial pursuit of reading Malthus one January night in 1804.[18]

If Southey became a byword for political apostasy after accepting the poet laureateship in 1813, his fellow Laker, William Hazlitt, was by contrast known for the enduring and unyielding conviction of his radicalism, a creed by which he died in penury in London in 1830. For Hazlitt, as for Coleridge, Wordsworth, and Malthus himself, 1798 was a turning point; as he recalled in one of his most famous essays, "My First Acquaintance with Poets" (1823), "1798 (the figures that compose that date are to me like the 'dreaded name of the Demogorgon')." The year took on such proportions because it was then, as the impressionable twenty-year-old son of a Unitarian preacher, that he first met and came under the spell of Samuel Taylor Coleridge, a spell that would determine in its first flush and later recantation the tenor of his life's work. In truth, much of Hazlitt's radicalism had already been instilled in him, both by his experience of the persecution experienced by his father in the "Church and King" riots of the hysterical 1790s and by his personal loss of faith in 1794/1795. And yet Coleridge's influence hastened the process of self-discovery, propelling his journey to find his own unique voice as a journalist, intellectual, and campaigner. The first fruits of this journey were, in a sense, disappointingly abstruse, coming as they did in the form of a philosophical treatise, *An Essay on the Principles of Human Action* (1805), printed in just 250 copies of which very few sold. And yet the *Essay* contained the core of Hazlitt's enduring beliefs, notably the tenet that disinterested behavior is inherent to humans, such that generosity of spirit and action is natural both individually and socially and is, in fact, our self-interest as well as our instinctive tendency. It was this unshakeable conviction that led to Hazlitt's staging of the most extensive, aggressive, bitter, and indeed eloquent campaign to be raised against Malthus by any of the romantic authors.[19]

Hazlitt's campaign against Malthus began in 1807 with an invitation from the rural campaigner William Cobbett to contribute to his *Political Register*. The *Register* was, in Cobbett's own somewhat immodest words, "an instance of success unparalleled in the history of periodical literature," and Hazlitt leapt at the chance by contributing a set of three essays attacking Malthus. Hazlitt repaid Cobbett's faith amply, jettisoning the abstruse style of his *Essay* in favor of the "vintage, rabble-rousing" prose that would characterize much of his greatest writing for the next quarter century. It was by some margin "Hazlitt's most accomplished composition thus far." The success of these essays inspired him to pen two further essays rebutting Malthus and a set of published annotations to the *Essay* akin to Coleridge's private scribblings, the whole being published the same year by Longmans as a weighty octavo volume of nearly four hundred pages, *A Reply to the Essay on Population*.[20]

Much of the substance in the *Reply* was anticipated by Southey's writings, by Coleridge's comments, unpublished and verbal, and by the comments of Thomas de Quincey (to whom we will turn next); indeed, there were spats between the Lakers as to priority and intellectual property in these ideas and arguments, but there can be no doubt that Hazlitt's *Reply* was the most substantial, comprehensive, and brilliant of the romantic ripostes to Malthus. Hazlitt reiterated the arguments that it was political organization, not nature, that limited population size, and that there were still large tracts of land that were all but uninhabited. He rehearsed the point that passion was not beyond our control, a physical necessity to whose empire we were all slaves, and suggested that, in making such arguments, Malthus was a sycophant to the rich and propertied who ignored his basic calling as a clergyman to see in the increase in human population an increase in the quantum of human good dispensed by God's grace. What was remarkable here was not so much the argumentation that

Hazlitt deployed as the philippic and literary modes through which he denounced Malthus and his ideas. In terms of philippic, even Southey, having abused Malthus in personal terms, drew back in his 1804 review (perhaps heeding Coleridge's advice) by suggesting that "the folly and wickedness" of the *Essay* had led to his "tone of contemptuous indignation," but that he accepted that "Mr. Malthus is said to be a man of mild and unoffending manners, patient research, and exemplary conduct." Hazlitt brooked no such equivocation. For him, in the age of gothic fiction of the sort that had turned Catherine Morland's head, Malthus positively fed on his own ghoulish imagination: "there is something in the prospect of dearth and barrenness which is perfectly congenial to the disposition of Mr. Malthus." Having preached "the virtue of celibacy with such success to others, he [Malthus] found it no longer necessary to practise it himself." Finally, there was the wonderful irony of Hazlitt's representation of Malthus as someone unable to suppress his sexual desires. Hazlitt had become a lifelong habitué of prostitutes after his first encounters as a schoolboy in 1794 and admitted his sex drive was "a perpetual clog and dead-weight upon reason." In print, however, he rounded upon Malthus, suggesting that his doctrine about the empire of sexual desire reflected not society and the record of history, but his personal concupiscence as "a man of a warm constitution, and amorous complexion" who could resist other temptations but to whom "the women are *the devil.*" The abuse of Malthus's character and ideas was brilliantly figured through literary references: Malthus was Don Quixote tilting at windmills, his was a Swiftian tub thrown out to distract us, and his doctrine was a reworking of the misanthropy of the Houyhnhnms in *Gulliver's Travels.* Allusions also likened Malthus to Mr. Shandy and to Colonel Trim in *Tristram Shandy,* the upshot being that the *Essay* was "a new Iliad of woes." Hazlitt was, of course, one of the great instigators of the nineteenth-century tradition of literary criticism in the periodical papers, updating the genre from its origins in the works of Addison and Johnson. Neglected though this has been, his first great outing in this guise was contained in his rebuttal of Malthus.[21]

Where Hazlitt combined invective, eloquence, and argument, he produced some of the greatest radical journalism in the English language, such as his denunciation of Malthus's ideas early in the second essay as the "little, low, rankling malice of a parish-beadle, or the overseer of a workhouse . . . disguised in the garb of philosophy . . . in which false logic is buried under a heap of garbled calculations, such as a bad player might make at cribbage to puzzle those with, who knew less of the game than himself." In lighter vein, and a set piece worth quoting at length, is Hazlitt's brilliant example of just how unreal Malthus's claims of the irrepressible sway of lust are in civilized society:

> Almost every little Miss, who has had the advantage of a boarding-school education, or been properly tutored by her mamma, whose hair is not of an absolute flame-colour, and who has hopes in time, if she behaves prettily, of getting a good husband, waits patiently year after year, looks about her, rejects or trifles with half a dozen lovers . . . and *all the while behaves very prettily;* till she is at last smitten with a handsome house, a couple of footmen in livery, or a black-servant, or a coach with two sleek geldings, with which she is more taken than with her man:—why, what an idea does Mr. Malthus give us of the grave, masculine genius of our Utopian philosophers . . . that they will not be able to manage these matters as decently and cleverly as the silliest women can do at present!

And yet, we should not dismiss Hazlitt's *Reply* as an exercise in literary excess with little originality. On the contrary, amid the rhetorical pyrotechnics, Hazlitt toward the close of the *Reply* anticipated elements that would resurface in the thought of Karl Marx. Hazlitt argued, for example, that in Malthus's account there was "always a certain quantity of misery *in bank* . . . a sort of out-guard or forlorn hope, to ward off the evils of population from the society at large." Reinterpreted systematically as a feature of the capitalist mode of production, this would appear as the "reserve army of the unemployed" in classical Marxism. Hazlitt also gestured toward a labor theory of value, anatomizing Malthus's binary of a virtuous owning class and "idle people called *the poor.*" Such a supposition only made sense if "a landed estate was a machine that did its own work; or . . . was like a large plum-cake, which the owner might at once cut up into slices." Hazlitt's *Reply,* then, was a unique fusion of insight, invective, and imagination; it is one of the most extraordinary and overlooked classics of the romantic tradition.[22]

There is something symbolically appropriate in the fact that the final Laker we should mention, Thomas de Quincey, despite living in the Lakes, was somewhat immune to their charms by virtue of his shortsightedness. Like Hazlitt, he narrated his first encounter with the poetry of the *Lyrical Ballads* in 1799 as "the greatest event in the unfolding of my mind," and he came to own Dove Cottage in 1810 in succession to Wordsworth. De Quincey, however, was not quite such a "party man"; he was always at some intellectual distance from the platform established by Coleridge and Wordsworth. And this is reflected both in his attitude to political economy in general and his response to Malthus in particular. Even if the depiction of the Lake Poets as hostile to political economy is oversimplified, only De Quincey actually read and absorbed the works of that tradition, and indeed came to contribute several books and articles devoted to the subject. His attraction to political economy is first recorded in 1811, at exactly the same time as his relations with Wordsworth and Coleridge became strained. As such, De Quincey's efforts to establish his own independent authorial voice were closely tied to his competencies in a field disdained by his fellow Lakers.[23]

De Quincey recognized that the criticisms Coleridge leveled against Malthus, for all their venom, lacked any actual understanding of his arguments, dismissively suggesting in his 1823 essay entitled "Malthus" that "Mr. Coleridge . . . probably contented himself *more suo* with reading the first and last pages of the work." In this De Quincey was about right; the marginalia by Coleridge in Southey's copy of the *Essay* did not extend beyond the first thirteen pages. Though he was a convinced disciple of Malthus's friend and critic David Ricardo, to the extent that he wrote a marvelously stilted defense of his doctrine of value in dialogue form, De Quincey held a view of Malthus that was more qualified and balanced than that of any other early romantic. Above all, De Quincey rebutted the idea touted by Hazlitt, Southey, and Coleridge that Malthus was a mere plagiary, taking all his core ideas from earlier writers such as Robert Wallace. On the contrary: "none of these writers did actually touch the central point of the doctrine . . . none of them deduced from it those corollaries as to the English poor laws—foundling hospitals—endowments of cottages with land—and generally of all artificial devices for stimulating population" that Malthus had detected. As such, De Quincey concluded of Malthus that "his originality is incontestable." And yet overall De Quincey was damning of Malthus in line with his advocacy of Ricardo's work: Malthus's work was in the "spirit of high promise and trivial performance," his argumentation such that "chaos would appear a model of order and light" in comparison. Most dramatically of all, De Quincey accused Malthus of "the greatest logical oversight which has ever escaped any author of respectability." What was this great oversight? To argue that in a perfect society people would still be under the sway of sexual desire such that population would rise again.[24]

De Quincey's deeper immersion in the literature of political economy than that of his romantic predecessors meant that his attacks on Malthus were more targeted, more terse, and, frankly, less interesting than those ventured by the other members of the Lake School. Coming at the end of this intellectual pedigree, De Quincey is something of a sterile hybrid of the rhetoric of the Lakes and the argumentation of the Ricardians. He is also the logical end point of this tradition of critique, living as he did to see Marx and Darwin in print, and thus to witness the dawning of the mid-Victorian age of optimism that resonated as discordantly with the project of the *Lyrical Ballads* as it did with Malthus. And yet, taken in the round, the thirty years from the publication of the *Lyrical Ballads* had seen the Lake Poets mine an extraordinarily rich vein of social, poetic, and moral criticism in their attacks on Malthus, who had truly been their malign muse.

Later Romanticism and Malthus

It has always been difficult to discern a core that unites "the romantics." Marilyn Butler suggests, in fact, that we can more meaningfully disaggregate English romanticism into "early" and "late" variants: the early, Lake Poets to whom we have directed our attention thus far, and the late, Marlow school centered on Keats, Shelley, Byron, and Peacock. This later school of romantics differed from its predecessor in its fascination with eroticism, in its classicism, in its irreligion, and in its lack of interest in the landscape. And these fascinations were interlinked; if in the *Lyrical Ballads* it was landscape that led to God, for the Marlow school it was a classical eroticism that would bring humanity to understand its true nature, which was to break free of the shackles of church and state. For Butler, if the *annus mirabilis* of the first school was 1798, that of the later romantics was 1817, when Shelley moved to Marlow (where his friend Thomas Peacock was already based) and discovered his mature, radical voice. By this time, Malthus was a household name, in good part due to his very public vilification by the Lake Poets. For his clericalism, his moderation, and his doctrine, Malthus was also an inevitable target for members of Butler's Marlow school. In fact, if one is looking for an Ariadnian thread linking the early Lakers and their more radical successors, hostility to Malthus and his doctrines is one of the few plausible candidates.[25]

If Hazlitt figured Malthus as a Dr. Jekyll and Mr. Hyde, with a respectable frontage couched in the language of political economy hiding a morbid fascination with lust, misery, and suffering, Percy Bysshe Shelley inhabited an imaginative world from early childhood haunted by such phantoms, fears, and figments. His intense willfulness and imagination were coupled to an abiding fury at injustice and cruelty, gained in good part through his own experiences at Eton, where he became acquainted with the works of Condorcet and William Godwin, whose radical efforts, so successfully quashed by Malthus, were all but forgotten by 1807–1809, when Shelley encountered them. Shelley's youthful experiences resulted in a mind that was to be radical and fantastical in equal and extreme measure, and that reached its maturity a decade after his Eton days. Shelley had, of course,

packed more into the intervening decade than most of us would in a lifetime, the most notorious moment being his elopement with Godwin and
Mary Wollstonecraft's daughter, the future author of *Frankenstein,* Mary
Shelley. By 1817, when Shelley settled in Marlow, familial bridges had
been rebuilt, in good part because William Godwin, impoverished and
forgotten, now required his son-in-law to bail him out financially.[26]

It was at this point that Shelley's attention turned to radical politics:

> As he settled into the spring at Marlow, he turned the whole question of
> radical political and social change over in his mind and began to read fur-
> ther studies of the French Revolution. More and more he came to believe
> that the way in which he and his contemporaries interpreted the French
> Revolution would decide the way in which they would fight for or oppose
> the present struggle for democratic reform.

Perhaps unsurprisingly, such a set of preoccupations in Godwin's son-in-
law put him on a collision course with Malthus, the great critic of the
French Revolution, whom Shelley described in a letter as "the apostle of
the rich." As William Godwin became increasingly consumed by his response to Malthus's destruction of his reputation, a project that would
culminate in the sprawling six-hundred-page tract *Of Population* (1820),
which his friends applauded and the reading public ignored, so too Shelley began to attack Malthus, but in ways that were brief, caustic, and
damning. Shelley's public pronouncements on Malthus are encoded in
the prefaces to two of his great poetical dramas, whose aim was to rein-
vigorate modern society and its mores through allegorical reworkings of
ancient themes. In the preface to *The Revolt of Islam* (1818), Shelley
singled out Malthus as one of those whose "sophisms . . . [are] calculated
to lull the oppressors of mankind into a security of everlasting triumph,"
but it was two years later in the preface to *Prometheus Unbound* that his
radical platform and its relationship with Malthus were most clearly anatomized. Here, Shelley argued that he was living in an age of great writers,
those whom we retrospectively label as "the romantics." For him, the lesson of history was that one finds such bunchings of genius only at moments of revolutionary social change, the last being the age of "the sacred
Milton," the English Civil War. The poetical flourishings of Shelley's own
age, therefore, we had "reason to suppose, [were] the companions and
forerunners of some unimagined change in our social condition or the
opinions which cement it." Shelley unambiguously placed his own work
in the company of those with "passion for reforming the world." And lest
flat-footed critics struggle to see how reform was engendered by poetical
reworkings of the Prometheus myth, Shelley made it crystal clear:

it is a mistake to suppose that I dedicate my poetical compositions solely to the direct enforcement of reform. . . . My purpose has hitherto been simply to familiarize the highly refined imagination of the more select classes of poetical readers with beautiful idealisms of moral excellence; aware that, until the mind can love, and admire, and trust, and hope, and endure, reasoned principles of moral conduct are seeds cast upon the highway of life which the unconscious passenger tramples into the dust, although they would bear the harvest of his happiness.

To enforce the point, he concluded with a pithy binary between the utopian and the pragmatic approaches to social reform, nailing his own colors clearly to one of these masts: "I had rather be damned with Plato and Lord Bacon than go to Heaven with Paley and Malthus."[27]

While literary critics have found innumerable possible allegorical personifications of Malthus in *Prometheus Unbound,* we are on safer ground in saying that Shelley's longest engagement with Malthus came in the same year (1820) in the form of his radical tract *A Philosophical View of Reform,* but would remain unpublished for exactly a century. *A Philosophical View,* "undoubtedly one of the most remarkable political documents written by any poet of the romantic period," was profoundly informed in its structure and argument by the progressive, reasoned theodicies of Condorcet and Godwin discussed in Chapter 2, but it showed some of the jaundice that the thirty-plus years since the onset of the French Revolution had created in even the most sanguine of radicals. Like Condorcet, Shelley wanted to plot the progress of freedom and the emancipation of societies from tyrannies, both political and religious, but he also had to acknowledge the tenacity of priestcraft and conservatism. And yet for Shelley, the American War of Independence showed that such reform could be achieved and now stood as "the victorious example of an immensely populous, and as far as the external arts of life are concerned, a highly civilized community administered according to republican forms." As Shelley wrote, he detected that England was now "at a crisis in its destiny" parallel to that America had faced a half century previously. The point English society needed to reach through this crisis was profoundly Godwinian: it consisted in "every individual giving his consent to the institution [of government] and the continuous existence of the social system which is instituted for his advantage and for the advantage of others," the result being "equality in possessions." In addressing who could guide us on this path to reform, the path to realizing that which "Godwin has with irresistible eloquence systematised and developed," Shelley formulated a version of what was to be one of his most lasting contributions to the English political and literary imagination in its published form in his *Defence of Poetry* (written 1821, published 1840): "poets and philosophers are the unacknowledged legislators of mankind." It is they who direct us toward a more just society. But it would take the right kind of philosophers and poets to do this given the tenacity of conservatism, and it was precisely Malthus whom Shelley targeted as the wrong kind, as nemesis to his emancipatory hubris. In its anticlerical vigor and its celebration of sexuality as vital to emotional emancipation, Shelley's attack on Malthus was a perfect short summary of late romanticism and its distance from the Lake Poets. Malthus was attacked as "a priest of course, for his doctrines are those of a eunuch and of a tyrant." But what made his doctrine so pernicious to Shelley was not so much that Malthus wanted the poor "stript naked by the tax-gatherer," nor that they would be "reduced to bread and tea and fourteen hours of hard labour" by his creed. No, it was that he would cut "the last tie by which Nature holds them to the benignant earth . . . the one thing which made it impossible to degrade them below the beasts," that is, "the soothing, elevating and harmonious gentleness of . . . sexual intercourse." By demanding that the poor abstain from sex and marriage until they had the means to support their progeny, Malthus proposed to set the poor asunder from the love, hope, and trust Shelley had spoken of in *Prometheus Unbound*. Malthus was precisely an acknowledged legislator of mankind; his doctrines trampled into the dust life's meaning and the possibility of human emancipation through sexuality and justice. At England's crisis point, Malthus was the poison, not the cure.[28]

Although Shelley and Thomas Love Peacock were close friends and lived in close proximity in Marlow, Shelley's temperament and that of his friend were profoundly different. Shelley's flame would burn brightly and be extinguished at the tender age of twenty-nine, while the more gentle Peacock would live to the ripe old age of eighty. Where Shelley's mode of expression was lyric, poetic, classical, and impassioned, Peacock's character led him to prose, detachment, and satire. And yet, as with satirists from Juvenal to *Private Eye,* Peacock aimed his mocking glance at that which he found morally venal; Malthus was one of those targets. In the year that Shelley moved to Marlow, 1817, Peacock published what was without question his most sprawling and least successful satirical novel, *Melincourt*. In literary terms, *Melincourt* is a failure on several levels: in its attempt to blend romance and satire, in its bizarre orangutan, Sir Oran Haut-ton, and in its rather strange prolongation long after the plot resolution is painfully obvious. Another main source of weakness is the inconsistency of its core characters, none more so than Mr. Fax. Mr. Fax is Peacock's comic characterization of a committed Malthusian, but by the end of *Melincourt* he is one of those who helps to find our abducted heroine, Anthelia, and ensures she marries the virtuous Mr. Forester. Mr. Fax is also made to hold doctrines directly opposite to those Malthus held, notably encouraging luxury in the rich and attacking paper money. And yet Peacock does in the character of Mr. Fax manage to lay bare some of the reasons that he, like Shelley, disliked Malthus. Mr. Fax is cold and detached from the consequences of his philosophy in terms of real human suffering: "the champion of calm reason . . . He looks on the human world . . . as a mathematician looks on his diagrams." As a consequence, Malthus/Fax must be misanthropic: evoking Aristotle's biological definition of human beings and Diogenes the Cynic's reworking of it, Mr. Fax opines that "the world is overstocked with featherless bipeds." As such, Fax "decidedly venerate[s]" spinsters, bachelors, and all who avoid procreation, advocating "rigid celibacy." This allows Mr. Fax to propose a mathematical criterion by which the success of a society can be measured by political economists: "the only true criterion of the happiness of a nation was to be found in the numbers of its old maids and bachelors." Peacock's positive answer to Malthus, the utopia he is advocating with Bacon and Plato, is found in his depiction of the rural estates of *Melincourt*'s hero, Mr. Forester. Mr. Forester is inspired (as was Malthus's father) by Rousseau's critique of luxury and advocacy of the rural, but unlike Rousseau has actually enacted these beliefs in his estate. Here, there is no "lordly mansion asserting its regal pre-eminence over the dwellings of its miserable vassals" but instead neat cottages, fertile gardens for the laborers, and a happy equality. As Mr. Forester explains his system of political economy to an increasingly enraptured Anthelia, it differs decidedly from Mr. Fax's: "the three great points of every political system are the health, the morals, and the number of the people. Without health and morals the people cannot be happy; but without numbers they cannot be a great and powerful nation." For all its artistic failures, *Melincourt* pitched a cold, commercial, and life-denying Malthus against the promise of a better society of equality, prosperity, and population growth. In its depiction of Malthus as an advocate of cities, commerce, and luxury, *Melincourt* was profoundly misleading, but by 1817 the real doctrines of Malthus and those attached to his name were diverging, resulting in the creation of a monstrous shibboleth, "Malthusianism," at some distance from anything Malthus had actually advocated. *Melincourt* participated in this process, to which we will return in chapter 6.[29]

Byron does not accommodate the attempts to delineate a core of shared meaning in romanticism: M. H. Abrams does not even bother to include him in his reading of romanticism as "natural supernaturalism," and

Marilyn Butler explicitly acknowledges his marginality in her survey of the field. It seems as if, aping Goethe's comment on Venice, Byron can only be compared unto himself. And yet he does share a hostility to Malthus with those we have canvassed to date. If *Melincourt*'s critique of Malthus suggested that his detachment was callous, it also implied that a society that adopted his doctrines was morally bankrupt, was driven by money not morality, by cash not kindness. Also inspired by a satirical muse, Byron's *Don Juan* (1819–1824) was to drive home the same message in its later cantos when Don Juan reaches England: "these are fiercely moralistic cantos in which Byron exposes the hypocrisy and double-thinking underpinning the whole structure of English public life." Part of that structure was Malthus, whom Byron targeted in what is undeniably the most brilliantly witty of all the attacks he faced from the romantics.[30]

In the English cantos of *Don Juan*, Byron both uses Malthus to expose the hypocrisy of English society and condemns him for hypocrisy. Taking Malthus the man first, Byron reactivates a criticism we have already seen leveled at him by Hazlitt; that he has preached celibacy and happily married on the proceeds: "Without cash, Malthus tells you, 'take no brides,' " and yet "Malthus does the thing 'gainst which he writes." But it was Malthus's utility as a guide to the commercial nature of English mores in the realm of marriage that Byron keyed in on most extensively. Byron had fled to Italy by the time he wrote *Don Juan*, hounded by allegations of incest and persecuted by the opprobrium of a censorious English society appalled by his rakishness and by rumors of his bisexuality. In *Don Juan* he wanted to fire back at that society, to convict it of deceit, and one of the key lines of criticism he generated was that English sexuality was both depraved and a purely commercial transaction, however much it alleged love, religion, and family lay at its heart. In terms of depravity, the English had recourse to prostitutes and rent boys routinely, so why attack him for the same?

> Of those pedestrian Paphians [i.e., prostitutes], who abound,
> In decent London when the daylight's o'er.
> Commodious, but immoral, they are found
> Useful, like Malthus, in promoting marriage

In kinship with his friend Shelley, Byron advocated sexuality as a basic component of human expression. He also supported its inevitable results in terms of progeny (although his personal record as a father to Claire Clairemont was less than impressive). He was, as he put it in *Don Juan*, in favor of "philo-genitiveness." But it was Malthus, not the poets, who was the more sure guide to how English society actually worked on By-ron's account. For the poets:

> "Love rules the camp, the court, the grove," "for love
> Is heaven, and heaven is love." So sings the bard,
> Which it were rather difficult to prove
> (A thing with poetry in general hard)

For Byron, Malthus's deflation of this bombast was a more transparent window onto society:

> But if love don't cash does, and cash alone.
> Cash rules the grove and fells it too besides.
> Without cash, camps were thin, and courts were none.
> Without cash, Malthus tells you, "take no brides"

Byron compressed much of the romantic critique of Malthus into one brilliant stanza in canto 15 of *Don Juan*. For the romantics, Malthus's religion was a sham. The mathematical language in which he clothed his argument was merely a cover for its inhumanity; he was an apostle of the rich who justified their selfishness while taking away the right to marry, have sex, and rear families, without which the life of the poor was intol-erable and meaningless:

> Had Adeline read Malthus? I can't tell.
> I wish she had; his book's the eleventh commandment,
> Which says, "thou shalt not marry," unless well.
> This he (as far as I can understand) meant.
> 'Tis not my purpose on his views to dwell
> Nor canvass what "so eminent a hand" meant,
> But certes it conducts to lives ascetic,
> Or turning marriage into arithmetic.[31]

Malthus and the Romantics—"Nature Seems Made up of Antipathies"

Malthus's ideas, writing style, morality, and personality riled all the ro-mantics in different ways. Paradoxically, their attempts to damn and de-stroy him gave Malthus a degree of notoriety the works of a political economist could never have attracted in and of themselves. If Samuel Johnson was right that "It is advantageous to an author, that his book should be attacked as well as praised. Fame is a shuttlecock. If it be struck only at one end of the room, it will soon fall to the ground. To keep it up it must be struck at both ends," the thrashings of the romantic poets against Malthus's ideas kept them in the air and made their author famous. They also started the process by which "Malthus" became a bogeyman to be berated. If Southey and Hazlitt engaged with and attacked "Malthus," by the age of Shelley, Peacock, and Byron, it was increasingly the specter of "Malthusianism" that was the butt of their critique.[32]

But why were the romantics, for all their divergences, united in their hostility to Malthus? The answer seems to lie in an insight from Hazlitt's remarkable essay "On the Pleasure of Hating" (1826): "Nature seems (the more we look into it) made up of antipathies: without something to hate, we should lose the very spring of thought and action." Romantic images of nature were on a collision course with Malthus, and Malthus's modes of argumentation appeared to the romantics as a distillation of the ills of their society. If the Lake Poets saw nature as redemptive, they saw in Malthus a fundamentally irreligious image of nature as niggardly. If the later romantics saw in sexuality a reconnection with our true nature and thence with the natural world and our fellow humans, they saw in Malthus's repression of sexuality a prudishness that was self-serving and life-denying. Malthus, then, catalyzed an "elective hostility" (to reverse Goethe's polarities) out of which sprang the formulation of romantic credos from Wordsworth to Byron.[33]

And yet we must beware of couching this as a clash between a pure vision of untainted nature to be protected, preserved, cherished in the romantics and an exploitative vision of nature as a bundle of resources to be plundered at whatever social and ecological cost in Malthus. While Jonathan Bate has tried to effect such a binary, perhaps with good cause as an attempt to make us think about values in our age, it is not a historically accurate framing of the clash between Malthus and the romantics. Above all, such a formulation ignores the extent to which the romantics were either Christians (Coleridge and Southey) or lapsed Christians who retained many of Christianity's values (Hazlitt). What this displaced Christianity meant was that the romantics advocated procreation, being fruitful and multiplying, as good, and that they were perfectly willing to accept that the resultant expansion in the population of the globe entailed subduing other societies and cultivating ever-larger swathes of our earth. If, then, the romantic poets cherished the natural world, they saw no contradiction between this and an ethic of utilization, an ethic that subjugated both the earth and other peoples to its logic. The tracks of intellectual history are not so straight and simple as to lead from Wordsworth to the Green Party, and from Malthus to capitalism and climate change.

The genealogy of our attitudes to nature and the economy is not merely comprised of two motorways leading us to the promised land or off a cliff, and in our route maps we should acknowledge that Malthus and the romantics can be placed on many of these highways and byways.

If nature is made of antipathies, Blake and Hegel in their different ways suggest that such binaries can be productive of a dialectical advance in our reasoning. If, with the romantics, we need to be able to respect nature, we also need to be able to extract a living from that nature as material beings. If the romantics attended more to how to respect nature than how to extract a living from it, as we have seen they most assuredly did not deny the legitimacy of the latter question. And Malthus assuredly loved and respected nature as his picturesque tours show, even if his life's work attended to the question of assigning value to nature as a bundle of resources. Two centuries later, we would be better advised to see the merits in both strands of work rather than merely to reenact their hostility. As we look for ways to respect nature and to use it with a population of 7 billion, we should look to find sympathy rather than antipathy between the modes pioneered by Malthus and the romantics. As part of this project, we need to investigate the emergence of the economic mode of understanding nature. Key to this genealogy is the later writing of Malthus. For, throughout the forty years that the romantics were assailing Malthus, he himself was advancing his understanding of natural resources, population dynamics, and issues of resource allocation. In the process, he became one of the founders of economics as the study of how nature and society interact successfully. It is to this that we now turn.[34]

CHAPTER FIVE

Malthus and the Making of Environmental Economics

Taking Bentham's Path

If we return from the vituperation cast at Malthus by the romantics to the man himself, in the immediate aftermath of the publication of the *Essay*, he set about two projects, both of which were evidently designed to fuel a more mature, considered version of the arguments rehearsed in polemic style in 1798. First, and pretty much the next thing we know of Malthus after the day in June 1798 when his epochal work was published, we find him writing to his father the following February asking if he can acquire a considerable number of books. While the details need not detain us here as we will address this issue presently, all the books Malthus sought were pioneering tracts in local- and national-scale demographic data gathering. Clearly, Malthus was beginning detailed researches into how populations actually worked to buttress the empirical demonstration of his argument. Second, within four months of writing this letter, Malthus was setting sail from Great Yarmouth for his first trip abroad. We have already seen in Chapter 3 that by 1795 Malthus was a keen observer of local prices and factories in addition to striking the pose of the gentleman seeking picturesque pleasure; four years later, the notes Malthus took during his first European trip were far more extended and serious, coupling as they did economic and demographic analysis on the one hand with an attentiveness to climate, weather, and their impact on human societies on the other.[1]

There is a fairly clear parallel between the activities undertaken by Malthus in the year immediately following the publication of the *Essay* and those of his soon-to-be self-declared nemesis, Samuel Taylor Coleridge. Like Malthus, Coleridge had been acquiring and voraciously reading books, notably importuning Malthus's publisher Joseph Johnson for a copy of the *Essay* within weeks of its publication. Furthermore, Coleridge had already taken the course Malthus was to take some eight months later, using the same ferry route from Yarmouth to Hamburg in September 1798 for his first continental sojourn, accompanied by William and Dorothy Wordsworth. Indeed, a perusal of Malthus's *Essay* was one of his last pieces of reading before setting sail. But as John Stuart Mill was to remark in 1840, "every Englishman of the present day is by implication either a Benthamite or a Coleridgian; holds views of human affairs which can only be proved true on the principles either of Bentham or of Coleridge." For all that Malthus and Coleridge had taken the same route to Hamburg, their journeys would now diverge, literally and intellectually. Malthus would decidedly take Bentham's path in the terms of Mill's binary. In more strictly historical terms, for Malthus in the 1790s this path was framed not by Bentham but by the Christian utilitarianism he had imbibed in Cambridge from William Paley. Literally, paths diverged because, from Hamburg, Coleridge and Wordsworth continued down the Rhine while Malthus took the path "less traveled by," heading eastward to Scandinavia and Russia, areas very little visited by enlightened English travelers. Intellectually, paths diverged still more profoundly. Coleridge and the Wordsworths went in search of German romanticism. While Dorothy Wordsworth's *Journal* shows an interest in prices, it is mainly to interrogate whether they were being fleeced as unsuspecting English tourists. And while Coleridge announced his intention to collect German population statistics to test the worth of Malthus's ideas, it was Malthus and not Coleridge who was to engage in that project, with precisely the texts for which he had asked his father in February 1799. The real quarry of the romantics was not to be found in prices and population, but in poets. The high point of the Wordsworths' trip was meeting Friedrich Klopstock, luminary of the German poetic scene. More studious and wealthy, Coleridge registered as a student at Göttingen University, went to lectures by Blumenbach, and studied the pioneering romantic aesthetics of Lessing. By contrast, while Malthus met the enlightened literati of the cities and towns he traveled through in Scandinavia, his main intellectual interests were in recording prices and population dynamics, in visiting factories and mines, and in observing the impact of climate and weather on the human habitation of the earth. Simply put, Malthus's Benthamite path led him in search of information, not imagination, and would do for the remaining thirty-six years of his life.[2]

The first fruits of the path Malthus took would emerge five years and one day after his first venture into print in the form of the 1803 edition of the *Essay*. As Malthus said at that time, while the book still retained the title from 1798 "in its present shape it may be considered as a new work." Editions with further expansions and adjustments would emerge throughout the rest of Malthus's life in 1806, 1807, 1817, and 1826. In addition to this, Malthus was to pen numerous pamphlets, essays, and learned reviews in the fields of statistics, demography, and political economy, and to consolidate his thoughts in one other great work, his *Principles of Political Economy* of 1820. Bringing together decades of observation and information gathering, Malthus's later career may be seen—anachronistically but productively—as forging a form of "environmental economics," in that his persistent concern with natural resources and with land, and with the economic, social, and political conditions of their usage was far greater than that of any other classical economist of his age.[3]

In this chapter, we will follow the path Malthus trod with such steady application throughout his life. We will first look at Malthus's patient collection of information both in the form of direct observation and in the form of the gathering of data, statistical and discursive. Once we have seen how Malthus gathered his information, we will turn to the use he made of it, to the arguments he constructed in the later editions of the *Essay*, in his *Principles of Political Economy*, and in his more occasional pamphlets around the nexus of the economy and the environment.

Observing Economies and Environments

Malthus left a fairly full diary of his 1799 trip to Scandinavia, although no material survives about what he may have seen in crossing to Russia. From this diary we can build a detailed picture of his concerns as a traveler. Much of the material fits neatly into the image one might have of what a Benthamite political-economic traveler might be preoccupied with, but as we shall see, he was unusual in the extent to which he tied the traditional fare of political economy to a close observation of the natural world's fluctuations and their impact on economic and social life.

Looking first at Malthus as a political-economic traveler, we can pick out three categories of concern to which Malthus recurred as he traveled through the Swedish empire: prices, production, and population. In terms of prices, Malthus attended—as had Dorothy Wordsworth—to the price of produce as he traveled, but in a rather less self-interested fashion. The Wordsworths had traveled in the autumn of 1798, and the winter that ensued had been one of the most severe in living memory, poor crop yields coupling with extreme cold to imperil the impoverished and the needy. Traveling in the following summer, Malthus was keen to track down the impact of the bitter winter just passed on prices and provisions. Thus in Altona, a town just outside Hamburg that the Wordsworths had also frequented, Malthus noted that "during the last hard winter (harder than was ever remembered) no distress was suffered for want of provisions" on account of the fact that "the government lays in a store of Corn & sells it to the poor at a reduced price during the winter." As we will see, fifteen years later Malthus would again engage with questions of protectionism and state regulation of essential food resources in addressing the utility of the English Corn Laws. Here, however, he merely reported the effect of such regulation on prices: the regulation had held the price of corn down, where the hard winter had led the price of unregulated goods to rocket upward in Altona, the price of meat doubling, as had that of butter, while coffee and sugar prices had tripled. And it was not simply the price of goods that Malthus monitored as he traveled; he showed a concern for the rates of interest at which money was lent and the mechanisms that enabled and regulated the provision of credit in the great commercial and maritime entrepôt of Hamburg. Malthus noted that the rate of interest on money lending was a staggering 11–12 percent as he passed through, this being ascribed to a shortage of money thanks to English borrowing by Pitt's government to finance military machinations against the French.[4]

In terms of produce, Malthus attended consistently to the natural and manufactured goods of the territories through which he was traveling. As an example, we can take Malthus's comments when he visited the town of Trolhatta (Trollhätten, seventy-five miles north of Gothenburg in Sweden) in June 1799. Here, Malthus investigated in detail the large waterfalls that today power Sweden's largest hydroelectric power stations, but in his era the concern was with canalization of the river to allow for the transportation of goods. From there, Malthus went on to inspect a sawmill, one of many he would see in Scandinavia given the role of timber export in the Swedish economy at this time. Malthus inspected the machinery in some detail, not being aware of any in England, noting how "the whole machinery is set in motion by a common undershot w[h]eel, the two handles of which move up & down the saws." If sawmills exemplify the working up of primary produce, Malthus also showed a healthy interest in extractive industries, most notably in a long discussion of the silver mines at Kongsberg in Norway. After discoursing of how much silver the mines produced, the hours and laboring conditions of the miners and the mineralogical school associated with the mines, Malthus descended into the mine itself on July 3, noting that "the strata of earths lye East & West, the veins of silver N & S. The richest veins are those which descend towards the south, & particularly when they are found in a stratum with Mundic or pyrites." Malthus was also aware that the silver mines were depleting a radically limited resource, for where once they had employed 4,000 men and coined $300,000 per annum, by the time of his visit only some 2,300 were employed, producing $100,000. Similar issues of resource scarcity had come to light earlier in Malthus's trip while he was staying in Gothenburg, where he met a merchant who collected a rare moss from the Trondheim area of modern Norway that made a scarlet dye: "when it was first discovered the price was only 3£ the tun, & is now 28. Formerly there was much of it about Gotheborg; but it is now nearly all picked, & it seems to grow very slowly." Finally, Malthus also showed a keen alertness to the condition of soils and agriculture as he traveled. Early in his journey, for example, he noted in comparative vein that the lands just outside Hamburg were "flat corn country—a little like Cambridgeshire. Observed rye in ear" and, later on the same day, "the cattle appeared very small and poor." Similar comments pepper the travel diaries that Malthus left us.[5]

Finally, and unsurprisingly given his desire to produce a more authoritative version of the *Essay*, Malthus also attended to population dynamics in Scandinavia. In line with the direction in which his thought moved between the first and the later editions of the *Essay*, Malthus's main preoccupation as he traveled was with the ways in which Scandinavian population was checked by preventive rather than positive means. In particular, he noted that military service of up to seven years could be visited upon any member of the laboring classes until the age of twenty-eight and that resultantly, "marriage therefore is generally delayed till this period is past, which forms a kind of preventive check to popn." Malthus also noted that changing social mores had led to the abolition of military service with a consequent fear that this would lead to younger, more prolific marriages, undermining what Malthus said was, "in my opinion the cause why the lower classes of people in Norway are in a much better state than could be expected from the barreness of the country." And yet, for all that the focus of attention was on social, preventive checks to population, Malthus was still aware that modern European societies had not escaped the thrall of the positive checks of disease, famine, and war, noting in Gothenburg that the lack of available sailors was ascribed to recent wars with Russia wherein "they calculate that . . . near a hundred thousand men were lost." All of this material was transferred wholesale into the second and subsequent editions of the

Essay (in book 2, chapters 1–3), providing empirical substance to Malthus's demographic claims.[6]

Some of the examples discussed from Malthus's travel diaries already make it clear that he was preoccupied not simply with the staple fare of political economy, but with the relationship between production, prices, and population on the one hand and the physical environment in which economic activity took place on the other. The attention to dwindling silver reserves, to changing prices, to the availability of moss, to crops, and to food price regulation all show Malthus working at the nexus between the economic and the environmental. And reverting to the travel diaries with this in mind shows that Malthus was preoccupied with climate and weather and their relation to production and distribution. In common with many contemporaries, Malthus was a keen amateur weather recorder, and thus he took a thermometer on his travels, which he nursed through several accidents and that left him crestfallen when it finally became dysfunctional. Until that time, the travel diaries are peppered with temperature recordings, these normally being accompanied by comments on wind strength and direction. And these weather recordings, which previous scholars have tended to ignore, did serve a purpose in the broader pattern of Malthus's thought, both as a traveler in particular and as a scholar more generally. At the start of his trip, Malthus noted, "as we are travelling to the North . . . it appears to be a good opportunity of observing the comparative forwardness of the spring in the difft. countries thro which we pass, & I mean to pay some attention to this subject." He was good to his word, noting when "Wych Elms" were budding, the blossoming of whitethorns, the lack of apple trees growing in Kongsberg, and a host of such minute observations about climate, seasonality, and the natural products of the earth.[7]

What is most remarkable in Malthus's Scandinavian journal and most betokens his mature habits of thought are the moments where these two strands of his observations—the economic and the environmental—are brought to bear on one another. In this regard, the most extraordinary passage is that on the economy of the most northerly point Malthus was to reach, Trondheim in modern Norway. Here, Malthus noted that checks to population had apparently been relaxed by the elimination of military service, but that this had been balanced by rapid increases in food cultivation. So far, this was closely parallel with the findings Malthus had made farther south in Sweden, but his informers led Malthus to believe the situation was rather different at a more northerly latitude and that "should a bad year come, the people in consequence of the increased popn would suffer most extremely." Why? "From the remote situation of

Drontheim, it is extremely difficult to obtain relief in time by importation, in case of the failure of crops; and the uncertainty of the climate renders a failure of the crops always possible, however flattering appearances may be." Malthus then traced the fact that, to counteract the increased food security risk posed by a remote location, the government had promulgated that farmers had to stockpile rather than sell excess produce. He also noted that, in the vicinity of Trondheim, the population-resource dynamic varied enormously in different environments, discerning that on the coast marriages took place early and that in bad fishing seasons famine could be acute, while in some of the inland valleys south of Trondheim food yields could be startlingly plentiful despite the high latitude as they had "a most fertile soil, & being shut out from all winds, retain heat very much; & as the sun is so long above the horizon, & the thermometer during the short night often does not sink lower than 60, it may easily be imagined how rapid must be the vegetation." This was part of a more general pattern that a German merchant noted for Malthus during his stay here, that "the winters were much less cold & the summers less warm than formerly. When he first came the land round Drontheim was very little cultivated & almost entirely covered with woods." It was only at this time that individual scholars, notably in the "ecological laboratories" of colonial islands and also in the Scottish Highlands, began to connect deforestation to climate change, and while Malthus by no means made this connection from the reportage he collected at Trondheim, he did begin to see that latitude and location mattered to economic production, that government regulation could fundamentally adjust population, production, and distribution, and that these two sets of concerns interacted in complex ways. The entries Malthus made in his diary in Trondheim in the middle of July 1799, then, pioneered a more complex, multifaceted approach to the interrelation of economy and environment than that which had made Malthus's name thirteen months earlier. However heralded has been the latter and however forgotten the former, the rest of Malthus's career was to be spent working out the intimations of an environmentally astute, physically grounded form of economic and social analysis that is presaged in Trondheim more than in Okewood.[8]

After 1799, Malthus's life was to be punctuated by tours, both within Britain and beyond in Europe. He never left a diary of comparable depth and detail, however, to that we have just been scrutinizing for his Scandinavian trip. Instead, we have preserved shorthand notes, fragmentary registers of transactions, anecdotes, and the like. While they need not detain us for long given their occasional and predominantly recreational rather than intellectual nature, it is worth noting that, abbreviated as they are, each of Malthus's tours appears to have seen him recording information about economics, demography, and the physical environment on the model we have seen in the Scandinavian trip. Thus, as did so many of his contemporaries, Malthus took advantage of the lull in the Napoleonic Wars marked by the 1801 Treaty of Amiens to tour the continent, visiting France and Switzerland. In the Jura, Malthus was harangued about the evils of early marriage, a harangue that went down in family folklore as it was heard by Malthus's future wife, Harriet Eckersall, and was incorporated in the 1803 edition of the *Essay*. Similarly, Malthus's 1810 visit to northern England and Scotland saw him commenting approvingly of Scottish poorhouses as "only to be considered as a refuge from starving," while his other visit north of the border sixteen years later, the last trip for which we have any written record, saw him attending to wages in a context he memorably described as "the crash . . . to credit and confidence." A year previous to this, in 1825, Malthus and family had gone overseas, taking a continental tour to shake off the misery of losing their youngest daughter, Lucy, to tuberculosis, and here again Malthus habitually recorded details about farming, crop yields, food prices, and labor costs. Finally, in the *Edinburgh Review* of 1808, Malthus had noted the lack of reliable information about Ireland and "the necessity, indeed, of making the British public more familiar with the state of Ireland." Nine years later he himself went to Ireland, staying with relatives, and noted again the condition of the land, population, and economy and their interrelation in a letter to David Ricardo, his summary being: "great marks of improvement were observable . . . [but that] the predominant evil of Ireland . . . [was] a population greatly in excess above the demand for labour, though in general not much in excess above the means of subsistence on account of the rapidity with which potatoes have increased under a system of cultivating them on very small properties rather with a view to support than sale."

What each of these fragments gestures toward and the Scandinavian journal evinces at greater length is the extent to which Malthus's intellectual efforts were grounded in patient firsthand observation of empirical details, these being built up by some form of induction into a more general understanding of the complex interrelations between economy and environment. In this Malthus was self-consciously at some distance from the more theoretically driven agendas of other contemporary political economists, most notably his friend and sparring partner David Ricardo, who quite rightly divined that "our differences may in some respects, I think, be ascribed to your considering my book as more practical than I intended it to be. My object was to elucidate principles." This attention to the empirical in all of its complexity was one of the ways in which, even if Malthus did in the terms of Mill's binary take a Benthamite path, he was anything but attuned to the abstract theorizations of Bentham. This empiricism did not only manifest itself in personal observation but also in the other project of inquiry Malthus signaled in 1799, his concerted attempt to collect, collate, and conceptualize the broader swathe of observational material about demography and economics, descriptive and statistical, that his contemporaries were accumulating. This was to be the second empirical bedrock of his analysis of economy and its environmental groundings.[9]

Reading about Economies and Environments

In the preface to the 1803 edition of the *Essay*, Malthus emphasized its predecessor's occasional and ephemeral origins, being "written on the spur of the moment, and from the few materials which were within my reach in a country situation." He also formalized what the letter to his father four years earlier had signaled, his desire to "give . . . a more practical and permanent interest" to the *Essay* by turning his "reading towards an historical examination of the effects of the principle of population." Malthus admitted that this intention had led him to a wide range of reading as he "found that much more had been done than I had been aware of, when I first published the essay." Bibliographical work confirms the truth of Malthus's modest prefatory statements: where the 1798 *Essay* only cited eleven other works, this went up by an order of magnitude for the 1803 edition, which cited 125 books and pamphlets, and then there was a gradual accretion of additional material in the later editions of the *Essay*, finally reaching some 162 works for the sixth and final, 1826 edition.[10]

The nature of Malthus's reading is indeed such as was gestured to in his preface, consisting in the main of travel accounts, pioneering works of Enlightenment social analysis and theory, and demographic, statistical, and economic tracts of the sort he had requested from his father in 1799. In terms of travel accounts, Malthus's global survey of the checks to ancient and far-flung civilizations in book 1 of the *Essay*, for example, made extensive use of the journals of James Cook in depicting the population dynamics of islands in the Pacific, and likewise drew upon Mungo Park to discuss the situation in central Africa. For other areas, he was more directly dependent on the syntheses offered by those Enlightenment scholars who either went to far-flung locations as part of the expanding British Empire, as in his use of William Jones's work on Indian culture, or who were enlightened denizens of those locations, as in his use of the work of Benjamin Franklin, or, finally, who collated information in the service of theories about the progress of society, as in William Robertson's history of the Americas, which Malthus drew on extensively in depicting that part of the globe. The economic and other tracts Malthus relied on were the most extensive category of all, covering the agricultural surveys of authors such as Arthur Young and Joseph Townsend, the pioneering demographic analyses of parish registers by Thomas Short and of the nascent British census material by Frederick Eden and John Rickman. Parallel demographic and economic analyses for other European states were also consulted and referenced by Malthus, including works by Durand on Switzerland, Peuchet on France, and Süssmilch on Germany.[11]

If Malthus's reading makes him sounds like a conventional representative of the late Enlightenment literati, simply becoming more thorough with the passage of time, a position he was very much placed in by his 1798 *Essay* as we saw in Chapter 3, this is misleading. His use of the emergent material from the first census of 1801 and of further information from each subsequent census, coupled with his deployment of other aggregate social data point to the other side of Malthus's scholarly persona as a pioneering social statistician. Why was Malthus so fascinated by statistics? Obviously, his Cambridge education had given him a considerable mathematical competence, but for him, social statistics filled the gap in our knowledge of mankind to which he had pointed in the 1798 *Essay*. Statistics, by viewing society as an aggregate, gave us the beginnings of a history of the poorer classes of society whose world had been ignored by narrative history: "this branch of statistical knowledge has of late years been attended to in some countries, and we may promise ourselves a clearer insight into the internal structure of human society from the progress of these inquiries." Malthus made use of as wide a range of statistics, mainly demographic but also economic, as he could gain access to in all his later works, starting with the 1803 edition of the *Essay*. Thus he considerably extended the treatment of fertility rates and consequent likely time spans for a doubling of the population in 1803 (book 1, chapter 4), most notably by showing the ways in which the degree of excess of births over deaths impacted on those time spans. And while Hazlitt's gibe that this was mere elementary mathematics has some purchase, Malthus patiently went through the details of his calculations to aid readers who were less well versed in mathematics than himself (a category into which Hazlitt himself fell!), but who wanted to understand the demographic and social issues at stake. If the treatment of fertility was merely mathematical, the subsequent section on mortality in book 1, chapter 6, was by contrast squarely statistical, drawing on the work of Süssmilch to investigate the varied rates of mortality over time in advanced European societies. For Malthus, this analysis reinforced his contentions from the first edition of the *Essay,* but with an empirical weight his abstract speculations had not achieved in 1798: "In contemplating the plagues and sickly seasons which occur in these tables, after a period of rapid increase, it is impossible not to be impressed with the idea that the number of inhabitants had, in these instances, exceeded the food and the accommodations necessary to preserve them in health." Tables of mortality, then, confirmed for Malthus the operation of "positive checks." Malthus kept a weather eye out for such information throughout his lifetime, seizing, for example, on Alexander von Humboldt's *Essay on New Spain* for his article entitled "Population" in the 1824 edition of the *Encyclopaedia Britannica* as providing "the first [demographic facts] of any consequence which the public has yet received of a tropical climate."[12]

Malthus's attention also went beyond demographic facts to other material, notably price series data of the sort we have seen him interested in during his Swedish tour. Malthus's long correspondence with David Ricardo, for example, is peppered with inquiries about prices and international trade, and indeed the friendship between the two great political economists began with a letter from Malthus about Jamaican prices. As Malthus summarized this concern in the *Quarterly Review* of 1823, "at all times an extensive collection of facts relative to the interchange of the various commodities of the commercial world . . . cannot but be of great importance to the science of political economy." Perhaps unsurprisingly, Malthus's most extended use of statistical data came in his analysis of the emergent material from the English censuses as he looked to the population dynamics of his own nation in later editions of the *Essay*. The 1803 edition of the *Essay* incorporated material from the 1801 census returns as interpreted by John Rickman, while the fifth and sixth editions updated the analysis in the light of the 1811 and 1821 data respectively and of the analytical possibilities such multiple temporal points of reference began to open up. Again, Malthus saw in the census data a striking empirical confirmation of the tenor of his more abstract argument about population and resource dynamics from 1798. The census abstracts revealed "marriages . . . are to the whole population as 1 to $123^{1/5}$, a smaller proportion of marriages than obtains in any of the countries [of Europe] . . . except Norway and Switzerland," and yet in fertility and resource terms even with "not more than half of the prolific power of nature . . . called into action . . . there are more children born than the country can properly support."[13]

The details of Malthus's interpretation of the census will detain us later, but as we here treat how Malthus used data, it is pertinent to note that a large proportion of his treatment of the English census data in fact addressed not whether it confirmed or refuted his positions regarding population-resource dynamics, but its sources of error and the robustness of its findings, for this opens up the final element of Malthus's critical use of sources. Malthus did not simply collate and deploy the emergent body of numerical social data sets; he also methodologically investigated the robustness of the figures such data sets generated. In the case of the English censuses, Malthus was clear, notably from the emergence of the 1811 data onward, that while the general pattern of rapid population growth and the contours of births, marriages, and deaths were apparent and well established, the detail was inaccurate due to initial errors in the 1801 census and defective enumerations in all the census returns. Malthus speculated at length on the methodological corrections that would reconcile the data from the successive censuses with the greatest ease and precision. And this opens up the element of Malthus's work that is most neglected by those who only read the *Essay* in its 1798 version rather than its successors, or who understand Malthus through his romantic critics rather than his own words. Where thanks to the 1798 *Essay* Malthus became notorious for his deployment of two simple ratio calculations— an arithmetic progression for food production and a geometric progression for potential population growth—in all his subsequent writings Malthus became notorious (to the distraction of friends and critics alike) for his desire to dwell in detail and avoid abstract and simple mathematical generalizations about social and economic patterns. Of Malthus's ambivalence about categorical social statements, Robert Torrens famously wrote in 1815 that "it is a singular fact, and one which it is not improper to impress upon the public, that, in the leading questions of economical science, Mr. Malthus scarcely ever embraced a principle which he did not subsequently abandon." As Malthus himself put it at its starkest in the opening of his *Principles of Political Economy:* "The principal cause of error, and of the differences which prevail at present among the scientific writers on political economy, appears to me to be a precipitate attempt to simplify and generalize." He went on to say, in a startling reversal of the Newtonian simplicity of the 1798 *Essay* that amounted to a recapitulation of his desire as a Cambridge undergraduate to study applied rather than pure math, that while "we cannot too highly respect and venerate that admirable rule of Newton, not to admit more causes than are necessary to the solution of the phenomena we are considering . . . the rule itself implies, that those which really are necessary must be admitted. Before the shrine of truth, as discovered by facts and experience, the fairest theories and the most beautiful classifications must fall."[14]

This methodological advocacy of complexity and caution in the use and analysis of data in the *Principles* may be said to relate back to the realization Malthus came to in his analysis of population, economy, and environment in Trondheim of complex mutual interrelations as a key to social and economic analysis. Certainly, an awareness of multiple causes and the need to avoid precipitate generalization guided Malthus in all his analyses of statistical data series. This manifested itself in a set of habitual responses Malthus displayed toward data and the claims made about it. First, and as we have already seen with respect to English census data, he always questioned the likely accuracy and grounds for enumerative errors in statistical data. Second, Malthus always looked cautiously for temporal and spatial variability in data sets. For mortality, for example, he stated as a general point that "political calculators have been led into the error of supposing that there is, generally speaking, an invariable order of mortality in all countries; but it appears, on the contrary, that this order is extremely variable; that it is very different in different places of the same country." And this was exactly what his analysis of the census data on mortality for England revealed, with rates of up to 1:50 in the countryside as opposed to under 1:21 in London making their aggregation not simply meaningless but downright misleading: "When the mortality of the human race, in different countries, and different situations, varies so much as from 1 in 20 to 1 in 60, no general average can be used with safety in a particular case, without such a knowledge of the circumstances of the country . . . as would probably supersede the necessity of resorting to any general proportion." Likewise Humboldt's data was praised by Malthus for showing that a different mortality and fertility regime existed in the tropics: "the proportion of the births to the population is extraordinarily great, and the proportion of deaths very considerable, showing, in a striking point of view, the early marriages and early deaths of a tropical climate, and the more rapid passing away of each generation." Finally, as well as questions of false aggregation, Malthus was keenly aware that he was working in the era of the birth of large-scale social statistics, and that this meant that inadequate time series data sets existed to be sure of their reliability or of the "normal" variability in indicators of economic and demographic change. Discussing epidemics, for example, he argued that scholars looking at birth:death ratios tended habitually "to estimate these proportions from too short periods, and generally to reject the years of plague as accidental," where their recurrence meant they were an integral part of the long-term demographic balance.[15]

In sum, Malthus in his later life was a keen, assiduous, and yet also cautious collector and critic of social, economic, and demographic data in the varied forms of personal observation, extensive reading, and scrutiny of the burgeoning statistical information emergent at the turn of the nineteenth century. After what we might call his "Trondheim moment," Malthus clearly turned his back on the simplicity and the sensationalism that his abstract mathematical argument of 1798 had relied upon and that had made his name, preferring a cautious and careful empiricism. And in the service of this empiricism, what did he craft?

Malthus's Mature Thought

Malthus's later writing career spanned over a quarter century, and thus, as intellectual historians would remind us, we need to beware the "myth of coherence," the idea that all of his ideas shared a tight focus that amounted to a singular doctrine. That said, however, and giving due weight to Torrens's criticism of Malthus's intellectual vacillations, for our purposes we can suggest that Malthus's later career showed a set of consistent tenors of thought about political economy and resource issues that guided his response to the specific socioeconomic questions of his era such as the Corn Laws and the Poor Laws.[16]

Malthus's two major treatises after 1798—the later editions of the *Essay* and his *Principles of Political Economy*—can be seen as linked meditations on the interconnection between land, sustenance, and resources on the one hand, and population, wealth, and its allocation on the other hand. In the *Essay,* this was framed as the issues raised by "the constant tendency in all animated life to increase beyond the nourishment prepared for it," a familiar depiction of the question of scarcity closely allied with that from 1798, but in the *Principles* this was abstracted and generalized into the opening formulation that political economy cannot be an exact, mathematical science because it addresses at its core "the agency of so variable a being as man, and the qualities of so variable a compound as the soil." That Malthus himself saw a tight interrelationship between the projects he addressed in both of his major later works is made clear in the *Principles,* where he tackled just that question by suggesting that the *Essay* had "endeavoured to trace the causes which practically keep down the population of a country to the level of its actual supplies," while his *Principles* endeavored to show "what are the causes which chiefly influence these supplies, or call the powers of production forth into the shape of increasing wealth." At its simplest, then, Malthus depicted his two key works as different angles on the same nexus, the *Essay* focusing on the demand side and the *Principles* on the questions posed by the supply side.[17]

In addressing this nexus, Malthus placed at the heart of the analysis "land" in the *Essay* and, expanding his net somewhat, "wealth" in the *Principles*. It was land and its produce that determined potential wealth, and it was land that limited demand in the ways positive or preventive that the demographic analysis of the *Essay* depicted. In 1803, Malthus argued that "the great position of the [seventeenth-century French] Economists will always remain true, that the surplus produce of the cultivators is the great fund which ultimately pays all those who are not employed upon the land." Malthus's deployment of the term "land" here was different from and broader than that which would spring to mind today as his final major publication, *Definitions of Political Economy* (1827), made clear in defining the term as "the soil, mines, waters, and fisheries of the habitable globe. It is the main source of raw materials and food." In short, all of those primary, extractive, and agricultural details that had attracted the eye of the itinerant Malthus on his Scandinavian jaunt a quarter century earlier were issues pertaining to the land in these terms. In the *Principles*, Malthus's preferred term switched from "land" to "wealth," in part as he recognized more clearly that economic analysis should key around the insights of Adam Smith (as whose disciple he constantly positioned himself), not the French *economistes*. And yet the focus on the material grounding of wealth remained: "I should define wealth to be, those *material* objects which are necessary, useful, or agreeable to mankind. . . . A country will therefore be rich or poor according to the abundance or scarcity with which these material objects are supplied, compared with the extent of territory." This attention to land/material objects as the definition of true wealth led Malthus to make a threefold distinction between immaterial goods, material goods, and goods that, while material, had no economic value as such. While the bulk of Malthus's analysis would attend to material goods of value as the subject matter of political economy, he addressed the other categories briefly as well. Immaterial goods that were useful or delightful to mankind might include "gratifications derived from religion, from political and civil liberty . . . from music, dancing, acting," but such goods, while valuable, were not capable of being quantified, and as such were beyond the remit of political economy. Goods that, while useful, could not be exchanged had, for

Malthus, "value in use," and here he agreed with Ricardo, whom he cited approvingly in denominating "air, water, the elasticity of steam, and the pressure of the atmosphere" as such goods. They were deemed uniform and not limited in supply, and thus outside the remit of political economy. Obviously, in the present day environmental economics is driven by the insight that such goods are, *per contra*, limited and capable of improvement or degradation by our usage and thus need to be given a value in exchange, not just in usage. Malthus was aware that extractive industries such as sawmills could damage the surrounding countryside, but it would take the extractive volumes of the twentieth century to bring such resources as air and water within the ambit of economic analysis. Where Malthus drew the line between "land" as having "value in exchange" and air, water, and so forth as only having "value in use" was that the former was scarce, and as such the insights of our own era amount to no more than a repositioning of where this line sits.[18]

Reverting to Malthus's categories rather than our own, land was a scarce resource with value in exchange: "the extent of the earth itself is limited, and cannot be enlarged by human demand. The inequality of soils occasions, even at an early period of society, a comparative scarcity of the best land." Thus rent, the value in exchange of the product of the land, was not a consequence of monopoly, the social construction of limits, but of natural differentials in soil fertility that were "the gift of nature to man" or, in more grandiose fashion, that "which God has bestowed on man." This was one of the positions adopted by Malthus that would most strongly arouse radical ire, as we shall see. Being a scarce resource with value in exchange would not in and of itself make land a category of more importance to the political economist than any other such resource, but that Malthus detected two characteristics that made land unique. First, in an advanced organic economy, land did not just produce one good but multiple goods, all of which were necessary rather than merely beneficial to human existence: "land does not produce one commodity alone, but, in addition to that most indispensable of all commodities—food, it produces the materials for clothing, lodging, and firing." As such, and unlike all other goods, the supply produced by the land would generate its own demand: "Land produces the necessaries of life—produces the means by which, and by which alone, an increase of people may be brought into being and supported. In this respect it is fundamentally different from every other kind of machine known to man." That demand, of course, was generated by the principle of population as analyzed in the *Essay*; once land could generate an increase in supply, population would immediately advance to absorb that increase. The second way in which land was unique revolved around questions that might, with pardonable anachronism, be called "food security." If land was, as we have just seen, that "by which alone" people could be supported, securing its product was paramount to the state and society and could trump the normal dictates of political economy surrounding free trade: "security is of still more importance than wealth." Malthus's thoughts on this topic were driven by contemporary concerns surrounding the utility or otherwise of the Corn Laws, the legislation that restricted importation of corn until the price in Britain rose above £4 per quarter. Malthus, in a move that bespoke his independence of thought and also alienated him from much of the Whig establishment, supported the Corn Laws on the grounds of food security. For him, "the nature of things has, indeed, stamped upon corn a peculiar value." As a result, it would be imprudent to rely on the importation of corn and other primary produce for several reasons. First, to be reliant on corn imported from other nations meant that, even if it were cheaper in the short run, its supply was less assured in the case of either the exporting nations seeing an increase in their own demand or of political hostilities with that nation. Writing in the same year as Waterloo and after decades of attempted grain embargos and blockades by Napoleon, Malthus in his 1815 pamphlet *The Importation of Foreign Corn* pointed out that in a free market, "if our ports were open," Britain would see her "principal supplies of grain . . . come from France." But, as France had recently enacted a law limiting the export of corn in years of scarcity, the result would be that "all assistance would be at once cut off . . . and we should have to look to other quarters, from which it is an established fact, that large sudden supplies cannot be obtained." Further, if the countries such as the Baltic states, Russia, and America were to be relied on for corn, as they diversified through the demand that, as we have seen, Malthus thought the land was unique in generating, they would build more highly developed commercial and manufacturing sectors. The result of this would be to redirect their agricultural surpluses toward their home market, leaving Britain as a corn importer painfully exposed to scarcity despite having the ability to pay for food supplies. Coupled with the political vulnerability to which Britain would be exposed as an importer in a system of international trade in primary produce, Malthus feared that such a position would also lead to political unrest at home. Malthus took it as a general position that "an excessive proportion of manufacturing population does not seem favourable to national quiet and happiness" in his first pamphlet on the Corn Laws and unpacked this idea at greater length in the 1815 tract mentioned before. Taking it as axiomatic that "the labouring classes" are "the foundation on which the whole [social] fabric rests," Malthus argued that the importation of corn, dependent as it was on the state of legislation, international relations, and scarcity in other countries over which Britain could have no control would indeed lead to cheaper minimum corn prices, but that the amplitude of price variation would be increased in such a system; and he demonstrated this on the basis of price series data for the era 1792–1805, when import dependency was greatest. Such fluctuations would impact most on the laboring poor and could easily become a catalyst to social unrest. Malthus's third and final point was that such dependence on overseas supplies might be necessary to small commercial nations or those with impoverished soils, say, Venice or the Netherlands, but this was not the case for Britain, where "the present commercial system . . . throws a country into this state, without any physical necessity for it."[19]

The point Malthus reached with regard to the question of food security as refracted through the lens of the Corn Laws is an important one, for it shows that while, in Mill's binary, he took the Benthamite path, he was by no means the heartless utilitarian of romantic and Dickensian caricature. On the contrary, and as he put it in concluding the point about British trade with which the previous paragraph ended, profit maximization via free trade, if it led to such consequences, "cannot be founded on the genuine principles of the wealth of nations." The verbal resonance here with Adam Smith was quite deliberate on Malthus's part; he saw himself as the inheritor of Smith's tradition where political economy was subsumed into the broader project of determining the "science of the legislator," or, true to his Cambridge roots, of building a Christian utilitarianism. As such, one can find passages where Malthus sounds intensely utilitarian—"what is morality, individual or political . . . but a calculation of consequences?"; "the principle of utility . . . [is] the great foundation of morals"—but in the texture of his thought as a whole, political stability and social cohesion are the aim of that utilitarianism; the operation of a free market is not the sovereign road to Malthus's brand of utilitarianism: "the happiness of a society is, after all, the legitimate end even of its wealth, power, and population." As his obituarist in the *Edinburgh Review,* William Empson, opined, Malthus was the "right sort" of utilitarian. This also explains Malthus's mature view on the desirability or otherwise of population growth. In a blending of Christian humanism with utilitarianism very much inspired by the thought of William Paley, Malthus argued that the correct index of social happiness was not the number of births per se as traditional political argument had suggested (see chapter 1), but "the number of children born . . . which survived the age of infancy and reached manhood" for it was only such individuals who could live meaningful, fulfilled lives and thereby "contribute their share to the resources or the defence of the state." As such, and in stark contrast to the received stereotype of him, Malthus welcomed population increase as conducive to social and personal good "when it follows in its natural order," by which he meant when there had been a "permanent increase of agriculture." Malthus accepted that an increase in population could stimulate increased food production (an argument to which we will return in discussing the critics of Malthusianism) and more generally that the two "re-act upon each other" but generally felt agriculture the stimulus to permanent increase in population, where population increase could lead to increased production but might equally lead to increased food scarcity.[20]

This complex, Christian utilitarianism also provides an Ariadnian thread through Malthus's mature thought on the question of resource scarcity. Malthus still took it as axiomatic that a social theorist had to analyze human existence, "living as we do in a limited world," a world "not furnished by nature in unlimited abundance." And yet the limits Malthus attended to in his later thought were not absolute but instead those created by social circumstances. Thus there was an acceptance of the point that—as we have seen—Southey and others would make against him (even before they had made it!): "there are many parts of the globe, indeed, hitherto uncultivated, and almost unoccupied." Likewise, even if areas had been occupied and cultivated, agricultural improvement meant that they could reasonably be expected to yield more per unit area: "no country has ever reached, or probably will ever reach, its highest possible acme of produce, it appears always as if the want of industry, or the ill-direction of that industry, was the actual limit to a further increase of produce and population, and not the absolute refusal of nature to yield any more." And yet, as Malthus went on, none of this "removes the weight of a hair from the argument" about the reality of resource scarcity for him. Why?[21]

The answer to this question lies in Malthus's forging of the concept of "effective demand," a concept familiar in modern-day economics, coupled to his belief in what we might call "legitimate supply," a concept that stemmed from his Christian utilitarianism. Addressing the unfamiliar concept first, merely to point to lands that were uncultivated across the globe was not to establish any form of right to use them given the consequences of such usage on their inhabitants. In stark contrast to the jingoistic imperial rhetoric we have seen Southey adopt on this issue, Malthus's tone was one redolent of the Christian critique of empire, this despite his employment from 1805 as a professor by the English East India Company. For how, Malthus asked, could large uncultivated tracts be brought into productive usage? The possible answers were twofold. First, "exterminating, or driving into a corner where they must starve . . . the inhabitants of these thinly-peopled regions" something that "must be questioned from a moral view" but that he saw as a process already being visited upon the native Americans in the United States of America as its civilization expanded westward. Second, to educate those indigenous peoples such that they could cultivate their lands more effectively and respond to global demand, a process that would "necessarily be slow; and during this time, as population would regularly keep pace with the increasing produce," such increases would no sooner be made than they would be absorbed. If societal development would be extremely slow, as the stadial theories of the Enlightenment suggested, and if the annexation of lands was morally repugnant, and if such insights were, as Malthus suggested, "applicable to all the parts of the earth, where the soil is imperfectly cultivated," then the mere existence of barren areas on the globe or indeed within a nation did not per se mean there was a legitimate supply with which to respond to the demand for the resources of the land that the principle of population would generate.[22]

The argument on which Malthus focused, however, with regard to resource scarcity and that which had by far the greater impact on the history of ideas was that surrounding "effective demand." Simply put, the fact that on the one hand there might be a supply of uncultivated or undercultivated land and that, on the other hand, there could be people who were in need of the resources which that land might produce did not necessarily mean that this supply and demand would be brought together successfully: "If want alone, or the desire of the labouring classes to possess the necessaries and conveniences of life, were a sufficient stimulus to production, there is no state in Europe, or in the world, that would have found any other practical limit to its wealth than its power to produce; and the earth would probably before this period have contained, at the very least, ten times as many inhabitants as are supported on its surface at present." For Malthus, "want" as a physical desire does not equate to "demand" as an economic category: "the desire of any individual to possess the necessary conveniences and luxuries of life, however intense, will avail nothing towards their production, if there be no where a reciprocal demand for something which he possesses. A man whose only possession is his labour has, or has not, an effective demand for produce according as his labour is, or is not, in demand by those who have the disposal of produce." The concept of effective demand or more often the lack thereof is punctuated throughout Malthus's analyses of population-resource dynamics in both the later editions of the *Essay* and his *Principles,* being his main analytical tool for explaining how scarcity functioned in a world that was not at its absolute limit in terms of resource utilization. Effective demand explained the distinction between temporarily and enduringly sustainable population increases in Sweden. Lack of effective demand drove the sluggish population growth in the resource-rich corn regions of Russia. Effective demand was the key to interpreting Alexander von Humboldt's findings in New Spain of a region of unparalleled natural fertility, yet one where population was slow to expand, the system of large landholdings meaning there was no need for labor and thus no income for laborers to purchase with. Effective demand also explained the very different population and landholding dynamics of Ireland, where a diet centered on the potato as a staple and where a mosaic of tiny, self-sufficient landholdings meant people could sustain themselves but neither produce for nor demand from commodity markets, keeping them in a cycle of populous near-poverty. And yet the example to which Malthus recurred most often and with most feeling was the question of effective demand in his home nation.[23]

Malthus, writing a quarter century after Adam Smith, could confirm with confidence that Britain was the "limit case" of a commercial society with a slimmed-down and efficient agricultural sector and an increasingly preponderant manufacturing economy: "about the middle of the last century, we were genuinely . . . an agricultural nation. . . . We have now, however, stepped out of the agricultural system into a state in which the commercial system clearly predominates." Comparatively, even within the advanced economies of Europe, Britain was the "country [with] the most manufacturing ever recorded in history." True to his empirical bent, Malthus also backed up these impressionistic claims with such data as he could access: if Süssmilch suggested that the maximum amount of urbanization he could find was a ratio of 3:7, in Malthus's England the census of 1811 revealed a ratio of agricultural to other employees of 2:3. This had all been facilitated by what can retrospectively be called an "agricultural revolution," but that Malthus with rather less reification saw as "the extraordinary improvements, and prodigious increase of produce that have taken place latterly in some districts." Malthus was aware that if such improvements could be extended from the light soils of Norfolk to the rest of Britain, "the quantity of additional produce would be immense, and would afford the means of subsistence to a very great increase in population." The problem was that for any such extension to create the real conditions for an enduring, stable expansion of population would demand a violation of either legitimate supply or effective demand. On the supply side, to ensure the maximization of the produce of land would necessitate that government control what people produced, something that "evidently could not be done without the most complete violation of the law of property, from which everything that is valuable to man has hitherto arisen."[24]

Malthus's main preoccupation, however, was with the question of government intervention to generate effective demand via the Elizabethan Poor Laws. While it has been too easy for neoconservatives in our age to latch onto Malthus as an opponent of government intervention thanks to his castigation of "the wretched system of governing too much," we have already seen that his actual views were far more complex than this suggests and far less hostile to state regulation for the public good in the case of the Corn Laws. And yet for Malthus the Poor Laws were simply infeasible; they were as deluded as Godwin's and Condorcet's systems of perfectibility that he had vanquished in 1798, only far more modest and plausible, and accordingly far more insidious. Viewed through the lens of effective demand, the Poor Laws were a self-defeating attempt to turn the need for sustenance by the poor into an effective demand by government subsidy, and they attracted Malthus's ire and his rhetorical fury in a way no other topic did in his mature, post-1798 oeuvre. Thus for Malthus, the Poor Laws were a complete denial of all that Adam Smith in particular and political economy more generally had shown of the operation of markets; he was flabbergasted that people "should still think that it is in the power of justices of the peace, or even of the omnipotence of parliament, to alter by *fiat* the whole circumstances of a country." The "obstinacy," or, as we would now term it, price inelasticity, of demand for corn meant that all Poor Law intervention could do was increase the effective demand of those receiving parish relief at the expense of those "immediately above the poor" and thereby create a poverty trap that increased the real price of food but not effective demand. In a rare reversion to his younger satirical style of declamation, Malthus said the Poor Laws were "as arrogant and as absurd as if it had been enacted that two ears of wheat should in future grow where only one had grown before. Canute, when he commanded the waves not to wet his princely foot, did not in reality assume a greater power over the laws of nature." The overseers of the poor could not magic from thin air an ongoing demand for labor, and it was only this that could create effective demand for underemployed labor. The words of statute could not trump the realities of economic circumstance. And it was in this context that Malthus penned words in his 1803 *Essay* that have dogged his reputation ever since, bespeaking, as they appeared to, a callous indifference to the survival of the poor. Malthus's comments on "Nature's mighty feast" were equivalent in their infamy to Burke's "swinish multitude":

> A man who is born into a world already possessed, if he cannot get subsistence from his parents on whom he has a just demand, and if society do not want his labour, has no claim of right to the smallest portion of food, and, in fact, he has no business to be where he is. At nature's mighty feast there is no vacant cover for him. She tells him to be gone and will quickly execute her own orders, if he do not work upon the compassion of some of her guests. If these guests get up and make room for him, other intruders immediately appear demanding the same favour. The report of a provision for all that come fills the hall with numerous claimants. The order and harmony of the feast is disturbed, the plenty that before reigned is changed into scarcity; and the happiness of the guests is destroyed by the spectacle of misery and dependence in every part of the hall, and by the clamorous importunity of those who are justly enraged at not finding the provision which they had been taught to expect. The guests learn too late their error, in counteracting those strict orders to all intruders, issued by the great mistress of the feast, who, wishing that all her guests should have plenty, and knowing that she could not provide for unlimited numbers, humanely refused to admit fresh comers when her table was already full.[25]

This sounded none too "humane" to Malthus's critics, and he immediately removed this passage in the next, 1806, edition of the *Essay*. This does not appear to have been a mere embarrassed expediency on Malthus's part. On the contrary, even in the case of the Poor Laws, Malthus the economic theorist could be trumped by Malthus the humane utilitarian. Thus before his infamous "mighty feast" passage, in a tract of 1800, *An Investigation of the Cause of the Present High Price of Provisions*, Malthus castigated the effects of the Poor Laws in terms familiar from the versions of the *Essay* both subsequent and prior to its publication for spreading poverty across a wider surface, but relented in admitting that while poor relief had increased the price of corn and led to grumbling among the laboring classes, "it was undoubtedly owing to this price that a much greater number of them has not been starved" and that, as such, "no inference . . . [should] be drawn against what has been done for the relief of the poor in the present scarcity." Even at his most trenchant, then, Malthus never forgot his humanity despite the caricature critics and supporters alike would construct.[26]

The Forgotten Malthus

That even on the subject on which he was most impassioned and unrelenting, the Elizabethan Poor Laws, Malthus can be found to vacillate, to find specific good in a system of whose general and theoretical ills he was wholly and unstintingly convinced, could be seen as pointing to the truth of Torrens's barb about his haverings. And yet, more charitably and more truthfully, Malthus showed (and was reflexively aware of demonstrating) the laudable quality of allowing empirical evidence to overcome general theorizations, of desiring to think humanely, practically, and specifically about the nexus of society, economy, and environment. As his obituarist William Empson suggested, Malthus was "not fond of [political] storms, as the petrel is said to be," but he always addressed them without party prejudice and in a spirit of "quiet civil courage." This unwavering focus on the specific and the practical was a consistent factor across Malthus's career, from his words as a frustrated Cambridge undergraduate desiring a more practical form of mathematics in 1786, through his more literary persona in the 1798 *Essay,* where he had cited approvingly Pope's *Essay on Man*—"What can we reason but from what we know," down to his strictures in later life that were expressed more prosaically: "the first business of philosophy is to account for things as they are." As he put it in the preface to his 1803 *Essay,* it would have been easy for him to adopt a "masterly air," to make his principle of population "an impregnable fortress," but "abstract truth" palled in the face of considering the practical consequences of that principle, consequences that lacked the simplicity and purity of conclusions following from first principles. It was here, as the 1798 *Essay* mutated into its 1803 successor via the experience of Scandinavian travel and omnivorous data collection, that Malthus's utilitarianism diverged from the abstract rigor of the Benthamite variant.[27]

More importantly, however much Malthus may have shifted ground on the practical issues of the day such as the Corn Laws and the Poor Laws, and however much his definitions of key economic terms such as land and wealth evolve over time, we can in fact find in his work a consistent set of core beliefs. For Malthus, land was the prime source of wealth and had to be placed at the very center of any form of political economy, and it was effective demand, not mere need or desire, that could unlock that source in an advanced, commercial economy. Policies that ignored this or came from an earlier stage of socioeconomic development such as the Poor Laws were bound to fail. And yet however much political economy as an abstract system might abhor interruptions to free trade, political economy as a pragmatic science for the legislator had to look at the consequences of such interruptions in the round, taking into account their social and moral consequences as well as the mere question of economic maximization. It was on these grounds that Malthus came to defend the Corn Laws, much to the horror of the Whig liberal establishment, and even to see some small good in the operations of the Poor Laws in 1798–1799.

The exceptionally severe winter of 1798–1799, the winter in which Coleridge and Wordsworth traveled and whose consequences Malthus diligently inquired after as he traveled through Scandinavia the following summer, led him to prioritize humane utility over the market qua panacea. If Malthus took the Benthamite path, he had enough sympathy and imagination not to wholly renounce Coleridgean qualities of thought.

Of course, to summarize Malthus's core beliefs by styling him an "environmental economist" is misleading, but it also captures an important truth. Malthus did not cognitize the airs, waters, and ecosystems of our earth as limited; he was no more an environmental economist than Wordsworth was a Friend of the Earth. It is more historically accurate to say that Malthus was the individual in the canon of so-called "classical economists" who cleaved most strongly to the argument that emanated from the seventeenth-century French *economistes* that the land—taken in a wide sense—was the origin of all value, even in a society he recognized as rapidly moving toward having a preponderance of its population and wealth in the manufacturing and commercial sectors. This is not, of course, environmental economics per se, but it is a form of economics more insistently attuned to the environment, to the limits and opportunities the physical world presents to human societies, than any other that was forged in his own era or for many decades thereafter.

CHAPTER SIX

Malthus and the Victorians

Malthus's Moment

Malthus died on December 29, 1834, suddenly, and most probably of a heart seizure. At the time of his death, Malthus had been staying with his wife's relatives in Claverton, and his visible life thus forms a circle, ending where first we had sight of it, on the banks of the Avon, just outside Bath. Richard Graves's "Don Roberto," the fighting boy, had fought his way by the intellect, too, such that by 1834 Malthus's fame and indeed notoriety spread its tentacles throughout English life. Where Malthus's biographer's claim that his name was (in its adjectival form of "Malthusian") as common in the period as "Freudian" would be a century later, might be taken as *parti pris,* it is confirmed in part by the fact that Sigmund Freud would still be jousting with Malthusianism a century later. There would be "Malthusian moments" in later decades which we will address subsequently; this was "Malthus's moment." It is worth going on a brief whistle-stop tour of Malthus's fame in the decade or so either side of his death, both as it limns a portrait of Britain around the time of Victoria's accession and as its contours were to shape and guide reactions to Malthus throughout the long era of her reign.[1]

The last decade or so of Malthus's life saw him propelled to public fame, to prestigious awards, and to the role of a political policy advisor. Thus Malthus was twice called to give evidence to parliamentary select committees, one concerning machinery and its impact on the laboring classes in 1824, and one concerning the likely efficacy of a scheme of Irish emigration on that country's economic prospects. In the same decade, Malthus was a founding member of the Political Economy Club, a dining society that has been seen as the first attempt to give some scholarly coherence to the study of economics; was elected as a Fellow of the Royal Society; and was given a stipendiary prize by the Royal Society of Literature. In the final year of his life, Malthus was also instrumental in the establishment of the Statistical Society of London (the forerunner of today's Royal Statistical Society). Malthus, then, was a node in the networks of social science that were forming in the early decades of the nineteenth century. And yet none of these accolades and obligations gives any sense of the sheer notoriety of Malthus at this time. For this, we can turn briefly to literature.[2]

We have already seen the romantic vilification of Malthus in Chapter 4, but this was itself part of a far broader literary response to his ideas that peaked in the 1830s and 1840s. In our world, economists and demographers are unlikely to be the subject of a play; not so Malthus! While it may strain the designation "literature" in terms of quality, in 1831 William Cobbett published a play, *Surplus Population and the Poor Law Bill*, in his *Political Register*. It was reprinted in 1835 and, at the time of the "Swing" riots, was suppressed on Cobbett's account by "the aristocracy, parsons and money-mongers" of Tonbridge Wells, who feared it could arouse insurrection in the county. The play itself is a rather thin farce, the lascivious Sir Gripe Grindum hoping to have his wicked way with the fair milkmaid Betsy Stiles. Sir Gripe hopes that his Malthusian friend, Squire Thimble, has an effective contraceptive—his "remedy against breeding"—not realizing that Thimble's "remedy" is merely a treatise on population control, a subject on which he waxes catastrophic: "Nothing can save our country but plague, pestilence, famine and sudden death. Government ought to import a ship-load of arsenic." On Cobbett's death, some forty-five thousand copies of this fairly lame play were reportedly sold, proof of both his fame and that of his butt, Malthus. Cobbett had repeatedly attacked Malthus in print, acknowledging the intensity of his vitriol in an open letter of 1819: "I have, during my life, detested many men; but never any one so much as you." In his most famous book, *Rural Rides* (1830), Cobbett devoted a long elegy entitled "The Valley of Avon" to refuting "the monster MALTHUS," trying to show by the size of the churches of the Avon Valley above Salisbury and by the decayed mansions that the rural population had once been much greater, that agricultural productivity far outstripped need, and that, therefore, the reason for rural poverty was the siphoning of money and food by "pensioners, parsons, or dead-weight people" to "the infernal WEN" of London.[3]

Cobbett argued that "MALTHUS . . . considers men as mere animals . . . and we now frequently hear the working classes called 'the *population*,' just as we call the animals upon a farm, *'the stock*.'" This line of critique of Malthus, framing him as seeing human beings as mere animals, resurfaced in two contexts, one chilling and now forgotten, the other perhaps Malthus's most famous turn on the literary stage. Forgotten now but a *succès de scandale* in its own age, in 1838 there appeared a purportedly serious treatise, *On the Possibility of Limiting Populousness,* by one "Marcus" (the verbal echo of whose name with Malthus was clearly deliberate). Marcus rebuked Malthus for his "timidity" in addressing solutions to the population pressures he had highlighted and argued for the public-spirited to unite to control the "'pauper herd' by suffocating its superfluous infants in chambers of 'gaz.'" Marcus was clearly a Chartist working in the mode of Swift's *Modest Proposal,* and his ideas were reprinted in 1839 as part of a major Chartist publication, *The Book of Murder.* Given the ways in which Malthusian reasoning, refracted through the lens of eugenics, would lead to Auschwitz within a century of Marcus's work, this was a frightening anticipation of barbarities to come. But if this was the specter of Malthusianism future, in the immediate context of the start of Victoria's reign, far more telling were Charles Dickens's spirits of Christmases past, present, and future in his *Christmas Carol* (1843). In the opening stave of the book, Scrooge is visited by two "portly gentlemen, pleasant to behold" who ask him for a little Christmas charity for the poor. Scrooge replies that he already pays toward the local prison and the Union workhouses and that this is sufficient. When pressed that many would rather die than be consigned to the workhouse, Scrooge's infamous reply is couched in deliberately Malthusian terms: "'If they would rather die,' said Scrooge, 'they had better do it, and decrease the surplus population.'" By the end of the book, the Spirit of Christmas Present gives Scrooge Dickens's reproof to his unfeeling hubris: "'Man,' said the Ghost, 'if man you be in heart, not adamant, forbear that wicked cant until we have discovered what the surplus is, and Where it is. Will you decide what men shall live, what men shall die?'"[4]

In 1834, the *Times* had put Cobbett's and Dickens's point as vituperatively as either of them could, animadverting on the "accursed heresy pervading all the trash of Malthus, Martineau and their disciples—the heresy that poverty is a crime." And yet this very criticism also points to the fact that Malthus had his literary defenders as well, the most notable of whom was the popular writer Harriet Martineau. If Cobbett's *Surplus Population* comes from a literary world alien to us, a play about population policies, so too do Martineau's popularizing tracts about economics, demography, and public policy, the *Illustrations of Political Economy* (1834). The *Illustrations* are twenty-four short stories where common people discourse of economics, and all, as Martineau put it in her *Autobiography,* "to exemplify Malthus's doctrine." In the present day, it is hard not to share the contemporary critic Edward Bulwer-Lytton's incredulity at narratives such as that in Martineau's "Weal and Woe in Garveloch," where "half starved fishermen take the most astonishing views on the theory of population." And yet Martineau's tracts did remarkably well in their own age, their monthly installments being estimated to sell at least ten thousand copies. Malthus also acknowledged the efforts of Thomas Chalmers, "my ablest and best ally" in propagating and defending his ideas. Chalmers, a staunch Scottish Evangelical, couched his support for Malthus in firmly theological as opposed to literary terms, but as Boyd Hilton has shown, it was precisely such an evangelical environment that set the dominant terms for discussion in the decades around the time of Malthus's zenith and death, and that unified supporters such as Chalmers and Martineau with opponents such as Dickens and the Chartists.[5]

One of the reasons Malthus was talked about so much in the literature of the time was that his words were perceived to have an impact in the real world of politics and public events. He may only have appeared in the House of Commons twice, and both on occasions where he professed a lack of expertise, but Malthus was perceived to color the ways in which politicians thought and acted as can be seen by looking at several areas of public activity around the time of the accession of Victoria. First, the census. The census had been instigated in 1801 in good part thanks to the efforts of John Rickman, albeit in the context of the fears about population growth inspired by Malthus's *Essay.* Rickman was a friend of Robert Southey's, and they exchanged letters about their cordial dislike of Malthus, Rickman speaking darkly of the "heavy grudges" he owed Malthus before opening an all-out attack on Malthus as having "profited more than the public by the upside-down speculations he began to produce 25 years since" and as "not likely to dogmatize less because he knows less." And yet if the architect of the census disliked Malthus, the public perception was of the census as a tool of Malthusian logic, being used as it was to identify and enumerate groups as "problematic" or "surplus" populations. The Office of the Registrar General was formed in 1837, and the census of 1841 asked for massively increased amounts of data from households, this being a product of "the statistical movement of the 1830s," which was "dominated by Whigs who had largely accepted the Malthusian variety of political economy."[6] Even more closely associated with Malthus by the public mind of the time was a second area of public policy, the New Poor Law of 1834. It was this legislation establishing workhouses that led to Malthus's notoriety in Dickens's Scrooge. In truth, historians have shown that Malthus's direct influence on the framing of this legislation was minimal, but his work was an important part of the intellectual arsenal of the "rising generation of conservative scholars who emerged at Oxford and Cambridge from the 1790s" who did frame it.[7] It was Edwin Chadwick who actually wrote the Royal Commission Report on the Poor Laws, and Chadwick's name is also indelibly linked with the public health movements that sought to improve urban sanitation in Britain in the 1830s and 1840s. In this third area of public policy, Chadwick, "himself no Malthusian," worked to combat the Malthusian climate of ideas wherein death was seen as easing the pressure of surplus population in favour of a vision of people as "the stuff of industrial growth . . . their premature deaths . . . as so much lost profit" and to envisage "disease as a product of ill-considered arrangements, not, as the Malthusians would, as proof of . . . an imbalance between population and food." Indeed, the severely rational Chadwick's vision of public health in the cities easily morphed into a more utopian vision where sewage recycling and sanitation would create "a post-Malthusian world where every being generated the fertilizer to sustain its own existence."[8] This utopianism contrasted painfully with the situation across the Irish Sea in the 1840s, where the demographic disaster of the Great Irish Famine unfolded. While quantitative analysis can show that the Famine was not caused by excess population and was not, therefore, an exemplar of Malthusian "positive checks," it was routinely understood in those terms at the time and contributed to the sense of Malthus's ubiquity. Thus an 1823 Select Committee on the condition of the poor in Ireland went so far as to directly quote Malthus in its analysis, while the architect of the Irish Poor Law of 1838, George Nicholls, framed the problem of Irish poverty in terms directly lifted from Malthus as one created by "superabundant population" and extreme subdivision of the land.[9]

Malthus, then, was everywhere in the debates and policies of the 1820s, 1830s, and 1840s. And yet it has been argued that his influence waned rapidly, and this for both intellectual and substantive reasons. Intellectually, it has been suggested that by the time of the publication of *The Origin of Species* in 1859 Malthus was a forgotten figure, the specter of starvation and overpopulation having receded in the face of an expanding empire and increasing prosperity. And substantively, this prosperity has been traced to Britain's emergence from an "advanced organic" economy reliant on fixed energy from the sun in the form of crops and fodder to a "mineral based" economy which could extract coal at ever-increasing rates and thus soar free from the negative feedback loop between population and food resources that Malthus had anatomized. Simply put, Malthus wrote at just the moment when the socioeconomic dynamics he analyzed were being superseded. But did Malthus really shuffle from the public stage as quickly as all this? Was he eclipsed, or did he become the éminence grise behind the scenes? To pursue this question, I want to follow three strands of discussion. Once we have followed them, a very different image of Malthus's role in Victorian intellectual life will emerge.[10]

"From Corn upon Coal": Malthus and the Birth of Modern Economics

That Malthus was at the core of debates in political economy during his lifetime is not surprising. His correspondence with David Ricardo was a model of scholarly courtesy, and a set of commentators and critics—names forgotten to the present day such as Ravenstone, Ensor, Sadler, and Everett—took it for granted that they had to joust with Malthus's achievement. That Malthus continued to exert a powerful influence on political economy right through the nineteenth century to its emergence as a professional university discipline of economics at the turn of the twentieth century is less well known, but can be made apparent by referring to three of the great figures of nineteenth-century economic thought.[11]

John Stuart Mill is remembered as a political theorist and the exemplar of the "public moralists" of the Victorian age. And yet a major part of his achievement was as a political economist, his *Principles of Political Economy* of 1848 going through numerous editions until his death in 1873 and selling more than one hundred thousand copies in that time, a staggering achievement for a long, dry work of instruction. The achievement of the *Principles,* moreover, was more than one of sales; it "was to be a guiding light for all serious students of the science . . . for the next two decades" and was, indeed, only fully eclipsed when Alfred Marshall published his *Principles of Economics* in 1890. Mill was born in 1806, and his youthful response to Malthus was somewhat schizophrenic. Thus, in his posthumously published *Autobiography* (1873), Mill acknowledged that the circle of "philosophic radicals" in which he grew up, under the aegis of his father, James Mill, took "Malthus's population principle . . . quite as much [as] a banner" as any other doctrine, arguing that the lot of the poor could be improved through "a voluntary restriction of the increase of their numbers." For Mill this was using Malthus "in the contrary sense," that is, against himself, arguing for the use of contraception, not delayed marriage. In a more satirical vein, the same ambivalence toward

Malthus surfaced in one of Mill's early essays, "The *Quarterly Review* on Political Economy" of 1825. Here, Mill took an essay by Malthus and reviewed it under the conceit that it was written by someone aping Malthus's style to ridicule him by the absurdity of the opinions offered. For Mill, the writer was a reactionary who "being unable to drag back the public mind a thousand years . . . are fain to try whether they can drag it back fifty." And yet even here, Mill paid Malthus the veiled compliment of acknowledging that his work on population and on the theory of rent comprised two of the three most important contributions to modern economics.[12]

Mill's *Principles of Political Economy* was to perpetuate this ambivalence, firmly enshrining Malthus in the pantheon of economic analysis for the mid-Victorian era while also using him for radically different ends from his own. The core of this response to Malthus is best encapsulated by Mill himself, in his autobiographical anatomy of the guiding thread of his *Principles* as being a distinction

> [b]etween the laws of the Production of Wealth, which are real laws of nature, dependent on the properties of objects, and the modes of its Distribution, which . . . depend on human will. The common run of political economists confuse these together . . . ascribing the same necessity to things dependent on the unchangeable conditions of our earthly existence, and to those which, being but the necessary consequences of particular social arrangements, are merely coextensive with these.

And true to this, in the *Principles* Mill engaged in a "briefer examination" of population questions on the grounds that "the discussions excited by the Essay of Mr. Malthus have made the truth . . . fully known." He also argued that Malthus's global survey of the dynamics of population and resources in books 1 and 2 of the later editions of the *Essay* "may even now be read with advantage." Mill could accept Malthus on population as a matter of production, but his drift toward an increasingly socialist position meant he demurred over the distributional responses to this. Thus he could condemn cheap attacks on "hard-hearted Malthusianism," he could rail against the empty hand-wringing "sentimental horror of Malthus" of his contemporaries, and he could agree with Malthus that if the poor had fewer children, their socioeconomic position would improve, while suggesting that this should be achieved in ways very different from those Malthus had advocated. On the one hand, in his early career Mill was apparently arrested but not charged for distributing birth-control literature, this being a good way to achieve family limitation to his mind, even if it would have horrified Malthus. On the other

hand, at the very end of his life, Mill's posthumous "Chapters on Socialism" (1879) suggested that while the years intervening since his arrest
had seen the pressure of population diminish, "there is much to be said
for Socialism" as the least socially divisive means by which this pressure
could be allayed in the long run. Over the course of the half century of
his life as Britain's most representative public moralist, then, Mill danced a
particular two-step with Malthus, refusing the cheap route of condemnation and indeed embracing the principle of population, while simultaneously rebutting the policy implications that Malthus had sketched and
that so many in the affluent classes were happy to adopt in mid-Victorian
society. For all his ambivalence, therefore, Mill's career as a public moralist cannot make complete sense without reference to his dialogue with
Malthus.[13]

Perhaps the apogee of Mill's public career came as MP for Westminster. It was in that capacity that, on April 17, 1866, he "commended to
the notice of hon. members a small work entitled *The Coal Question*,
by Mr. Stanley Jevons." *The Coal Question* had been published the year
previously, and had immediately attracted the attention of the prime minister, William Gladstone, who wrote in February 1866 that he had "pe-
rused it with care." Careful reading of Jevons soon led to concern, a Royal
Commission on Coal Supplies being promulgated by June of the same
year. What had Jevons written, why did it strike such a chord, and how
did it relate to Malthus?[14]

William Stanley Jevons tends to be remembered now by historians of
economics as one of the first to insist on the use of mathematical nota-
tion in economic analysis and as a key player in the "marginalist revolution" that changed how economics was practiced in ways to which we
are still inheritors. He is also now heralded by environmental economists
for his fledgling attempts to relate economic behavior to climatic change,
most notably in his statistical work tying sunspot cycles to variations in
corn prices via weather patterns.[15] *The Coal Question* was his breakthrough work, however, and has neatly been characterized as "an extended exercise in Malthusian projection." Jevons took "the principle of
population as established by Malthus in his celebrated essay," but added
a simple point: "what is true of the mere number of the people is true of
other elements of their condition." By this, Jevons meant that as population increased, so did resource use. Where Malthus had expected this to
lead to a negative feedback via food limits, Jevons was aware he was living in a new environmental-cum-economic regime: "Our subsistence no
longer depends upon our produce of corn. The momentous repeal of the
Corn Laws throws us from corn upon coal." *The Coal Question* backed

this up with exhaustive tables of population growth extracted from census returns, of coal reserves and rates of usage, of industrial production, of imports and exports. And yet however convincing were the figures trotted out by Jevons the statistician, it was Jevons the doomsayer who captivated the public imagination with the sorts of dire warnings that Malthus had been seen to generate two generations earlier. As the conclusion to his reasonings, Jevons suggested that if population was increasing and their use of coal was increasing per capita, coal was not an escape to freedom but a *pis aller* because it presented "a certain absolute and inexorable limit." Britain was now reliant on others for food and was buying this by exporting a finite resource, coal. In the same register as Tennyson or Matthew Arnold, Jevons could only see one outcome: "In the increasing depth and difficulty of coal mining we shall meet that vague, but inevitable boundary that will stop our progress. We shall begin as it were to see the further shore of our Black Indies. The wave of population will break upon that shore, and roll back upon itself." It was this dire prediction that had led to the flutterings in the parliamentary dovecotes. Malthus's fears about corn from the 1810s, suitably updated to a coal-based economy in the 1850s, rode again in mid-Victorian Britain. Peak oil and global population growth would see them emerge again a century later.[16]

Jevons died young, drowning in 1882 at the age of forty-six. And yet by that time, the mantle of the leading economic thinker in the British context had already passed elsewhere, coming to rest as it would do for the better part of a half century with Alfred Marshall. Marshall's great contribution was to steer the disparate inquiries that had been known since Adam Smith's time as "political economy" to the shores of scientific respectability as "economics," a subject whose modern place in the school and especially the university curriculum owes a great deal to him. And in his navigation from old to new, to economics as the science of a mass, industrial, and commercial society, Malthus was an essential interlocutor. A year after publishing his seminal work, *Principles of Economics* (1890), Marshall encapsulated the overall aim of the book:

> The book was written to express one idea, & one only ... it is the main product of my lifes [sic] work, & the raison d'être of my appearing as a writer. That idea is that whereas Ricardo & Co maintain that value is determined by the Cost of production, & Malthus, MacLeod, Jevons & (in a measure the austrians [sic]) that it is determined by utility, each was right in what he affirmed but wrong in what he denied. They none of them paid, I think, sufficient attention to the element of *Time*.[17]

This sense of a babble of contributors being organized into some semblance of coherence was one to which Marshall frequently reverted. How did Malthus fit in?

Rather akin to Mill, Marshall acknowledged Malthus as "the starting point of all modern speculations" on population growth and its economic implications, suggesting his findings "remain substantially valid." Where his analysis had gone awry was in its failure to anticipate the technological advances enabled by coal, but "it was not Malthus's fault that he could not foresee the great developments of steam transport by land and by sea, which have enabled Englishmen of the present generation to obtain the products of the richest lands of the earth at comparatively small cost." Writing a quarter century after Jevons, however, Marshall was still keenly aware of the Malthusian specter raised in *The Coal Question*, accepting that British society had "dodged the demographic bullet" but that another bearing its name was likely to be fired at some point: "it may be possible for an increase in the population to cause a more than proportional increase in the means of subsistence. It is true that the evil day is only deferred"; however, as where agricultural yields are renewable, "the produce of mines is merely a giving up of their stored treasures." Furthermore, and taking the analysis beyond the point Jevons had reached, Marshall realized not just the inevitable future exhaustion of the mineral resources on which British prosperity and population were built, but the environmental and social costs of the way in which the Malthusian bullet had been dodged for the better part of a century. Marshall, "the former 'slum boy'" from Bermondsey, saw that squalid cities and urban poverty were the outcome of the industrialized, mineral economy of the nineteenth century, arguing in a section with the suggestively Malthusian title "Limits of Man's Power to Hasten Progress" that the poor were growing up "under unwholesome influences which had enfeebled the frame of their minds and their bodies." The problem was not, at this stage, securing subsistence in the sense of actually bodily sustenance, but making life tolerable and meaningful: "the evils caused by close packing" of the poor in the great cities of Britain led to their degeneration and moral "death," "simply because of the law of diminishing returns with reference to fresh air, and pure and free recreation." In this, Marshall echoed the concern Mill had raised a half century earlier in his *Principles of Political Economy* that even if the economy could sustain more people, there was "little reason for desiring it" as it would come at the expense of a world

[w]ith every rood of land brought into cultivation, which is capable of growing food for human beings; every flowery waste or natural pasture ploughed
up, all quadrupeds or birds which are not domesticated to man's use extermi-
nated as rivals for food, every hedgerow or superfluous tree rooted out, and
scarcely a place left where a wild shrub or flower could grow without being
eradicated as a weed in the name of improved agriculture.

A solution inspired by Marshall, and one that is still imprinted on the
circumference of London's sphere of influence today, was the construction of Garden Cities that would, in Ebenezer Howard's pioneering analysis of 1898, draw off excess, unhealthy population from the great urban
centers without re-creating the boorish, underpopulated environments of
the countryside.[18]

From Ebenezer Scrooge to Ebenezer Howard, therefore, Malthus remained at the heart of Victorian economic analysis. His ideas concerning
population dynamics were accepted almost without demur, and the escape
to a mineral-based economy was seen within a generation of Malthus's
death as a postponement of the problem he posed, not its removal, and one
that created vast social and environmental problems to boot. Coal, and
the empire and emigration that it fostered and knitted together, might have
changed the look of the economic landscape, but the bedrock geology on
which it was built remained firmly Malthus's.

Prophets, Socialists, Utopians: Radical Responses to Malthus in the Victorian Age

If Malthus's *Essay* emerged, as we saw in Chapter 3, as a response to the
Enlightenment utopian ideals of the perfectibility of mankind, it is not
surprising that thinkers in the utopian tradition spent considerable energies refuting his claims. In Malthus's own lifetime, the chief target of his
fire, William Godwin, produced a colossal tract, *Of Population,* in 1820,
that attracted little serious attention, while a few years earlier the industrialist and social reformer Robert Owen produced his *New View of
Society* (1813–1816), seeing an educated working class as the way out
of the Malthusian dilemma, these ideas spawning considerable legions
of Owenite followers, most of whose practical efforts at reform found-
ered in quick time. It was as the Victorian age dawned that three strands
of radical criticism of Malthus gained steam—one prophetic, one socialist, and the last utopian—their combined achievement, paradoxically,
being to keep to the fore of public consciousness the ideas of the man
they sought to refute.[19]

First, the two great seers, those prophets of doom in an age of industrial malaise, Thomas Carlyle and John Ruskin, both responded to Malthus's ideas, one far more directly than the other. Carlyle's first great work, *Signs of the Times,* emerged before Malthus's death in 1829, and showed an ambivalence about industrialization just as had Malthus himself. Carlyle recognized that he was living in a "Mechanical Age" and saw it had some advantages, notably in evading the jaws of the Malthusian logic of poverty: "how much better fed, clothed, lodged and, in all outward respects, accommodated, men now are." But for all that "we war with rude nature and . . . come off always victorious," the "outward" side of mankind was not for Carlyle the only, or even the most important, gauge of their well-being. On the contrary, it was mankind's inward or spiritual life that had decayed in this mechanical age. In anatomizing and abhorring this world, Carlyle routinely condemned statistics and steam, utilitarianism, Irish laborers, and laissez-faire economics. It is not surprising, then, that he also leveled his sights at Malthus in perhaps his two most famous publications, *Sartor Resartus* (1833–1834) and *Chartism* (1839). Carlyle's immortal denigration of economics as the "dismal science," a phrase that has passed into our collective consciousness, was first coined in his evenhandedly weary condemnation of the Malthusian debates of the 1830s in *Chartism:* "The controversies on Malthus and the 'Population Principle,' 'Preventive check' and so forth, with which the public ear has been deafened for a long while, are indeed sufficiently mournful. Dreary, stolid, dismal, without all hope for this world or the next, is all that of the preventive check and the denial of the preventive check." By far Carlyle's most brilliant response to Malthus, however, came earlier, in *Sartor Resartus,* which reopened a line of criticism we have seen in Hazlitt, extending it to brilliant satirical effect as a tool of social critique. In *Sartor,* Malthusianism is imagined as a species of madness, something worthy of the attentions of Freud or the padded cell, personified in the form of Hofrath Heuschrecke and his "Institute for the Repression of Population." Those consumed by Malthus, like Hofrath, display: "A deadly fear of Population . . . undoubtedly akin to the more diluted forms of Madness. Nowhere . . . is there any light; nothing but the grim shadow of Hunger; open mouths opening wider and wider; a world to terminate by the frightfullest consummation; by its too dense inhabitants, famished into delirium, universally eating each other." For Carlyle, this state of mind is a system of "Helotage," a revival of the Spartan system where the Helots who served the warrior class were "speared and pitted . . . when they grew too numerous." If such is the view of a Malthusian, they should reserve "some three days annually" to shooting the "abled-bodied Paupers that had accumulated." And, in a Swiftian parody of utilitarianism that tied Malthusian arguments about the Poor Laws with concerns about excess population, in such a schema, "the very carcasses would pay for it. Have them salted and barrelled could not you victual therewith, if not the Army and Navy, yet richly such infirm Paupers, in workhouses and elsewhere, as enlightened Charity, dreading no evil of them, might see good to keep alive?" For Carlyle, the solution lay in emigration to the vast, uninhabited parts of the globe, and in a spiritual system that respected the divinity in human beings rather than understanding them exclusively through the dehumanizing logics of steam and statistics.[20]

Carlyle's star shone brightly for but a brief while. His attacks on the Irish and his unrepentant refusal to come in line with the "public mind" of the Victorian age left him increasingly isolated and embittered by the 1850s. By that time his mantle as a Christian seer, as a prophet of a rounded, humanizing vision of social life and as a jeremiad against the limitations of commerce, industry, and economics had passed to John Ruskin, who turned his critical fire on Malthusian ideas in the 1860s. If one looks at the monumental thirty-nine-volume Cook and Wedderburn edition of Ruskin's works (1903–1912) through the lens of its nearly seven-hundred-page-long index, one would be forgiven for thinking Malthus passed Ruskin by as he does not merit an entry. And yet while Ruskin never named Malthus, he did level his sights at Malthus in the book he thought most likely to perpetuate his name to future generations, *Unto This Last* (1860; published in book form, 1862). At the core of Ruskin's argument was a redefinition of "value" away from the narrow vision of Ricardo's and Mill's utilitarian political economy. Ruskin wished "such well-educated merchants" (a dig at Ricardo) knew enough Latin to recall that "valor/valere" meant to be strong in life, such that "THERE IS NO WEALTH BUT LIFE." Immediately after issuing this vatic pronouncement, Ruskin turns to its application in Malthusian realms, opining that "in all the ranges of human thought I know none so melancholy as the speculations of political economists on the population question." If all wealth is life, the "maximum of life can only be reached by the maximum of virtue," this not necessarily being equivalent as the utilitarians implied with merely maximizing the number of beings clothed, fed, and housed on the globe. Thus for Ruskin the "population question" was "not how much habitable land is in the world, but how many beings ought to be maintained on a given space of habitable land." Industrialization might allow for massive numbers to survive, but this was a future of "diminished lives in the midst of noise, of darkness, and of deadly exhalation." Against this dystopian world presaged by narrow visions of "wealth," Ruskin pitched an environmentally regenerative vision of a society with "a wise population" which sought "felicity as well as food" by not just exploiting the land but instead by "'rejoicing' in the habitable parts of the earth." As Ruskin closed out this vision, his political economy circled around to join the aesthetics and art criticism that had made his name in *Modern Painters* in ways that curiously parallel the calls for environmental regeneration we have already seen in Mill, Marshall, and the political economy tradition he despised:

> As the art of life is learned, it will be found that all lovely things are also necessary; -the wild flower by the wayside, as well as the tended corn; and the wild birds and creatures of the forest, as well as the tended cattle; because man does not live by bread only, but also by the desert manna; by every wondrous word and unknowable work of God.[21]

By the time Ruskin pitched his Christian environmental economics against the utilitarian destruction of human meaning, a more lasting critique was already emerging from the pens of Friedrich Engels and Karl Marx that also took on Malthus. Engels's initial attacks on Malthus were surprisingly close to Ruskin's in their Christian overtones, criticizing his work as a "repulsive blasphemy against man and nature" and seeing in his work "merely the economic expression of the religious dogma of the contradiction between spirit and nature." In fact, of course, Engels then moved the attack on Malthus in new directions, seeking to show that it was neither nature, as Malthus suggested, nor the blinkered social psychology of "steam and statistics," as Carlyle and Ruskin had suggested, which created the "problem" of population. On the contrary, excess population was essential to the functioning of a capitalist economy whose rhythm of boom and bust necessitated that at all times, bar those of peak economic activity, there must be "an unemployed reserve army of workers." If Engels wrote all of this in the 1840s, it was in the 1860s that Marx leveled his sights on Malthus's *Essay* in *Capital* as "nothing more than a schoolboyish, superficial plagiary," the fame of which was "due solely to party interest," Malthus's "party" being that of his own class as "a parson of the English State Church." Where scholars have pointed out Engels's indebtedness to Malthusian ideas of population and Marx's indebtedness to his idea of effective demand, Marx focused on his conflict with Malthus; there could be no universal law of population as Malthus had suggested, each mode of production having its own "special laws of population." Malthus had correctly seen the "disharmonies" capitalism created by its inevitable tendency to cycles of boom and bust, but by packaging this as a law of nature, he had mystified its social origins in defense of the interests of the landed aristocracy and the bourgeoisie. Engels, in a letter of 1881, looked forward to the day when communism arrived, feeling that he was on its "eve." And when it came, Europe would be *certain to require* a large increase of population." But once this had been achieved, the harmonious communist society it produced would be able to "regulate the production of human beings . . . it will be precisely this society, and this society alone, which can carry this out without difficulty."[22]

The heady millenarianism of Marx and Engels had a massive impact on late-nineteenth-century society in Europe and across the Atlantic, with many variants of socialism being spawned, some remembered, some forgotten. It is worth just pausing on three of these socialisms as they took on Malthus. In France, the anarchist Pierre-Joseph Proudhon wrote a furious denunciation of Malthus in that most revolutionary of years in the nineteenth century, 1848. Proudhon opened with Malthus's "nature's mighty feast" image from the 1803 *Essay*, and said that Malthus's influence in midcentury France was pervasive: "all that has been done, said, and printed today and for the last twenty years has been done, said, and printed in consequence of the theory of Malthus." The 1848 Revolution was France's protest against this Malthusian monopoly, his "theory of political murder" and "cannibalism," and in its defeat, "who will tell me that the principle of Malthus is not the whole of the counter-revolution?"[23] Thirty years later, another anti-Malthusian radicalism emerged. Henry George is all but forgotten today, and yet in the 1880s he was a cause célèbre. His fame rested on his analysis of the failings of industrialization, *Progress and Poverty* (1879), a work that sold a staggering 2 million copies by the time of his death in 1897 and has been described as "the most widely read book on economics in the nineteenth century." It was in book 2 of *Progress and Poverty*, "Population and Subsistence," that George took on Malthus. Malthus's ideas had persisted despite refutation because they were "eminently soothing and reassuring to the [ruling] classes" and made poverty and want "the inevitable results of universal laws with which . . . it were as hopeless to quarrel as with the law of gravitation." Where George was novel was in his analysis of the way out of this impasse, and it was this that led to his enormous and now-forgotten popularity. For George, the solution lay in "land nationalisation," the idea that if the state took control of all property, it could painlessly and peacefully ensure that all gave according to their skills and received according to their needs.[24] By the 1890s, it was the gradualist socialism of the Fabian Society (which history has treated far more kindly than the now-forgotten George) that had more purchase on the radical agenda. The Fabians also turned their fire on Malthus in their benchmark text *Fabian Essays in*

Socialism (1889). While the Fabians were to fracture into competing groups on questions of population as so many others, in the *Fabian Essays* George Bernard Shaw's essay on economics saw overpopulation as real, but a product of the misery in which the poor were mired. As workers were "degraded" by the factory conditions, so the rich left them "throw[n] back, reckless, on the one pleasure and the one human tie left to them—the gratification of their instinct for producing fresh supplies of men." In a strong echo of Carlyle in *Chartism*, Shaw went on that for the rich to then cry murder about "over population" was pointless: "your slaves are beyond caring for your cries: they breed like rabbits; and their poverty breeds filth, ugliness, dishonesty, disease, obscenity, drunkenness, and murder." Socialism was the answer to this situation: it would nationalize the land as George had recommended and thereby show that "the source of our social misery is no eternal well-spring . . . but only an artificial [social] system." And thus at century's end Carlyle's gibe against Malthus would be upended, Fabianism making economic science, "once the Dismal, now the Hopeful."[25]

If Shaw and Engels thought themselves on the brink of socialist evolution and revolution respectively, others plotted through political fiction what the new society would look like and how it would view its benighted nineteenth-century ancestors. There was a slew of utopian literature in the final decades of the nineteenth century. Most important in relation to Malthus was Edward Bellamy's *Looking Backward* (1887), in which Julian West, a wealthy East Coast American, falls asleep in 1887 and wakes up in 2000. He finds himself in a society formulated after a socialist transformation that lives in ecologically attuned harmony with its environment. The citizens of 2000 can recall that in the "old society" "the driver was hunger" and its consequence was human and environmental despoliation, but for them cooperation has replaced competition. And in a society where education has been extended to women in equal measure with men, marriage is only entered into for love, ensuring the production of a small, stable, and advanced population. *Looking Backward* was a triumphant success, and Bellamy spent the final ten years of a life cut short elaborating its arguments. In this regard, he took on Malthusian criticisms of imagined utopian futures explicitly in a journal he founded, the *New Nation* (1891–1893). In an essay entitled "To a Disciple of Malthus," Bellamy argued that "nationalism"—the nationalization of land and labor—would not lead to a Malthusian apocalypse as with increasing wealth and education in the new nation would come the delay of marriage prophesized in *Looking Backward* and the displacement of the pleasures of sensualism in favor of more intellectual and exulted pleasures. In words echoing Godwin and George Bernard Shaw, Bellamy concluded:

> The reason the poor and ignorant classes are so dominated by the sexual impulse is the rudeness and narrowness of their lives, and the lack of the wide and numerous diversions of thought and interest which culture and refinement open to their possessors. In proportion as the mind and taste are developed, human beings are freed from the bondage of cruel bodily appetites. . . . [T]he population of the world today is greater than it will ever be again.

In fact of course, by 2000 AD, Julian West would have woken in a world with 5 billion souls on the planet and one where utilitarianism and utopianism were still in painful dialectic. He would also have woken in a world where Malthus remained on the agenda while his creator, Bellamy, was a minor footnote. But that is a story for a future chapter.[26]

Malthus and Evolution: Friction and Its Frictions

Writing to commemorate the fiftieth anniversary of the publication of Charles Darwin's *Origin of Species* (1859), the codiscoverer of evolution by natural selection, Alfred Russel Wallace, highlighted three contexts he shared with Darwin that led to this set of ideas. Beetle collecting and travel need not concern us here, but Wallace gave pride of place to their shared encounter with Malthus:

> Both Darwin and myself . . . had our attention directed to the system of *positive checks* as expounded by Malthus in his "Principles of Population." The effect of that was analogous to that of friction upon the specially prepared match, producing that flash of insight which led us immediately to the simple but universal law of the "survival of the fittest," as the long sought *effective* cause of the continuous modification and adaptations of living things.

Darwin made similar if more plain comments in his *Autobiography* about reading Malthus in 1838 "for amusement" but finding here "a theory by which to work." The Darwin industry has, of course, analyzed the Malthusian moment narrated here by both Darwin and Wallace in great detail and demonstrated that this is not a mere retrospective fabrication: the discovery of Darwin's notebooks show Darwin did in fact read Malthus when he said, while Wallace's inspiration was always clear from his direct references to "geometrical ratios" in his breakthrough essay, "On the Tendencies of Varieties to Depart Indefinitely from the Original Type" of 1858. And yet Wallace's retrospection, like most in the genre, did smooth over and simplify the different Malthusian legacies to nineteenth-century ideas of evolution that he and Darwin engendered. By following these split legacies, we can chart a third route through the Malthusian labyrinths of Victorian life.[27]

Darwin was the more "straight" Malthusian of the two. On his return from the *Beagle* voyage in the mid-1830s, he had become enmeshed via his brother in the London circle around Harriet Martineau, whose Malthusian popularizing we have already encountered. This was, as we saw, the moment when Malthus's influence was at its peak, and Darwin was close to the eye of the storm in his acquaintance with and entrancement by the Martineau circle. And thus his autobiographical comments about stumbling upon Malthus "by chance" are somewhat misleading; he was bound to encounter Malthus's ideas by the company he kept. But this in and of itself cannot explain the profundity of Malthus's impact on Darwin's ideas, which has led one commentator to say, "it is just that Thomas Malthus be ranked as contributor rather than catalyst to Darwin's new understanding." Malthus's direct appearance on the stage in *The Origin of Species* (1859) is brief, the struggle for existence being styled as "the doctrine of Malthus applied with manifold force to the whole animal and vegetable kingdoms." And in slight variants, both the joint paper with Wallace that announced the theory of evolution by natural selection in 1858, and the "big species book" on natural selection that Darwin shelved in order to get the *Origin* out before Wallace could preempt his ideas, stated that the struggle for existence in the natural world had first been "philosophically enunciated by Malthus." The difference was that, the natural world lacking the preventive checks Malthus had uncovered in "advanced" societies, his positive checks worked "with tenfold force" in the populations studied by the biologist. If the *Origin* was controversial, Darwin's 1871 text, *The Descent of Man*, caused still more furor by extending core evolutionary ideas to the realm of mankind. And here Darwin followed the binary Malthus had established between early and primitive societies, where the positive checks were to the fore, and advanced societies where preventive checks had been installed by the operation of societal reason. In a long passage on rates of population increase, Darwin, more than thirty years after his Martineau-inspired stumbling upon Malthus, praised "the ever memorable 'Essay on the Principle of Population,'" going on to suggest, in line with the latest anthropological researches, that Malthus had only failed in his analysis of primitive societies in underestimating the impact of infanticide as a positive check.[28]

Just after this praise of Malthus in *The Descent of Man*, Darwin acknowledged the point at which his ideas diverged from those of Wallace: "I cannot, therefore, understand how it is that Mr. Wallace maintains that, 'natural selection could only have endowed the savage with a brain a little superior to that of an ape.' " Behind this polite bewilderment lay a major difference in how Wallace and Darwin came to understand the position of mankind vis-à-vis evolution that led them to very different imaginings of Malthus. Darwin believed that evolution provided the motor by which humankind had achieved its position as "the most dominant animal that has ever appeared on the earth." As a consequence, he saw mankind as still under the sway of the same natural forces such as Malthusian population pressure that impacted on all other plants and animals, however much their operation had been modified by social advance as Malthus had shown. Wallace, by contrast, thought that human mental development had gone way beyond what natural selection could explain and had become self-sustaining, thereby lifting mankind above the aegis of the forces of natural selection. As Wallace put it in his singlemost popular essay, "The Origin of Human Races," in 1864: "Man has not only escaped 'natural selection' himself, but he actually is able to take away some of that power from nature which, before his appearance, she universally exercised. We can anticipate a time when the earth will produce only cultivated plants and domestic animals; when man's selection shall have supplanted 'natural selection.' " Until that time, Wallace saw a split world. On the one hand was the biological world, where plants and animals were still subject to the positive checks Malthus had depicted, a position he held onto right up to and including his last published book about evolution, *The World of Life* (1910). On the other hand, the world of mankind being beyond that process, Wallace saw Malthusian reasoning in this arena as stifling, reactionary, and plain wrong.[29]

The "human" side of Wallace's extraordinarily fertile intellectual analysis was consistently intertwined with the utopian and socialist strands discussed in the previous section. Wallace was bowled over by Henry George's *Progress and Poverty,* trying in vain to convert Darwin, who confessed that "books on political economy . . . produced a disastrous effect on my mind." He also became the founding president of the George-inspired Land Nationalization Society in 1881, holding the post until his death in 1913. The bedrock of these reformist tendencies was a radicalism that had been kindled by Wallace's teenage exposure to the anti-Malthusian efforts of Robert Owen, and the "tipping point"—the "time I declared myself a socialist"—was the publication of Bellamy's *Looking Backward*. Where Wallace's Owenism, his support of George and Land Nationalisation, and his "conversion experience" on reading Bellamy all put him at implicit loggerheads with Malthus, after his declaration of socialist conviction, Wallace chose to take on Malthus directly in what he

considered his finest anthropological study, "Human Selection" (1890).
Here Wallace argued in a medley on themes from George and Bellamy,
that "once we have cleansed the Augean stable of our existing organization," the Malthusian dilemma would be dissipated: universal education
in a society where "all are relieved from sordid cares and the struggle for
mere existence" would only see marriage come about far later, dissipat-
ing any putative population pressure. Starvation in Ireland and poverty
in England's cities were caused by private land ownership, not overpopulation. Wallace further concurred with Ruskin and Jevons (in their very different registers!) in lamenting the litany of environmental and resource
depletion that had been wrought by modern, industrial capitalism: "by
destroying for ever a considerable and ever-increasing proportion of the
mineral wealth of our country, we have rendered it absolutely less habitable and less enjoyable for our descendants." Goods such as minerals
"must be considered to be held by us in trust for the community and for
succeeding generations." It was only with land nationalization and socialism that such environmental stewardship could be engendered; they
would allow us to evade the illusory pressures of Malthusian self-interest
and be a just reflection of the fact that humans had escaped the arc of
evolutionary pressures by which Malthus and his inheritors (including
Darwin) misleadingly still believed us to be entrapped.[30]

Where once historians tended to focus on the "respectable" Wallace as
an evolutionary biologist and to shuffle his other ideas off to the historical attic of embarrassing detritus better left unexplored, modern historians realize both that his ideas were a complex, coherent web, and that his
socialist-cum-utopian views about humanity's place in the evolutionary
process were by no means uncommon. It is worth briefly looking at two
further such "unorthodox" evolutionists and their responses to Malthus.
Wallace in his "Human Anthropology" essay drew explicitly on Herbert
Spencer's theory of population. Spencer coined the term "survival of the
fittest" and pioneered the idea of "social evolution" in the 1850s, before
Darwin or Wallace put pen to paper. Spencer had been educated just
downstream from Malthus's stomping ground of Claverton in the village
of Hinton Charterhouse outside Bath, and he first emerged on the public
stage defending the New Poor Laws. Moving to London, Spencer developed the idea of evolution as a cosmic process of development, an idea
he championed throughout his career, leading George Eliot's husband-
to-be, George Lewes, to quip that with Spencer everything evolved except his own theory. Eliot's life at this time was enmeshed with Spencer's:
it was alleged that a brief liaison collapsed due to Spencer's refusal to
marry someone he found physically ugly, but more importantly Eliot was

editing the *Westminster Review* in succession to John Stuart Mill in the early 1850s, and it was here that Spencer published his first great statement of social evolutionary doctrine, the "Theory of Population." Characteristically, the essay synthesized a vast amount of recent biological and demographic argument and data, developing an ultimately utopian image of social demography completely at odds with received Malthusian wisdom. Spencer argued that over the long term, life saw the increasing coordination of organisms and that this ever-advancing complexity was the gauge of sociobiological progress. For Spencer, all species tended toward a population equilibrium in which the ability of the individual to survive was balanced by the power of propagation. The more complex the species, the greater was the power of the individual to survive and the less was there a need for reproduction. For the human species, Spencer diagnosed a temporary imbalance, the power of reproduction being greater than was required given the advances achieved in social individuation. In Godwinian terms, Spencer concluded that over time, the intensity of the passions would wither in line with social advance, and thus the reproductive excess would be dispelled, bringing the human species back to equilibrium. Spencer's personal prickliness and his inability to accept the most trifling of criticisms made him anything but at equilibrium with his own society, and yet he was widely respected as one of the "public moralists" of his age, and his ideas reached a large audience at the end of the century through the writings of the utopian evolutionist and town planner Patrick Geddes. More of an outsider was Peter Kropotkin, a Russian émigré who had fled to London via a French jail. Where Darwin took the social dynamics anatomized by Malthus and found them in the natural world, Kropotkin took the utopian social evolutionary cosmologies of Spencer and Wallace and found them in the natural world. In a set of essays of 1888 for the influential journal the *Nineteenth Century* that were later published in book form as *Mutual Aid* (1902), Kropotkin argued that the Darwinian-Malthusian image of nature as a struggle for existence, a war resulting in the survival of the fittest, was erroneous: based on his work in the Russian steppes, Kropotkin noted, "better conditions are created by the *elimination of competition* by means of mutual aid and mutual support." And he had no doubt that it was Malthus, not Darwin, who was to blame for this error, Darwin in his *Descent* having, according to Kropotkin, produced "data disproving the narrow Malthusian conception of struggle" while failing to remove "the old Malthusian leaven" from his thinking. As Daniel Todes has shown, Kropotkin's argument was simply the best known from an Anglophone perspective of a series of Russian attacks on Malthus's ideas and their warping effect on ideas of evolution, with Leo Tolstoy, for example, framing Malthus as "a very poor English writer, whose works are all forgotten, and recognized as the most insignificant of the insignificant."[31]

And yet what might be termed the "utopian" or Wallacean, strand of the social analysis of evolution was in fact by far the less vigorous one. Spencer, Kropotkin et al. were by and large drowned out by the multitude of those who followed Darwin's more straightforwardly Malthusian line in the evolutionary study of society. Indeed, it has even been suggested that "social Darwinism" is a misleading sobriquet and that "scientific Malthusianism" may more accurately express the efforts to apply evolutionary ideas to the study of society as "[m]uch of what we associate with the concept had been in formation for over half a century by the time the *Origin of Species* appeared in 1859. . . . Darwin's discoveries occasioned no revolution in social theory, but instead involved remapping . . . a pre-existing structure of ideas based largely . . . upon a Malthusian and economic metaphor of the 'struggle for existence.' " If it was Spencer who coined such phrases as "struggle for existence," they received their most famous treatment in the squarely Malthusian social analysis of the man known as "Darwin's bulldog," Thomas Henry Huxley. At a personal level, Huxley embodied Malthusian values of thrift, energy, and prudential restraint; emerging from "the slums that made Dickens shudder," Huxley was a self-made man, and he delayed his own marriage for more than four years in an attempt to accumulate enough money to make ends meet when family obligations were visited upon him. Huxley fought his way to wealth and respectability by pugnacity in the cause of Darwinian science, his defining moment coming when he took on Bishop Wilberforce in defense of Darwinism against orthodox Christianity in a debate in Oxford in 1860. Huxley's intellectual engagement with Malthus came some thirty years after this celebrated encounter. By the late 1880s, Huxley was a grandee of the British scientific establishment, but eminence had not led to the loss of abrasiveness. On the contrary, spurred by depression engendered by the death of his beloved daughter Marian, Huxley penned two devastatingly bleak and intensely Malthusian exercises in social Darwinism, "The Struggle for Existence: A Programme" (1888) and *Evolution and Ethics* (1893). Both were founded on a set of core beliefs that bolted "straight" Malthusian ideas together with core Darwinian concepts. First, in nature "all living things tend to multiply without limit, while the means of support are limited." This resulted in "a cosmic process" best characterized as "the struggle for existence." Second, what allied Huxley with Darwin and Malthus and distanced him from Wallace was the contention that such dynamics still applied to modern human societies. Using the sorts of trade and census data Jevons had drawn upon thirty years earlier, Huxley argued that Britain had a population of 36 million, which was expanding by three hundred thousand every year, and further that "at the present time, the produce of the soil does not suffice to feed half its population." As a result, "lo! In spite of ourselves, we are in reality engaged in an internecine struggle for existence with our presumably no less peaceful and well-meaning neighbours." Finally, this reality meant utopian visions were, as Malthus had said of Godwin and Condorcet, a delusion, or, as Huxley put it himself, "the optimistic dogma that this is the best of all possible worlds will seem little better than a libel upon possibility." In such a context, social engineering of the sort advocated by Henry George and others in the socialist tradition was meaningless: "no fiddle-faddling with the distribution of wealth, will deliver society from the tendency to be destroyed by reproduction from within itself."[32]

In truth, Huxley only expressed more trenchantly and unremittingly ideas in general circulation throughout English, European, and American intellectual circles. In Germany, for example, Malthus-derived Darwinian ideas of the ubiquity of the struggle for existence were described as "a badge and common property of our age" and guided the work of the leading popularizer of Darwin, Ernst Haeckel, who preferred to package this struggle in the even more suggestively Malthusian phrase "the competition for the means of subsistence." In the United States, William Sumner founded his ideas for the study of sociology likewise on the ineluctable truth of the pressure population places on resources and the struggle emergent therefrom, defining sociology as "a science which deals with one range of phenomena produced by the struggle for existence, while biology deals with another." By the time Sumner wrote this in 1881, American intellectuals had already been addressing themes inspired by Malthus for decades, the complex debates in antebellum society about the demographic and racial implications of slavery having been conducted in the light of the *Essay* throughout the 1840s and 1850s.[33] The complex skein of debates that Darwin and social Darwinism provoked, the two strands that Darwin and Wallace began to thread through nineteenth-century life, then, led to a propagation of Malthus's ideas unimagined in his own lifetime.

The Ironic Adjective: Malthus and Malthusianism

Thus far, we have pursued three separate strands to follow Malthus's reputation in the Victorian age—political economy, radicalism, and evolution. To keep these strands separate has involved some considerable artifice or indeed simple artificiality for they in fact interpenetrated completely. To complete the picture and make all these strands come together, it is worth contemplating the emergence of "Malthusianism," the polite contemporary euphemism for debates about, and encouragement of, birth control and contraception, which occurred in the 1870s and continued into the twentieth century. While the *Oxford English Dictionary* shows that the word "Malthusian" had been in circulation as early as 1805 in Southey's letters, at that time it meant literally a "follower of Malthus." In the 1870s, however, it came to bear an additional meaning as a supporter of birth control to the point where the term became predominantly a synonym for that position. While history is full of terminological ironies, this is a considerable one: Malthus himself always adopted the orthodox Christian and Anglican position that chastity was "the only virtuous means" of limiting family size and was therefore opposed to birth control, which he only ever alluded to in print by an oblique reference to "improper arts." And yet within a half century of his death, Malthus's name in adjectival form came to be routinely linked with practices whose name he dared not speak.[34]

"Malthusian" as a term came into currency after the scandal of the prosecution of Charles Bradlaugh and Annie Besant for selling literature that offered contraceptive advice in 1877. While that prosecution ultimately failed on a technicality, in its aftermath the two defendants were at the heart of a group who founded the Malthusian League, a society dedicated to the cause of legalizing birth control literature and encouraging public discussion of suitable means of limiting family size, which would take an active part in British society for half a century. In the debates that circulated around the Malthusian League, we can see the three strands followed in this chapter interweave and interact. Under Bradlaugh initially and then the Drysdale family, the Malthusian League was committed not just to birth control, but also to expounding the ideas embodied in Malthus's *Essay*. The League, then, was not merely "Malthusian" in the new sense of advocating birth control, but also in the earlier sense of the term as followers of Malthus. In this spirit, the League adopted seven principles on its foundation in 1877, four of which "sounded like quotations from T. R. Malthus." This adherence to Malthus's shade stayed with those we might call the "core" members of the Malthusian League throughout its lifetime, those who ran the Council of the League, Drysdale admitting as late as 1913 that the League would have been more successful "had the doctrines of Malthus not been insisted upon," Malthus's mere name being enough to make the poorer classes hostile to their mission even if they favored birth control. And yet the League did

insist upon Malthus's doctrine in its extraordinary efforts at public pros-
elytization, which included printing an estimated 3 million pamphlets
between 1879 and 1921, publishing a regular journal, the *Malthusian,* and
encouraging the formation of sister societies across the globe, an enumera-
tion of 1911 suggesting that Malthusian Leagues now existed in "Hol-
land, Germany, France, Austria, Spain, Brazil, Belgium, Switzerland, Cuba
and Portugal."[35]

If the League's Council adhered to both senses of "Malthusian," others
demurred in ways derived from views regarding radicalism, economics,
and evolution. Thus Charles Darwin himself refused to support Bradlaugh and Besant at the trial, which led to the formation of the League,
despite their subpoenaing him, on the grounds that contraception would
"spread to unmarried women & w^d destroy chastity on which the family
bond depends; & the weakening of this bond would be the greatest of all
possible ends to mankind." Simply put, here as elsewhere, Darwin remained a Malthusian in the original sense of the term and refused to bolt
on the newly emergent meaning of the 1870s. Huxley adopted the same
position, ensuring, as his biographer suggests, "the undefiled purity of
Malthusian views, dreading Bradlaugh's sexual contagion which would
rot the respectable evolutionary edifice" he had worked so hard to erect.
And if the "orthodox Malthusianism" of Huxley and Darwin led them to
oppose the Malthusian League, there were also interesting filiations with
socialism. Where mainstream socialism in its Marxist, utopian, and land
nationalization variants had, as we have seen, opposed Malthus, the Malthusianism of birth control was another matter. Thus the publisher of the
Malthusian journal, George Standring, was also responsible for the *Fabian News,* being an active supporter of both causes who worked for
their rapprochement. The potential for a socialist Malthusianism was also
highlighted by Annie Besant, who, in the years after her trial with Bradlaugh in 1877, diverged considerably from him in intellectual terms, such
that by 1886 she could publish an essay, "The Law of Population and Its
Relation to Socialism," in defense of the contention that "there is no necessary antagonism between prudential restraint of population and Socialism, and that indeed such prudential restraint must be a vital condition of the success of any Socialist community." Arguing that "the remedy
for over-population proposed by Malthus was a thoroughly bad one," she
went on to suggest that contraception, rather than delayed marriage and
restraint within marriage, would lead to smaller families "in preparation
for the class struggle that lies before us." More common was an antipathy,
however, between socialism and the Malthusian League, Henry George
being an entrenched opponent as were those at the heart of the Fabian

Society such as Shaw and the Webbs. Someone who joined both groups and then managed to leave them both was H. G. Wells, who became vice president of the Malthusian League in 1915, only to leave it in 1917 over its opposition to socialism, a trajectory similar to that he followed with respect to the Fabians. Final efforts at connection down the axis of socialism and Malthusianism were made by the philosopher Bertrand Russell's wife with respect to the fledging Labour Party, Ramsay Macdonald quashing them in 1925.[36]

Malthusianism could make strange bedfellows. Rounding out our picture, we can join Sigmund Freud to Darwin and Ramsay Macdonald in the roll call of its opponents. In his vital early essay "Sexuality and the Aetiology of the Neuroses" (1898), Freud argued directly against Malthusianism. The essay is the first where Freud tentatively launched "a therapeutic procedure which I propose to describe as 'psycho-analytic.'" The bulk of the paper was a defense of the idea that there are two categories of neuroses, "neurasthenic" ones developed by sexual habits acquired during maturity, and "psychoneurotic" ones deriving from childhood experiences that lie behind the conscious memory of the patient. Freud would become most famous, of course, for his analysis of the latter, and already in 1898 he flagged "a book on the interpretation of dreams on which I am now engaged," his *Interpretation of Dreams*, which would emerge two years later. But in 1898, his main focus was the sexual neuroses acquired in maturity, his neurasthenic category. For Freud, while "the problem of Malthusianism is far-reaching and complicated," he had no doubt that it would lead to hysterical and neurotic outcomes. While "in any marriage Malthusian preventive measures will become necessary at some time or other," they had damaging consequences: "Everything is harmful that hinders the occurrence of satisfaction. But, as we know, we possess at present no method of preventing conception which fulfils every legitimate requirement—that is, which is certain and convenient, which does not diminish the sensation of pleasure during coitus and which does not wound the woman's sensibilities." In concluding his discussion of Malthusianism, Freud presaged the thesis of his masterpiece, *Civilization and Its Discontents* (1930), suggesting that in the need for advanced societies to create modes of population limitation, "we may with justice regard civilization, too, as responsible for the spread of neurasthenia."[37]

Malthusianism and the Malthusian League show the complex filiations of Malthus's ideas in the last decades of the nineteenth century. Socialism, utopianism, economics, evolution, and psychoanalysis intertwined in ambivalent patterns of affirmation and rejection. And these were not just about "Malthusianism" qua birth control, but also about the contested legacy of Malthus himself, around the politically charged resonances of his mere name. On the one hand, the adherence of the Malthusian League to Malthus himself led to its tortuous and ultimately failed interactions with socialism, Fabianism, and the Labour Party. On the other hand, the adherence of the League to birth control led to the hostile reaction from Darwin, Huxley, and their disciples on the grounds that such policies would undercut the motive force of Malthus's struggle for existence, this being the engine of societal development. By wanting to fudge Malthus and Malthusianism, the Malthusian League managed to alienate all. But in that very fudge and the sheer centrality of Malthus to late-nineteenth-century debates lies the reason why all the strands we have addressed in this chapter saw the need to engage with the League if only to disown it.

Éminence Grise or Age of Eclipse?

As we cast our eye back over the six or seven decades after Malthus's death, was he indeed the man of the moment in the 1830s and 1840s, only to sink like a stone beneath the waters of public debate in Victorian England? Or was he a shadowy specter haunting the Victorian imagination in a time of imperial plenty? As has become apparent, Malthus was neither: he certainly did not disappear from the intellectual radar, but nor was he a mere gray figure in the wings. On the contrary, Malthus's ideas were constantly and explicitly discussed and debated, derided and defended in all quarters of the intellectual life of Britain. Furthermore, where at his death Malthus's reputation was mainly confined to the British Isles, by the turn of the twentieth century he was being attacked in Russia, defended in the United States, and having public health leagues named after him in Brazil. Malthus had become a well and truly global brand in a way that would only come around again in the 1960s.

How important was Malthus to the Victorian life of the mind? While there is no way history can provide a definitive answer to the question, perhaps an indication can come from two lists and two utopians. Lists first. George Bernard Shaw once wrote that there were three great masters of invective in the nineteenth century: Karl Marx, John Ruskin, and William Cobbett. Moving a century forward, in his infamous essay "What Is an Author?" the French poststructuralist philosopher Michel Foucault argued that there were only three great founders of new ways of describing the world in the nineteenth century: Marx, Darwin, and Freud. Not only did all five names on these lists tackle Malthus head-on, but so did their two compilers, Shaw as part of his Fabianism (as we have seen), and

Foucault in his Freud-inspired *History of Sexuality* project as well as his analysis of the emergence of population as an object of state control in his lectures at the Collège de France. And the utopians? Despite a lifetime's opposition to Malthus, Henry George correctly opined that the ideas Malthus created were "held and habitually reasoned from by many who have never heard of Malthus and who have not the slightest idea of what his theory is." Where this chapter has addressed the direct engagements with Malthus in the nineteenth century, they are but the tip of the iceberg. More direct praise came from H. G. Wells, whose attitudes toward Malthus were far more "conflicted" than those of George. Writing at the dawn of the new century in his 1901 *Anticipations,* Wells argued that in the progress toward a new, utopian republic:

> The first chapter in the history of this intellectual development, its definite and formal opening, coincides with the publication of Malthus's "Essay on Population." Malthus is one of those cardinal figures in intellectual history who state definitively for all time, things apparent enough after their formulation, but never effectively conceded before. . . . Probably no more shattering book than the "Essay on Population" has ever been, or ever will be, written.

Wells squarely figured Malthus's great achievement as being to show us that "the main mass of the business of human life centres about reproduction" but took this in directions we have not canvassed in this chapter except tangentially at its opening. For Wells, Malthus showed us that the state must control reproduction. Over the course of the hundred years since Malthus had written, Wells detected that "the average of humanity has positively fallen" resulting in "the spectacle of a mean-spirited, undersized, diseased little man, quite incapable of earning a decent living even for himself, married to some underfed, ignorant, ill-shaped, plain and diseased little woman, and guilty of the lives of ten or twelve ailing ugly children." The way out? "To have perhaps half the population of the world, in every generation, restrained from or tempted to evade reproduction. This thing, this euthanasia of the weak and the sensual, is possible." What Marcus had advocated in satirical vein in 1838 was argued for here in deadly earnest. Within a generation of Wells's *Anticipations* and under a century after Marcus, "chambers of gaz" would become a reality. It is to Malthus's part in this unfolding story that we now turn.[38]

CHAPTER SEVEN

Malthus and the Dismal Age

Doleful Anticipations at the Century's New Dawn

If we left H. G. Wells at the close of the previous chapter imagining grand futures for Malthus as the prophet of the twentieth century, there was an equally strong case for anticipating his disappearance from public debate as the new century dawned. For Wells himself was hardly a "representative" figure, however well known. On the contrary, "anxiety about overpopulation" was "the key to Wells's reading of modern history." This anxiety emerged from Wells's home environment: growing up in Bromley in Kent in the 1860s and 1870s, Wells's childhood saw the arrival of the railways and the development of the area; fields turned into suburbs, hedgerows to houses as London, the hub of a vast empire, spread its tentacles ever farther across southeast England. The resultant sense of mass society, of a teeming population eradicating England's green and pleasant land, colored Wells's work. No wonder his anticipations were so Malthusian. Panning out from the individual and autobiographical to the social and structural, however, there were three powerful reasons to expect Malthus's eclipse in the public consciousness.[1]

First, if Malthus had a great impact on the economic-cum-demographic debates of the Victorian age, there was clear evidence that he was increasingly a figure of historical interest only in those arenas. The last decades of the nineteenth century had seen the rapid "professionalization" of economics as a discipline, a process we touched upon in Chapter 6 in looking at the work of Alfred Marshall. The success of this process led, paradoxically, to Malthus's eclipse. Malthus the economist had been absorbed so thoroughly into the emergent disciplinary history that everyone "knew" his insights without actually reading his words. The same sense of Malthus as increasingly a figure in the history of ideas rather than a contributor to current debates could be gleaned from his absorption into intellectual life in Oxford at the turn of the century. Most important here were two pioneering economic historians at Balliol College. Arnold Toynbee has gone down in history as the scholar who coined the phrase "industrial revolution" as a shorthand for the massive changes that took place in the century after Malthus's birth. In Toynbee's *Lectures on the Industrial Revolution* (1884), he addressed Malthus's contribution to understanding these epochal changes. Toynbee gave a fairly "straight" exposition of Malthus's ideas, but was quite clear that they were of historical interest only for two main sets of reasons. First, the core idea of Malthus's work—that population tends to outstrip resources—was empirically false for late Victorian Britain, where "the average quantity of food consumed per head is yearly greater; and capital increases more than twice as fast as population." Second, Toynbee suggested that in a Britain with mass emigration to the Americas, with mass food importation from the same continent, and with increasing use of contraception to restrict family size (something that, for Toynbee, "excite[s] our strong moral repugnance"), Britain now faced a wholly non-Malthusian problem: "a stationary population is not a healthy condition of things in regard to national life; it means the removal of a great stimulus to progress." Toynbee was tragically cut down, apparently by excess work, at the age of thirty. By contrast, Toynbee's exact contemporary—they were both born in 1852—and fellow Balliol man, James Bonar, would live a long and productive life as an economic historian, dying in the depths of World War II, in 1941. Historians have noted that Bonar was heavily influenced by Toynbee in his work popularizing political economy. Less noted is the fact that Bonar's main scholarly achievement, his work on Malthus's life and ideas, also shares in Toynbee's image of Malthus as of historical interest only. Bonar published the first biographical assessment of Malthus since the obituaries by his friends in the 1830s in the form of *Malthus and His Work* in 1885, the year after Toynbee's lectures on the Industrial Revolution reached the public. In *Malthus and His Work,* Bonar tracked down previously unpublished letters and traced Malthus's reputation among the romantics and economists. All this was a prolegomena to a complete biography of Malthus that Bonar penned, revised, but never published (it is now preserved at the University of Illinois, Urbana-Champaign). Lurking behind Bonar's biographical projects was a sense that Malthus could now be treated impartially; the storms of controversy that Malthus had aroused were past, such that he could now be viewed with the dispassionate eye of the historian.[2]

The second reason Malthus could plausibly have been expected to recede into history as a new century dawned is tied with the questions of contraception that aroused Toynbee's repugnance. As we saw in Chapter 6, one key reason why Malthus remained a hot potato in the Victorian Age was the connection forged between his name and projects to empower people to limit their family size. This changed quite rapidly in the first decades of the twentieth century, thus decoupling Malthus from a highly charged debate. If Toynbee had written of the Industrial Revolution in the 1920s rather than the 1880s, for example, he would almost certainly have used the phrase "birth control" rather than "Malthusian" to describe practices of family limitation, a change in linguistic practice that has been comprehensively traced by Richard Soloway, who concludes that: "Neo-Malthusianism in the 1920s was abruptly shunted aside and overwhelmed by new populationist interests and personalities whose broader concepts of sexuality and fertility control reflected more accurately the problems and values of the present and the likely realities of the future." A new generation of birth control advocates, led by Margaret Sanger in the United States and Marie Stopes in the United Kingdom, actively "rebranded" ideas of family limitation away from any even nominal connection with Malthus and Malthusianism. In 1919, one of the stalwarts of the Malthusian League, Binnie Dunlop, praised the new generation in telling terms. Writing to Marie Stopes on the publication of her phenomenally successful book *Married Love* (1918), he argued: "Like Malthus, you might well spend the remainder of a long and happy life bringing out new editions of your Essay with more and more data and evidence. *STOPES LAW. And it supplements the Laws of Malthus.*" At the dawn of the twentieth century, clearly, Malthus's tie with family limitation had been superseded; he could shuffle off the stage to graceful retirement in the biographical pastures of James Bonar.[3]

Lurking behind these intellectual currents was the most powerful reason to anticipate Malthus's departure from political debate, a reason that was all about the realm in which Malthus had made his name—brute demographic realities. For that which Toynbee intimated in the 1880s, and which had in fact been occurring across the advanced industrial economies of Europe and North America from the 1870s, was widely known about by the onset of the twentieth century: a precipitate decline in the birth rate meant that a new demographic regime was emerging where population was projected to be at most static and quite possibly declining within decades. While the ways in which Malthus was entwined with discussions of population collapse, crisis, and the like will be addressed later in this chapter, at this point it is fair to say that many might have found here a prima facie case to regard his insights as increasingly redundant. If Malthus was the prophet of population's inexorable tendency to push against resource limitations, the late nineteenth century saw birth rates fall and thereby refuted his vision of a lawlike inevitability to this process. Reflecting back at the end of the period covered in this chapter, for example, Guy Chapman in *Culture and Survival* (1940) framed a historical transition from a "first population problem," the Malthusian dilemma of excess fertility in the face of scarce resources, to "the second population problem," "the maintenance of the population at a level which will permit it to enjoy a standard of life no less than that it enjoys at present." Chapman concluded his imagining of demographic Armageddon with a prediction that "Nature appears as if about to take her revenge, and to turn the material aspirations of millions into the dust of vanished hopes." While Chapman's tone might be ascribed to the outbreak of war, his fear that population decline was the new, very non-Malthusian terror were more widespread, less sensational, and of a far more venerable pedigree; predictions of "race suicide" in the context of declining birth rates peppered the popular press and more academic writings in the 1920s and 1930s. Ultimately, such predictions were grounded in the twin impacts of a declining birth rate and the massive loss of life experienced in World War I. In post–World War I Britain, the National Birth Rate Commission and the Registrar General, for example, both meditated on the fact that at least a half million children had not been born in the war years due to the inevitable fall in birth rates with men away fighting, not to mention the loss of life and health caused by the war itself, this being estimated at more than seven hundred thousand men killed and more than twice that number wounded. Even as august and sober a body as the Birth Rate Commission was "haunted by a morbid image of full coffins and empty cradles." This, coupled with parallel demographic projections suggesting that Germany had lost more than 2.5 million potential births in the war and Austria-Hungary 1.5 million, led a leading American scientist to proclaim that "we are unquestionably witnessing the most stupendously interesting step of human evolution since that which differentiated man from the anthropoid."[4]

And yet for all these good reasons why H. G. Wells's anticipation of Malthus's significance to the first half of the twentieth century might, perhaps should, have been misplaced, he was in fact to be proved right. As we shall see, the key public debates that thread through the first half of the twentieth century linking economics, resources, population, and the environment all drew on Malthus as far from a historical curio. Richard Overy has characterized the interwar years in Britain as "the morbid age," an era obsessed with what Lewis Mumford called "the soothing words, *downfall, doom, decay.*" Likewise, John Carey sees in this era an intellectual culture in Britain of misanthropy, fueled by fears of the cultural and environmental destruction wrought by mass society. Projecting onto the larger canvas of Europe as a whole, John Burrow has anatomized what he sees as a crisis of reason pervading the intellectual history of the age. One can perhaps suggest that Malthus, whom as we noted in Chapter 6, Carlyle saw as the epitome of the "dismal science" of political economy, resonated with Overy and Carey's "dismal age" and thus retained his relevance. We can trace Malthus's impact through four doleful debates that did much to define the "dismal age." Suitably enough, they can be arrayed as four dismal "Ds": degeneration, depression, development, and dictatorship.[5]

Degeneration: Malthus and the Demography of Decline

If European birth rates were declining from the 1870s, census-taking activities ensured that scholars and politicians knew about this in quick time. The census also ensured that there was a clear understanding of the sectional nature of that decline: simply put, the decades either side of 1900 saw an awareness that the working classes retained a high birth rate while more affluent classes were barely replacing their numbers generation on generation. In this context, demography entwined with social Darwinism in the form of eugenics. "Eugenics" as a term was coined by Darwin's cousin Sir Francis Galton in the 1870s. The core concern of eugenics was that the less able were reproducing while those of higher intelligence were not, the likely aggregate result being, according to Galton and his numerous followers, that the "human stock" would degenerate in terms of intellectual and cultural "quality." While there were many faces to the debate about human degeneration, how was Malthus implicated? In a remarkable book published in 1977, the left-wing journalist Allan Chase traced a predominantly American history of eugenics and its chilling consequences in terms of forced sterilization and legalized demographic dictatorship. The book, some seven hundred sprawling pages tracing events over the century from Galton to its publication, was issued under the title *The Legacy of Malthus.* Chase meant the title literally, claiming that "all of the Malthusian 'Natural Laws' ordaining the permanence of poverty and illiteracy were, of course, the start of scientific racism in Europe." Chase's depiction of Malthus is a woeful set of distortions: there is no evidence Malthus thought "God had imparted a Divine Revelation about population" to him, nor that he knew "history had long since disproven his great 'discovery.'" Malthus assuredly did not believe poverty was due to "hereditary low nature" as he had no discernible conception of hereditable intelligence, unsurprisingly given when he wrote. And yet we cannot merely dismiss Chase's core idea of an interconnection between Malthus and eugenic anxieties about a degenerating population. On the contrary, they were mutually interwoven, albeit in ways far more subtle than *The Legacy of Malthus* disclosed.[6]

Malthus may have had no conception of "hereditary inheritance," but he was aware of the idea of selective breeding. It was this awareness that led to his only plausibly "eugenic" comment in the *Essay*. While scotching the utopian ideas of Godwin and Condorcet about the perfectibility of mankind, he did concede that it "does not . . . seem impossible, that by an attention to breed, a certain degree of improvement, similar to that among animals, might take place among men." Malthus went on to make two important qualifications. First, that such an approach would amount to "condemning all the bad specimens to celibacy," something he found both implausible and unpalatable. Second, and in complete contradiction to the eugenic movement a century later, Malthus said of such selective human breeding: "whether intellect could be communicated may be a matter of doubt: but size, strength, beauty, complexion, and perhaps even longevity are in a degree transmissible." Malthus, then, was really trying to hedge his argument about human improvement against the charge of pessimism in 1798, but his comments were picked up on in the post-Darwinian context of eugenics. The first generation of eugenicists such as Galton were profoundly hostile to neo-Malthusianism as leading prudent and therefore "superior" groups to have a lower birth rate than the poorer classes with a deleterious impact on average levels of intellect. As Galton summarized, Malthusian delayed marriage was "a most pernicious rule of conduct in its bearing upon race." Galton approved of Malthus's advocacy of delayed marriage for the poor as a way of limiting their family size and impact on the collective stock but doubted its realism. If Malthusian remedies were likely to be pernicious, however, Galton admired Malthus personally, calling him "the rise of a morning star before a day of free social investigation." Likewise, as Chase points out, in 1923 the first issue of a new academic journal, the *Annals of Eugenics*, founded by Galton's pupil and successor Karl Pearson, featured a portrait of Malthus, whom it lauded as "Strewer of the Seed which reached its Harvest in the Ideas of Charles Darwin and Francis Galton." As with most intellectual movements, and as befits an argument obsessed with heredity, the eugenicists were keen to form a "pedigree" for their own endeavors, and clearly both Galton and Pearson sought to marshal Malthus into that lineage.[7]

How was Malthus invoked in the debates that raged in the first decades of the twentieth century about dwindling populations and degenerating stocks? A tour of several European nations gives us some insight into Malthus's continued relevance to demographic and social debates in the interwar years. In France in the aftermath of World War I, politicians turned their backs on Malthus's argument. Where before the Great War France had had one of the most active neo-Malthusian birth control movements in Europe, estimates that some 1.3 million French soldiers had died in the war led to a seismic shift in attitudes. Abortion and the sale of contraceptives were outlawed in 1920 in a bill whose preamble made France's newfound hostility to Malthus explicit: "In the aftermath of the war, where almost one and one-half million Frenchmen sacrificed their lives so that France could have the right to live in independence and honor, it cannot be tolerated that other French have the right to make a livelihood from the spread of abortion and Malthusian propaganda." By the 1930s, however, the onset of economic depression led to a rehabilitation of Malthus in France. With a stagnant global economy, a shrinking population could suddenly be seen as a strength or at least a way of minimizing the problems of unemployment and excess population: "The conclusions drawn by many French eugenicists from the Depression were therefore Malthusian—that is, the problems were the result of demography and economics. In words that would have made Malthus himself smile (albeit grimly), French eugenicists described a world with too many mouths to feed and too few resources. A new word entered French eugenic vocabulary—'overpopulation.' "[8]

Italy followed a similar pattern, with late-nineteenth-century Malthusianism being overturned in favor of pronatalism. After the First World War, and notably once Mussolini came to power in the mid-1920s, a concern with a decline in the birth rate led to strong pronatalist policies that explicitly rebutted Malthus. The formalization of this policy came in a 1927 speech by Mussolini, "Numero come Forza" (Strength in numbers). An explicit attack on Malthus came at what was Mussolini's great set piece of fascist demography, the 1931 Rome Population Conference. Whilst Mussolini disappointed the audience by not attending in person, he did edit the keynote speech delivered by his chief demographer, Corrado Gini, "instructing the latter to remove a passage praising Malthus." As a result, Gini opened his speech by opining that "for too long students of population problems have based their discussions on Malthusian premises" as opposed to the fascist doctrine enunciated in "Numero Come Forza." Italian hostility to Malthus was fortified not just by Il Duce, but also by the Vatican. Mussolini had signed the Lateran Treaty in 1929, creating concord between the Italian state and the Roman Catholic Church, and it was in this context that Pope Pius XI published his encyclical "Casti Connubii" in 1930, affirming Catholic support of the traditional family and abhorrence of birth control as "a new and utterly perverse morality" tempting "the flock committed to our care" to "poisoned pastures." Where, appropriate to its genre, Pius's encyclical does not mention Malthus by name, his status as poisoner of the pastures had already been made explicit twenty years earlier in the officially sanctioned English language *Catholic Encyclopaedia* (1907–1914). While the entry entitled "Theories of Population" canvassed Malthus's ideas evenhandedly, its conclusions were unequivocal: "The most notable results of the work and teaching of Malthus may be summed up as follows: he contributed absolutely nothing of value to human knowledge or welfare. . . . [H]is teaching has directly or indirectly led to a vast amount of social error, negligence, suffering, and immorality."[9]

A tour of the population policies of advanced industrial economies of the interwar years could go on to the Soviet Union, where, akin to France, contraception was banned in a Socialist pronatalist drive and, on the other side of the ideological divide, to the United States, where eugenic fears of degeneration led to a program of compulsory sterilization for "defectives" that affected up to sixty thousand by its cessation in the 1970s, this being coupled with racialized Malthusian fears that removing positive checks would lead to an "outward thrust of surplus colored men" that would swamp the White World, an alarmist fantasy made popular in works such as Lothrop Stoddard's *The Rising Tide of Color* (1920) and Madison Grant's *The Passing of the Great Race* (1916). Instead, we will return to Malthus's homeland of England, and look in more detail at how Malthus was implicated in the interacting fears about declining population and degenerating stock in the first half of the twentieth century.[10]

In the aftermath of the Great War, there was a combined concern about numbers and quality. Regarding numbers, it was argued that the advent of Malthusianism in the aftermath of the 1877 Besant-Bradlaugh trial had cost England dear. The Reverend James Marchant in two popular tracts, *Cradles and Coffins* (1916) and *Birth-Rate and Empire* (1917), argued that Malthusianism in the form of declining birth rates and putative sterility caused by the use of contraceptives had cost England up to 20 million people in fifty years. The reduced birth rate had removed the Malthusian population pressure, which many saw as a positive spur to

British imperial success. Summarizing this argument in 1914, Ethel Elderton's *Report on the English Birth Rate* suggested that only population
pressure had "carried an English population as the great colonizing force
into every quarter of the globe, and it may be that coming centuries will
recognize the Bradlaugh trial as the knell of the British colonial empire—
and as the real summons to the Slavs, Chinese and other fertile races to
occupy the spare places of the earth." This was a concern about eugenic
quality as well as demographic quantity: it was widely believed that as
the unfit had been invalided out of the Great War, the genetically fit had
been selectively culled by that war. As Lloyd George famously encapsulated the resultant problem for the English after the Treaty of Versailles,
you could not run an A1 empire with a C3 population. Imperial themes
easily mixed with providential ones, the Anglican Church holding to a
line not wildly dissimilar to that we have already seen the Vatican adopt.
One might treat the Reverend William Barry's 1905 declaration regarding birth control that "Malthus reigns instead of Christ" as eccentric, but
for the fact that the 1908 Lambeth Conference as the formal mouthpiece
of Anglicanism made strikingly parallel pronouncements in fearing that
"there is the world danger that the great English-speaking peoples, diminished in number and weakened in moral force, would commit the
crowning infamy of race-suicide, and so fail to fulfil that high destiny to
which in the Providence of God they have been manifestly called."[11]

Eugenic fears of swamping were assuaged by the 1931 census, which
showed working-class fertility on the decline, but this was replaced by
the concern that if all sectors of English society saw a declining birth
rate, the English population would in due course decline as well. Did the
censuses bespeak "race suicide," what we might call a "reverse Malthusian mathematics?" As Soloway puts it: "the fear of depopulation which
erupted in the 1930s was another phase in the recurring continuum of
pessimistic demography which had started with Malthus when the birth-
rate was soaring." In 1926, the Registrar General confirmed that on the
basis of current vital statistics, the English population would be in absolute decline by 1951. This story caught the public imagination, the *Observer* editorializing that "our swarming is over, the expansion of England . . . is at an end." Most influential, however, was Enid Charles's
1934 book, *The Twilight of Parenthood*. Charles explicitly played the
same geometrical demographic card Malthus had in 1798, only in reverse: "The population of Great Britain may or may not at any future
time be halving itself in a generation. Our present knowledge makes such
a possibility less incredible than any of the 'nightmares of population'
which Malthus depicted." And if one had geometrical decline rather than

Malthusian expansion of population, the dwindling was just as staggering, of course, as had been Malthus's resource conundrum: Charles pointed
out a current population of 45 million in 1933 would, *ceteris paribus,* be
reduced to 6 million in two hundred years, to 45,000 in three hundred
years, and to the princely total of 8 within four hundred years! Charles
did not, of course, believe that such a decline would actually come to
pass, but the press caught the tone of hysteria in headlines about the falling birth rate such as "The Peril of the Empty Cradle" and, with war
looming in 1938, "British Wives Help Hitler." In this context, the BBC
hosted a series of radio lectures on the subject of population in 1937; the
press made the general public au fait with a new term of art, "demography"; and there was a repeated insistence that people were preferring
personal affluence over family responsibilities, or "Baby Austins to babies."
If the hysteria and humor make the debate seem lightweight retrospectively, it was anything but: William Beveridge declared himself a convert
to the cause of bolstering the family on the basis of projections of national
population decline. On these grounds he would formulate his comprehensive social insurance policies in the so-called "Beveridge Report" of
1942. Emerging from the war, Beveridge would want to make a Britain
of babies in Baby Austins.[12]

The sheer intensity with which debates about demographics and degeneration penetrated English intellectual life and were still refracted
through a Malthusian lens can be seen by finally attending to Aldous and
Julian Huxley. We encountered the Malthus-driven pessimism of their
grandfather, T. H. Huxley, in Chapter 6, his framing of the "struggle for
existence" sparking a torrent of commentary. A half century later, both
Aldous and Julian Huxley reverted to questions concerning population
and society, albeit in a very different vein driven by the debates about
population decline and degeneration that had come to the fore in the interim. Aldous Huxley is without doubt the better known of the brothers
today, and this primarily for *Brave New World* (1932) despite his prodigious output as a novelist and essayist right through from the 1920s to
his death in 1963. *Brave New World* is, of course, shot through with the
concern for social engineering of the population, opening as it does in the
"Central London Hatchery and Conditioning Centre," where children
are born with precise genetic makeups to produce a range of talents from
controlling intellects to humble drones. And to avoid pregnancy for those
who have not been genetically engineered to prevent it, Huxley intro-
duces a suggestively named "Malthusian Belt," Lenina's being described
as "a silver-mounted green morocco-surrogate cartridge belt . . . with the
regulation supply of contraceptive." While commentators have pointed

to Huxley's prescience in the 1930s about elements of the society we now inhabit, notably its ruthless commercialization of all elements of life right down to a country walk, he did not have to be too inventive to create the demographic world of the Malthusian Belt. There was, as we have seen, both intense debate around eugenic social policy and a routine connection between this and Malthusian ideas of birth control. And if Huxley's "Malthusian Belt" was a pure fiction, others coined such phrases in good earnest, Dr. F. J. McCann, the gynecologist who presided over the predominantly Catholic "League of National Life," arguing in the early 1930s as Huxley wrote, for example, that contraceptives induced a form of sterility he called a "Malthusian uterus." If Aldous Huxley has gone down in the public memory as a dystopian critic of eugenics, this is only because his wider work on population questions, "the hidden Huxley," has gone undetected. For in the 1930s, while penning *Brave New World,* Aldous also wrote essays for popular journals advocating compulsory sterilization of "defectives," viewing the despoiled countryside as evidence that Britain's population was in excess of its optimum, and prophesizing that the more educated, especially the white race, faced extinction within a few short generations. Aldous's vision was curiously akin to that anticipated by H. G. Wells; it also bore close kinship with that of his older brother, Julian. If Aldous is the more celebrated brother today, in the 1930s Julian Huxley was the better known of the two, his popularizing approach to biology and social issues leading readers of the *Spectator* to rank him as one of Britain's "five best brains." Julian, a brain again, also featured in the World War II radio program *The Brains Trust,* which contemplated social futures for Britain in the depth of conflict. When he turned to population issues, Julian, like his brother, blended eugenics and concerns about conservation with Malthus. As he put it in his autobiographical *Memories,* by 1922 he realized that demographic growth would lead to "deforestation, shortage of food, gross overcrowding and other troubles. Malthus had arrived at the same conclusion." But throughout his long career, Julian advocated very non-Malthus-based solutions; Malthus's reliance on individual restraint in marriage was deemed unworldly, and state-sponsored planning was advocated in its stead. Where after World War II this would be advocated in consensual terms, in the 1930s Julian envisaged an authoritarian state as the answer to demographic and other social dilemmas, arguing for the irrelevance and inefficiency of democratic approaches in his disturbingly titled and timed book *If I Were a Dictator* (1934). In a world where, as he put it in 1930, "some people are born talented, others are born morons," eugenic engineering by an all-powerful state could remedy the problem. Where the "public"

Aldous Huxley could almost be taken to have parodied his brother's literal ideas to dystopian effect in *Brave New World,* the "hidden" Aldous of course subscribed to startlingly similar beliefs. If T. H. Huxley had composed a threnody in minor key depicting a blind, amoral nature locked in vicious Malthusian struggle, then, suitable to the age of anxiety about demographic degeneration and decline, his grandsons in the 1930s produced a requiem for humanity or the white races whose only hopeful notes lay in population planning and social control.[13]

Depression: "Jeremiah Malthus" and Malthus

It is a minor footnote in the history of the Bloomsbury Group that Aldous Huxley cut his teeth in its company intellectually, cycling while an Oxford undergraduate during the Great War to join Lady Ottoline Morrell's soirees at Garsington. Julian Huxley could also look back on visiting Aldous at Garsington and therefore intersecting with the Bloomsberries. Far more central to the history of Bloomsbury, of course, was John Maynard Keynes, whose intellectual engagements with Malthus from around 1912 until his death in 1946 were perhaps the most sustained and important reasons for Malthus's continued public prominence in the interwar years. Malthus has been described by Keynes's biographer Robert Skidelsky as his "favourite economist," a judgment that was more wittily endorsed by Keynes's Cambridge undergraduates who affectionately knew him as "Jeremiah Malthus." Above all, in two sharply separate engagements with Malthus in the early 1920s and the early 1930s, Keynes would make Malthus relevant to the modern era, reworking the meaning of Malthus's ideas to accord with the needs of the times as he perceived them. Donald Winch rightly calls this a "Keynesianising" of Malthus and warns that Keynes's Malthus is not necessarily the same as Malthus himself. And yet there can be no doubt of the intellectual impact of this new Malthus.[14]

Keynes's interest in Malthus started after he left a civil service job in the Indian Office and returned to Cambridge as a lecturer in Alfred Marshall's economics department. One of his roles was to lecture on population, in which context he started to think and write about Malthus, leaving draft lecture notes from 1912 and 1914. Much that Keynes wrote about Malthus and population before World War I was fairly conventional: a declining birth rate showed "Malthus's psychological assumptions" were dubious, and differentials in fertility between the educated white population and others were of eugenic concern "from a racial point of view." Where Keynes stood out was in his belief that Malthus's views

were about to come back to direct relevance, that in the early 1910s society was "perhaps now at the moment of turning" where the terms of
trade would move against manufactures relative to agricultural produce.
The 1914 lecture in particular unpacked an argument that Britain had
escaped from Malthus's law of diminishing returns by relying on a glo-
balizing food trade in the second half of the nineteenth century, but that
beyond the tipping point on which the nation teetered, this globalization
would come back to haunt us. As the terms of trade moved against manufactures due to global population increase, Britain could no longer ensure
her food security (an argument we have seen Malthus make in the context
of the Corn Laws) as other nations could price her out of the food market.
At the very least, and avoiding sensationalism, Keynes judged that "the
problem [of food supply] . . . is made much worse and far harder of solution by having become, since Malthus's time, cosmopolitan."[15]

Keynes's transition from a minor albeit highly regarded Cambridge
lecturer to a public sage and celebrity was negotiated by his role in the
Treaty of Versailles. Keynes was part of the British delegation to Versailles, but resigned in spectacular fashion in protest at what he considered the punitive nature of the reparations being imposed upon Germany.
And so, as the treaty was coming to fruition in 1919, Keynes sat down
instead to write the polemic against it that would make his name, *The
Economic Consequences of the Peace*. The specter of Malthus was at the
very core of the success and infamy of this pessimistic tract for its times.
Malthus drives the second chapter of *Economic Consequences*, although
in truth there was little here that Keynes had not already said to undergraduate audiences before the outbreak of war. The argument Keynes ran
was that the war was at least in part a consequence of Europe having
reached the tipping point he had discussed in his 1914 lecture. Malthus
had come back to haunt society, and the result was a collapse into continental conflict. Chapter 2 of *Economic Consequences* is a potted history
of, as its title enunciates, "Europe before the War." In this context, Keynes
argues that the fifty years prior to the outbreak of war were "unstable
and peculiar" because "the pressure of population on food . . . became
for the first time in recorded history definitively reversed." If "Malthus
disclosed a devil" in 1798, the years after 1870 had been able to leave
that devil "chained up and out of sight." In this scenario, it was rapid
German population growth from 1870 that unleashed that devil again,
for it was only by operating "continuously and at full blast" that Germany could "find occupation at home for her increasing population and
the means of purchasing their subsistence from abroad." In this context,
Keynes returned to his tipping-point thesis to find one of the points of

tension that led to war: "the law of diminishing returns was at last reasserting itself." Keynes intoned in Delphic terms that "the great events of history are often due to secular changes in the growth of population and other fundamental economic causes" and depicted not one but two such events resulting from the adverse swing in terms of trade between food and manufactures. The Great War itself had been sparked by the ever-intensifying pressure on the European economies to feed their populations, but a smaller-scale result of the same pressure was manifested in "the extraordinary occurrences of the past two years in Russia," a revolution that Keynes opined "may owe more to the deep influences of expanding numbers than to Lenin or to Nicholas."[16]

Keynes's vision was not uncontested at the time. Perhaps the most high-profile critique came from Sir William Beveridge, and it put the Malthusian component of Keynes's case on trial. We have already noted that Beveridge by the early 1920s feared "race suicide," not overpopulation, and developed the elaborate schema of social security that immortalized his name in the United Kingdom twenty years later to address this concern. Unsurprisingly, then, Beveridge took issue with Keynes's argument that a fifty-year window when the pressure of population on resources had relented had now been closed. Writing in 1923 for the most important economics journal of the age, Beveridge used his presidential address to the British Association for the Advancement of Science to controvert Keynes's Malthusian specters. Above all, for Beveridge, "the problems of unemployment and of over-population are distinct; they are two problems, not one." The existence of structural unemployment in the early 1920s was a result of the economic frictions in the transition to a postwar economic footing. They did not justify what Beveridge modeled as a form of collective paranoia: "many, perhaps most, educated people are troubled by fear that the limits of population, probably in Europe and certainly in this country, have been reached." In this context, Beveridge saw Keynes as acting irresponsibly in letting "Malthus's devil" loose again; merely by invoking Malthus, Keynes had ipso facto let his shade haunt the educated imagination: "The question is not indeed whether Malthus's Devil is loose again. Mr. Keynes has seen to that; he stalks at large through our lecture-rooms and magazines and debating societies. The question is rather whether Mr. Keynes was right to loose this Devil now upon the public." Reviewing the statistical data on secular trends in food prices and the relative prices of foodstuffs and manufactures, Beveridge's answer was a resounding "no." Birth rates were falling and had been since the 1870s, real wages had consistently increased, and the world still exhibited massive uncultivated tracts. In sum, Beveridge found "no ground for Malthusian pessimism," "no justification for Malthusian panic." While most commentators then and since have seen Beveridge's rebuttal of Keynes's argument as decisive, Keynes did venture a reply. He argued that the bigger picture was one where to deny the significance of Malthus to contemporary debate was pernicious. Citing press clippings from the most important newspapers of the age—the *Guardian,* the *Daily Mail,* the *New Statesman,* and so forth—Keynes showed that they all saw Beveridge as having scotched "the bogey of an overcrowded earth, first raised by the short-sighted Malthus." By contrast, the newspapers had all failed to note Beveridge's concluding acceptance that:

> Nothing that I have said discredits the fundamental principle of Malthus, reinforced as it can be by the teachings of modern science. The idea that mankind, while reducing indefinitely the risks to human life, can, without disaster, use to the full a power of reproduction adapted to the perils of savage or pre-human days, can control death by art and leave birth to Nature, is biologically absurd. The rapid cumulative increase following on any practical application of this idea would within measurable time make civilisation impossible in this or any other planet.

In this context, Keynes suggested that Beveridge was more irresponsible to threaten to dispense with Malthus's devil than he had been to disclose it. As fate would have it, however, Malthus was very much not dispensed with thanks to Beveridge's intervention; on the contrary, his relevance was about to be enforced with a new intensity.[17]

We have already seen that a number of versions of Malthus were doing the rounds in the 1930s, most, like those developed by the Huxley brothers, negotiating a compromise between anxieties about decline and degeneration on the one hand and eugenic, planned solutions on the other. And yet the version of Malthus that was to be both the most original and to have the greatest impact on both the life of the mind and public policy over the ensuing half century was that created by Keynes in response to the economic reversals that we collectively label as "the Depression." This "new" Malthus was to bear striking resemblance to Keynes himself as a Cambridge seer in the wilderness, plotting a radical new path, the taking of which could avoid collective destruction. His portrait was limned in Keynes's 1933 biographical essay "Thomas Robert Malthus: The First of the Cambridge Economists," and in the texture of his epochal work of economic theory, *The General Theory of Employment, Interest and Money* (1936).

Keynes had held a biographical interest in Malthus since his earliest days as an economics lecturer, his 1914 lecture on population containing recognizable passages that would be recycled in the 1933 biography. Furthermore, from at least 1922, Keynes had been giving a version of his biographical sketch of Malthus as a seminar, notably to the Political Economy Club in Cambridge. Over time, however, his emphasis shifted such that by its publication in 1933, the portrait of Malthus was also an unveiling of elements of the system Keynes would formalize as a response to mass unemployment in the Depression in his *General Theory* three years later. Keynes's Malthus above all is praised for his combination of philosophical acuity and attentiveness to real life, the exact combination any economist should exhibit. Thus Keynes praised Malthus's first, 1798, edition of the *Essay* as "for posterity a far superior book" to the later, more dense versions as it was "*a priori* and philosophical in method." And yet it was equally the case that Malthus's philosophical approach was not an example of scholastic rigor decoupled from reality, but was concerned with how economies actually functioned: "Malthus, by taking up the tale much nearer to its conclusion, had a firmer hold on what may be expected to happen in the real world." It was this apparently paradoxical combination of the a priori and the empirical that Keynes came to frame as definitive of a "Cambridge economist," Malthus being the first and Keynes (implicitly) the culmination: a Cambridge economist was "a great pioneer of the application of a frame of formal thinking to the complex confusion of the world of daily events." In this, if Malthus was the prototype of the exemplary/Cambridge economist, his nemesis was his good friend David Ricardo, whose precision was in the service of an abstract, unreal model of the economy: of the respective merits and subsequent impact of the two economists Keynes passed a celebrated judgment that would be echoed closely in his *General Theory:* "one cannot rise from a perusal of this correspondence without a feeling that the almost total obliteration of Malthus's line of approach and the complete domination of Ricardo's for a period of a hundred years have been a disaster to the progress of economics." For Keynes such a judgment could be made in strictly economic terms: "if only Malthus, instead of Ricardo, had been the parent stem from which nineteenth-century economics proceeded, what a much wiser and richer place the world would be today." The core insight that Keynes offered to substantiate his claim about the respective merits of Malthus and Ricardo was Malthus's discovery of the "principle of effective demand," which would become the lynchpin of Keynes's *General Theory.* This was mentioned briefly in the 1933 biography and expanded on in the context of Keynes's contribution to the celebrations of the centenary of Malthus's death in 1934. Keynes's centennial address was published in the *Economic Journal* of 1935 and discussed the "brilliant intuitions" of Malthus's realization, in the context of the economic depression that beset Britain in the age of the Napoleonic Wars, that inadequate demand in the form of excess saving could lead to unemployment. The palliatives that Keynes alleged Malthus advocated were an example of just how much in the mid-1930s Keynes used Malthus as a cipher for the ideas he would champion in his *General Theory:* "a spirit of free expenditure, public works and a policy of expansionism."[18]

A year after the publication of his centennial address about Malthus, Keynes stepped out from the shadow of his historical portraiture to publish the *General Theory,* a reworking of Cambridge economics in the new age of economic depression. Ricardo's "classical" economics assumed supply created its own demand, but this only worked in conditions of full employment. Malthus had shown that such conditions could fail and thereby begun the "scientific explanation of unemployment." Any more comprehensive, or "general," economic theory had to address the fact that full employment was only a rare and special condition of an economy: more generally, equilibrium was where aggregate demand and aggregate supply intersected, and to artificially raise or lower demand would, via production, adjust supply as well. As such, in his opening comments Keynes made it plain that *"effective demand . . .* is the substance of the General Theory of Employment." Bookending the *General Theory,* Keynes in conclusion suggested that the state needed to increase its involvement in manipulating the economy via taxation and investment to ensure that effective demand was kept at a level to prevent the sorts of mass unemployment that had been witnessed in the early 1930s. The overall rationale here was closely akin to that laid out in *The Economic Consequences of the Peace:* state intervention, the anathema of Victorian laissez-faire, was "the only practicable means of avoiding the destruction of existing economic forms in their entirety." Writing in 1936 with Hitler and Mussolini enhancing their power bases, Keynes recognized that "dictators . . . find it easy to work on the natural bellicosity of their peoples," but thought that "facilitating their task of fanning the popular flame, are the economic causes of war, namely, the pressure of population, and the competitive struggle for markets." The Keynes of the *General Theory* was clear that population pressure was not likely to be the catalyst to war as it had been on his reading of the events of 1914–1919; on the contrary, it would be ineffective demand, the struggle for markets. It was in this context that in 1937, a year after the emergence of the *General Theory,* Keynes in his Galton Society lecture to the Eugenics Society—"Some Economic Consequences of a Declining Population—shifted his Malthusian ground. Where in 1919 he had detected the perils of overpopulation and collapsing terms of trade for food only to be decisively refuted by Beveridge, twenty years later a stationary population threatened inadequate effective demand to provide the employment on which social stability was predicated. Predictably, Keynes managed to frame this in terms of Malthus's life and changing attitudes as much as his own:

> We have now learned that we have another devil at our elbow at least as fierce as the Malthusian—namely the devil of unemployment escaping through the breakdown of effective demand. Perhaps we could call this devil too a Malthusian devil, since it was Malthus himself who first told us about him. For just as the young Malthus was disturbed by the facts of population as he saw them round him and sought to rationalise that problem, so the older Malthus was no less disturbed by the facts of unemployment . . . when Malthusian devil P is chained up, Malthusian devil U is liable to break loose.[19]

Development: The Old Devil and Three-Quarters of the World

Thus far, one piece of the jigsaw puzzle that comprises Keynes's picture of Malthus has been left untouched. If we return to his 1914 lecture on population, Keynes argued not only that Europe was at a tipping point, being about to revert to a desperate struggle to keep its population fed, but also that "three quarters of the world have never ceased to live under Malthusian conditions." The three-quarters in question, was, of course, what subsequent generations would label as the "developing" or the "Third" World, and which Keynes, true to the parlance of his era, tended to term "the East." Keynes discussed in particular China and India. China will figure briefly in our story in Chapter 8, but for the present the focus rests on India and the ways in which Malthus was implicated in the modern construction of the idea of a global binary between rich and poor countries. Keynes provides a decent entrée to the discussion, for he framed a binary where Malthus's "old devil" of overpopulation applied in the East at the same time as he was building his idea that the West was following a different Malthusian logic, whether that was in terms of a period of respite from Malthus that was now at a dangerous turning point, his vision in the 1920s, or in terms of a different and new Malthusianism of insufficient demand, as in the 1930s. In either case, there was an essential difference between East and West, and this difference could be understood in terms derived directly from Malthus. This also allowed Keynes to figure life as cheap in the East and valuable in the West: Keynes had worked in the India Office and incorporated statistics about mortality from that experience in his 1914 lecture. If Asia floundered in "a surfeit of population," plague such as that which visited the Punjab in 1901–1911, killing, in Keynes's account, 10 percent of the population, could be framed as a "beneficent visitation."[20]

The discourse upon which Keynes drew in the first decades of the twentieth century was of some antiquity by this time, and its origins have been traced by some to the intertwining of political economy with the English incursion in India through the East India Company. In this context, Malthus's role as professor of political economy at the East India College in Haileybury from 1805 until his death three decades later has been seen as important. In fact, however, what we know of the political-economic teaching of "Old Pop" (as Malthus was affectionately known by his pupils) at Haileybury suggests that he mainly instructed his pupils in the ideas of Adam Smith's *Wealth of Nations,* not in his ideas about population-resource issues from the *Essay.* As such, we should not imagine regiments of Malthus's disciples filing into colonial India thanks to his direct indoctrination. If Malthus's ideas did impact upon the English colonial understanding of Indian population and resource questions, this should be seen to emanate from the general cultural circumstances of Victorian intellectual life sketched in Chapter 6, not the specific efforts of Malthus himself. And there is plenty of evidence to suggest that exactly such a Malthusian worldview did influence the colonial understanding of India, helping to establish the conditions in which Keynes would view the subcontinent in terms of a surfeit of people, their lives beneficently cut short by positive checks. As governor general of India from 1876 to 1880, for example, the Earl of Lytton argued in conventional Malthusian fashion that the Indian population "has a tendency to increase more rapidly than the food it raises from the soil." As Mike Davis has shown in terrifying detail, Lytton, a minor romantic poet always in Tennyson's shadow, was by his time in India subject to violent mood swings and incipient insanity; he lavished monies on the enthronement of Queen Victoria as empress of India at the same time as tens of thousands of Indians were dying of famine. The famine relief offered to the starving by Lytton's administration was less in terms of calorific intake than that Hitler gave to those interned in Buchenwald concentration camp. It would be easy to frame Lytton as a lone, demented maniac, but it is more plausible to see his attitudes to Indian subjects as part of a far broader cast of mind held by those without his mental instability. Lytton's policies were bolstered by official reports flooding in from across the subcontinent such as the following in 1877: "Southern India has enjoyed peace and tranquillity for many years during which the increase of population up to the limit of the sustaining power of the soil has been unchecked. . . . [T]he limits of increase of production and of population have been reached." As this comment makes clear, English administrators could even claim that the "Roman peace" brought to India by English rule was demonstrated by famine: removing the positive checks of war and addressing those of plague by modern medicine had led to a population explosion that only famine now could curtail in the absence of Malthusian family limitation. Modern economic analysis of Indian famines by Amartya Sen makes it clear they were events where the absolute quantities of food produced would have been sufficient to avoid starvation, but "entitlement," the ability to successfully demand food, was being undercut by the integration of production into a globalized market economy. As such, Indian colonial rule created a "late Victorian 'proto-third world' " whose functioning was legitimated by what has been called a "myth of 'Malthusia.' " Myths, of course, are their own realities; they act on the unfolding of historical events. By framing India as a "less developed world," in Malthus's terms as "overpopulated," English colonial administrators learned to respond in certain ways that had tragic consequences through the course of colonial rule. We can gain a window onto this process by tracing Winston Churchill's entanglement with Malthus and India.[21]

On Churchill's own account of his youthful years, *My Early Life* (1930), he was something of a disappointment at Harrow, bright but prickly and noncompliant. His formal education having gone awry, Churchill departed for India in the 1890s with a military commission and a yen to make his name by writing about colonial affairs and military engagements on the subcontinent. It was here that Churchill began to educate himself or, as his son Randolph put it in his massive biography, "he thus became his own university." Winston dated the change more precisely in *My Early Life:* "it was not until this winter of 1896, when I had almost completed my twenty-second year, that the desire for learning came upon me." Churchill outlines a wide course of reading he undertook while staying in Bangalore, this taking in historians such as Gibbon and Macaulay, philosophy in the form of Plato, and so forth, but our particular concern is with the fact that he read "Schopenhauer on Pessimism; Malthus on Population; Darwin's Origin of Species," a suitably dismal trio for the dismal age. It appears that the effect of this reading was to give Churchill a cast of mind in witnessing mass death in India that was comprehensible in the light of the more general colonial response to India outlined above, viewing plague as a "positive" check both in the sense Malthus intended and in Keynes's sense from 1914 as "beneficent." Thus two years after reading Malthus, Churchill framed a plague in India as one where "a philosopher may watch unmoved the destruction of some of those superfluous millions, whose life must of necessity be destitute of pleasure." Strangely, and as we will see shortly, this sense of positive checks as beneficent is one Churchill would share with Adolf Hitler.[22]

Returning to a career in English politics, Churchill came to adopt the form of Malthusian "split vision" we have seen in Keynes, arguing that there were different forms of population problem in East and West, in developing and advanced nations. For Europe, Churchill was anxious, true to the age, about declining birth rates and a degenerating "racial stock." In 1912, for example, he attended the First International Congress of Eugenics in his capacity as one of the vice presidents of the Eugenics Education Society. One reason Churchill was thus honored was probably his efforts in 1910 as home secretary to persuade Asquith of "the need for forcible sterilization and incarceration of the feebleminded and insane." By the outbreak of World War II, Churchill, shifting in the face of the depopulation scares of the 1930s, was anxiously juxtaposing the low birth rate in England with what he perceived as the excess fecundity of Russia and Asia in an article for the popular *News of the World,* thereby marginalizing his eugenic concerns of the 1910s and highlighting the disjunction between the world of the East, where Malthus still reigned as he had discovered in the 1890s, and the West, where race suicide loomed even as Europe descended into a conflict that could hasten that process.[23]

It was this binary that Churchill adopted, which was to play out so tragically in the depths of the war when food shortages emerged on the subcontinent in 1942–1943. Modern economists see the 1942–1943 Bengal famine as, in Amartya Sen's words, "a 'boom famine' related to powerful inflationary pressures initiated by public expenditure expansion." Simply put, the Indian economy was expanding rapidly in the context of its mobilization to produce food and manufactures for the British war effort. Britain was to repay the cost of these products after the war concluded, and in the interim Indians could spend on credit monies owed to them. When food shortages started to be encountered in 1942, the British government continued to insist that grain exports to Europe be maintained to bolster the war effort. As a result, inflationary pressures spiraled in India itself, meaning that many lacked the purchasing power to access even subsistence levels of food. In 1943, grain was being shipped from Australia to Europe as well, being stockpiled to aid the Mediterranean campaigns; as such, supplies went directly past India but were never diverted to relieve the emergent crisis even though there was spare shipping capacity at the time to allow for this. In fact, Churchill diverted some of this shipping glut to ensure he could "restore white bread to the United Kingdom" to boost morale on the home front. Why? Much of the answer must lie in the Malthusian mentality of Churchill and his key advisors, Frederick Lindemann (Lord Charwell) and Leo Amery (secretary of state for India). All were able to make a categorical division in their minds and their morals between an overly fecund East and the needs of an advanced West. Lindemann, who was Churchill's key policy advisor, a man of whom C. P. Snow (to whose own Malthusianism we will return in Chapter 8) was to say that he had "more direct power than any scientist in history," argued in orthodox Malthusian fashion that "shortage of food is likely to be endemic in a country where the population is always increased until only bare subsistence is possible," thereby ignoring the export-orientated pressures that had led to the failure of subsistence entitlements. Leo Amery as secretary of state was privately aware of this but publicly blamed famine on Indian overpopulation. Churchill himself tended to frame famine as something that British colonial rule had eliminated from the subcontinent, "until the horrors of war and the dislocations of war have given us a taste of them again," thereby casting famine as a visitation from history as opposed to economic policy. Privately in the War Cabinet he was more uncompromising, refusing Amery's requests in 1943 for emergency relief on the grounds that "Indians [are] breeding like rabbits and being paid a million a day by us for doing nothing about the war." Some 3 million souls died in the Bengali famine of 1942–1943; this may have been made more palatable to Churchill by figuring them as mere rabbits in the Malthusian headlights of inevitable starvation; posterity and economic theory judge them with rather more honestly.[24]

Dictatorship: Hitler and "Positive" Positive Checks

If Churchill's Malthusian policy in India was assuredly not his finest hour, the confrontation with Hitler's Germany was one where, viewed through the lens of Malthus, the two men shared similar doctrines. If the first half of the twentieth century is cast as the age of great wars, these events were often framed in terms that owed much to Malthus. We have already seen the pivotal role Keynes accorded to population pressure in triggering World War I. He was by no means alone in tying population pressure to conflict: the Malthusian League, for example, ran what it called a "Malthusian War Map" in the 1914 edition of its journal, *Malthusian,* to make the point that the Great War was in fact a war of the low-birth-rate nations—France, Belgium, and the United Kingdom—against the predatory high-birth-rate nations of Austria, Hungary, and Germany. Only Russia did not fit the schema, but as with Keynes, the Revolution allowed it to be slotted in retrospectively with the aggressor nations with high birth rates. And if one might expect the Malthusian League to view matters thus, others chimed in on the same theme. A range of Malthus-inspired terms were used to explain the war: "War was explained in distinctly modern socio-biological terms as adaptive behaviour springing from territorial urges, crowding, competition for resources and reproductive advantage." By 1931, scholars were similarly framing the Manchurian War between Japan and China as fueled by the pressure of predictably expanding Asiatic populations.[25]

If many commentators viewed overpopulation as a "problem" and a cause of war, German discourse viewed matters differently, a strong pro-natalism dominating discussion from the age of the Franco-Prussian War through to Hitler's demise. Where Keynes had focused on the rapidly increasing German population as an engine pushing Europe into conflict in 1914, German discussion focused not on her total population increase in the period 1871–1910 from 41 to 65 million, but on the fact that there was a serial decline in birth rates, this amounting to a 70 percent decrease from 1870 to 1930. As such, the fact that Germany had experienced mass starvation due to food shortages in World War I did not dent the demand for policies to increase the birth rate. The Weimar government was keen to increase the birth rate—it was one of the few policies Hitler would maintain intact—but also attended to the quality of German "stock." The tone of concern was captured by that tract for the gloomy times, Oswald Spengler's *Decline of the West* (1918–1923):

> All Civilizations enter upon a stage . . . of appalling depopulation. The whole pyramid of cultural man vanishes. It crumbles from the summit, first the world-cities, then the provincial forms and finally the land itself, whose best blood has incontinently poured into the towns . . . the spirit of Civilization . . . so, doomed, moves on to final self-destruction.

It was in this context of pronatalism coupled with gloom about the decay of the best blood in the enervating city that Hitler was to rise to power. Hitler was inspired by Spengler, but his disastrous failure to renew the German "blood" in the rabble-rousing of the Munich Beer Hall Putsch of 1923 led to his incarceration in Landsberg Prison. It was while in Landsberg that Hitler styled himself as a philosopher, just as Churchill had done in Bangalore. And the two shared not only the insecurities of the autodidact, but also an encounter with Malthus at this formative moment.[26]

While working on his intellectual testament in Landsberg, *Mein Kampf,* Hitler was visited by the German geopolitician Karl Haushofer, who introduced him to the works of Malthus. Hitler's reading practices were notoriously desultory, so how much of Malthus he actually read will never be known, but he did immediately scribble Malthusian comments in a notebook whose tenor would echo down the ensuing two decades in the population policies of the National Socialist Party. Blending Haushofer and Malthus, Hitler labeled the page in his notebook "Das Hunger als Macht" (Hunger as Power) framing "the Goddess of Want" as the "Greatest world power." He divided his categories, suggesting hunger could be "paralysing deadening" but equally "Stimulating." Further down, he also answered the rhetorical question, "Is scarcity a natural phenomenon?" by saying "possible . . . but might also be artificial, if someone benefited from its effects." The ensuing leaf of the notebook continued to another theme to which Hitler already recurred obsessively, "Jewish fraud," tying this to Malthusian resource questions in two ways. First, Hitler suggested that the politician can use "Hunger as a means to an end" and that "Hunger abets the sword." He also envisaged that in the "fight for world domination by Jewry" their control of markets as moneylenders meant that "Confusion of thought is helped by physical degeneration obtained through hunger in the form of lasting 'price increases.'" These notes are very fragmentary, and any attempt to string them together to have a clear meaning risks both granting them too much coherence and viewing them in the light of what came. But at the very least they show that Hitler's encounter with Malthus while languishing in Landsberg in 1924 led him to tie together hunger, war, power, and the Jews. And such concerns did immediately figure in *Mein Kampf,* where Hitler opined in fairly conventional Malthusian terms that: "The productivity of the soil can only be increased within defined limits and up to a certain point. The necessities of life, however, are rising more rapidly than the numbers of the population—requirements in food and clothing." Where Hitler departed from the conventional Malthusian message was in the policy implications he took from these limits. Where most saw Malthus as meaning that population must therefore be checked, the staunch pronatalist in Hitler went on in *Mein Kampf* to look for ways in which the limits could be circumvented by territorial expansion. As his argument has been summarized: "Only two courses remain open to guarantee 'work and bread' for a rising population: either to acquire new territory on which each year the superfluous millions can be settled, thereby perpetuating the nation's self-sufficiency in food; or so to organise industry and commerce as to increase exports and attempt to live off the proceeds. The sounder argument is undoubtedly the first." As Hitler's notebooks had suggested, then, Hitler saw positive checks as "positive": hunger would abet the sword, being a means to the end of his expansionist fantasy of the Third Reich and its turning of the tide against the "fight for world domination by Jewry."[27]

In power from 1933, Hitler acted consistently with regard to population questions, his approach in most regards enacting the vision glimpsed in fragmentary form from his notebook entries and *Mein Kampf*. To turn visions and high rhetoric into pragmatic policy, the National Socialists had recourse to the logic of statistics to allow for "the total registration and classification of the population." As Friedrich Zahn, president of the German Statistical Society, remarked in 1940: "In its very essence, statistics is closely related to the National Socialist movement. The State holds population policy in especially high regard. It is no longer a mere quantitative population policy, but has developed into a qualitative and psychological one. This requires a thorough knowledge of statistics in order to aid our Fuhrer in his work." The "qualitative" element of this policy, of course, was to divide the populace in Spenglerian-cum-eugenic fashion into the German people, who were to be encouraged by a pronatalist policy, and the defectives, Jews, and others who were framed as a population problem. And it was these "non-Germanic" elements of the population who were most frequently modeled in terms derived indirectly from Malthus as "useless eaters" and as an example of the tendency to over-population. A Malthusian framing of the problem was especially common in the "Generalgouvernement," the part of Poland that was not formally incorporated into the Reich in 1939. Thus in July 1940 the head of demography for the Generalgouvernement, Fritz Arlt, said the area suffered from "the problem of overpopulation" and advocated that emigration offered no solution, preferring "some within the subjugated groups . . . [to] die off." While Poles were part of this vision, it was the substantial Jewish population that was the main target. By October 1940, a paper on "Jewry in the eastern European sphere" made the solution more plain:

> The Jewish question . . . has become a first degree problem of mass population policy. It takes its place next to the difficult population policy questions involving the agrarian over-population of this area, and, over the long term, calls urgently for a solution. These masses of Jews are today largely without any productive employment or their own means of subsistence. . . . This gives rise to one long-term goal: the demographic cleansing of this area.

The "Final Solution" could thus be viewed through a Nazi-Malthusian lens as producing two benefits to the Reich. First, it reduced demand for food and other resources from those of non-German blood. In tandem with Nazi "cleansing" came the statistical assessment of resources saved, the most remarkable tabulation being that by Edmund Brandt, which looked at how much the 70,273 people killed in the period from January 1940 to August 1941 would have consumed in the forthcoming decade. Brandt subdivided by food type, arguing, for example, that 5,902,920 kilograms of marmalade would be saved thereby, not to mention nearly 1 million reichsmarks worth of cottage cheese. As Aly and Roth summarize this work, "the calculations of the net value of humans . . . led to the fact that killing, statistically speaking, was viewed as an accomplishment, since living human beings showing negative productivity were economic dead weights." Second, this reduction in demand for resources allowed for a pronatalist policy for Germans and for them to emigrate to the new German lands in the East once suitable vacancies had been made: "the east was a safety-valve . . . now that Germany had some 'elbow room.'" The landscape of the German eastern front would be remodeled by forced labor, mainly Jewish. This labor would die in the process of creating a new greater German landscape of farms and villages (Auschwitz itself was built on reclaimed marshland in Upper Silesia), which would turn civilization back from the brink of Spengler's nightmare of world cities, depopulation, and final decay. In many ways, then, Hitler's dismal demography was the outcome of a desire to turn the putative tide of degeneration that had preoccupied the age, not its antithesis.[28]

Compulsory sterilization. Avoidable famine. Auschwitz. We have come a long way from an amiable Surrey cleric in this chapter, and it would be all too easy for an apologist for Malthus to deny any connection. But equally, even if overblown in places, Allan Chase's *The Legacy of Malthus* does grasp the kernel of an important point when it says "Malthus . . . made societal aggressions against the poor . . . emerge in the consciousness of the educated and affluent classes as perfectly proper and natural approaches." Even if Malthus's name and language were more often invoked than his work was read, and even if, when he was read by individuals such as Churchill and Hitler, it is not clear that the humanity and complexity of his arguments were ever understood, it remains the case that strong and direct connections can be drawn between his work and some of the most abhorrent moments in twentieth-century history. No one can be held to account for their posthumous reception, yet it behooves the intellectual historian and their readership to face that reception head-on.[29]

And what of the new dawn that followed Hitler's demise? If Malthus was implicated in the dismal age, would the optimism of the postwar era see him marginalized? Would a more just peace at Yalta, the birth of a United Nations with power as well as vision, and the development of Keynesian management of the global economy lead to the jettisoning of Malthus's message? If, as Harold Macmillan argued in winning the 1959 British election, "you've never had it so good," would the era at last lead to Malthus shuffling off the stage? Quite on the contrary, Malthus was about to enter an age of celebrity.

CHAPTER EIGHT

Malthus the Transatlantic Celebrity

Celebrity and the Malthusian Moment

In 1978, a book called *The 100* emerged, a printed version of a parlor game many of us must have played over the years ranking the most important people of all time. Malthus came in at number 80, sandwiched between Niccolo Machiavelli and John F. Kennedy, well above both Lenin and Mao. Not bad for the curate from Okewood! The summary of Malthus's achievements in the book was unremarkable, but the inclusion of Malthus raises the questions this chapter will address. *The 100* was an American publication, which immediately opens up new questions for our narrative about when, precisely, Malthus came to have an impact on that side of the Atlantic, our story to date having been predominantly British and to a lesser extent European. And, more important than this question of geography, how had Malthus come to be seen as such an important figure in the postwar decades?[1]

Was Malthus really as significant to the culture of the decades after the conclusion of World War II as *The 100* suggested? Undoubtedly, there were massive global increases in population and resource use going on that could raise the Malthusian specter; there was "something new under the sun" in the twentieth century's use of the global environment, and that was particularly true from 1950 on, the rate of population growth after that time being 10,000 times that experienced under hunter-gatherer social systems and 50–100 times that achieved by the development of settled agriculture. The result of this was that the twentieth century used more energy than all of human history up to 1900 combined.

Furthermore, not only were unprecedented numbers using unprecedented quantities of resources, but also there was an unprecedented drive to collect and ability to process data about such global facts. With national governments, the United Nations and other international organizations collecting massive data sets and digesting their meaning through reports and policy documents, scholars, writers, and politicians had an unmatched ability to track the interactions between population and resource usage that defined the Malthusian territory. And as one makes a preliminary reconnoiter of the intellectual culture of the decades in question, it is remarkable how many Malthusian themes emerge. We can take a brief tour of the evidence to support this claim before turning to the more precise question of how Malthus himself (rather than a broader culture of Malthusianism) was configured in the era circa 1945–1990.[2]

First, newspapers and other public digests were both hungry for information about, and eager to produce stories that addressed, Malthusian questions concerning the balance between population and resources. The *Times* of London, for example, ran a story on the bicentenary of Malthus's birth depicting him, as the headline had it, as "a realist proved right," while on the eve of the Rome population conference of the United Nations in 1974 the same paper argued that "the situation envisaged by Malthus, where runaway population expansion is held in check only by famine, disease and war, has already come to pass in Bangladesh." Equally, the *Times* could also report on Lord Rothschild's Godwinian "prospect of a brave new world" that would circumvent Malthus in 1975 and assert on the tenth anniversary of Mauritian independence that the island's recent demographic history was "Malthus refuted." Such stories tended to feed in turn on the aforementioned burgeoning of demographic data made available by research groups such as the Population Reference Bureau, whose news releases on the topic mushroomed from 231 per annum in 1952 to nearly 6,000 per annum a decade later. Clearly, any putative "population explosion" was at least matched in intensity by closely interrelated "information" and "news" explosions.[3]

The easy availability of data about population and resource matters also helped to spark imaginative literature addressing Malthusian themes. The title essay in V. S. Naipaul's *The Overcrowded Barracoon* (1972), for example, took a less rosy view of life on Mauritius from that of the *Times*, suggestively formulating that "it was on Mauritius that the dodo forgot how to fly, because it had no enemies: the island, 720 square miles, was once uninhabited. Now, with more than a thousand people to the square mile, the island is overpopulated." Less based on reportage and far more dark were the musings of Anthony Burgess in *The Wanting Seed* (1962), his companion piece to *A Clockwork Orange* (also 1962), addressing, as Burgess noted in a 1983 foreword, "a phenomenon I had been well aware of while living in the East—the population explosion and the shrinking of the world's food supply." The novel imagined a future in which "England . . . suffered from the pullulation of India," its central government sending young men to fight a war in Ireland (topically enough for the 1960s) from which none were ever allowed to return because, unbeknown to themselves, they were fighting their own countrymen in a bid to remove excess population by a thoroughly Malthusian positive check of warfare. *A Clockwork Orange* was, of course, by far the more successful part of Burgess's dystopian diptych, in large part thanks to Stanley Kubrick's 1972 film version, but perhaps Kubrick's greatest success, *2001: A Space Odyssey* (1968), was itself set in a world where, as the narrator put it, "by the year 2001, overpopulation has replaced the problem of starvation." If Kubrick jointly wrote *2001* with one of the doyens of science fiction writing, Arthur C. Clarke, it expressed views strongly held by Clarke's great rival for that crown, Isaac Asimov. Asimov eschewed writing about futuristic scenarios of overpopulation in his science fiction, but in his nonfiction writing, he consistently suggested that we faced apocalypse: "my island of comfort is but a quiet bubble in a torrent that is heaving its way downhill to utter catastrophe. . . . The matter can be expressed in a single word: Population."[4]

If references to popular culture suggest that Malthusian concerns were purely held by the general public, this would be highly misleading; in fact, and on the contrary, Malthus remained at the heart of scholarly debates in the postwar era as well. Naipaul's reportage about Mauritius as an "overcrowded barracoon," for example, closely followed the depiction of that nation fleshed out by the distinguished economist James Meade. Meade would win the Nobel Prize for economics in 1977, but in 1966, as president of the Royal Economic Society, he marked the bicentenary of Malthus's birth by reaffirming his significance as "possibly the most important political-social-economic development in the world today is the quite unprecedented explosion of population," a contention he then analyzed with respect to Mauritius. Other Nobel laureates in economics would continue to debate Malthus down the decades. Thus 1998's winner, Amartya Sen, took important inspiration from Malthus's *Investigation of the Cause of the Present High Price of Provisions* (1800) as he built his "entitlement approach" to famines, an approach that has led him to strongly attack Malthus's work as he has built his ideas of freedom leading to development. Following a similar trajectory, 1992's laureate, Gary Becker, has framed his "family economics" as working in a field where "aside from the Malthusian theory of population change, economists hardly noticed the family prior to the 1950s." Becker goes on to adjust Malthus's ideas, suggesting that expenditure on families in advanced societies can go up even as family size goes down "because children's education and other human capital increase." As such, Becker argues a "Malthusian theory can explain changes in human populations during much of recorded history" but not in the present, hence his argument in a 1994 *Business Week* essay, "Let's Diffuse [sic] the Population Bomb—with Free Markets," that state-directed Malthusian population policies are bound to misfire, Further back in time, both the joint winners at Stockholm in 1974, Gunnar Myrdal and Friedrich Hayek, had engaged with Malthus despite their political antipathies. Myrdal began his career in the context of depopulation fears in 1930s Sweden, being the first to design the pronatalist state spending incentives that Beveridge then brought to Britain, but in the postwar era his attention switched to the developing world and his views on population dynamics changed. This is witnessed by Myrdal's mammoth project with the 20th Century Fund, *Asian Drama,* which discussed Malthus in concluding that "the population explosion is the most important social change that has taken place in South Asia in the post-war era." By contrast, Hayek came to admire the demographic work of the anti-Malthusian Julian Simon and to argue toward the end of his life that market demand, not governments, should determine population size: "Malthus's theory made a reasonable first approach . . . but modern conditions make it irrelevant."[5]

The scholarly reception of and engagement with Malthus and Malthusian themes of overpopulation and resource depletion was by no means concentrated in economics alone. The celebrated novelist, academic, and public commentator C. P. Snow, for example, noted in a 1968 lecture that his famous depiction of a separation of the "two cultures," the sciences and the arts, had suffered "a curious and culpable omission" in its failure to address "the growth of population." The lecture, *The State of Siege,* written amid the burst of student protests around the globe, rectified that omission in plotting a "food-population collision" that should give "young people . . . a cause . . . Peace, food. No more people than the earth can take. That is the cause." A decade earlier, Bertrand Russell, a Bloomsburyite looking at the world as it entered the 1960s, likewise saw "two antithetical dangers," those of the H-bomb and of the population bomb, arguing that, though antithetical, they were connected: "nothing is more likely to lead to an H-bomb war than the threat of universal destitution through over-population." In the same year that Russell's words were published, a philosopher whom he saw as a phony, the existentialist

Jean-Paul Sartre, gave an interview in *Le Monde* arguing that "hunger is the only thing, period." And it is remarkable just how widespread was the agreement on the significance of this issue, from the anthropologist Laurens Van Der Post, through writers such as André Maurois to the pioneering ecologist H. T. Odum and the celebrated biologist E. O. Wilson, whose jointly authored *Theory of Island Biogeography* was built on Malthusian foundations. Historians likewise returned to Malthus at this time, the advent of modern, quantitative historical demography coming in the 1960s through the pioneering work of Peter Laslett and Tony Wrigley on which we drew so extensively for our portraiture in Chapter 1. Even those who wanted to unpick the critical consensus around Malthusianism, of course, engendered its fame by the energies they expended on its analysis, notable here being the Marxist unravelings of Malthusian ideology by the historian E. P. Thompson and the geographer David Harvey and the genealogical unpicking of Malthusianism contained in the work of Michel Foucault.[6]

The broad platform of interest in Malthusian issues in the postwar era also expressed itself in a desire to actually read Malthus's words rather than merely using his name. The *Essay* had always remained available to an English-language audience, notably via regular reprinting of the Everyman edition of Malthus's 1803 version. Responding to the wide circulation of Malthus's name in the 1950s, the Everyman edition was furnished with a new introduction in 1958, albeit one that still suggested Malthus had eleven children rather than the actual three. A year later, the University of Michigan Press produced an edition of the first, 1798, edition of the *Essay*, introduced by the economist Kenneth Boulding, who was one of the first to coin the soon-fashionable term "Spaceship Earth." The visibility of Malthus in public debate finally encouraged both of the great transatlantic producers of "classics" for the general public to include Malthus's 1798 *Essay* in their rosters, Penguin producing a U.K. edition in 1970 under the editorship of the philosopher Antony Flew, while W. W. Norton entrusted the same task to the literary scholar Philip Appleman. In just over a decade, then, accessing a reliable edition of Malthus's *Essay* became radically easier for scholars and general readers alike.[7]

And yet all of this is merely to *evidence* Malthus's celebrity in the postwar age and to confirm the representativeness of the assessment contained in *The 100*; it does not in any way *explain* it. Why was there this massive explosion of interest in Malthus and Malthusianism? Where it is easy to understand how, at the peak of Malthus's public career in the 1830s, there was the "Malthus moment" identified in Chapter 5, why did the 1950s to the 1970s see a second "Malthusian moment" in a society so different from that about which he wrote? To start to answer these questions, we need to look to the set of debates, mainly American, that took off in the immediate aftermath of World War II as the (atomic) dust settled. A set of ecologists, biologists, food scientists, and like-minded scholars started to raise a public alarm about nothing less than the future sustainability of life on the globe, and this set in motion a flurry of interest—public and political, literal and literary—that peaked in the late 1960s and early 1970s, and that, throughout the period, was also vehemently contested by those who saw in all this a scam, a mere bogeyman being paraded to scare the ignorant. It was in this maelstrom that Malthus became a household name, and it is to this maelstrom that this chapter is devoted.[8]

Detecting a Malthusian Bomb aboard Spaceship Earth, 1945–1965

As we saw earlier, Malthus was intensely interested in demographic data coming back from the fledgling United States of America and used it to construct the "limit case" of population doubling rates in the *Essay*. And yet while there was a fairly rapid response to Malthus on the other side of the Atlantic, it was in the main negative in the decades of his lifetime, in good part because the population pressures of which he spoke made no sense in an extensive, sparsely populated nation. By the mid-nineteenth century, however, Malthus was making his impact on debates about demography and the descent into Civil War. Census data was used to speculate about how an independent South might be swamped by a black population within decades, such scare tactics being freely traded by both sides. Sustained engagement with Malthus's ideas, however, came in the fin de siècle period: as public debate started to center around the "closing of the frontier" and what that meant for American identity in the wake of Frederick Jackson Turner's frontier hypothesis, and as Theodore Roosevelt and others began to talk of the need for conservation, so American discourse began to revolve around population reaching limits in terms of space and resources. This national fear was soon projected onto the international stage as an explanation of the events of the Great War. Three names stand out for forging this argument in the interwar years and thereby presaging the postwar debates that would ensure Malthus's age of transatlantic celebrity. First, the influential Johns Hopkins biologist Raymond Pearl was tireless in trying to turn around what he saw as the "fashion somewhat to deride Malthus," arguing instead that "Malthus reasoned about the future course of population with a logic which was in most respects faultless." Pearl saw human populations as exhibiting the same dynamics he witnessed as a biologist and was in no doubt that World War I was, as we have already seen Keynes argue from the economic perspective, a consequence of Malthusian overpopulation. The Harvard chemist and plant scientist Edward East offered the same diagnosis of the war in his 1925 study *Mankind at the Crossroads*. East had read Malthus during the war, and opened his study praising Malthus for "demonstrating statistically and maintaining against all comers" the basic truth "concerning the concrete evils arising from population increase." But East's real concern was forward-looking: "if world saturation of population, which approaches speedily, is not prevented, in its train will come more wars, more famine, more disease." Finally, Warren Thompson was a pioneering demographer whose first book in 1919 was entitled *Population: A Study in Malthusianism*, but whose major impact came in a 1929 text, *Danger Spots in World Population*, which identified geopolitical "hot spots" where conflict looked likely thanks to population pressures. Suitably updated, *Danger Spots* reemerged in the postwar period as *Population and Peace in the Pacific* (1946) and then as *Population and Progress in the Far East* (1959), each iteration bolting Malthusian fears about population onto new geopolitical circumstances and explicitly tying all of this back to Malthus himself. The structure of argumentation that Thompson forged has been dubbed "population-national security theory": as we shall see, this "theory," or rather, this loose and flexible constellation of linkages, was immensely influential with policy makers and ensured that Malthus was talked of in the corridors of power in ways not dreamed of since the Malthus moment identified at the beginning of Chapter 6.[9] Further, suitably updated, this theory and its Malthusian moorings are still very much with us today.

The efforts of Pearl, East, and Thompson may have presaged, but they did not prepare anyone for the way in which "Malthusian worries . . . exploded in the United States after World War II." *Time* magazine wrote in perplexity in 1948 about the way in which "the ghost of a gloomy British clergyman, Thomas Robert Malthus, was on the rampage" while the *Economist* ran a piece in the same year entitled "Malthus Goes West." Four years later, the *New York Times* agreed about the "revival of the Malthusian doctrine" but went beyond *Time* by adding a cause—or rather, two named causes—for the otherwise inexplicable phenomenon: "we owe this revival to Fairfield Osborn ('Our Plundered Planet') and to William Vogt ('Road to Survival') who have been followed by economists, public health officials and governments with predictions of misery."[10]

William Vogt came from a background in ecology. During the war, Vogt's interests turned to mankind's impact on the environment, and this led to his publication in 1948 of *The Road to Survival*, a tract about population and resources that was translated into nine languages and was so popular as to be serialized for Americans in *Reader's Digest*. Vogt's core concern was that mankind's ability to manipulate nature had increased dramatically without a matching awareness of the biotic limitations that nature presented, limits that could lead to an apocalyptic outcome. He noted "a few rare individuals" who had seen the problems that industrialization would pose, naming Franklin and Jefferson, but singling out Malthus as the most insightful of the Enlightened trio. He added, however, that "not even Malthus foresaw that in the core of increasing 'production' there was hidden the worm Ouroboros, the worm that would finally consume the earth." The 1949 English edition added to this genealogy, suggesting that the British "more than any other people of modern times have developed a world-wide understanding." The roll call of British luminaries of globalism was initiated for Vogt by Malthus and went on to include Darwin and Galton as well as John Boyd Orr, all of whom engaged with Malthus's legacy. And yet for all this intellectual foresight, Vogt depicted Britain as the paradigm of the societal collapse impending from the reckless expansion of population regardless of resources. Britain's population was now so large that it "cannot possibly produce enough food at home to support what we consider a decent standard of living." The predicted outcome was one of the many arresting images that projected *The Road to Survival* into the public consciousness of the era: "we may well see famine once more stalking the streets of London. And hand in hand with famine will walk the shade of that clear-sighted English clergyman, Thomas Robert Malthus." Vogt's book made an impact not just due to its gloomy predictions, but also because it spoke to the emergent political context of the Cold War. Vogt deployed an image that was highly popular throughout these decades in suggesting that with population growth, "man's destructive methods of exploitation mushroom like the atomic cloud over Hiroshima." In this context, Vogt depicted the state socialisms of China and the Soviet Union as especially problematic given their Marxist hostility to Malthusian reasoning and argued that democracy was essential to defusing the population bomb as it was "better than any other system of government that now exists, [in that] it can bring to *all* its people the realisation that their lives and their civilization are profoundly shaped by their environment." In an anticipation of the language of "Spaceship Earth" that would become popular in the 1960s, Vogt concluded by suggesting that only democracy could make people realize that "we all form an earth company" whose road to survival demanded a consensual respect for biotic limits and an accordant control of population growth.[11]

In the same year, 1948, Fairfield Osborn produced a parallel tract, *Our Plundered Planet,* that achieved at least equal success, being translated into thirteen languages. Osborn had a background in biology and was by this time president of the New York Zoological Society. He shared many themes with Vogt, depicting World War II as in fact two wars, one being military, the other, "man's conflict with nature." And, varying the theme that we have already seen in both Vogt and Bertrand Russell, he opined gloomily that "these are momentous days and many things can happen to check population growth, even including the devastating use of atomic bombs." As this use of the unavoidably Malthusian term "checks" might imply, especially when coupled to the declaration that population pressure is "perhaps the greatest problem facing humanity today," Osborn was an admirer of the insights of Malthus. While Malthus—the "gloomy doctor," as Osborn called him—had not foreseen how global trade and transport could circumvent resource imbalances, his basic insight remained valid: "there is a discernible rhythm between the accelerated tempo of trade and the accelerated tempo of human reproduction. Shades of Dr. Malthus! He was not so far wrong."[12]

The path Vogt and Osborn first laid in U.S. thought was soon a well-trodden one. A few examples will have to suffice to give a flavor of this. The Hugh Moore Foundation issued a pamphlet in 1954 called *The Population Bomb,* a title Paul Ehrlich (or rather his publisher, Ian Ballantyne) would immortalize fifteen years later, but this first "bomb" did well enough, more than 1 million copies having been distributed in eleven editions within a decade. A year later the Harvard botanist Karl Sax published another arrestingly titled tract about population, *Standing Room Only,* which stated bluntly that "the Malthusian laws of population growth are as valid today as when they were formulated." Sax was as alert to the political consequences of accepting Malthus in the Cold War era as Vogt, attacking both the Catholic Church and communists for denigrating Malthusian insights. One of the few contributions not to come from someone trained in biology or ecology came from the pen of the literary scholar Philip Appleman. As we have already noted, Appleman would go on to use his literary skills to edit Malthus's *Essay* for Norton a decade later, but in 1965 he produced a book about global population problems, *The Silent Explosion* (1965). The book had a short endorsement from Julian Huxley, and in it Appleman explained that his interest in the issue of global population had been raised while working for the International

School of America, especially by experiencing the slums of India. After an epigraph from Keats, *Silent Explosion* began in a tone both elegiac and apocalyptic: "at Sealdah Station, Calcutta, misery radiates outwards. . . . In a few years, the children who survive these conditions will stop playing and become adults; that is, they will grow taller and thinner and stand in the streets like ragged skeletons, barefoot, hollow-eyed, blinking their apathetic stares out of gray, dusty faces." For Appleman, the message to take away from this dystopian epiphany was an acceptance of Malthus as the "first [who] brought attention to the now familiar predicament: population tends to increase faster than the means of subsistence."[13]

Apocalyptic ruminations tend to have a limited shelf life, and it is easy for us, a half century later, to see in all this anything-but "silent" explosion of Malthusian concern something more akin to science-fiction-driven hysteria than sober reality. At the time, however, the concerns and predictions of Vogt, Osborn et al. were taken in good earnest. Aldous Huxley, for one, was convinced that the population problem had traversed the divide between science fiction and fact as he returned a quarter century later to the concerns he had first aired in *Brave New World* (1932). *Brave New World Revisited* (1959) is a far more sober work, which aimed to compare the futuristic fantasies he penned in the 1930s with the world as Huxley saw it from his retreat in California. And in this context, where *Brave New World* had imagined a world where contraception—Malthusian Belts—led to an optimal and controlled population, Huxley now saw that "in the real contemporary world, the population problem has not been solved. On the contrary, it is becoming graver." All other global problems were played out against this "grim biological background" in the "Age of Overpopulation." And like Osborn, whose *Our Plundered Planet* he reviewed enthusiastically, Huxley saw the politics to this situation, suggesting a sequence with "overpopulation leading through unrest to [communist] dictatorship." More succinctly, and as he put it in a *New Yorker* interview in 1957, the Cold War world was "Malthus's nightmare come true." In this belief, Aldous was united with his brother Julian, who took on the role of secretary general to UNESCO in the immediate postwar period. In this position, Julian Huxley wrote a "philosophy" for the group in 1945 keyed around Darwin and population control as leading to peace "through the reduction of tensions due to overpopulation and to damage to man's environment." Huxley's time at the UN saw him travel the globe, and his autobiography, *Memories* (1973), shows him consistently viewing the developing world in Malthusian terms, with the Egypt of 1948 haunted by "the spectre of overpopulation," Haiti likewise, and, above all, India exhibiting "the general unwantedness of the swarming population." It was in this context that Huxley wrote a number of essays in the 1960s addressing population questions and affirming the centrality of Malthus's ideas: "Malthus thus marks the beginning of the modern era in demography. . . . These ideas have very important implications at the present moment." Julian Huxley was the first to take the climate of Malthusian fear and translate it into the arena of global governance concerns via UNESCO. His tenure at UNESCO would be short-lived, but the process of conjoining policy and population that he began would be central to national and international governance in the decades that followed. It would be the United States as a global superpower who would take this nexus farthest.[14]

In 1949, Harry S. Truman announced the vision for his presidency in the form of a "four point plan." Central to the plan was the idea that the spread of global communism should be halted by technology transfers from the United States. Lurking behind this was the sequence that we have seen Aldous Huxley envisaging, from overpopulation to undernourishment, from undernourishment to unrest, and from unrest to communism. To nip such a trajectory in the bud, U.S. administrations from Truman to Carter targeted the use of food aid and the development and dissemination of high-yielding species to achieve a "green revolution." This "supply side" approach to the problem was, from the late 1950s, tied with a "demand side" solution seeking to control population growth by linking aid packages to the adoption of birth control programs. And on both sides of this Cold War "blueprint for hungry nations," Malthus was an oft-cited inspiration. On the demand side, this becomes most apparent from the speech that Norman Borlaug gave in 1970 when accepting the Nobel Prize for Peace. Borlaug had been at the heart of the "Green Revolution," working on the Mexican Agriculture Program of the Rockefeller Foundation from 1943, developing high-yielding wheat species that were soon to be carried to Asia as the seeds (literally) of a solution to the population problem. And yet from the perspective of old age, Borlaug could frame his "Malthus-busting" achievements in wholly Malthusian terms. He argued that from the Neolithic to the present, civilization had been a struggle between "two opposing forces, the scientific power of food production and the biologic power of human reproduction." If the supply-side solutions of the Green Revolution had bolstered the forces of production, this provided only a "breathing space" of thirty years at most, before such advances were swallowed by the power of reproduction, "the menace of the population monster." It was this menace that had necessitated a "demand side" approach as well. Key here was the so-called "Draper Report," named after William H. Draper, who chaired a committee on U.S. aid programs in 1958–1959. The committee report, which has been dubbed "the Magna Carta of U.S. population policy," was suggestively titled *The Population Explosion* and argued that global economic aid was futile unless tied to binding demands for developing nations to adopt birth control. It was in the mid-1960s, during the presidency of Lyndon Baines Johnson, that this issue reached a denouement: in his 1965 State of the Union address, Johnson spoke of "the explosion in world population and the growing scarcity in world resources" as the key issue facing the world and said that "less than five dollars invested in population control is worth a hundred dollars invested in economic growth." And yet Johnson was still seen as too slow to accept Malthusian logic, the *New York Times* running an article the following year, "Johnson vs. Malthus," urging him to accept that economic development could never occur "in a world where the Malthusian specter, more terrible than Malthus ever conceived, is so near to being a reality."[15]

This Malthusian moment in development policy came to a head around fears that India was plunging into a nightmarish famine due to rampant overbreeding. India had long been at the heart of U.S. fears as a massive but democratic nation whose descent into communism would be a disaster of epic proportions in the Cold War. Truman had initiated large-scale wheat transfers to India in 1951 to prevent Indians becoming "pawns of the Kremlin," and by the mid-1950s more than $6 billion of wheat was being transported to the subcontinent every year. From the perspective of Washington, this seemed fatally insufficient in 1966–1967, President Johnson declaring the situation to be a thoroughly Malthusian "race between food supplies and population." On the ground, however, the Indian government saw matters very differently, declaring that they were experiencing scarcities but no conditions of absolute starvation. If, as the historian Nick Cullather has suggested, the Indian "famine" of 1966–1967 is more accurately seen as the "imagineering" of "the green revolution legend" through an invented "brush with . . . [India's] Malthusian limit," not a decade earlier the world failed to notice perhaps the greatest single case of famine in human history, a very real "anti-Malthusian brush" spawned by and in communist China. India, as we have seen, had long since become the paradigm of Malthusian overpopulation for individuals such as Appleman and Huxley, but this, of course, was because they could easily visit the subcontinent. It is only in recent years that the full story of the famine caused by Mao's policies in China has been revealed to the rest of the world. Launching the Great Leap Forward in the late 1950s, Mao declared "there is a new war: we should open fire on nature." As a result, the Chinese state embarked on large-scale deforestation and manipulation of water courses. One element of the policy was an orthodox Marxist eschewal of the "population problem" as a failure of capitalism, not a natural inevitability: as Mao put it in 1949, the idea that "food cannot keep up with increases in population" was "the absurd argument of bourgeois Western economists like Malthus." The communist state of China would see large-scale population growth, that population then achieving gargantuan environmental modifications to sustain itself in the face of capitalist hostility. As a popular slogan of the time had it, *Ren Duo Liliang Da* (with many people, strength is great). This view was opposed by one of China's most distinguished academics, Ma Yinchu, president of Beijing University, who published his *New Demography* in 1957. Basing his argument on the 1953 census, Ma Yinchu argued that rapid population growth was negating economic development and therefore urged the state to encourage family limitation methods and delayed marriage. By 1960, Ma Yinchu was forced to resign in the wake of a campaign that had seen him denounced as a Malthusian. As well as thousands of officially sanctioned posters declaring Ma Yinchu a Malthusian being spread across the Beijing University campus in 1958, there was much play with his name, suggesting "as for Ma Yinchu's *New Demography*, does it really belong to the Ma family of Marx or to the Ma family of Malthus [?]." While Ma was banished into rural exile, Mao's "war with nature" continued, but as Frank Dikotter's chilling rendering of accounts shows, "Mao lost his war against nature. The campaign backfired by breaking the delicate balance between humans and the environment, decimating human life as a result." While we will never know what the adoption of Ma Yinchu's ideas might have done to change this, nor precisely how many died in Mao's Great Leap Forward, we can, Dikotter says, "conservatively put the number of premature deaths at a minimum of 45 million for the great famine of 1958–62." For twenty years after World War II, politicians and ecologists, writers and philosophers, spoke of and worked to avoid a population explosion, but the only time the bomb really went off in that era, no one felt the fallout beyond China's boundaries.[16]

Detonating the Population Bomb: The New Malthus Goes Viral, 1965–1980

The late 1960s and early 1970s were the great age of the "new" Malthusianism, which must be distinguished from both the intense debates about Malthus in his own age and those that swirled around the phrase "Malthusian" as a synonym for "birth control" in the late nineteenth century.

The new Malthusianism was tied closely to ecology, interacting in a tense and often hostile fashion with the two disciplines with which Malthus's work had previously been most closely connected, namely demography and economics. It also attracted political and public attention to an unprecedented extent. This was an age when some 20 million people in the United States participated in Earth Day on April 22, 1970, protesting and partying to raise awareness about the fragility of the global environment, something that the iconic Apollo 8 "Earthrise" image poignantly symbolized. A key part of maintaining "Spaceship Earth," it was suggested, was population control: "Stop at Two" was the slogan on balloons floating through the skies of great American cities on that day. There was serious discussion among scholars and in the press about the practicality of putting sterilizing agents in the water supply to control population growth, and the national newspapers were galvanized by the comments of one Stephanie Mills at her graduation from Mills College, California, in 1969. Mills, a concerned twenty-one-year-old, caught the mood of the youth of the nation, suggesting that "we are breeding ourselves out of existence." She envisaged that her lifetime would see "widespread famines and possible global plagues" and posed the question Burgess had in his *Wanting Seed:* "Will I be forced to become a cannibal?" Mills recognized that all this "was foreseen nearly two centuries ago" by Malthus.[17]

Mills's apocalyptic speech was not, however, inspired by Malthus so much as a far more proximate cause, the California-based biologist and ecologist Paul Ehrlich. Mills vowed not to have children; Ehrlich and his wife and coauthor, Anne, had one child before he had a vasectomy. Unlike Malthus, a father of three, there would be no charges of hypocrisy for the new Malthusians. If anyone was the doomsaying doyen of the new Malthusianism, it was Ehrlich. Ehrlich was influenced by the first phase of the postwar revival of Malthus, acknowledging the impact of Vogt and Osborn on his ideas as a biology graduate student in the 1950s, and would be the single-most important catalyst for the second peak phase when Malthusianism "went viral." Ehrlich's fame was squarely grounded in his 1968 work *The Population Bomb,* "the most famous population treatise since Malthus," a book that has sold some 3 million copies and that catapulted its author onto the public stage via many television appearances. *The Population Bomb* has been vilified by its critics, being given an honorable mention in the *Human Events'* list of the "Ten Most Harmful Books of the Nineteenth and Twentieth Century." The main reason for *The Population Bomb*'s notoriety is undoubtedly its apocalyptic tone, which Mills and so many other "baby boomers" picked up on in giving Ehrlich "rock star appeal" by the time of Earth Day. It opened with an arresting claim—"the battle to feed all of humanity is over"—before a famous set piece in the mold of Burgess, Appleman, and Huxley about Indian overpopulation in Delhi: "people eating, people washing, people sleeping.... People defecating and urinating.... People, people, people, people." Ehrlich's conclusion struck a chord with the age: "we must all learn to identify with the plight of our less fortunate fellows on Spaceship Earth if we are to help both them and ourselves to survive." And yet for all that, Ehrlich was and remains happy to be labeled a "neo-Malthusian," *The Population Bomb* never in fact mentioned Malthus, not once in its two hundred pages. Ehrlich ascribes this lacuna to the constraints of time, the book being written in great haste, to constraints of space, and to the fact that he had assimilated Malthus's ideas and did not need to cite them directly. Ehrlich would in later works mention Malthus directly, notably in his response to Earth Day, *How to Be a Survivor* (1971), which attacked state socialism for ignoring Malthus's insights and in his twentieth-anniversary reappraisal of *The Population Bomb*, *The Population Explosion* (1990), which again opened in arresting fashion, suggesting that in 1968 "the fuse was burning, now the population bomb has detonated." As a way out of the problem, Ehrlich recognized the centrality of economics by 1990 (although he had, as we shall see, several spats with economists en route) and here credited Malthus as the "economist ... who first recognized the key role played in human affairs by population growth."[18]

What we might call the "paradox" of Ehrlich's "new Malthusianism," that he was labeled a Malthusian but rarely directly discussed Malthus, also applies to a number of the other key actors in the era such as Ehrlich's great rival as a celebrity ecologist, Barry Commoner, and the founders of ecological economics, Kenneth Boulding and Herman Daly. Perhaps the most influential single book other than Ehrlich's in the population-resource scenario genre was the so-called Club of Rome's computer-generated projection, published in 1972 as *The Limits to Growth*, which likewise exhibits Malthusianism with only the smallest hint of Malthus himself. The book is peppered with graphs, all of which show declining resource stocks and increasing population and consumption demands, the only question being when the two sets of curves would cross fatally, and whether, as Ehrlich believed, that date had passed some time previously. *The Limits to Growth* has been called "Malthus as ghost in the machine," but in fact it mentions him only once in a concluding litany of those who had seen the need for a "nongrowing state for human society."[19]

Thus far the new Malthusianism, then, appears to truly make of Malthus a ghost in the machine—a nonpresent presence. And yet there were two other major contributors to the ecological debates of the age who directly engaged with Malthus and saw him as a great progenitor of their arguments, Georg Borgstrom and Garrett Hardin. Borgstrom was a Swedish biologist with a particular interest in plant breeding who, unlike Norman Borlaug, was led in a pessimistic direction, seeing it as impossible for food production to keep pace with population growth. It was this pessimism that led to him being cast in classical terms as the "Swedish Cassandra" or, in more gothic vein, as the "Gothenburg Alarm Clock" for his doomsaying. While based in Sweden, Borgstrom deliberately did not discuss Malthus, fearing his scientific credibility would be undercut by being associated with that name, but by the 1960s, when based in the United States, Borgstrom became far more willing to create a direct lineage to Malthus. As part of this, Borgstrom and his wife translated Malthus's *Essay* into their native Swedish in 1969, another of those moments of making Malthus's words directly available in this era that we have already traced for the Anglophone tradition, but his major engagement with Malthus came in two highly successful books, *The Hungry Planet* (1965) and its companion volume, *Too Many* (1969). *The Hungry Planet* is all but forgotten today, but it was a huge success in its own age, being translated into six languages, and it has a fair claim to have more direct conceptual impact on modern debates about climate, population, and resources than any of the work of Ehrlich et al. Borgstrom recognized that Malthus has been "ridiculed" but argued that he was in fact right to suggest that population can double every twenty-five years for the simple reason that certain developing countries were exhibiting precisely that demographic regime. The reason no one had recognized Malthus's insights was that developed countries had been able to exploit resources around the globe, not simply those on their own lands: here Borgstrom developed the ideas of "ghost acreage" and "population equivalents," which, suitably updated, still inform our ideas about "carbon footprints" in the present day. The ghost acreage was the actual number of acres needed to feed a population, taking into account all their resource usage including that beyond the boundaries of their own nation, while population equivalents added to the human population of a nation the animals it relied on for food to give a full ecological population. It was in this context that, as Borgstrom put it in *Too Many*, "the correctness of the basic assertion of Malthus becomes most evident." If we lived on "Spaceship Earth," as Borgstrom accepted in an image that was quickly becoming hackneyed, the rapid expansion of global population and the still more rapid expansion of population equivalents left the Gothenburg Alarm Clock ready to toll its final, apocalyptic chime: "we have gone far beyond the feeding resources of our globe. We need to declare the Great War for Human Survival—but it is getting late. Time is running out on us. It is five minutes to twelve."[20]

Even more conceptually wedded to Malthus was the Californian biologist Garrett Hardin. In 1964, he published a collection of essays about population and birth control that gave Malthus center stage, but Hardin was really shot to fame (or, more accurately, propelled to infamy) by an article he published in *Science* in 1968, "The Tragedy of the Commons." The tragedy of the title was the inevitable fate of global population–resource crisis, which current ways of cognitizing the environment and the family would engender. As in a Greek tragedy, the Fates had set humanity on a course to doom. For, if families were allowed to breed without restriction, both individually and collectively, and if they did not have to ensure that they had the means of survival, the state and the global food-aid community doing this instead, people would breed excessively. And if the environmental resources people had to use to feed this population were not given any value by market processes, they would be depleted, destroyed, and wantonly polluted until our biotic life-support systems collapsed. In all this, Hardin recognized Malthus as his precursor, both in seeing that population growth would easily outpace resources, and in arguing that state relief created the problem rather than alleviating it. Hardin was not the Cassandra of Santa Barbara, however, because he offered a way to avoid this tragedy, a way of defying the Fates: remove the freedom to breed, mutually agree upon mutual coercion. Hardin courted the opprobrium of the liberal intelligentsia by this move, paralleling the anger Malthus had unwittingly sparked by his Poor Law proposals and his "nature's mighty feast" image. Hardin succeeded in stirring a hornet's nest and spent much of his career restating the same points. For our purposes, the most important of these restatements was what he described as a book-length attempt to explain the argument of the *Science* paper, *Exploring New Ethics for Survival: The Voyage of the Spaceship Beagle* (1972). *Spaceship Beagle* was a summation of so many of the currents of the new Malthusianism, being an ecological sci-fi novella playing with the image of "Spaceship Earth" and published for a general audience by Penguin Books. In Hardin's future, a group of hardy souls had boarded the titular spaceship looking for new worlds for a burgeoning human population to inhabit. On earth, societies had recklessly ignored biotic limits to growth and the need for coercive population control, preferring a technological quick fix and stringent silencing of ecologists with their inconvenient truths, the first to go being Paul Ehrlich himself, "tarred and feathered by the Youth for American Freedom . . . [and] thrown ignominiously into the Fort Mudge Memorial Dump." The quest for new planets proving hopeless—as Hardin had, in more serious mood, shown in a paper called "Interstellar Migration and the Population Problem" (1959)—at the end of the novella, Spaceship Beagle returns to earth some five thousand years later. While circling their ancestral home, the astronauts speculate as to whether nuclear destruction has wiped people from the planet, or whether feral remnants of humankind will remain, like Swift's Houhnynyms looking at humans. Amid this debate, one pipes up that "what was most lacking on earth all along was simple courage to face the truth." In Freudian vein, such truths were repressed, the supreme example being "from the man who began it all, Thomas Robert Malthus," who had cut his "nature's mighty feast" passage after 1803 despite the truth it encapsulated. For Hardin, then, and for many of his generation, the question of future options for mankind boiled down to a simple binary: apocalypse now or Malthus.[21]

Forty years on, it is all too easy to see Hardin's *Spaceship Beagle* as laughably crass, as akin to an especially clunky episode of *Star Wars* penned by a biology professor. But we would be wrong to project this onto the era at which it was targeted, because it is clear that politicians took the new Malthusianism very seriously indeed. A good starting point is another product of the "future shock" genre, William and Paul Paddock's *Famine 1975!* (1967), which opened with powerful images of cities in the grip of yellow fever, predicting that what had happened to U.S. cities in the nineteenth century would be visited upon the Madrases and Recifes of this world in the ensuing decade due to excessive population growth. In response, and accepting what they saw as Malthus's core insights, the Paddocks advocated a policy of "food triage": the United States should focus its energies on food aid for countries where the population growth rate could be quelled and leave others to their fate as beyond salvation. Unlike Hardin, Ehrlich et al., however, the Paddock brothers were not academic ecologists; they had worked in plant science and policy and in international diplomacy respectively. The "Malthusian imaginings" of *Famine 1975!* came directly from the corridors of power, the idea of food triage, indeed, having first been broached by the Draper Report of 1959. And these concerns were represented both at the highest levels of U.S. political life and in U.S. legislation of the era. The Wilderness Act of 1964, for example, was passed to "assure that an increasing population . . . does not occupy and modify all areas within the United States." In tandem with this, it was in the mid-1960s that legislation was brought in to control U.S. population growth, especially facilitating access to abortion and birth control as a federal right, this concern being fueled by the so-called Gruening Hearings of the U.S. Senate in 1965, whose multiple volumes of testimony were published under the title *Population Crisis*. As successive presidents, Lyndon Johnson and Richard Nixon both accepted, in the latter's words, that population growth was "one of the most serious challenges to human destiny in the last third of this century." Years later, Jimmy Carter declared after his defeat by Ronald Reagan in the election of 1980 that "dealing with limits" had been "the subliminal theme" of his presidency. And in the interim, further legislation addressing this theme had been passed, perhaps most importantly Nixon's 1969 Natural Environment Policy Act, which made it a responsibility of the federal government to "achieve a balance between population and resource use."[22]

All of this new Malthusian policy swirl is best seen in a short 1974 pamphlet, *Malthus and America,* issued by the Committee on Agriculture of the U.S. House of Representatives. In 1974–1975, the Paddocks' dire warnings in *Famine 1975!* seemed perilously close to the mark as the United States experienced exceptionally poor harvests and evidence of food shortages for the first time in living memory. And all of this, of course, in a context where the previous year had seen the OPEC oil crisis create other resource-related fears of geopolitical meltdown. *Malthus and America* was released at this moment when, in its words, "the world food supply-demand equation is perilously balanced" and "Americans were forced to cope with scarcities and found it none too pleasant." The pamphlet addressed, as a subtitle had it, "Who Is This Thomas Malthus and What Did He Say?," arguing that declining death rates rightly led to a "revival of concern about the ability of the world to feed its people" in the face of "the unrelenting geometry of human growth." But in the main the luminaries cited in the pamphlet were drawn from the more recent vintage of new Malthusians: ideas of food triage from the Paddocks were canvassed, as were Garrett Hardin's ideas about a global commons and that a limited world demanded a "lifeboat ethics" where the developed world drew up the ladders rather than seeing the ship of state sink under the demographic swell. *Malthus and America* was finely poised, raising the question of whether this was "an echo from the grave of Thomas Malthus or is it merely another cry of 'wolf'?" Clearly, however, U.S. presidents quite as much as Stephanie Mills at her college graduation worried and acted on the question *Malthus and America* posed in conclusion: "Will Americans discover too late that Thomas Malthus is a 200-year-old alarmist whose time has finally arrived."[23]

Defusing the Nonsense Explosion, 1945–1980

With the U.S. government taking Malthus seriously, with science fiction writers and college graduates in their droves talking about and reading Malthus, with predictions of imminent famine on the doorstep and biotic collapse across the seas, with the clock of demographic Armageddon about to strike, Malthus's inclusion in the hundred most important people in history was perhaps none too surprising. But Malthus's celebrity was also fueled by another group not mentioned to date to whom we must now turn: those who denied that we teetered on the brink of disaster. For every ecologist who saw population disaster, there was a demographer such as Frank Notestein wondering why zealots such as Hardin seemed to feel "it takes massive advertising to sell both soap and . . . ecological necessity." For every prediction of famine by 1975, there was a countervailing suggestion such as that made by John Maddox in 1972 that "the problems of the 1970s and 1980s will not be famine and starvation but, ironically, problems of how best to dispose of food surpluses." For every evocation of zero population growth, there was the response that, again in Maddox's words, this "seems like patronizing neo-colonialism to people elsewhere." And was this Ehrlich's population explosion or, as Ben Wattenberg replied in 1970, "the nonsense explosion"? There was, then, a strong vein of anti-Malthusian response in the postwar decades which, as we shall see, engaged with Malthus directly.[24]

If Vogt and Osborn foresaw impending Malthusian disaster in 1948, their opponents replied in quick time, the geographer Earl Parker Hanson publishing in the following year *New Worlds Emerging*, "an optimist's bid for a hearing" in the face of "the lugubrious wailing of the Neo-Malthusian Jeremiahs." Rejoining the attack against "hysterical books" trotting out "the old, mechanistic Malthusian doctrine," Hanson's epilogue, "Redemption from Fear," took on Vogt directly, arguing that he forgot Goethe's wisdom that "Where danger lies, there also grows the saving power," which for Hanson lay in free-market capitalism. Similarly, the Nobel Prize–winning biologist John Boyd Orr, who also served as the first director general of the United Nations' Food and Agriculture Organisation (FAO) (1945–1948), articulated a positive, technological response to food-shortage issues at the same time that his opposite number in UNESCO, Julian Huxley, was gripped by Malthusian fears of inevitable population overshoot. After stepping down from this role, Boyd Orr penned a panoramic mission statement about what mankind must do to avoid atomic war, *White Man's Burden* (1953). For Boyd Orr, the choices faced in the early 1950s were stark:

Modern science has the answer to Malthus, but it has to be applied on a world scale. Much of the industrial output now devoted to armaments would need to be diverted for the purpose. And so we come back to the fundamental question. . . . Will governments co-operate to apply science to promote the welfare of the peoples of the world, or, in rival groups, apply it to their mutual destruction?

Living in the shadow of atomic war, Boyd Orr had no doubt that we could avoid the population bomb thanks to advances in plant science, but like his Malthusian adversaries argued that the two bombs needed to be defused in tandem.[25]

The FAO also was a congenial home from the mid-1950s for the Danish economist Ester Boserup. If Borgstrom was the Swedish Cassandra, in Boserup he found an opponent, although one would hesitate to call her a Danish Pollyanna. For Boserup's optimism that increasing numbers of humans did not merely drain or draw upon limited resources, but could also lead to technological innovations, especially in the realm of agrarian change, was built on the basis of years of practical work in the field in a wide range of developing countries. In 1957, Boserup went to India to work on Gunnar Myrdal's project for the 20th Century Fund that would eventuate in the previously discussed epic *Asian Drama*. Boserup's encounter with India, however, would take her on a different, anti-Malthusian path and lead her to resign from Myrdal's team. As she narrated this in her autobiography, her epiphany came in the fields of rural India, a counterbalance to the "slum narratives" of Huxley, Ehrlich, and others that figured so prominently among the new Malthusians:

I travelled by car and train from New Delhi in North India to Nagpur in the middle of India . . . and on the way I observed that in a large area some of the small fields had a second crop, while the neighbouring were left fallow. In Nagpur, I asked the Indian experts why the cultivators did not all add to their income with a second crop, and was told that I had passed the coalmine district, where better incomes could be earned in that season in the mines.

Boserup's epiphany was to discover that as populations increase, they respond to economic incentives, and that the many ways in which they respond include intensifying their agriculture, changing their diet in the light of new patterns of supply and demand, or, as in her Indian fields, changing the portfolio of their employment to ensure their food entitlement. Once Boserup left Myrdal's project in 1960, she had time to write up her anti-Malthusian insight, publishing her landmark *Conditions of Agricultural Growth* in 1965. In *Conditions*, Boserup opened with a depiction of "the approach of Malthus," which saw food supply as inelastic, as unable to alter rapidly, before arguing on the contrary that "population growth is here regarded as the independent variable which in turn is a major factor in determining agricultural developments." The terms of the debate were, of course, slightly artificial: as we have seen, Malthus had proposed in 1798 that "necessity has been with great truth called the mother of invention," a phrase that came in the postwar decades to epitomize Boserup's repudiation of Malthus, but she was right to see that the Malthusian doomsayers of the period tended to ignore this part of his argument, which she then revitalized. Although she did not show awareness of this, Boserup was more an "anti–new Malthusian" than she was an opponent of Malthus per se.[26]

Boserup was far too much the grounded anthropologist to be an anti-Malthusian Pollyanna; someone who traveled equally widely but was far more in his own bubble—or dome—was the architect and futurist R. Buckminster Fuller. Fuller is remembered today for his geodesic domes such as that at Montreal's Expo 67, structures that were icons of faith in science, progress, and modernity, but he spent at least as much of his energy mapping futures in print as in glass and steel, taking on the new Malthusians in the process over their doomsaying futuristic scenarios and their vision of a fragile Spaceship Earth. Key to Fuller's utopianism was to switch the application of technology to improving the quality of life and away from an arms race, this allowing the "eliminating [of] fundamental causes of war, ie 'you or me to the death . . .' a seemingly scientific fact established by Malthus." Fuller's two key futuristic tracts, *Operating Manual for Spaceship Earth* and *Utopia or Oblivion,* were both published in 1969 in a straight conflict with the peak of new Malthusianism as represented by Ehrlich's *Population Bomb.* Fuller accepted the premise that "Spaceship Earth" needed to be tended and viewed as a fragile whole, but "saw that Malthus could be fundamentally wrong because his thoughts were devoid of any sense of technology's more-with-lessing." We had been given fossil fuels as the spaceship's "self-starter" but must then switch to renewables to keep the craft moving forward. And the signs were there that humanity was learning to live in harmony with earth: "the population explosion is a myth. As we industrialise, down goes the annual birth rate." Fuller even developed his own computer programs to model this at the University of Southern Illinois, where he held tenure, the doleful predictions of *Limits to Growth* being jettisoned in favor of a very different program, "The World Game—How to Make the World Work," which would show how resource use could be made maximally efficient and thereby give all a high standard of living. Part seer, part scientist, Fuller joined the roll call of those who had developed utopian responses to the Malthusian specter, a genealogy that linked Condorcet and Godwin as Malthus's catalysts to Carlyle, Ruskin, and Henry George.[27]

And yet the man who brought together all these strands of anti-Malthusianism and by his pugnaciousness and self-publicity added immeasurably to Malthus's fame would probably have seen much of what Fuller wrote as sheer baloney. For he was a pragmatic economist who traded in the tracking of prices, not plotting future courses for Spaceship Earth. That man was the economist Julian Simon. In many ways, Simon's anti-Malthusianism was merely a rehash of themes we have already seen, notably Boserup's critique of the idea that increasing population should merely be seen in terms of diminishing per capita returns, and the argument witnessed in Boyd Orr and others that technological innovation made resources not fixed natural entities but expanding social ones. What Julian Simon added technically was an economist's unwavering focus on resource and commodity prices as the indicator of scarcity and abundance; what made him the anti-Malthusian cause célèbre was a rhetoric as high-flown as that wielded by the new Malthusians.

Simon had a good conversion narrative to tell: on his own autobiographical account, he had set out in 1966 to follow Ehrlich's path, to "use my skills in economics and marketing to help the world contain its 'exploding' population'"; this would be "my life's work." Simon started from the received wisdom about the economics of population, which "has hardly changed since Malthus," and asserted that increasing population size led to a declining standard of living, but encountered what Huxley famously called the great tragedy of science, "the slaying of a beautiful hypothesis by an ugly fact": "the available empirical data do not support that theory." The data Simon would spend the rest of his life emphasizing was that regarding standards of living and resource prices. If the new Malthusians were right, the rapid increase in global population and consequent resource usage should lead to both declining standards of living and increasing resource costs, where price series data from Malthus to the present showed quite the opposite trend. Why? For Simon the answer lay in the human capacity to innovate and make technological advances, which meant resources were not a fixed denominator to be divided by a growing demographic numerator.[28]

Where Simon has been simplistically pitched as an "anti-Malthusian," he was more accurately an opponent of the new Malthusians, his attitude toward Malthus himself being far more respectful. Simon accepted entirely that "Malthus was the fount of the systematic economic study of population," thereby placing his own work in a direct genealogy with

Malthus's. He also distinguished the Malthus of the 1798 edition of the *Essay*, from the Malthus of the later editions, aligning himself—and indeed Malthus—with the latter position to suggest that "Malthus himself was a powerful critic of 'Malthusianism.'" In the populist language of Simon's *The Ultimate Resource*, this was figured as follows:

> We must recognize what Malthus came to recognize. After he published the short simplistic theory in the first edition of his *Essay on Population* and after he had the time and inclination to consider the facts as well as the theory, he concluded that human beings are very different from flies or rats. When faced with the limits of a bottle-like situation, people can alter their behaviour so as to accommodate to that limit. . . . And people can alter that limit—expand the "bottle"—by consciously increasing the resources available.

Here is Simon's creed "in a bottle." Starting from this belief, Simon made headline-grabbing claims in *The Ultimate Resource*, deliberately sounding paradoxical. Most notorious was his claim that "natural resources are not finite. Yes, you read correctly." By this arresting claim, Simon meant something far less original, something we have already seen claimed by several postwar anti-Malthusians: if humans can innovate to find new ways of using the earth, there is no meaningful sense in which we are running down a fixed stock of resources. On this basis, Simon also took on what we have seen was a rhetorical favorite of the new Malthusians, castigating the "notion of our planet as 'spaceship earth,' launched with a countable amount of each resource and hence having less minerals per passenger as the number of passengers is greater" as "dramatic but irrelevant," the only theoretical limit being the amount of energy derived from the sun.[29]

The target of Simon's screed was not, then, Malthus, but what Simon saw as the misuse of his earlier, ultimately discarded ideas from 1798 by the alarmist Malthusians of his own age, especially Paul Ehrlich. For behind Simon's economic rhetoric he disclosed what might be deemed a "humanist" attitude: "The longer I read the literature about population, the more baffled and distressed I become that one idea is omitted. Enabling a potential human being to come into life and to enjoy life is a good thing. . . . [W]e need another person for exactly the same reason we need . . . Ehrlich. That is, just as the . . . Ehrlichs of this world are of value to the rest of us, so will the average additional person be of value." As we shall see, Ehrlich would beg to disagree, forcibly. And in that disagreement, the coming together of new Malthusians with their critics, the "Malthus craze" of the postwar years would peak.[30]

Betting and Beating the Bastards: Wagering on Malthus

The Malthus craze came to a peak in three very public, very famous collisions between Julian Simon and the neo-Malthusians. By the late 1970s, Julian Simon was already a regular columnist and contributor to national newspapers, his essays and articles about him appearing in the *New York Times,* the *Washington Post,* and the *Boston Globe,* among other places. His arguments lent scholarly support to a position that the new breed of conservatives had been peddling for the better part of the 1970s. Notable in this regard was Ronald Reagan, who had initially been part of the wave of Californian concern about population and resources in the 1960s that had been galvanized by Ehrlich and Hardin, before a dramatic volte-face when he became governor of California, this being signaled in a 1971 speech delivered to petroleum industry bosses. Reagan began to argue that coercion around population issues was the slippery slope to tyranny, and that American liberties were being jeopardized. Simon's arguments fit neatly with neoconservative free-market economics, arguing as they did that individual ingenuity, not state compulsion, was not merely the road to survival, but the freeway to prosperity. It was on these grounds that by the UN's 1984 population conference, with Reagan in the White House, the United States would come to argue that population growth was neutral as regards its impact on economic affairs, a proposition that would have been unimaginable under successive postwar presidents from Truman to Carter. Reagan's journey with regard to population issues was mirrored by that of William Buckley Jr., founder of the right-wing *National Review* and, by the 1970s, the face of neoconservatism on U.S. television. As Carson's *Tonight Show* had publicized *The Population Bomb,* propelling Ehrlich to fame, so Buckley's *Firing Line* gave Simon a platform to debate and disseminate the arguments from *The Ultimate Resource* in a program broadcast on November 8, 1981. The program was entitled "Answer to Malthus" and saw Simon and Buckley in broad agreement about resource and population questions, while the new Malthusians were represented by Mark Green, a Cornell-educated lawyer who cited the work of the Worldwatch Institute, the *Limits to Growth* team, and the Jimmy Carter–commissioned *Global 2000* report to suggest a gloomier picture. Simon was unmoved by the serried ranks of experts Green lined up, indeed the very number and repetitiveness of their doomsaying suggested "the sad fact . . . that we do not seem to learn from these kinds of mispredictions. We've been making the same kinds of predictions since Malthus," and they have all been wrong.[31]

If "Answer to Malthus" was a very public debate between Simon and the new Malthusian position, it had not actually involved any of the key players responding to Simon and, thanks to Buckley's stance as the interviewer, had been somewhat stacked in Simon's favor. A direct engagement between Simon and the new Malthusians had, however, already been staged a year earlier with the deck stacked in very much the opposite direction, in the pages of *Science,* one of the world's most prestigious journals. Simon put together an essay suggesting that many of the claims about resource shortages and population overshoots were not simply hysterical, but deliberately ignored macroeconomic data about prices that refuted them. The essay, with the typically provocative title "Resources, Population, Environment: An Oversupply of False Bad News," was accepted for publication early in 1978, but took an unprecedented two-and-a-half years to appear in print as the editor of *Science* realized what a controversial issue he was handling. Letters and phone calls came and went and still the essay had not made it into print. Reputedly, the editor Philip Abelson said of his delaying, "I've got to crap or get off the pot." Abelson finally made his decision, and Simon saw his incendiary essay in print in the July 27, 1980, edition of *Science* and said to himself, "I beat the bastards." Opening with the claim that "bad news about population growth, natural resources, and the environment that is based on flimsy evidence or no evidence at all is published widely in the face of contradictory evidence," Simon went on to attack Ehrlich's *Population Bomb* as a prime example of the problem, ignoring as it did that "per capita food production has been increasing at roughly 1 per cent yearly" for a quarter century. And once more, Simon attacked the notion that population growth can only lower per capita income: this might be the case while those expanding numbers were dependents, "the point was crystal clear to Malthus even without a complex model," but when "once the children grow up, however, and become producers as well as consumers, their impact on per capita income reverses. . . . Population growth and productivity increase are not independent forces running a race."[32]

If Abelson was worried what would happen when he published Simon, his concerns were well founded. Even Simon, no stranger to controversy, noted "there was an explosive reaction"—his very own "publication bomb." Some of these brickbats Simon treasured in a perverse way, proudly citing on the dust jackets of his later books comments such as "the man's a terrorist" and that his work was "schizophrenic nonsense and baloney . . . sabotaging the human race." But the main response came in the pages of *Science* itself, which hosted a ten-page set of responses, "Bad News: Is it True?" in its issue of December 19, 1980, the responses being longer than the initial article. A gamut of biologists, development economists, geographers, and ecologists responded to Simon, but most importantly, Paul and Anne Ehrlich together with their colleagues and regular coauthors John Holdren and John Harte replied. Their response keyed on Simon's alleged naïveté about ecological processes as an economist and concluded that "even if one were to accept the maximization of the mass of human protoplasm sustainable on earth as a goal superordinate to all others, it would be a monstrous error to think that this goal could be realized without the services derived from largely unmanaged biogeophysical processes." Privately, Paul Ehrlich's response was far less measured, purportedly wondering how Simon's work got through peer review and likening it to a "cargo-cult" that assumed resources would miraculously fall from the skies.[33]

If Simon did not necessarily "beat the bastards" thanks to his *Science* article, it certainly raised the profile of anti-Malthusianism to an unprecedented height. And it formed a heady cocktail when combined with the third collision point with the neo-Malthusians, the so-called "Ehrlich-Simon" bet of 1980. This bet has acquired a certain notoriety over the years, although it was, as should be clear by now, merely one of a number of flash points between an assertive new Malthusianism and a neo-conservative, populist anti-Malthusianism. Oddly enough, given the celebrity of Simon and Ehrlich and the fame this episode has acquired, the "bet" between them began with a scholarly spat in a minor journal, *Social Science Quarterly,* in March 1981, three months after the *Science* exchange. Ehrlich published an essay about the meaning of environmental problems for the social sciences, starting in what Simon would identify as "vintage Ehrlich" rhetoric with the apocalyptic dictum that "in my opinion, and that of virtually every ecologist I know, humanity is now faced with an unprecedented escalation of environmental disruption, a situation that threatens the persistence of civilization as we know it." Ehrlich was especially dismissive of economists as "utterly ignorant of the constraints placed upon the economic system by physical and biological factors." Simon would see in this a call to arms, focusing on price and yield data to suggest that apocalypse was not imminent due to human ingenuity. The new move in the debate came halfway through the paper: "This is a public offer to stake $10,000 . . . on my belief that the cost of non-government controlled raw materials (including grain and oil) will not rise in the long run." Ehrlich responded with his customary asperity about both Simon's rhetoric and the bet. Regarding his style, Ehrlich coded an ad hominem attack on Simon in his response: "I will not hesitate to use words like 'desperate,' 'dangerous,' 'grim' and 'unprecedented' in describing today's human predicament. Nor will I eschew words like 'wrong,' 'incompetent' or even 'moronic' in describing the works or views of others when the shoe fits." And of the bet, Ehrlich, with his colleagues and the coauthors of his response to Simon in *Science,* John Holdren and John Harte, accepted "Simon's astonishing offer before other greedy people jump in." They offered a formal bet around the ten-year changes in the traded price of chromium, copper, nickel, tin, and tungsten. Even this shared agreement to a wager was the subject of controversy and acrimony, the pages of *Social Science Quarterly* seeing vacillations about the details of the bet and accusations of "bombastic challenges" while letters were also exchanged to thrash out terms and conditions. And yet at last this very high-profile scholarly spat eventuated in a formal contract in 1980 about future metal prices between the parties, who "never met in all the years they have been excoriating each other," the winner to be determined in 1990.[34]

Bickering and the Bet: The Fizzling of the New Malthusianism

Unsurprisingly, perhaps, neither party took the making of the wager in the autumn of 1980 as a cue to cease their clashes, nor would they agree about the meaning of its outcome. Indeed, battle was rejoined not only in the debate on Buckley's *Firing Line* show, but also in a predictably fruity 1982 spat between Simon and Garrett Hardin in an interview that was published in the neoconservative journal *Public Opinion.* At this time, *Public Opinion* was edited by Ben Wattenburg, author of the 1970 attack on Ehrlich's "nonsense explosion," and in what Simon called, "a lovely stroke" that also nailed the journal's colors to the anti-Malthusian mast, he once again turned up journalistic trumps in titling the exchange "Is the Era of Limits Running Out?" Hardin, undaunted, lambasted Simon's optimism and suggested that his views were only influential with "budget evaders, car salesmen, realtors, advertisers, land speculators."[35]

And so matters have gone on down the years from the bet to the present. All passion has never quite been spent in this very noisy dialogue of the deaf, and Malthus has remained part of the shouting match. Thus Garrett Hardin has in both *Living within Limits* (1993) and *The Ostrich Factor* (1998) invoked Malthus, in the former suggesting as a categorical fact that "biology and most of the evidence from human experience supports the Malthusians." *The Ostrich Factor*'s engagement with Malthus was rather greater: once again shuttling between science fiction and science as he had in *Spaceship Beagle*, Hardin here invented a dialogue with a Martian to get a dispassionate view of earth's plight. In a chapter entitled "A Martian's View of Malthus," the problem becomes clear and is strikingly unaltered from Hardin's 1972 formulation: Malthus had formulated an unpalatable truth in 1803 about the lack of covers at nature's mighty feast and society has repressed it. As Hardin's very Malthusian Martian has it: "earthlings indulge in well-intentioned acts only to see misery increased." Similarly entrenched new Malthusian statements have emerged from the *Limits to Growth* team and the Ehrlichs, both of whom have described their famously doleful predictions of the late 1960s and early 1970s as too optimistic when faced with the grim realities of the present day.[36]

But what of the Ehrlich-Simon "bet?" As 1990 rolled round, who won? April 1990 saw a massive "Earth Day," which, with some 200 million participants the world over, was an order of magnitude larger than that very Malthusian moment on April 22, 1970. Ehrlich was once again plastered over the media, promoting his updated Malthusian *Population Explosion* and alluding to Simon in his alleged comment about "the ultimate resource—the one thing we'll never run out of is imbeciles." Simon, on his own characteristically self-deprecating account, spoke to an audience of sixteen on that day. And yet it was Julian Simon who won the bet, Paul Ehrlich sending him a check for $576.07 in the autumn after the razzmatazz of Earth Day 1990 had faded. Simon had correctly predicted that the basket of five metals Ehrlich and his Californian new Malthusians had selected would, taken in toto, fall in market price over the decade. And yet where the making of this bet had been much hyped in 1980, its conclusion went all but unnoticed for three sets of reasons. First, it seems that two decades of bickering between entrenched positions had left both the general public and the scholarly community fairly anaesthetized to the result of the bet. A dialogue of the deaf is not very interesting listening to bystanders who are able to hear both sides. Second, the conclusion of the bet merely led to more bickering among the participants. Thus the new Malthusians argued that Simon was "lucky," that his own favored metal, copper, had gone up in price over the decade, and that the main reason they had lost was recession, increasing oil prices that had reduced demand for metals meaning, paradoxically, that they had lost the bet because of resource scarcity. Third, and perhaps most important, the terms of debate were shifting away from those pioneered in the 1950s and publicized so effectively in the "Ehrlich wars" of the 1970s such that the bet had outlived its usefulness by the time it matured. When Julian Simon offered a new bet to Paul Ehrlich in 1995 via an article in the *San Francisco Chronicle,* Ehrlich responded by generating fifteen global indicators he was willing to wager on, the first five of which related to global temperatures and to atmospheric levels of carbon dioxide, nitrous oxide, ozone, and sulphur dioxide. This was in line with Ehrlich's immediate response to losing the bet in 1990:

> The bet doesn't mean anything. Julian Simon is like the guy who jumps off the Empire State Building and says how great things are going so far as he passes the 10th floor. The resource that worries me the most is the declining capacity of our planet to buffer itself against human impacts. Look at the new problems that have come up: the ozone hole, acid rain, global warming. . . . If we get climate change and let the ecological systems keep running down-hill, we could have a gigantic population crash.

The terms of debate, then, were shifting from the biotic to the atmospheric, from ecosystems to climate change. As we shall see, it is in these terms that Malthus figures in the debates of the present day.[37]

CHAPTER NINE

Malthus Today

The Quiet Bicentenary and Green Shoots

For a historian to write of the present immediately puts one in mind of Samuel Johnson's once-celebrated and now-notorious judgment of women's preaching being like unto a dog walking on its hind legs: "it is not done well; but you are surprised to find it done at all." And yet just as we now live in a world where Johnson's beloved Anglican Church has many able women preachers, so it behooves the logic of this book to follow the trajectory of responses to Malthus down to the present day. As such, this final chapter offers notes about the ways in which Malthus's name and ideas are being used in contemporary discourse, cognizant that the dominant shapes in these discussions may become more readily apparent to future commentators with the passage of time.[1]

A good starting point is the bicentenary of the publication of the *Essay*, 1998. Where such anniversaries tend to see a fair amount of academic and media ballyhoo for the great writers and their works, Malthus's bicentennial passed off with minimal fuss. After all the high-profile debates, vitriol, and media coverage in the 1970s, 1998 saw all quiet on the Malthus front, the distinguished demographer Geoffrey McNicoll voicing a question this silence implicitly engendered: "should Malthus therefore be retired . . . with the acknowledgement that the issue is all but dead—a piece of intellectual history rather than a continuing controversy?" Of a piece with this comment were two further straws in the wind: first, the death of Julian Simon in February 1998, which added to the sense of a Malthusian high point now long since gone, and the fact that the Penguin Classics edition of Malthus's *Essay* dipped in annual sales below one thousand copies in the same year that its original celebrated its bicentenary. If such anniversaries normally spark renewed interest, the hard facts of sales figures spoke of an apparently terminal decline in interest in Malthus. Reinforcing this sense of decay, the environmental activist Bill McKibben was surely right to detect in the same year that Malthus's "stock is especially low." If *The 100* had been rewritten in this particular year, it is hard to imagine that Malthus would have made the cut.[2]

Why had Malthus's work fallen into such relative oblivion at this time? While some of this might be accounted for by the overexposure his work had experienced in the previous decades, the main reason must lie in the sense that his concerns had been addressed and the population problem had been conquered. Global population growth slowed from 2 percent per annum in 1965–1976 to 1.2 percent now, the number of people added to that population annually peaking in 1987. In response to this sense that global population was stabilizing, population control fell down the list of global priorities: there has been no United Nations conference on population since that in Cairo in 1994, and spending per capita on family planning programs has diminished considerably, in most parts of the world by over 50 percent in the decade 1996–2006. Unsurprisingly, as population was seen as a problem solved, so the man most associated with posing the population problem fell from favor. If population control was a done deal, Malthus was a spent force.[3]

Or was he? We can also in fact see green shoots in Malthus's role in global policy debates emerging in these same years either side of the new millennium, a new role built around reconceptualizations of the categories of "population" and "environment" from their usages in the 1970s to new modes suitable to an age where climate change is a central preoccupation. Thus, referring back to the commentators mentioned above, McNicoll resoundingly answered his own question by arguing that Malthus should not be retired: "a solid empirical stance and a clear-eyed, sceptical assessment of institutional possibilities seem to be the main hope for negotiating a route forward. Malthus . . . would make a dour companion—but an invaluable one." Likewise for McKibben, the fall in Malthus's stock could only be a temporary one as "Malthus never goes away." And McKibben then framed the "return of Malthus" for our era in suitably apocalyptic terms: "the next fifty years will be crucial to our planet's future. . . . How many people we have on this planet during that half-century will go a long way toward determining how deep the damage is." Both of these assessments of Malthus's continued relevance into the new millennium were made in the context of acceptance of and concern about climate change. McKibben framed our present moment as the beginning of "Earth 2," a world where the old rules about human-environment interactions no longer held good: where the generation that spawned the Ehrlich-Simon debates addressed how humans *modified* natural processes, now we have to accept and respond to the fact that we *dominate* the globe. This is not mere journalistic hype: on the contrary, McKibben was picking up on the emergent scientific consensus that we live in an age that can be labeled the "anthropocene," a new, quasi-geological era where the biggest impact on environmental systems, climatic and biotic, is that created by human societies. In framing this anthropocene, Malthus's bicentennial saw the publication of an address by the president of the American Association for the Advancement of Science (and now scientific advisor to President Obama), Jane Lubchenco, calling for a "new social contract for science," concluding that "in view of the overarching importance of environmental issues for the future of the human race, all graduates from institutions of higher learning should be environmentally literate." Lubchenco specifically addressed issues about population earlier in her address. And from the side of students of demography came the same call at the same moment of Malthus's bicentennial: in her 1998 Presidential Address to the Population Association of America, Anne Pebley opened and closed with reference to Malthus in a talk entitled "Demography and the Environment." Simply put, if we do indeed live in the age of the anthropocene, the number of human beings on the planet and the intensity of their impact on planetary environmental systems become of importance to the studies of both natural and social scientists alike in ways more profound and thoroughgoing than ever before. This puts Malthus squarely back on the agenda rather than in the retirement home. To see how this is the case, we will first trace the new debates about "population" and" environment" that have emerged over the past two decades in the context of concerns over climate change and attend to how they have used Malthus. We will then go on to see how these analyses have catalyzed a set of broadly Malthusian concerns about possible demographic, food, and environmental "checks" that might derail modern societies, these checks being framed in the post–9/11 world as threats to security. In sum, as we shall see, imaginings of global futures for the next half century revolve around a thoroughly Malthusian binary between positive and preventive approaches to envisaging global survival in the anthropocene.[4]

Population and Climate: New Malthusian Connections

If some perceived the end of Malthus's reign in the last years of the twentieth century due to the slowdown in global population growth, a more nuanced response is offered by present-day demographers. For we now live in a "two-speed" demographic world, globally speaking, with many parts of the developing world still seeing rapid population growth, while the developed world is witnessing dramatic declines in fertility, leading inevitably to both aging and shrinking populations. Both trajectories lead to Malthusian concerns.

On the one hand, population growth in the developing world leads to fairly "orthodox" Malthusian worries. While global population growth may have peaked a quarter century ago, for example, we still see the addition of nearly 80 million people annually. This led the distinguished naturalist and television star Sir David Attenborough recently to pen an unrepentantly Malthusian article, "This Heaving Planet," which argued that "the fundamental truth that Malthus proclaimed remains the truth: there cannot be more people on this earth than can be fed." Attenborough went on to call on us all to break the "taboo" on talking about population. More considered arguments come from demographers and development economists who address the two-speed issue, the fact that 99 percent of projected global population growth to 2050 will be in developing countries. In this context, it is only parts of the globe that are "heaving," that may see a Malthusian problem of population increase pressing on available resources. As such, present arguments have replaced the "global" Malthusian concerns of Paul Ehrlich with more "regional" or "national" ones. Regionally, it is Africa that is most regularly viewed in these terms: "Africa is a Malthusian train crash waiting to happen." And yet even this regional scale of analysis is too coarse to capture the more geographically nuanced realities most demographers detect. "Malthus's theorem may not be the global constraint that he imagined. But at the level that matters practically—the individual country—food production often does not keep up with population growth." As such, it is at the national scale that most look to find Malthusian problems emerging: there are what the World Bank demographer John May calls "demographic hotspots," nations such as Yemen.[5]

For every "hot spot" there is now a countervailing demographic "cold spot" in the developed world where fertility levels are below replacement, such that population is both aging and shrinking. And as with the hot spots, such cold spots are being detected on both regional and national levels. Regionally, Europe is the most obvious such location, its overall fertility rate leading to an intrinsic growth rate of -1.46 percent per annum, which, small-sounding as it is, "would bring a population to half of its original size in 47 years." And even within the cold spot of Europe, there are what might be called the "frigid" nations, notably Russia, whose rate of population decline is such as to "shrink a population to one third of its original size within 50 years." Russian president Vladimir Putin was moved in 2006 to call this "the most acute problem facing our country today." In more restrained academic language, it has been suggested that "there is hardly any historical precedent for such precipitous demographic collapse," while in journalistic rhetoric the population dynamics of such cold spots are framed in more apocalyptic terms: "Europe's demographic black hole. Doomsday for a continent." The future scenarios conjured up for Europe and other such cold spots are bleak or dystopian. The bleak scenario would see civilization itself collapse, not by the Malthusian positive checks of population overshoot that Jared Diamond has popularized in *Collapse* (2005), but by too effective a preventive check: "Civilizations have simply melted away because of poor reproductive rates." What might be left? "Europe could be transformed into a huge theme park, geared for the entertainment of curious visitors, comprising the newly rich of Asia." But as my usage of Malthus's language of "checks" in this context implies, contemporary analysis of demographic cold spots is as thoroughly Malthusian in its origins as is the study of hot spots. It is, of course, the analysis of an imbalance between population and resources created by the reverse geometrical progression that comes into play when population declines. Such scenarios, as we have seen in Chapter 7, were envisaged in the interwar years, when population last saw secular decline. Malthus in reverse is still most assuredly Malthus.[6]

If there is really a Chinese curse, "may you live in interesting times," demographically we are cursed: "dullness is not a risk over the next 50 years." Why? Combining the cold and the hot spots on our globe, Joel Cohen has pointed out that the first decade of the new millennium spanned "three unique, important transitions in the history of humankind":

> Before 2000, young people always outnumbered old people. From 2000 forward, old people will outnumber young people. Until approximately 2007, rural people always outnumbered urban people. From 2008 forward, urban people will outnumber rural people. From 2003 on, the median woman worldwide had, and will continue to have, too few or just enough children during her lifetime to replace herself and the father in the following generation.

The social, economic, and political implications of these momentous changes are all being examined through Malthusian frameworks, but before we turn to this, we need to address the ways in which population hot spots and cold spots are seen to impact on the environment.[7]

If Malthus attended to the balance between population and food availability at the heart of the postwar Malthusian revival, as we have seen in Chapter 8, was a widening of the "resources" seen as under strain due to population growth from food to nonrenewable resources such as those around which the Ehrlich-Simon wager revolved, and to renewable resources in the form of global ecosystems. In our own "anthropocenic" era, the balance of concern between renewable and nonrenewable resources has shifted, and there has been a further widening of the resources with which population must balance, subsuming ecosystems as part of a broader concern with global climatic systems. And yet the analysis offered remains fundamentally indebted to Malthus and the postwar iteration of Malthusianism.

Concern about rates of usage of nonrenewable resources has declined over the past few decades, perhaps in response to the success of Julian Simon's analysis of long-term price trends for metals. And yet two thoroughly Malthusian concerns remain about resource availability. First, with the continued population momentum of 80 million new people per annum (even if that number is falling year on year and should reach only 31 million per annum by 2045), can we continue to find new resources? More particularly, what of resources that exist and cannot be found, notably land for food and water? Even given projected improvements in agricultural yields, it is estimated that "an area roughly equivalent to the continent of Australia will need to be converted to crops" to feed the circa 2 billion extra people who will inhabit the planet by 2050. Perhaps even more pressingly, the combined global demand for water created by increased urbanization and the momentum of population growth means "a new Rhine-equivalent must be found each year." Second, even if we can find food, water, and other such resources, what of the materials we thereby produce in the form of waste and pollutants? As McKibben frames the issue: "It's not that we're running out of stuff; what we're running out of are what the scientists call 'sinks.' Places to put the *by-products* of our large appetites. Not garbage dumps—we could go on using Pampers till the end of time and still have empty space left to toss them away. But the atmospheric equivalent of garbage dumps." In the new millennium, then, the concern about the population-resource balance has shifted from nonrenewables to renewables and, within this, from the biotic to the atmospheric.[8]

If, as we have seen, the contemporary global demographic landscape is a binary one of the too many and the too few, current debates about the linkage of climate change and population depict a rather different but equally Malthusian scenario of the too many and the still more. To understand this, one needs to look at the so-called "IPAT equation" developed by Paul Ehrlich and his colleague and fellow wagerer (and now advisor to President Obama) John Holdren in 1971. The IPAT equation suggests that the impact (I) of a society on the environment is a function of population (P), affluence/consumption (A), and technology (T). In these terms, the "too many" of the developing world impact on global climate by their still considerable demographic momentum (P), while the "too few" of the graying nations are more than countering their declining population by their increasing levels of consumption (A). While acknowledging in its fourth assessment of 2007 that "GDP/capita and population growth were the main drivers of the increase in global emissions [of CO_2] during the last three decades of the 20th century," the Intergovernmental Panel on Climate Change (IPCC) has paid remarkably little attention to population issues. This will probably change for the fifth edition as more sophisticated work has shown both how population growth impacts on climate change and the relative importance of population growth and increases in per capita consumption. Population growth has a more than proportional effect on greenhouse gas emissions due to its correlation with urbanization and decreases in household size such that if global population could reach an equilibrium at 8 billion by 2050 rather than 9 billion, this would mitigate one-seventh of the total reduction in emissions recommended by the IPCC to stabilize climate change. And yet, as these figures suggest, population growth in developing countries is ultimately less important than reducing consumption in the affluent world in a scenario where 7 percent of the world's population produces 50 percent of greenhouse gas emissions. For factors other than greenhouse gas emissions that are pertinent to climate change, however, population growth remains a far more important factor: up to 80 percent of global deforestation, for example, can be linked to population growth, with similar stories being told for salinization of land due to irrigation and increased methane emissions due to livestock.[9]

Complexity and Security: The New Malthusian Checks?

The global demographic landscape, then, is more complex and diverse than that modeled in the immediate postwar decades, tending toward a binary scenario with both trajectories being read in terms inspired by Malthusian concerns. Furthermore, the Malthusian interconnections being traced between both demographical trajectories and environmental limitations are being channeled predominantly through the new lens of climate change, with both being seen to contribute to global challenges, albeit in different ways. As Joel Cohen has neatly summarized the situation: "Populations, then environment, economics and culture all interact *jointly*. Think of a string quartet: the combined effect exceeds that of any single player or pair or trio of players." To continue Cohen's metaphor, however, current analyses of these complex interactions seem predominantly to envisage not the smooth harmonies of a Haydn quartet but instead Mozart's so-called "dissonance quartet" or, more likely, the harsh sounds of Schoenberg. Put more literally, analyses of the interactions of population, economics, and environment over the past decade have been developed in the thrall of a suite of "security" fears developed in the wake of 9/11. A set of discourses about demographic, food, and environmental security have come to the fore that replay in various ways the concern Malthus expressed with the "positive" checks of famine, pestilence, and war. Opposing this analysis have been two strands of thought that, again, we have encountered at various points in our narrative. On the one hand, although I will not address this in detail, there have been continuations of the neoconservative rebuttal of Malthusian fears that Julian Simon pioneered. Thus Bjørn Lomborg's *Skeptical Environmentalist* (2001) has attracted a certain notoriety for its refusal to accept the legitimacy of fears of limits to growth and visions of consequent social breakdown. Lomborg's book has a motto from Julian Simon and adopts the same basic method: confounding fear on the basis of long-term price data. He also opens by analyzing the question, "Why do we hear so much bad news?," as did Simon's infamous 1980 essay in *Science,* before going on to say Malthus's ideas are "simple and attractive," but "the evidence does not support the theory." In the same mold is the neoconservative attack by Robert Bradley Jr. in *Forbes Magazine* on Barack Obama's economic policy as "a *Malthusian* New Deal . . . green Keynesianism . . . at odds with wealth creation and true recovery." Most grandiose of all in this vein is Robert Zubrin's remarkable attempt to update (albeit from the perspective of the opposite end of the political spectrum) the argument of Allan Chase's socialist *Legacy of Malthus* (1977), which was addressed briefly in Chapter 7. For where Chase traced a strand from Malthus to eugenics to Hitler, Zubrin brings the same pedigree to the present day via Ehrlich and proponents of climate change, depicting them all as "antihumanists" denying human creativity and the logic of the market. Malthus is given dubious pride of place by Zubrin as "the founding prophet of modern antihumanism." On the other hand, the security complex fearful of Malthusian checks is opposed by radical Marxist and feminist analysts for mystifying the social origins of the concerns about population imbalances, food supply, and resource conflicts, for seeing as natural limits what are in fact social constructions, a line of critique we have already seen pioneered by the romantics and by Marx himself.[10]

Returning to the nexus of demography and security, in 2010, the influential "crossover" journal for U.S. academics and politicians concerned with international relations, Foreign Affairs, carried a provocatively titled article, "The New Population Bomb." Its author, Jack Goldstone, is an academic at George Mason University, but also rather closer to the levers of power than this suggests, having served on the U.S. vice-presidential task force on state failures as well as acting as a consultant to the U.S. State Department and the FBI. Goldstone's key point, and one that has gone to the heart of recent U.S. international policy thinking, is that with a new "two-speed" demographic world, "twenty-first century international security will depend less on how many people inhabit the world than on how the global population is composed and distributed." As he has put it elsewhere, he foresees and indeed already discerns a world spotted with demographic "flash points and tipping points" where wars, civil unrest, and more nebulous security threats driven by population dynamics are emerging. As Goldstone summarizes, "taken together, these trends will pose challenges every bit as alarming as those noted by Ehrlich." Even if the global population bomb has been defused, then, a new set of demographic devices appear primed and ready to explode. For Goldstone, although he never invokes his name, the new millennium faces a new set of Malthus's "positive checks" of war and unrest.[11]

Goldstone is by no means alone in discerning these trends and warning of positive Malthusian demographic checks; on the contrary, his work in good part summarizes for politicians a set of concerns that have stretched back twenty years or so to a 1989 essay in the same journal, Foreign Affairs, by Jessica Matthews on "redefining security" for the post–Cold War era. Taken together, Richard Cincotta, another demographer working for the U.S. government, has neatly labeled this the "security demographic," the fear that in the post–Cold War era and in the wake of 9/11, threats to U.S. national security will be driven by smaller political groups, whose followers will come from four discernible demographic contexts.[12]

First, and the demographic feature that has attracted most attention from the security community, is the concern with so-called "youth bulges" in the developing world. Those countries that saw rapid population growth in the 1980s and 1990s now have "youth bulges," disproportionately large cohorts of men in the 15–29 age range. Post 9/11, this group has been depicted as the target group for radicalization against liberal democracies, especially the United States. Cincotta, for example, has run statistical analyses, his conclusion being that where this age group comprises 40 percent or more of the total population of a nation, that nation is twice as likely to see radicalization and civil conflict. A variant of this argument, the so-called "bare branches" idea, is deployed for nations where draconian population control policies have led to an imbalanced sex ratio in the younger age cohorts, most notably that engendered by Chinese one-child policies but also in India. In such a context, it has been argued that male aggression is being created by indulgent parenting and a lack of opportunities for socialization with women, the result being a potentially explosive cohort who lack social bonds and may therefore cause civil and international unrest. In a two-speed demographic world, a reverse demographic imbalance is feared in the aging populations of the developed world. Where stalwart anti-Malthusians have seen in these aging populations a refutation of the fears of the 1970s, security analysts find cause for concern that Malthusian positive checks will emerge by other means in such a scenario. Where an ever-enlarging elderly cohort creates an intolerably high "dependency ratio," huge numbers in old age needing care and social resources that the ever-narrowing base of the working population find it increasingly burdensome to maintain, it is argued that the potential is created for civil strife due to cleavages in generational needs and demands.[13]

The second arena of demographic security threats revolves around migration. A two-speed demographic world is seen to encourage mass international migration on a scale never seen before as the youth bulges of the poorer countries are drawn to the wealth and opportunities of the richer nations, whose aging populations need their labor to prop themselves up and reverse the increasing dependency ratio. If concerns about youth bulges have mainly centered around radicalization and threats to the United States, the migratory issue, while an important one for the United States on the Mexican border, is seen to be greatest for Europe. There is a dramatic demographic fault line between the twenty-five nations of Europe and its twenty-five neighbors. Europe is aging, and its population will at best be static over the next decades, while the predominantly Muslim nations of the Middle East and North Africa are seeing rapid growth; where the European population was twice the size of its hinterlands' in 1950, by 2050 its neighbors will have three times more people needing a livelihood. In this context, "demography's role in creating and resolving conflicts is likely to become increasingly pressing."[14]

The third new population bomb is tied to its two predecessors: urbanization. As we have already noted, the globe has now passed a watershed where the majority of its population lives in cities. The fear the security demographic poses is that both youth bulges in developing world cities and internationally migrant youth bulges in the urban areas of the advanced economies mean that "the world's megacities, with their surging populations, are powder kegs." The image conjured up is of a disempowered youth concentrated in urban slums or ghettos, which have suggestively been called "Malthustans," environmentally depleted urban areas where a radical, disaffected subculture can mobilize. Cincotta supports this dramatic claim statistically, arguing that nations seeing a rate of urbanization of 4 percent per annum or more are twice as likely to experience civil conflicts. And where a youth bulge and rapid urbanization combine, such security risks are only heightened.[15]

The fourth and final demographic security fear is the one most straightforwardly derived from Malthus himself: that nations which are still witnessing rapid population growth are also exhibiting a descent into the positive check of civil strife. Thus security analysts have noted that if the new millennium has seen warring hot spots in Iraq, Afghanistan, and the Sudan, "there is also a Malthusian slant on such events" as each of these nations "had striking population growth over the 1950–2005 period, much faster than the world as a whole." This, of course, updates Malthusian readings of war we have encountered being used to explain World War I and the Manchurian conflicts of the 1930s. But the most celebrated case where a Malthusian interpretation of excess population as the cause of social meltdown has been offered relates to the atrocities of the Rwandan civil war of 1994. In his influential book *Collapse* (2005), Jared Diamond addresses Rwanda as an example of how societies fall apart in a chapter simply titled "Malthus in Africa." In his acknowledgments, Diamond thanks Paul Ehrlich for reading his work in manuscript, and his opening to the Rwandan chapter strongly smacks of Ehrlich's revelation in Delhi in *The Population Bomb:* "East Africa's people also overwhelmed us, with . . . their sheer numbers. To read in the abstract about 'the population explosion' is one thing; it is quite another thing to encounter." Diamond goes on to argue that "modern Rwanda illustrates a case where Malthus's worst-case scenario does seem to have been right," by which he means that population overshoot led to hunger and thence to a war over resources whose effect was to act as a positive check on population growth by its severity. *Collapse* generalizes from the Rwandan case, suggesting that past unravelings of human civilizations have been caused by overpopulation and resultant starvation and war, and that we are likely to see future resource conflict and the threat of global collapse given rates of population growth and our demands on environmental resources.

Diamond's analysis has been hugely influential, the then U.S. secretary of state Warren Christopher modeling the Rwandan conflict as fueled by "depleted resources and swollen populations," for example. It has also been strongly contested by scholars who see Malthusianism as naturalizing what was in fact a social, political, and economic conflict. Just as Marx and the romantics saw Malthus as ignoring that capitalism creates the poor, so it is argued that Rwanda was in fact one of the most agriculturally successful nations in Africa; that it was the wealthy landowning group of Hutus who led the civil war, not those driven to desperation by a lack of food; and that it was the explosion of unresolved religious and ethnic tensions created at independence that led to the violence of the events of 1994. Similar ripostes have been offered to the other Malthusian fears of security demography: a youth bulge is not a problem per se; indeed, it can create a large working population and thereby a "demographic dividend" of economic advance as it did in Southeast Asia in recent decades. It is only where national and global economic inequalities leave such groups without opportunities that they may be modeled as problematic. The same applies for migration: migrants, when given suitable economic opportunities in receiving nations, can be used to remedy the problems of increasing dependency ratios, such that the security demographic's fear of migrants is little more than coded xenophobia. In each case, the response is that of Marx to Malthus: population does not create problems, nor do natural limits; they are made by an economic system that creates marginalized groups.[16]

If demographic security analysts fear descent into Malthusian positive checks due to unprecedented imbalances in global and national demographic structures, their arguments segue neatly into concerns about global food security. Over the past decade, there has been a discernible renewal of concerns about feeding the global population. Such discussion began for three interrelated reasons: first, as we have seen above, demographic momentum means we still see the need for huge increases in global agricultural productivity, which in turn rest on access to water, fertilizer, and other resources. Second, economic development, especially in Asia, has led increasing numbers to demand a "Western-style" diet that, with its emphasis on meat consumption, is far less efficient in terms of calories produced per acre than the diets it is superseding. And finally, the signs are that global growth in food yields per acre is tailing off as the Green Revolution, which we addressed in Chapter 8, reaches its limits and as investment in food research has dwindled as food availability, like population growth, fell from the top of the international political agenda in recent decades. One consequence of this renewed concern about food security was the endowment in 2010 by the Population Reference Bureau and the International Food Policy Research Institute of an annual "Malthus Lecture" to address "the connections among nutrition, food, agriculture, and population."[17]

Such a set of concerns may have been bubbling in the academic and policy literature for a decade or more, but they burst into public and political consciousness in 2007–2008 with the pronounced "spike" in global food prices. Estimates vary, but somewhere between thirty and forty-seven countries are said to have experienced food riots as a consequence. And in this context, unsurprisingly, Malthus has reemerged on the public stage as a prophet of food crisis. The Harvard historian and public intellectual Niall Ferguson reminded the readers of the *Daily Telegraph* in the United Kingdom and the *LA Times* in the United States "Don't Count out Malthus" in 2007 as the food price spike peaked: "as the world approaches a new era of dearth, misery and its old companion, vice, are set to make a mighty Malthusian comeback." *Time* magazine likewise acknowledged in 2011 "that Malthus was prescient." And the price spike has also led serious economists to rehabilitate Malthus: the *Wall Street Journal* reported in March 2008 that the 2001 Nobel Prize winner Joseph Stiglitz now sees limits to growth impending, while his successor as Nobel laureate in 2008, Paul Krugman, has gone further. In a speech in 2009, Krugman argued that the credit crunch and global economic depression should not be allowed to divert attention from long-term food supply problems: "The [credit] crisis will eventually end and when it does, we'll discover that neo-Malthusians were not wrong. Resource constraints plus bad policies are creating a major problem for the supply of food in the world. . . . Fundamentally we are moving towards a world where Malthusian type pressures are increasing and it's a problem."[18]

Krugman's mention of "bad policies" as well as "resource constraints" opens up the sorts of riposte offered by those who do not see the food crisis of 2007–2008 in Malthusian terms. As both Vaclav Smil and Jeffrey Sachs have emphasized, there is currently enough food produced in the world to feed around 10 billion people. On this analysis, then, the problem is one of resource distribution, not a Malthusian one of absolute resource shortages. As people demand Western-style diets and as increasing acreages of agricultural land are being used to produce biofuels rather than food, so it is argued that the "real threat is consumption patterns, not 'overpopulation.'" If such a perspective tends to lead to a critique of capitalism, there is also a free-market analysis of the food price spike that suggests it was the product of too much interference in the global food market, not of the market itself. It has been argued, for example, that there were large food stockpiles that the World Trade Organization would not allow onto the market in 2007–2008 and that major food-producing nations started to stockpile their products to address their own domestic food security concerns, such that "the simple Neo-Malthusian notion, that *aggregate* need is outstripping *aggregate* supply, is wrong." And yet even if the Malthusian analysis is "wrong," it is having a great impact on world affairs and actions at present. In a context where "the spectre of Malthusian famines has returned to haunt the world," even if that specter is arguably, as the term suggests, illusory, governments and corporations are acting upon it. Concerns about food security have led to up to 227 million hectares of land globally being bought by agencies and nations from outside the country in question to secure their access to food and resources. Malthusian fears about food security, which he articulated so eloquently in addressing the issue of the Corn Laws in his own age, are driving an unprecedented global "land grab" that internationalizes the ownership of agricultural resources in ways not seen since decolonization.[19]

Perhaps the most contentious area of all, however, is a field known as "environmental security," which has had demonstrable impacts on global policy makers. Environmental security concerns take on board Cohen's point about population, climate, agriculture, and culture being interlinked and make of this a "Security" string quartet that plays on the ways in which these variables might interact to create self-reinforcing vicious spirals of positive checks. As the language of checks suggests, and as we shall see, Malthus has been closely associated with the emergence of this complex of ideas over the past two decades. Indeed, Malthus has been depicted as the "father" of environmental security as "many of his concerns have been remarkably persistent in arguments about how environment should be linked to security."[20]

Environmental security as a discourse springs from the concern that the best available models of the impact of climate change on human populations, those offered by the IPCC, suggest multiple ways in which the suite of climate changes associated with increasing global temperatures may deleteriously affect human societies leading to the very Malthusian positive checks of pestilence, unrest, famine, and, potentially, apocalyptic global warfare. Starting with the predictions that have fueled environmental security, it is estimated, for example, that climate change will lead to a decrease in global food production due to shifts in temperature and changing rainfall regimes and that this will keep the numbers suffering globally from malnourishment at the order of 1 billion by 2050. Rising sea levels and other changes have been predicted to cause unprecedented waves of "environmental refugees," estimates of the scale of the issue ranging from 200 million to 1 billion people thus displaced by 2050. Climate change is also anticipated to create better conditions for a range of vector-borne diseases and thereby increase the incidence of deaths by these diseases as well as leading to circumstances in which more die of conditions related to heat stress. It is the social, economic, and political consequences of such predictions, coupled with the concerns we have already seen around global demographic momentum, around demographic imbalances, and around food supply and security that environmental security addresses.[21]

The most important pioneer of this type of inquiry is Thomas Homer-Dixon. In opening up the field in a pathbreaking essay in 1991, Homer-Dixon referred explicitly and repeatedly to Malthus. Writing in 1991, just a year after the maturation of the Ehrlich-Simon wager, Homer-Dixon argued that while "cornucopians" like Simon had been right to date, there were multiple reasons to assume that "Neo-Malthusians may underestimate human adaptability in *today's* environmental-social system, but as time passes their analysis may become ever more compelling." Homer-Dixon envisaged a global future where environmental degradation, accelerated by climate change in ways discussed in the previous paragraph, would lead to three forms of conflict: battles caused by simple scarcity, group ethnic conflicts caused by unprecedented global migration in the face of climate change, and wars caused by relative depravation, by the disparities between shrinking rich nations and populous poor ones. Climate change, food and resource shortages, and demographic imbalances would combine such that "whereas serious scarcities of critical resources in the past usually appeared singly, now we face multiple scarcities that exhibit powerful interactive, feedback, and threshold effects."[22]

Homer-Dixon's work was picked up on by the Bill Clinton administration, the U.S. president himself directly referring to it in a speech in 1994, arguing as a consequence that "you must reduce the rate of population growth." Homer-Dixon has gone on to act as an advisor to the CIA and the National Security Council, but his later work has struck a less directly Malthusian note, albeit still discussing population pressures and stresses. The impact of these ideas on the public stage came in fact not primarily from Homer-Dixon himself but from the popularization of his work in a February 1994 essay in *Atlantic Monthly* by Robert Kaplan, "The Coming Anarchy," which has been described as "probably the most influential essay" in the discussion of environmental security. It was also far more unrepentantly Malthusian than anything Homer-Dixon penned, and it is this that appears to have secured its influence in U.S. policy circles.

Kaplan, with no great display of modesty, opened by describing his essay as nothing less than a "report on what the political character of our planet is likely to be in the twenty-first century." To diagnose the future, Kaplan turned to Sierra Leone, seeing "the withering away of central governments, the rise of tribal and regional domains, the unchecked spiral of disease, and the growing pervasiveness of war." Lest the pedigree of such an analysis was lost on his readers, Kaplan made it explicit: "It is Thomas Malthus, the philosopher of demographic doomsday, who is now the prophet of West Africa's future. And West Africa's future, eventually, will also be that of most of the rest of the world." Four months later, Bill Clinton acknowledged, "I was so gripped by many of the things that were in that article." The message also dovetailed neatly with the environmental concerns of his vice president, Al Gore. As a result, a copy of Kaplan's essay was faxed to every U.S. embassy around the world as essential reading. Malthus had used the demographic work of Benjamin Franklin; now he was on Capitol Hill![23]

As with the discourses of demographic and food security, so the Malthusian language of environmental security has faced its critics. Statistically, scholars at Oslo's International Peace Research Institute have shown that there is no correlation between environmental degradation and the incidence of armed conflict in the era after 1945. Likewise, rather than being an "inconvenient truth," the resurgence of Malthus in U.S. policy circles has been seen from a Marxist perspective as very "convenient" for neoliberal agendas: "Homer-Dixon's is a conservative world view where the maldistribution of both power and resources is essentially naturalized and determined by the god of scarcity. . . . [T]he result is the greening of hate." And yet, for all this academic criticism, the Malthusian complex of environmental security developed in the 1990s is proving hugely influential, the 2008 National Defense Strategy enshrining that U.S. policy must respond to the fact that "over the next twenty years physical pressures—population, resource, energy, climatic and environmental—could combine with rapid social, cultural, technological and geopolitical change to create greater uncertainty."[24]

Malthus's Momentum: An Assured Futurity

For a historian to think about futurity is, to return to Dr. Johnson's aforementioned hound, perhaps akin to that dog trying to tap-dance on its hind legs: unlikely to succeed. Giving an address in Cambridge on the centenary of Malthus's death in 1934, John Maynard Keynes closed by suggesting that "a century hence, here in his Alma Mater, we shall commemorate him with undiminished regard." While we are currently twenty years shy of that anniversary, there are good grounds on which to conclude that even now we can be sure that Keynes's prophecy will come to pass. After all, amid the catalogue of uncertainties that the 2008 U.S. National Defense Strategy compiles there seems to be one certainty: that in the coming decades uncertainty will certainly keep Malthus and Malthusian reasoning at the heart of our debates about the interrelationships between population, environmental change, and sociopolitical responses. This is but one reason to see Malthus as having sufficient momentum to reach the midcentury, his influence undiminished.[25]

Part of Malthus's intellectual momentum relates to the "real-world" momentums of demography and the environment that have preoccupied us in this chapter. The trends in current demography will take decades to unravel, and their implications in terms of security and social change will be felt over the same timescale: "societies are being churned up in ways never seen in the more static pre-modern world. In the decades to 2050 these changing demographic patterns will, perhaps more than anything else, shape how the world changes." The same holds good for the causes of climate change: demographic and economic momentum means that scenarios of global warming and associated societal dislocations are bound to play out over decades to come. To the extent that Malthus stands as the grandfather of environmental security debates, "Old Pop" will remain a key sounding board into future decades.[26]

Putting aside real-world momentums, however, Malthus's impact into futurity also seems assured because the landscape of present-day debates about scenarios for the global future of humanity seems so strongly indebted both to his work, as canvassed in Chapter 3, and to the context of revolutionary optimism from which his work sprang, as canvassed in Chapter 2, discussion today revolving to an uncanny degree around the same binary of a conservative pessimism and a more revolutionary optimism. On the one hand, Malthus's name is frequently explicitly evoked by those who predict a gloomy future for mankind. Thus the influential public intellectual John Gray sees a future where wars "could have the effect of culling the population in the way Malthus described," views the American action in the Persian Gulf as "a classical Malthusian conflict," and concludes: "If you want to understand twenty-first-century wars, forget the ideological conflicts of the twentieth century. Read Malthus instead."[27] And if such journalistic rumblings sound lightweight, a rather more serious note of Malthusian pessimism was struck in 2009 by the United Kingdom's chief scientific advisor, Sir John Beddington, who argued that food and water shortages, depletion of energy sources, and climate change might act in a negative loop to create what he, in a re-working of the language of environmental security, called "a perfect storm of global events." In the speech in which Beddington first aired these ideas, he concluded: "we have got to deal with increased demand for energy, increased demand for food, increased demand for water, and we've got to do that while mitigating and adapting to climate change. And we have but 21 years to do it." And then Malthus came into his picture: "Are we all doomed? Is there any hope? Whenever I interview, people always mention Thomas Malthus and am I now a second Thomas Malthus? Not quite because I am reasonably optimistic." Beddington, then, used a Malthusian rhetoric of doom to counsel us to hope by means of action. Talk of positive checks in a perfect storm was in fact used to persuade us of the need for preventive checks addressing questions of food security and carbon footprint reductions.[28]

Equally serious, albeit coming in the reverse direction from Beddington, is Jeffrey Sachs, who acted as an advisor to U.N. Secretary General Kofi Annan. In his 2005 book *The End of Poverty*, Sachs argued that we can put an end to global poverty, concluding his call to arms by arguing that we should build an "enlightened globalism" rather than wallowing in parochial self-interest. And as an inspiration for such a globalism, Sachs singled out Malthus's old sparring partner the Marquis de Condorcet, who "brilliantly foresaw the role that science and technology could play for sustained social betterment." As Sachs concluded, "remarkably, contrary to the dark vision of Thomas Malthus, we can accomplish all of this." Former U.S. vice president Al Gore seems to agree, his 1992 *Earth in Balance* seeing in the formation of what he calls "a global Marshall Plan" a way to address climate change and economic development successfully, avoiding our previous recourse to "escap[ing] the Malthusian dilemma" by a Faustian pact with fossil fuels. More recently, however, Gore has been less certain of the ease with which we can circumvent Malthusian problems of population. Likewise, by 2008 Sachs had added a rather darker, Malthusian tone to his picture. In part, this was triggered by the food price hikes of the preceding twelve months, which led Sachs to pen an article for *Scientific American*, "Are Malthus's Predicted 1798 Food Shortages Coming True?," in which he acknowledged that whereas during his student years as an economist, "Malthusian reasoning was a target of mockery," the present situation suggested that "the Malthusian spectre is not truly banished—far from it." Sachs's rehabilitation of Malthus was extended in his book of the same year, *Common Wealth: Economics for a Crowded Planet*, which, as its subtitle suggests, now saw the stabilization of global population as a key desideratum.[29]

If Beddington has invoked the fear of positive checks to guide us to preventive ones, Sachs's has moderated his language of enlightened globalism in the face of the stark pressure of positive population and food checks that he now detects. But both are enmeshed in patterns of thought that are Malthusian, that come from the moment when Enlightenment social science came to address the meaning of the French Revolution. Perhaps both could agree with an uncertainty: "Have we beaten Malthus? After two centuries, we still do not really know." And it is for this reason that Malthus's future is assured. Malthus is not outdated, as Beddington and Sachs in their different ways show; the question is more what kind of Malthus we want as we seek to address the problems global society now faces. We will turn to this question in a brief, very unhistorical, epilogue.[30]

Epilogue

High Time for the Untimely Prophet

IN 2011, while I was deep sunk in the writing of this book, there was a sudden flurry of Malthus-related stories in the media as the globe's population overtopped the 7 billion mark. The date for this event was set with implausible accuracy as October 31 (the real date may have been as much as six months earlier or later than the selected date), while with an equally arbitrary eye for story making, one Danica May Camacho of the Philippines was nominated as the earth's seven-billionth living inhabitant (although others were thus nominated too). As will be unsurprising to those who have followed my narrative this far, Malthus was duly mobilized as part of the story line. We were told that Malthus thought that women have as many children as physically possible, that he underestimated human inventiveness, and that he argued "without providing any reasons." Somewhat embarrassingly, both *Reuters UK* and *Forbes* magazine in the United States ran stories on this event with the same headline, "7 Billion Reasons Why Malthus Was Wrong." In general, the tenor of the stories that ran on this date reinforced the same, very simple assertion: Malthus is wrong. And this is but the respectable tip of the iceberg in terms of contemporary commentary on Malthus, there also being a world of blogs and posts on the Internet condemning Malthus as a lackey of the establishment, trotted out to tell all-too-convenient falsehoods.[1]

And yet as I write this epilogue in the summer of 2012, there is also a rather different suite of stories circulating in the media. With the hottest summer on record devastating the U.S. cereal harvest for this year, the specter of global food shortages on the model of those experienced in the

2007/2008 "price spike" discussed in Chapter 9 looms. Comparisons have been raised with the "Dust Bowl" of the early 1930s, with newspapers starting to note "it will inevitably raise food prices and increase hunger worldwide," this being part of a more structural concern that we are "entering a new age of scarcity." Such stories suggest a simple and reverse message from those that ran for the 7 billion: Malthus is right, and, like the Grim Reaper in *Tristram Shandy*, will be tapping at your door any day now.[2]

Finally, and to complete my set, a few months back there was another little bubble of Malthusian stories when the U.K. Office for Budgetary Responsibility published a report suggesting that an aging population would add so much to the burden of state spending via health-care costs and pension payouts that an extra 5 percent of GDP would need to be set aside and that this would still leave the nation with an increase of around £750 billion in its national debt by 2050. The ever-increasing dependency ratio that the United Kingdom shares with the rest of the developed world would in this scenario lead the working-age population to be ever more burdened by their commitments. If they chose to respond to this by having fewer children themselves, the situation would spiral generationally without mass immigration. As a report in the *Daily Telegraph* suggested, in this context the dire predictions of Ehrlich's *Population Bomb* were preposterous: "time has turned the book, and its author, into an economist's joke." Here, then, Malthus is deemed right, but only if his geometrical ratio is understood in mirror image as the specter of depopulation and social implosion looms.[3]

To the intellectual historian, there is something bizarre but also very flattering about these responses to Malthus some two centuries after he wrote. Flattering, that people think Malthus matters so much that they choose to rebut him or to defend his shade so passionately. Bizarre, in that one can think of few comparable figures in the history of ideas in general, let alone in the history of economics or demography, who are treated in this way as offering a universal, transhistorical doctrine that every event in world population movements and food/resource supply trends can prove right or wrong. Few people tend, for example, to think of Adam Smith as proved right by the increases in global prosperity that capitalism has wrought, or indeed as proved wrong by the problems associated with that system such as the Great Depression that confronted Keynes or our current gloom in the wake of the credit crunch. The attitude taken toward Malthus, that he is "perpetually modern," that he is always to be found right or wrong in the light of current events, is one that the distinguished critic Sir Frank Kermode identified as marking out works that a society deems canonical. As Kermode showed, *Hamlet* has thus been found to offer new parables to each age, for example, precisely because it is presumed to be fresh and modern, to speak to our condition at least as much as to the era of its creation. Such an attitude of perpetual modernity is, of course, also definitive of religious texts and their significance to believers, be those texts the scriptures of orthodox religions (as, say, the Bible and the Koran) or of quasi-religions (one thinks of certain modes of reading Marx, Freud, and others in this regard). And yet there is one way in which the assertion of Malthus's perpetual modernity has proved rather different from those just mentioned: Christians read the Bible, Marxists pore over *Capital,* critics devour *Hamlet.* Malthus, however, seems all but unread in that the assertions the media and indeed many scholars have offered about what he "said" are so divorced from any clear sense of his life and of what he actually wrote. When a distinguished professional geographer, for example, can suggest in a study of global demography that Malthus's advocacy of family limitation was nothing more than "the sexual hang-ups of an economist of the cloth," we realize just how little both the scholar in question and his audience actually read the canonical individual he chooses thus to travesty. Malthus, then, ends in a strange limbo land as the "unread" classic. He is, to revert to my prologue, still hidden behind the door hinges of intellectual history.[4]

The aim of this book has been rather different with respect to Malthus. *Malthus* has sought to convey to its readers what Malthus actually wrote and the context in which he wrote it (Chapters 1–3 and 5). It has also sought to show how people who actually read Malthus's works responded to him over the two centuries since the publication of the *Essay,* placing the reception of his works in the contexts of shifting times and needs (Chapters 4 and 6–9). Both Malthus's achievement and his reception, then, have been placed in their respective historical contexts rather than seeking to adjudicate about matters of right or wrong, rather than asserting Malthus's perpetual modernity.

For a historian to offer prescriptions about how a figure from the past should be used is, to revert to Dr. Johnson's imagery from Chapter 9, rather like a dog tap-dancing on its hind legs while riding a unicycle: almost bound to fall flat on its face. And yet it seems worth risking the resultant bloody nose and offering a concluding unhistorical thought about a "usable" Malthus for our own age. We've already seen that Malthus is actively shaping the agendas that bring together climate change, demography, and public policy, notably through the discourse of "security," but which Malthus should we draw upon in our present-day debates? The Malthus on whom the media and public intellectuals are drawing to show him right or wrong is almost exclusively a caricatured version of the Malthus who penned the first edition of the *Essay* in 1798. In truth, the only other "usable" Malthus whom we have ever been offered over the past two centuries is that which Keynes constructed in the 1930s on the basis of a fairly tendentious reading of Malthus's *Principles of Political Economy*, as we saw in Chapter 7. But if most commentary (historical and current) revolves around the first edition of the *Essay*, as we saw in Chapter 3, the real Malthus of 1798 was in fact nowhere near as stark and simplistic in his analysis of the population-resource balance or in his policy prescriptions as modern reportage would have you believe. And yet there was a bold, polemical tone to this work that Malthus spent the rest of his life softening, qualifying, adjusting, and altering, as we saw in Chapter 5. After what we might style his "Trondheim moment" during his Scandinavian trip, Malthus consistently sought to emphasize and analyze the complexity of the interrelationships between the environment, population, socioeconomic structures, and policy responses. He was always willing to suspend theoretical presuppositions if they did not appear to work in real-world circumstances, as his ruminations on the Corn Laws and even on relief for the poor showed. If we want a "usable" Malthus as we address the nexus of demographic and environmental change in our own age, perhaps it can be found here in the later Malthus. Such a Malthus should be read rather than merely caricatured, and he should be read not through a "right-wrong" binary of timeless truth but for his temper of mind. In other words, where Malthus has normally been read in scriptural terms as right or wrong, he is better read as an "organon," a tool by which to reason. Malthus's devotion to empirical truth, his geniality and flexibility, all those admirable intellectual qualities that make his funereal inscription in Bath Abbey seem so dull, are perhaps where we should turn in our present discontents to find a very untimely prophet.

Notes

Prologue

1. Part of the epitaph can be found in Patricia James, *Population Malthus: His Life and Times* (London: Routledge, 1979), 460. An image of the tablet can be found at: http://en.wikipedia.org/wiki/File:Epitaph_of_Thomas_Malthus.jpg.

2. Malthus's life is treated most comprehensively in James, *Population Malthus.* Contemporary sources for Malthus's life are: William Otter, "Memoir of Robert Malthus," in Thomas Robert Malthus, *Principles of Political Economy,* 2nd ed. (repr., New York: Augustus M. Kelly, 1951), xiii–liv; and William Empson, "The Life, Writings and Character of Mr. Malthus," *Edinburgh Review* 67 (1837): 469–506.

3. Rosemary Hill, *God's Architect: Pugin and the Building of Romantic Britain* (Harmondsworth: Allen Lane, 2007), 2.

4. Paul Krugman, "Malthus Was Right!" *New York Times,* 25 March 2008, emphasis in original. This article can be accessed at: http://krugman.blogs.nytimes.com/2008/03/25/malthus-was-right/.

5. Excavations of this Malthusian regime are offered in: E. A. Wrigley, *Continuity, Chance and Change: The Character of the Industrial Revolution* (Cambridge: Cambridge University Press, 1988); E. A. Wrigley, *Energy and the English Industrial Revolution* (Cambridge: Cambridge University Press, 2010); Gregory Clark, *A Farewell to Alms: A Brief Economic History of the World* (Princeton: Princeton University Press, 2007); Edward Barbier, *Scarcity and Frontiers: How Economies Have Developed through Natural Resource Exploitation* (Cambridge: Cambridge University Press, 2011); and Oded Galor, *Unified Growth Theory* (Princeton: Princeton University Press, 2011).

6. Garrett Hardin, *Living within Limits: Ecology, Economics and Population Taboos* (New York: Oxford University Press, 1993), 91.

7. While *Malthus* takes in moments in the response to Malthus in countries such as France, Italy, and Germany, it mainly attends to the Anglophone response to Malthus. Even within this remit, little attention is given to the early American reactions to Malthus or to Anglophone colonial reactions. On the first of these topics, see James Russell Gibson, *Americans Versus Malthus: The Population Debate in the Early Republic, 1790–1840* (New York: Garland, 1989); and Dennis Hodgson, "Malthus's *Essay on Population* and the American Debate Over Slavery," *Comparative Studies in Society and History* 51 (2009): 742–770. On the second question, see Alison Bashford, "Malthus and Colonial History," *Journal of Australian Studies* 36 (2012): 99–110.

8. For two recent examples, see Danny Dorling, *Population 10 Billion: The Coming Demographic Crisis and How to Survive It* (London: Constable, 2013); and Stephen Emmott, *10 Billion* (London: Penguin, 2013).

1. Before Malthus

1. For Sterne's life, see Arthur Cash, *Laurence Sterne: The Early and Middle Years* (London: Methuen, 1975); and Arthur Cash, *Laurence Sterne: The Later Years* (London: Methuen, 1986).

2. Laurence Sterne, *The Life and Opinions of Tristram Shandy,* ed. Graham Petrie (Harmondsworth: Penguin, 1985), 36 and 89.

3. Ibid., 286.

4. Ibid., 69.

5. Ibid., 460–461, 42, 60–61, and 331.

6. Cash, *Sterne, Later Years,* 134; Cash, *Sterne, Early Years,* 61 and 82–83.

7. Cash, *Sterne, Early Years,* 134–135 and 158.

8. David Vaisey, ed., *The Diary of Thomas Turner 1754–1765* (Oxford: Oxford University Press, 1984), 1–5.

9. Ibid., 228.

10. John Beresford, ed., *The Diary of a Country Parson 1758–1802 by James Woodforde* (Oxford: Oxford University Press, 1935), 558, 571–572, 563, and 567.

11. W. H. Chaloner, ed., *The Autobiography of Samuel Bamford* (1849; repr., London: Frank Cass, 1967), 1, 5, and 58.

12. The current estimate is 5.917 million: E. A. Wrigley, R. S. Davies, J. E. Oeppen, and R. S. Schofield, *English Population History from Family Reconstruction, 1580–1837* (Cambridge: Cambridge University Press, 1997), 538, table 8.8. The same source gives us life expectancies in 1751 (294–295); rates of infant mortality (215, table 6.1); expectations of life age 25 (281–282, figure 6.14); and rates of female mortality in childbirth (313, table 6.29). See also Peter Laslett, *The World We Have Lost,* 2nd ed. (London: Methuen, 1971). The modern demographic data is drawn from the U.K. Office for National Statistics, death registrations summary tables, England and Wales, 2011 (provisional) at: www.ons.gov.uk/ons/publications/re-reference-tables.html?edition=tcm%3A77-265234.

13. Laslett, *World We have Lost,* chap. 4; Wrigley, Oeppen, and Schofield, *English Population History,* 135, 461, and 508; James Boswell, *London Journal, 1762–1763,* ed. Frederick Pottle (New Haven: Yale University Press, 1950), 237.

14. Wrigley, Oeppen, and Schofield, *English Population History,* 135, 140–141, 137, 194.

15. John Landers, *The Field and the Forge: Population, Production and Power in the Pre-Industrial West* (Oxford: Oxford University Press, 2003), 19–25 and 28; Wrigley, Oeppen, and Schofield, *English Population History,* 547–548.

16. Mary Dobson, *Contours of Death and Disease in Early Modern England* (Cambridge: Cambridge University Press, 1997), esp. pt. 3; John Landers, *Death and the Metropolis: Studies in the Demographic History of London, 1670–1830* (Cambridge: Cambridge University Press, 1993); Wrigley, Oeppen, and Schofield, *English Population History,* 273.

17. On advanced organic and mineral economies, see: E. A. Wrigley, *Continuity, Chance and Change: The Character of the Industrial Revolution* (Cambridge: Cambridge University Press, 1988); E. A. Wrigley, *Energy and the English Industrial Revolution* (Cambridge: Cambridge University Press, 2010); and Landers, *Field and Forge,* quote at 17.

18. Joel Mokyr, *The Enlightened Economy: An Economic History of Britain, 1700–1850* (New Haven: Yale University Press, 2009), 178, 194–195, 462. For current studies of calorific intake, see Craig Muldrew, *Food, Energy and the Creation of Industriousness: Work and Material Culture in Agrarian England, 1550–1780* (Cambridge: Cambridge University Press, 2011). On early modern mature heights for the English, see Roderick Floud, Robert W. Fogel, Bernard Harris, and Sok Chul Hong, *The Changing Body: Health, Nutrition, and Human Development in the Western World since 1700* (Cambridge: Cambridge University Press, 2011).

19. Mark Overton, *Agricultural Revolution in England: The Transformation of the Agrarian Economy, 1500–1850* (Cambridge: Cambridge University Press, 1996); G. E. Mingay, *Parliamentary Enclosure in England: An Introduction to Its Causes, Incidence and Impact 1750–1850* (London: Longmans, 1997).

20. On draining and deforestation, see H. C. Darby, ed., *A New Historical Geography of England after 1600* (Cambridge: Cambridge University Press, 1976), chapters by Darby and Prince. Data for coal from Ian Simmons, *An Environmental History of Great Britain: From 10,000 Year Ago to the Present* (Edinburgh: Edinburgh University Press, 2001), 120–121.

21. John Richards, *The Unending Frontier: An Environmental History of the Early Modern World* (Berkeley: University of California Press, 2003), 240. For market integration, see Ann Kussmaul, *A General View of the Rural Economy of England, 1538–1840* (Cambridge: Cambridge University Press, 1990).

22. Geoffrey Hawthorn, *Enlightenment and Despair: A History of Social Theory* (Cambridge: Cambridge University Press, 1976); Johan Heilbron, *The Rise of Social Theory* (Cambridge: Polity Press, 1995).

23. Montesquieu, *Persian Letters*, trans. and ed. C. Betts (Harmondsworth: Penguin, 1973), 202, 326n3, 203–204. For quantitative demographic work in Montesquieu's France and England, see Andrea Rusnock, *Vital Accounts: Quantifying Health and Population in Eighteenth-Century England and France* (Cambridge: Cambridge University Press, 2002).

24. Montesquieu, *Persian Letters*, 206, 211–212, 209, 219. Compare with book 23, "On Laws in Their Relation to the Number of Inhabitants," in Montesquieu, *The Spirit of the Laws,* trans. and ed. Anne Cohler, Basia Miller, and Harold Stone (Cambridge: Cambridge University Press, 1989), 427–458. On Smith, see Knud Haakonssen, *The Science of the Legislator: The Natural Jurisprudence of David Hume and Adam Smith* (Cambridge: Cambridge University Press, 1981). On the sinews of power, see John Brewer, *The Sinews of Power: War, Money and the English State, 1688–1783* (London: Unwin Hyman, 1989).

25. Mirabeau cited in Rusnock, *Vital Accounts,* 180; Benjamin Franklin, "Observations Concerning the Increase of Mankind" (1751), in Bernard Larabee et al. eds., *The Papers of Benjamin Franklin* (New Haven: Yale University Press, 1954–present), 4:225–234, quote at 228; David Hume, "Of the Populousness of Ancient Nations" (1752), in *Essays: Moral, Political and Literary,* ed. Eugene Miller, rev. ed. (Indianapolis: Liberty Fund, 1987), 377–464, quote at 388.

26. Hume, "Populousness," 448–452, quote at 451; Margaret Schabas, *The Natural Origins of Economics* (Chicago: University of Chicago Press, 2005), 2; Keith Thomas, *Man and the Natural World: Changing Attitudes in England, 1500–1800* (Harmondsworth: Penguin, 1984), 18.

27. Rusnock, *Vital Accounts;* James C. Riley, *Population Thought in the Age of the Demographic Revolution* (Durham, NC: Carolina Academic Press, 1985), chaps. 2 and 4, quote at 85; William Cowper, *The Task* (1785), bk. 1, line 749; Hume cited in James Bonar, *Theories of Population: From Raleigh to Arthur Young* (London: Frank Cass Reissue, 1966), 230–231.

28. Hume, "Populousness," 421. Rousseau's comment comes from the *Social Contract,* cited in Rusnock, *Vital Accounts,* 182. Süssmilch cited in Bonar, *Theories,* 148. For Petty and Halley, see Ted McCormick, *William Petty and the Ambitions of Political Arithmetic* (Oxford: Oxford University Press, 2009); and Alan Cook, *Edmund Halley: Charting the Heavens and the Seas* (Oxford: Clarendon Press, 1998), 198–200. For Fothergill, Black, Howlett, and Heysham and for the 1753 census debate, see D. V. Glass, *Numbering the People: The Eighteenth-Century Population Controversy and the Development of Census and Vital Statistics in Britain* (London: D. C. Heath, 1973) for commentary; and D. V. Glass, ed., *The Development of Population Statistics* (Farnborough: Gregg International, 1973) for reprints of their writings. On the final emergence of a census as well as D. V. Glass, see Kathrin Levitan, *A Cultural History of the British Census: Envisioning the Multitude in the Nineteenth Century* (New York: Palgrave, 2011).

29. Rousseau cited in Rusnock, *Vital Accounts,* 182; Süssmilch's global estimates discussed in Charles Strangeland, *Pre-Malthusian Doctrines of Population:*

A Study in the History of Economic Theory (1904; repr., New York: Augustus Kelley, 1966); quotation from Süssmilch is cited in Bonar, *Theories,* 148–150.

2. Prophets of Perfection

1. On "left" and "right" in English political discourse of this time, see James J. Sack, *From Jacobite to Conservative: Reaction and Orthodoxy in Britain, c. 1760–1832* (Cambridge: Cambridge University Press, 1993); and Robert Hole, *Pulpits, Politics and Public Order in England, 1760–1832* (Cambridge: Cambridge University Press, 1989).
2. William Doyle, *The Oxford History of the French Revolution,* 2nd ed. (Oxford: Oxford University Press, 2002) remains a good introduction. See, for the other points about these events, François Furet, *Interpreting the French Revolution* (Cambridge: Cambridge University Press, 1981); and Robert Darnton, *The Forbidden Best Sellers of Pre-Revolutionary France* (New York: Norton, 1996).
3. The demographic transition model is clearly explained in Massimo Livi-Bacci, *A Concise History of World Population,* 4th ed. (Oxford: Blackwells, 2007), chap. 4.
4. D. O. Thomas, *The Honest Mind: The Thought and Work of Richard Price* (Oxford: Oxford University Press, 1977), xxiii, and see chapter 15 for Price and Burke; Conor Cruise O'Brien, *The Great Melody: A Thematic Biography of Edmund Burke* (London: Sinclair Stevenson, 1992).
5. Thomas, *Honest Mind,* 139–140.
6. Richard Price, *Observations on Reversionary Payments,* 6th ed. (London: Cadell and Davies, 1803), 47, 27, 141. For Disney, see W. Bernard Peach and D. O. Thomas, eds., *The Correspondence of Richard Price,* 3 vols. (Cardiff: University of Wales Press, 1983–1994), 1:160–161.
7. Price, *Observations,* quotes at 141, 139, 40, 146, and 243. For Utopia, see Thomas More, *Utopia,* ed. George Logan and Robert Adams (Cambridge: Cambridge University Press, 1989), 18–19. For debates about luxury, see Maxine Berg and Elizabeth Elger, eds., *Luxury in the Eighteenth Century: Desires, Debates and Delectable Goods* (Basingstoke: Palgrave, 2003); and John Brewer and Roy Porter, eds., *Consumption and the World of Goods* (London: Routledge, 1993).
8. Price, *Observations,* 144, 145–146. See also Richard Price, "Britain's Happiness and the Proper Improvement of It" (1759), in D. O. Thomas, ed., *Price: Political Writings* (Cambridge: Cambridge University Press, 1991), 1–13.
9. Richard Price, "Observations on the Importance of the American Revolution" (1785), in D. O. Thomas, ed., *Price: Political Writings* (Cambridge: Cambridge University Press, 1991), 116–151, quotes at 148 and 119.
10. Price to Mirabeau, in Price, *Correspondence,* 3:230; Richard Price, "A Discourse on the Love of Our Country" (1789), in D. O. Thomas, ed., *Price: Political Writings* (Cambridge: Cambridge University Press, 1991), 176–196, quotes at 181, 194, and 195.

11. Price, *Correspondence*, 3:230. On Condorcet's death, see David Williams, *Condorcet and Modernity* (Cambridge: Cambridge University Press, 2004), 42–43. *Hamlet*, act 1, scene 5, line 77.

12. For Condorcet's early life, see Williams, *Condorcet and Modernity*, chapter 1; and Keith Michael Baker, *Condorcet: From Natural Philosophy to Social Mathematics* (Chicago: University of Chicago Press, 1975), chapter 1. French Newtonianism is analyzed in J. B. Shank, *The Newton Wars and the Beginning of the French Enlightenment* (Chicago: University of Chicago Press, 2008). French salon culture is depicted in Dena Goodman, *The Republic of Letters: A Cultural History of the French Enlightenment* (Ithaca, NY: Cornell University Press, 1994).

13. For the *Encyclopédie* and radicalism, see Robert Darnton, *The Business of Enlightenment: A Publishing History of the* Encyclopédie, *1775–1800* (Cambridge: Harvard University Press, 1979). For coining the term "social science," see Baker, *Condorcet*, 197–198. For Condorcet's doubts regarding democracy, see Williams, *Condorcet and Modernity*, 254–256; and for his application to social mathematics, see ibid., 105–106.

14. Condorcet, "Reception Speech at the French Academy" (1782), in Keith Michael Baker, ed. and trans., *Condorcet: Selected Writings* (Indianapolis: Bobbs-Merrill, 1976), 3–32, quotes at 21, 5, and 9. For Condorcet on the need for physical geographical information, see also Williams, *Condorcet and Modernity*, 198–200.

15. For Condorcet's umbrella and the conception of Eliza, see Williams, *Condorcet and Modernity*, 28, who also discusses Condorcet as icon, 4. The most thorough discussion of Condorcet and the Society of 1789 is in Baker, *Condorcet*, 272–285, quote at 273.

16. On Condorcet's newfound bellicosity after the king's flight, see Baker, *Condorcet*, 304–308; Burke's public comment comes in "Thoughts on French Affairs" (1791), in L. G. Mitchell, ed., *The Writings and Speeches of Edmund Burke*, vol. 8, *The French Revolution 1790–1794* (Oxford: Clarendon Press, 1989), 338–386, at 369. His private comment is from a letter of 1 June 1791 in *The Correspondence of Edmund Burke*, ed. T. W. Copeland et al. (Cambridge: Cambridge University Press, 1958–1978), 6:267–268. For Condorcet and the death penalty, see Williams, *Condorcet and Modernity*, 41.

17. For Condorcet's ideas in 1792–1793, see Baker, *Condorcet*, 316–322. For the *Journal of Social Mathematics*, see Baker, *Condorcet*, 330–340. For the Terror, Condorcet's flight, and capture, see Baker, *Condorcet*, 352; and Williams, *Condorcet and Modernity*, 42–43.

18. Antoine-Nicholas de Condorcet, *Outlines of an Historical View of the Progress of the Human Mind* (London: J. Johnson, 1795), 8 and 39 on settled agriculture; 245 for Bacon and science; 153 on medieval priestcraft. Obviously, much of Condorcet's historical account was highly indebted to the stadial theories of the Scottish Enlightenment, for which see Christopher Fox, Roy Porter, and Robert Wokler, eds., *Inventing Human Science: Eighteenth-Century Domains* (Berkeley: University of California Press, 1995); Larry

Wolff and Marco Cipolloni, eds., *The Anthropology of the Enlightenment* (Stanford, CA: Stanford University Press, 2007); and chapters by Richter, Mason, and Pross, in Mark Goldie and Robert Wokler eds., *The Cambridge History of Eighteenth-Century Political Thought* (Cambridge: Cambridge University Press, 2006).

19. Condorcet, *Outlines,* 287, 355, 410, 385.

20. C. Kegan Paul, *William Godwin: His Friends and Contemporaries* (London: Henry S. King and Co, 1876), 1:61, 1:62–63. Godwin's diaries are now being made available in an ambitious electronic project hosted by the Bodleian Library: http://godwindiary.bodleian.ox.ac.uk/index2.html. Likewise, Godwin's correspondence is also being edited anew: Patricia Clemit, ed., *The Letters of William Godwin* (Oxford: Oxford University Press, 2011–).

21. Kegan Paul, *Godwin,* 1:118; Peter H. Marshall, *William Godwin* (New Haven: Yale University Press, 1984), 121, 92.

22. Marshall, *Godwin,* 14–15; Kegan Paul, *Godwin,* 1:78; Marilyn Butler, *Jane Austen and the War of Ideas* (Oxford: Clarendon Press, 1975), 75.

23. Marshall, *Godwin,* 185; for chance medley method, 307; for Shelley and the elopement, 296; for the impact of the *Enquiry* on Shelley, 124; and for the put-downs of Godwin by the romantics, 172. Marriage as a system of fraud comes from William Godwin, *Enquiry Concerning Political Justice,* ed. Isaac Kramnick (Harmondsworth: Penguin, 1976), 762. More on the Shelley-Godwin issue can be found in William St Clair, *The Godwins and the Shelleys* (London: Faber and Faber, 1989).

24. Hazlitt's quote and the judgment of Godwin's importance are from Marshall, *Godwin,* 1. Godwin's "fantasy of reason" comes from Don Locke, *Fantasy of Reason: The Life and Thought of William Godwin* (London: Routledge, 1979). Godwin, *Enquiry,* 273, 274, 759, 760, 702, 703, and 704.

25. Godwin, *Enquiry,* 151, 768, 769, 775, 776, and 777.

26. Edmund Burke, "Reflections on the Revolution in France" (1790), in *The Writings and Speeches of Edmund Burke,* ed. L. G. Mitchell, vol. 8, *The French Revolution 1790–1794* (Oxford: Clarendon Press, 1989), 53–293. The "swinish multitude" comment is at 130; the material on French population size and Price is at 177–178.

27. Arthur Young, *Travels in France during the Years 1787, 1788, 1789,* ed. Constantia Maxwell (Cambridge: Cambridge University Press, 1929), 278.

3. Malthus's *Essay* and the Quiet Revolution of 1798

1. William Wordsworth, *The Prelude 1799, 1805, 1850,* ed. Jonathan Wordsworth, M. H. Abrams, and Stephen Gill (New York: Norton, 1979), 396 (1805 edition, 11:108–109); John Pullen and Trevor Hughes Parry, eds., *T. R. Malthus: The Unpublished Papers in the Collection of Kanto Gakuen University,* 2 vols. (Cambridge: Cambridge University Press, 1997–2004), 1:54–56 for letters from 1789; 2:4–11 for the sermon of the same year; quotes from 7 and 4 respectively.

2. Pullen and Parry, *Unpublished Papers,* 2:8, and 2:34.

3. Jane Austen, *Northanger Abbey* (Oxford: Oxford University Press, 1980), 87; Raymond Postgate, *1798: The Story of a Year* (London: Longmans, 1969), author blurb, 14, and 187; Deirdre Le Faye, ed., *Jane Austen's Letters* (Oxford: Oxford University Press, 1995), 30 and 22.

4. Austen, *Northanger Abbey*, quotes at 87 and 88. For Austen as antirevolutionary, see Marilyn Butler, *Jane Austen and the War of Ideas* (Oxford: Clarendon Press, 1975). For general discussion of the social and political climate of the 1790s, see Ian R. Christie, *Stress and Stability in Late Eighteenth-Century England: Reflections on the British Avoidance of Revolution* (Oxford: Clarendon Press, 1986). Primary sources showing this climate are conveniently excerpted in Iain Hampshire-Monk, ed., *The Impact of the French Revolution: Texts from Britain in the 1790s* (Cambridge: Cambridge University Press, 2005).

5. Thomas Robert Malthus, *An Essay on the Principle of Population* (1798), vol. 1 of E. A. Wrigley and David Souden, eds., *The Works of Thomas Robert Malthus*, 8 vols. (London: Pickering and Chatto, 1986), 31. For the Sedbergh encounter, see Pullen and Parry, *Unpublished Papers*, 2:29; and for Conniston, see 2:40.

6. For Daniel Malthus at Queen's College, see Patricia James, *Population Malthus: His Life and Times* (London: Routledge, 1979), 8. For George Austen, see Park Honan, *Jane Austen: Her Life* (London: Weidenfeld and Nicolson, 1987), 12. For Graves on the Malthuses, see Clarence Tracy, *A Portrait of Richard Graves* (Toronto: University of Toronto Press, 1987), 123.

7. James, *Population Malthus*, 8–16 on Daniel Malthus; G. B. Hill and L. F Powell, eds., *Boswell's Life of Johnson* (Oxford: Oxford University Press, 1934–50), 1:75 for the nest. Wesley quoted from Trevor Fawcett, ed., *Voices of Eighteenth-Century Bath* (Bath: Ruton Press, 1995), 134. For Don Roberto, see Parry and Pullen, *Unpublished Papers*, 1:5.

8. Tracy, *Portrait*, 147; Malthus, *Essay*, 26–27.

9. Graves on Rousseau is cited in Tracy, *Portrait*, 103; Gilbert Wakefield, *Memoirs of the Life of Gilbert Wakefield* (London: E. Hodson, 1792), 199 on Warrington; and 234–236 on Bramcote. Malthus on coal is in Parry and Pullen, *Unpublished Papers*, 1:11–15. Malthus on reasoning from nature is cited from the *Essay*, 123. Issues about oaths and offices are addressed in J. C. D. Clark, *English Society, 1660–1832: Religion, Ideology and Politics during the Ancien Règime* (Cambridge: Cambridge University Press, 2000); and, for their impact on dissenters, in Knud Haakonssen, ed., *Enlightenment and Religion: Rational Dissent in Eighteenth-Century Britain* (Cambridge: Cambridge University Press, 1996).

10. The depiction of student dissipation in Cambridge is taken from D. A. Winstanley, *Unreformed Cambridge: A Study in Certain Aspects of the University in the Eighteenth Century* (Cambridge: Cambridge University Press, 1935), 211–215. For revisionist views of the university, see John Gascoigne, *Cambridge in the Age of the Enlightenment: Science, Religion and Politics from the Restoration to the French Revolution* (Cambridge: Cambridge University Press, 1989); and Peter Searby, *A History of the University of Cambridge,*

vol. 3, *1750–1870* (Cambridge: Cambridge University Press, 1997). Malthus's Cambridge cited from Parry and Pullen, *Unpublished Papers*, 1:30, 1:31, and 1:34.

11. Parry and Pullen, *Unpublished Papers*, 1:53, 1:29, 1:36, 1:39, and 1:41.

12. Ibid., 1:40, 1:48; Winstanley, *Unreformed Cambridge*, 209. Malthus also discussed shooting and walking to instance the respective powers of mind and body in his rebuttal of Godwin in the *Essay*, 79–81.

13. Parry and Pullen, *Unpublished Papers*, 1:62.

14. Malthus, *Essay*, i.

15. Modern real estate agents' blurb for Okewood comes from Savills (http://media.primelocation.com/SAGR/SAGU/SAGU_287098/BROCH_01.PDF). Roland White, "Beyond the Brochure: The Okewood Hill Estate, Surrey," *Times* (London), 1 November 2009; H. E. Malden, ed., *A History of the County of Surrey: Volume 3* (London: Constable, 1911), sub "Wotton" (www.british-history.ac.uk/report.aspx?compid=42948); John Evelyn, *Diary*, ed. William Bray, rev. ed., 2 vols. (London: Dent, 1952), 1:3.

16. See Henry Malden, *A History of Surrey* (London: Elliot Stock, 1905), 260–277 for iron and deforestation; and 289–290 for numbers relieved by the Poor Laws. The 1840 and present census data are taken from the Vision of Britain website, which classifies Okewood under its modern census location, The Mole Valley (www.visionofbritain.org.uk/unit_page.jsp?u_id=10100227&x=3305661.14511&y=2763901.94986).

17. Pullen and Parry, *Unpublished Papers*, 1:41; Malthus, *Essay*, 29–30, a passage also picked up on by James, *Population Malthus*, 43–44, and whose validity is confirmed by the studies of changes in human height over the past two centuries in Roderick Floud, Robert W. Fogel, Bernard Harris, and Sok Chul Hong, *The Changing Body: Health, Nutrition, and Human Development in the Western World since 1700* (Cambridge: Cambridge University Press, 2011), 364–375. Dietary patterns are discussed in Malthus, *Essay*, 49; and Pullen and Parry, *Unpublished Papers*, 2:33–35.

18. Thomas Pakenham, *The Year of Liberty: The Story of the Great Irish Rebellion of 1798* (London: Phoenix 1992), 172 and 180 on 7 July. See Pakenham, *Year of Liberty*, 243–244 on Napoleon's fleet; and Hugh Gough, "The Crisis Year: Europe and the Atlantic in 1798," in Thomas Bartlett, David Dickson, Dáire Keogh, and Kevin Whelan, eds., *1798: A Bicentenary Perspective* (Dublin: Four Courts Press, 2003), 544–547. On mutinies, see N. A. M. Rodger, "Mutiny or Subversion? Spithead and the Nore," in Thomas Bartlett, David Dickson, Dáire Keogh, and Kevin Whelan, eds., *1798: A Bicentenary Perspective* (Dublin: Four Courts Press, 2003), 549. For Haiti and India, see Postgate, *1798*, 179ff., and 215–219. Numbers of English loyalists are from Pakenham, *Year of Liberty*, 233; and Farington from Kenneth Garlick and Angus Macintyre, eds., *The Diary of Joseph Farington, Volume 3* (New Haven: Yale University Press, 1979), 976–977, 1016–1018.

19. For food riots, see John Langton and R. J. Morris, *Atlas of Industrializing Britain, 1780–1914* (London: Methuen, 1986), 185; and John Rule and Roger Wells, *Crime, Protest and Popular Politics in Southern England, 1740–1850*

(London: Hambledon Press, 1997), 3. Rioting along the River Avon is detailed in Andrew Charlesworth, David Glibert, Adrian Randall, Humphey Southall, and Chris Wrigley, *An Atlas of Industrial Protest in Britain, 1750–1990* (London: Macmillan, 1996), 25–29.

20. For such protest generally in early modern culture, see E. P. Thompson, *Customs in Common* (London: Merlin Press, 1991); quote from Gough, "Crisis Year," 538.

21. Malthus, *Essay*, 54 and 5.

22. Ibid., 59. On the quantifying spirit, see the essays in Tore Frangsmyer, J. H. Heilbron and Robin Rider, *The Quantifying Spirit in the Eighteenth Century* (Berkeley: University of California Press, 1992).

23. Malthus, *Essay*, 5, 8, and 9.

24. Ibid., 14, 18, 19, 20, 26, 9, 15. Malthus's inclusivity is being recovered by modern scholarship: see Alison Bashford, "Malthus and Colonial History," *Journal of Australian Studies* 36 (2012): 99–110 from a postcolonial perspective; and Karen O'Brien, *Women and Enlightenment in Eighteenth Century Britain* (Cambridge: Cambridge University Press, 2009), 222–225, from a gendered perspective.

25. Malthus, *Essay*, 56–57, 60n, and 8.

26. Ibid., 83, 85, 89–90, 76–78, 65, 64–65, and 97.

27. Ibid., quotes from 33, 36–37, and 27. The longer trajectory of this debate is ably canvassed in Gareth Steadman Jones, *An End to Poverty? A Historical Debate* (London: Profile, 2004).

28. Malthus, *Essay*, quotes at 118, 117, 107, and 110. Malthus discusses Richard Price at 119–121.

29. Ibid., quotes at 86, 123, 124, 125, 127, and 126–127. For Malthus's religious beliefs, see A. M. C. Waterman, *Revolution, Economics and Religion: Christian Political Economy, 1798–1833* (Cambridge: Cambridge University Press, 1991); A. M. C. Waterman, *Political Economy and Christian Theology since the Enlightenment: Essays in Intellectual History* (Palgrave: Basingstoke, 2004); and Boyd Hilton, *The Age of Atonement: The Influence of Evangelicalism on Social and Economic Thought, 1785–1865* (Oxford: Clarendon Press, 1988). For William Petty's religious views and demography, see Ted McCormick, *William Petty and the Ambitions of Political Arithmetic* (Oxford: Oxford University Press, 2009)

30. The clerical and conservative nature of the English Enlightenment is best captured by J. G. A. Pocock, "Clergy and Commerce: The Conservative Enlightenment in England" in Raffaele Ajello et al., eds., *L'Età dei lumi: Studi storici sul settecento Europeo in onore di Franco Venturi* (Naples: Jovene, 1985), 1:523–562; and J. G. A. Pocock, *Barbarism and Religion*, vol. 1, *The Enlightenments of Edward Gibbon, 1737–1764* (Cambridge: Cambridge University Press, 1999).

4. Malthus as the Malign Muse of Romanticism

1. For the question marks around placing the *Lyrical Ballads* as the font of romanticism, see Marilyn Butler, *Romantics, Rebels and Reactionaries: English*

Literature and Its Background, 1760–1830 (Oxford: Oxford University Press, 1981), 57–58.

2. William Wordsworth, "Lines Written a Few Miles above Tintern Abbey" (1798), in Wordsworth and Coleridge, *Lyrical Ballads,* ed. R. L. Brett and A. R. Jones (Abingdon: Routledge, 2005), lines 63–66, 34–36, 95–103, 123–124, and 129–130. Note that "Michael" and "The Old Cumberland Beggar" first appeared in the second, 1800, edition of the *Lyrical Ballads.* See also Tim Fulford, "Apocalyptic Economics and Prophetic Politics: Radical and Romantic Reponses to Malthus and Burke," *Studies in Romanticism* 40 (2001): 345–368.

3. Coleridge to Dyer, 1795, cited in Nicholas Roe, *Wordsworth and Coleridge: The Radical Years* (Oxford: Clarendon Press, 1988), 212.

4. See Jonathan Bate, *The Song of the Earth* (London: Picador, 2000); and Jonathan Bate, *Romantic Ecology: Wordsworth and the Environmental Tradition* (London: Routledge, 1991). For a counterpoint, see Scott Hess, *William Wordsworth and the Ecology of Authorship: The Roots of Environmentalism in Nineteenth-Century Culture* (Charlottesville: University of Virginia Press, 2012).

5. For these variants of romanticism, see M. H. Abrams, *Natural Supernaturalism: Tradition and Revolution in Romantic Literature* (New York: Norton, 1973); M. H. Abrams, *The Mirror and the Lamp: Romantic Theory and the Critical Tradition* (Oxford: Oxford University Press, 1953); Jerome J. McGann, *The Romantic Ideology: A Critical Investigation* (Chicago: University of Chicago Press, 1983); James Chandler, *England in 1819: The Politics of Literary Culture and the Case of Romantic Historicism* (Chicago: University of Chicago Press, 1998); and Butler, *Romantics.* An important new argument about the romantics and political economy to which this chapter is indebted is offered in Philip Connell, *Romanticism, Economics and the Question of "Culture"* (Oxford: Oxford University Press, 2001). On the romantics and demography, see Maureen McLane, *Romanticism and the Human Sciences: Poetry, Population and the Discourse of the Species* (Cambridge: Cambridge University Press, 2000).

6. For the trip to Germany, see Richard Holmes, *Coleridge: Early Visions* (London: Hodder and Stoughton, 1989), 198; the publication schedule for the *Lyrical Ballads* is addressed at 199–200; and in Stephen Gill, *William Wordsworth: A Life* (Oxford: Oxford University Press, 1989), 150–151.

7. In the analysis that follows I am indebted to Connell, *Romanticism.* See also Christian Becker et al., "Malthus vs Wordsworth: Perspectives on Humankind, Nature and Economy. A Contribution to the History and the Foundations of Ecological economics," *Ecological Economics* 53 (2005): 299–310.

8. William Wordsworth, *The Prelude 1799, 1805, 1850,* ed. Jonathan Wordsworth, M. H. Abrams, and Stephen Gill (New York: Norton, 1979), quotations from the 1805 edition at 6:136–137; 10:805–810, 10:844, 10:903–904, and 6:150–155. For Euclid, avoiding holy orders, and poverty in Racedown, see Gill, *Wordsworth,* 107, 52, 96, and 152. For geometry as an intellectual bridge, see Roe, *Wordsworth and Coleridge,* 229.

9. Wordsworth, *Prelude,* book 12: quotations (respectively) from lines 76–77, 79–80, 185–188, 194–195, 197–201, 218–219, and 206–210.

10. Alan Hill, ed., *The Letters of William Wordsworth,* vol. 5, *The Later Years Part II 1829–1834* (Oxford: Clarendon Press, 1979), 405–406; W. J. B. Owen and Jane Worthington Smyser, eds., *The Prose Works of William Wordsworth,* vol. 3 (Oxford: Clarendon Press, 1974), 240–259.

11. Holmes, *Coleridge,* 21, 41, 39, 45, and 60. For Coleridge and Frend, see Roe, *Wordsworth and Coleridge,* 85–88.

12. H. J. Jackson, ed., *Samuel Taylor Coleridge* (Oxford: Oxford University Press, 1985): "Fire, Famine and Slaughter" (1797?), line 68; "Fears in Solitude" (1798), lines 90–94, 113–116, 186–188, 221, 223, and 225–226. For Coleridge and Wordsworth being suspected as French spies, see Roe, *Wordsworth and Coleridge,* 248–262.

13. For Coleridge reading and not reacting to Malthus in 1798, see Connell, *Romanticism,* 16–17. Holmes, *Coleridge,* 173, describes the *Rime* as a green parable. The reaction to the 1803 edition is contained in H. J. Jackson and George Whalley, eds., *The Collected Works of Samuel Taylor Coleridge, Marginalia Volume III: Irving to Oxlee* (Princeton: Princeton University Press, 1992), 805–809.

14. Kathleen Cockburn, ed., *The Notebooks of Samuel Taylor Coleridge,* vol. 3, *1808–1819* (London: Routledge, 1973), note 4183; Carl Wooding, ed., *Samuel Taylor Coleridge: Table Talk,* 2 vols. (Princeton: Princeton University Press, 1990), 1:323, 2:290, 2:366, and 1:324; Kathleen Cockburn and Anthony Harding, eds., *The Notebooks of Samuel Taylor Coleridge,* vol. 5, *1827–1834* (London: Routledge, 2002), note 6915.

15. Southey's comments are in Coleridge, *Marginalia,* 3:805.

16. W. A. Speck, *Robert Southey: Entire Man of Letters* (New Haven: Yale University Press, 2006), 30, 48, and 92–94.

17. Earl Leslie Griggs, ed., *Collected Letters of Samuel Taylor Coleridge* (Oxford: Clarendon Press, 1956–1971), 1039 (Letter 538 to Southey, 25 January 1804). For Southey's work for the *Annual Review* and the quotes here, see Speck, *Southey,* 104–106. Southey's review of Malthus appeared in *Annual Review,* January 1804, 292–301. I cite it from Andrew Pyle, ed., *Population: Contemporary Responses to Thomas Robert Malthus* (Bristol: Thoemmes Press, 1994), 116–137, quotes at 129, 136, and 128. For Southey's own comments on this review, see Robert Southey to John Rickman, 8 February 1804 in Kenneth Curry, ed., *New Letters of Robert Southey* (New York: Columbia University Press, 1965), 1:351.

18. Curry, *New Letters,* 1:327, 1:351, and 1:357. I quote Southey's *Quarterly Review* essay from Robert Southey, *Essays, Moral and Political* (London: John Murray, 1832), quotes at 1:149, 1:246, 1:79, 1:95, 1:94, 1:154, and 1:155.

19. William Hazlitt, *Selected Writings,* ed. Jon Cook (Oxford: Oxford University Press, 1991), 211. The biographical information about Hazlitt is taken from Duncan Wu, *William Hazlitt: The First Modern Man* (Oxford: Oxford University Press, 2008), 48–49, 60–61, 104, 63, and 102–105. See also William

Albrecht, *William Hazlitt and the Malthusian Controversy* (Albuquerque: University of New Mexico Press, 1950), 48, on the importance of Hazlitt's *Essay* to his life's controversy with Malthus.

20. William Reitzel, ed., *The Autobiography of William Cobbett: The Progress of a Plough Boy to a Seat in Parliament* (London: Faber and Faber, 1933), 92; Wu, *Hazlitt*, 115.

21. [William Hazlitt], *A Reply to the Essay on Population* (London: Longman, Hurst, Rees and Orme, 1804), quotes at 77, 307, 139, 140, and 94. The other points canvassed in this paragraph are addressed at 38 and 144ff. (political organization, not nature, creates the problem); 52 (we are not slaves to lust); 61 (Malthus as sycophant); 5 and 69 (Malthus ignores his clerical calling); 120 *(Don Quixote);* 85 (Swift's *Tale of a Tub*); and 35 and 54–55 (Malthus and *Tristram Shandy*). Southey's softer comments are in the 1804 "Review" at 137. For Hazlitt's sex drive, see Wu, *Hazlitt*, 59–60, from where the quotation is taken. For Hazlitt and political journalism, see Tom Paulin, *The Day Star of Liberty: William Hazlitt's Radical Style* (London: Faber and Faber, 1998).

22. [Hazlitt], *Reply*, 19, 52–53, 262, and 282.

23. Robert Morrison, *The English Opium Eater: A Biography of Thomas de Quincey* (London: Weidenfeld and Nicolson, 2009), 152–153 (shortsighted); 34 (response to 1798); 150 (Dove Cottage); and 156 (reading political economy).

24. Thomas de Quincey, *Politics and Political Economy* (Boston: Houghton Mifflin, 1877), 295–296 (Coleridge); 298 (Malthus's originality); 192 (trivial performance); 229 (chaos); and 292 (logical oversight). Coleridge, *Marginalia*, 808. See also Josephine McDonagh, "De Quincey, Malthus and the Anachronism Effect," *Studies in Romanticism* 44 (2005): 63–80.

25. Butler, *Romantics, Rebels and Reactionaries*, 127–137 and 165. On Shelley's move to Marlow, see Richard Holmes, *Shelley: The Pursuit* (London: Harper, 1994), 347–413.

26. See Holmes, *Shelley*, 2–4 for phantoms; and 26 for Eton. For Shelley and the elopement, see William St Clair, *The Godwins and the Shelleys* (London: Faber and Faber, 1989).

27. Holmes, *Shelley*, 366; Frederick L. Jones, ed., *The Letters of Percy Bysshe Shelley* (Oxford: Clarendon Press, 1964), 2:261; William Godwin, *On Population* (London: Longman, Hurst, Rees, Orme and Brown, 1820); Percy Shelley, "Author's Preface" to *The Revolt of Islam* (1818), in Thomas Hutchinson, ed., *The Complete Poetical Works of Percy Bysshe Shelley* (Oxford: Oxford University Press, 1914), 1:60; Percy Shelley, "Preface" to *Prometheus Unbound*, cited from Duncan Wu, ed., *Romanticism: An Anthology*, 3rd ed. (Oxford: Blackwell, 2006), 1091–1094.

28. For allegorical readings, see C. E. Pulos, "Shelley and Malthus," *Proceedings of the Modern Language Association of America* 67 (1952): 113–124. The praise for the *Philosophical View* is from Holmes, *Shelley*, 592; Percy Shelley, *A Philosophical View of Reform*, ed. T. W. Rolleston (1914; repr., Honolulu: University of Hawaii Press, 2004), 12, 29, 69, 70, 30, 51, 51, 51–52, and 52.

For Malthus and Shelley in general, see Maureen McLane, *Romanticism and the Human Sciences: Poetry, Population and the Discourse of the Species* (Cambridge: Cambridge University Press, 2000), 109–158.

29. For Peacock's life, see Carl Dawson, *His Fine Wit: A Study of Thomas Love Peacock* (London: Routledge, 1970); and Felix Felton, *Thomas Love Peacock* (London: Allen and Unwin, 1973). Thomas Love Peacock, *Melincourt or Sir Oran Haut-Ton*, ed., George Saintsbury (London: Macmillan, 1927), quotes from 56, 59, 60, 197, 200, and 201–205. The other components of Mr. Fax's character can be found at 189 (luxury); and 226ff. (paper money).

30. Fiona McCarthy, *Byron: Life and Legend* (London: Faber and Faber, 2003), 445–446. For Byron and Malthus, see Frederick L. Beaty, "Byron on Malthus and the Population Problem," *Keats-Shelley Journal* 18 (1969): 17–26.

31. Lord Byron, *Don Juan*, ed. T. G. Steffan, E. Steffan, and W. W. Pratt (Harmondsworth: Penguin, 1986), quotes (by canto, verse, and line) from 12.14.4, 12.20.8, 11.30.4–7, 12.22.7, 12.13–14, 12.14.1–4, and 12.38.

32. G. B. Hill and L. F. Powell, eds., *Boswell's Life of Johnson* (Oxford: Oxford University Press, 1934–50), 5:400.

33. William Hazlitt, "On the Pleasure of Hating" (1823), in Tom Paulin and David Chandler, eds., *William Hazlitt: The Fight and Other Writings* (Harmondsworth: Penguin, 2000), 435–436.

34. On Blake's dialectics, see Heather Glen, *Vision and Disenchantment: Blake's Songs and Wordsworth's* Lyrical Ballads (Cambridge: Cambridge University Press, 1983).

5. Malthus and the Making of Environmental Economics

1. John Pullen and Trevor Hughes Parry, eds., *T. R. Malthus: The Unpublished Papers in the Collection of Kanto Gakuen University*, 2 vols. (Cambridge: Cambridge University Press, 1997–2004), 1:63–65.

2. J. M. Robson, ed., *The Collected Works of John Stuart Mill*, vol. 10, *Essays on Ethics, Religion, and Society* (London: Routledge, 1985), 120–121. For enlightened travel to eastern Europe or the lack thereof, see Larry Wolff, *Inventing Eastern Europe: The Map of Civilization on the Mind of the Enlightenment* (Stanford, CA: Stanford University Press, 1996); and Brian Dolan, *Exploring European Frontiers: British Travellers in the Age of Enlightenment* (Basingstoke: Macmillan, 2000). For Coleridge's German population project, see Richard Holmes, *Coleridge: Early Visions* (London: Hodder and Stoughton, 1989), 234–235; and for his time at Göttingen, see 219–220. The Wordsworths' trip is recounted in Dorothy Wordsworth's "Journal of a Visit to Hamburgh" (1798), in E. de Selincourt, ed., *Journals of Dorothy Wordsworth* (London: Macmillan, 1952), 17–34.

3. Thomas Robert Malthus, *An Essay on the Principle of Population*, ed. Patricia James, 2 vols. (Cambridge: Cambridge University Press, 1989), 1:2. This is a variorum edition that shows all the changes Malthus made in the successive editions between 1803 and 1826.

4. On climate and history in 1798, see John Tyrell, *Weather & Warfare: A Climatic History of the 1798 Rebellion* (Cork: Collins Press, 2001); and Sherry Johnson, *Climate and Catastrophe in Cuba and the Atlantic World in the Age of Revolution* (Chapel Hill: University of North Carolina Press, 2011). Patricia James, ed., *The Travel Diaries of T. R. Malthus* (Cambridge: Cambridge University Press, 1966), 35–36 and 38.

5. James, *Travel Diaries,* quotes at 76–77, 115, 73, and 40–41.

6. Ibid., 59, 90, and 72. This material appears in James, ed., *Essay,* 1:148–180.

7. For weather recording in Malthus's age, see Vladimir Jankovic, *Reading the Skies: A Cultural History of the English Weather, 1650–1820* (Chicago: University of Chicago Press, 2000); and Jan Golinksi, *British Weather and the Climate of Enlightenment* (Chicago: University of Chicago Press, 2007). For Malthus's enthusiasm, see John M. Pullen, "Correspondence between Malthus and His Parents," *History of Political Economy* 18 (1986): 133–154 at 136–137. Observations from James, ed., *Travel Diaries,* 32, 34, 109, and 114.

8. James, ed., *Travel Diaries,* 152, 164, and 158. For ecological laboratories, see Richard Grove, *Green Imperialism: Colonial Expansion, Tropical Island Edens and the Origins of Environmentalism, 1600–1860* (Cambridge: Cambridge University Press, 1995) on tropical islands. See Fredrik Albritton Jonsson, *Enlightenment's Frontier: The Scottish Highlands and the Origins of Environmentalism* (New Haven: Yale University Press, 2013) on the Scottish Highlands.

9. For the Swiss harangue, see James, *Travel Diaries,* 296–298, and compare with James, ed., *Essay,* 1:226–228. The Scottish diary is quoted from James, *Travel Diaries,* 224, 261, and 264. For the loss of his daughter, see Patricia James, *Population Malthus: His Life and Times* (London: Routledge, 1979), 407. The continental journal is transcribed in James, *Travel Diaries,* 226–252. Thomas Robert Malthus, "On the State of Ireland 1" (1808), in E. A. Wrigley and David Souden, eds., *The Works of Thomas Robert Malthus* (London: Pickering and Chatto, 1986), 4:23. Malthus's comments to Ricardo about Ireland are in Pierro Sraffa, ed., *The Works and Correspondence of David Ricardo,* vol. 7, *Letters, 1816–1818* (Cambridge: Cambridge University Press, 1952), 175. Ricardo's characterization of his and Malthus's differences is in the same correspondence at 184.

10. James, ed., *Essay,* 1:1. For the bibliographical information, see Thomas Robert Malthus, *An Essay on the Principle of Population* (1798), vol. 1 of E. A. Wrigley and David Souden, eds., *The Works of Thomas Robert Malthus,* 8 vols. (London: Pickering and Chatto, 1986), 1:53–59.

11. James, ed., *Essay,* 1:47ff. (Pacific); 1:87 (Mungo Park); 1:113 (Jones); 1:30 (Franklin); and book 1, chapter 4 (Robertson).

12. The ignorance of the lower classes was discussed in 1798 in Malthus, *Essay,* 14–15. For statistics as the way around this problem, see James, ed., *Essay,* 1:21. Note that from the 1806 edition of the *Essay,* book 1, chapter 4, this chapter, "On the Fruitfulness of Marriages," was much reworked and appeared as book 2, chapter 9. For plagues and sickly seasons, see James, ed.,

Essay, 1:213. For Malthus on Humboldt, see Thomas Robert Malthus, "Population" (1824), in Wrigley and Souden, eds., *Works,* 4:179–243 at 189. Humboldt repaid the compliment, describing Malthus's work as "one of the most profound works in political economy which has ever appeared" in his *Political Essay on the New Kingdom of Spain* (1810–1811) (New York: AMS Press, 1966), 1:107.

13. Thomas Robert Malthus, "High and Low Prices" (1823), in Wrigley and Souden, eds., *Works,* 7:225–253 at 225; James, ed., *Essay,* 1:252 and 1:253.

14. On defective census entries, see James, ed., *Essay,* 1:268ff. Torrens is cited in James, *Population Malthus,* 265. For causes of error and Newton, see Thomas Robert Malthus, *Principles of Political Economy,* ed. John Pullen (Cambridge: Cambridge University Press, 1989), 5–6 and 7, passages worth comparing with Malthus's last major work, *Definitions in Political Economy* (London: John Murray, 1827), 168.

15. James, ed., *Essay,* 1:148; compare with Wrigley and Souden, eds., *Works,* 4:206. Malthus on mortality rates is from James, ed. *Essay,* 1:200. For Humboldt, see Wrigley and Souden, eds., *Works,* 4:189. For plague as not accidental, see James, ed., *Essay,* 1:300.

16. For the myth of coherence, see Quentin Skinner, "Meaning and Understanding in the History of Ideas," *History and Theory* 8 (1969): 3–53. The best survey of Malthus's political economy in context is Donald Winch, *Riches and Poverty: An Intellectual History of Political Economy in Britain, 1760–1834* (Cambridge: Cambridge University Press, 1996), 221–406. See also Samuel Hollander, *The Economics of Thomas Robert Malthus* (Toronto: University of Toronto Press, 1997).

17. James, ed., *Essay,* 1:10; Pullen, ed., *Principles,* 1 and 345.

18. James, ed., *Essay,* 1:393; Malthus, *Definitions,* 236; Pullen, ed., *Principles,* 28–29, compare with Malthus, *Definitions,* 234–235. Pullen, ed., *Principles,* 27–28 and 226; James, ed., *Travel Diaries,* 74.

19. Pullen, ed., *Principles,* 139, 140, 149, and 141–142; Thomas Robert Malthus, "The Corn Laws" (1814), in Wrigley and Souden, eds., *Works,* 7:87–109 at 100. For the peculiar value of corn, see James, ed., *Essay,* 1:428. Thomas Robert Malthus, "The Importation of Foreign Corn" (1815), in Wrigley and Souden, eds., *Works,* 7:151–174 at 157–158. For national quiet and happiness, see Malthus, "Corn Laws," 101; and for the social fabric, see Malthus, "Importation," 162. For Britain's commercial system, see James, ed., *Essay,* 1:404.

20. James, ed., *Essay,* 1:404, 1:328, and 2:104; William Empson, "The Life, Writings and Character of Mr. Malthus," *Edinburgh Review* 67 (1837): 469–506 at 478; James, ed., *Essay,* 1:261, 2:206, and 1:439–440.

21. Pullen, ed., *Principles,* 206; Malthus, *Definitions,* 11; and James, ed., *Essay,* 1:13 and 1:444.

22. James, ed., *Essay,* 1:13. For analysis, see Alison Bashford, "Malthus and Colonial History," *Journal of Australian Studies* 36 (2012): 99–110.

23. Pullen, ed., *Principles,* 348, on effective demand. See James, ed., *Essay,* 1:162 for Sweden; 1:103–104 for Russia; and Pullen, ed., *Principles,* 382–394 for New Spain; and 394–401 for Ireland.

24. James, ed., *Essay,* 1:400; Malthus, "Corn Laws," 102. Malthus discusses rates of urbanization in Pullen, ed., *Principles,* 380–381; and what we term the agricultural revolution in "Importation," 160 and 161. Violation of property is in James, ed., *Essay* 1:362.

25. Wretched system is James, ed., *Essay,* 2:140; and the critique of the Poor Laws at *Essay* 1:356, 1:361, and 1:350. The infamous "nature's mighty feast" section is from *Essay* 2:127–128. For neoconservative evocations of Malthus, the most famous in Britain was Sir Keith Joseph's 1974 speech that led to his castigation as a "saloon bar Malthus" and to Margaret Thatcher's ascent to power in his stead (see Dominic Sandbrook, *Seasons in the Sun: The Battle for Britain, 1974–1979* [London: Penguin, 2012], 233–234).

26. Thomas Robert Malthus, "An Investigation of the Cause of the Present High Price of Provisions" in Wrigley and Souden, eds., *Works,* 7:5–18 at 14.

27. Empson, "Life," 496. The frustrated undergraduate is in Pullen and Parry, eds., *T. R. Malthus: The Unpublished Papers,* 1:41. The Pope quotation is cited in Malthus, *Essay,* 62, and comes from *An Essay on Man,* 1:18. "Things as they are" is from Pullen, ed., *Principles,* 11. The 1803 preface is cited from James, ed., *Essay,* 1:2–3.

6. Malthus and the Victorians

1. On Malthus's death, see Patricia James, *Population Malthus: His Life and Times* (London: Routledge, 1979), 459–461; and on "Malthusian" being as ubiquitous as Freudian, 346.

2. James, *Population Malthus,* 351–358, 392–393, and 448–449.

3. William Cobbett, *Surplus Population and the Poor Law Bill: A Comedy in Three Acts* (1834; repr., Leeds: Pelagian Press, 1994), i, 25, 9, and 44; sales figures reported at ii. Cobbett's open letter to Malthus is cited in James P. Huzel, *The Popularization of Malthus in Early Nineteenth-Century England: Martineau, Cobbett and the Pauper Press* (Aldershot: Ashgate, 2006), 105. William Cobbett, *Rural Rides,* ed. George Woodcock (Harmondsworth: Penguin, 1985), 298, 304, and 307.

4. William Cobbett, "Mr. Cobbett's Taking Leave of His Countrymen" (1817), in Leonora Nattrass, ed., *William Cobbett: Selected Writings,* vol. 3, *Reform, 1810–1817* (London: Pickering and Chatto, 1998), 425. For Marcus, see Harold A. Boner, *Hungry Generations: The Nineteenth-Century Case against Malthusianism* (New York: Columbia University Press, 1955), 138–139; and Josephine McDonagh, *Child Murder and British Culture, 1720–1900* (Cambridge: Cambridge University Press, 2003), 101–112; Charles Dickens, *A Christmas Carol and Other Christmas Writings,* ed. Michael Slater (Harmondsworth: Penguin, 2003), 38–39 and 82.

5. *The Times* is cited in Huzel, *Popularization of Malthus,* 74, on whom I also draw here for Martineau's autobiographical comment, 57; for Bulwer-Lytton, 73; and for sales figures, 55. For Chalmers and Malthus, see Boyd Hilton, *The Age of Atonement: The Influence of Evangelicalism on Social and Economic Thought, 1785–1865* (Oxford: Clarendon Press, 1988), 65.

6. Rickman is cited from Orlo Williams, *Lamb's Friend the Census Taker: The Life and Letters of John Rickman* (Boston: Houghton Mifflin, 1912), 272 and 302; for the Malthusian logic of the census, see Kathrin Levitan, *A Cultural History of the British Census: Envisioning the Multitude in the Nineteenth Century* (New York: Palgrave, 2011), chapter 2, quote at 32.

7. See Peter Mandler, "Tories and Paupers: Christian Political Economy and the Making of the New Poor Law," *Historical Journal* 33 (1990): 81–103 at 86; and Peter Mandler, "The Making of the New Poor Law Redivivus," *Past and Present* 117 (1987): 131–157.

8. Christopher Hamlin, *Public Health and Social Justice in the Age of Chadwick: Britain, 1800–1854* (Cambridge: Cambridge University Press, 1998), 33, 91, and 293.

9. For quantitative analysis of the Irish Famine showing it was not a consequence of Malthusian overpopulation, see Joel Mokyr, "Malthusian Models and Irish History," *Journal of Economic History* 40 (1980): 159–166; and Joel Mokyr, *Why Ireland Starved: A Quantitative and Analytical History of the Irish Economy, 1800–1850* (London: George Allan and Unwin, 1983), 30–80. For the Select Committee and George Nicholls's Malthusianism, see David Nally, *Human Encumbrances: Political Violence and the Great Irish Famine* (Notre Dame, IN: University of Notre Dame Press, 2011), 50–52 and 106–109. See also Eric Ross, *The Malthus Factor: Poverty, Politics and Population in Capitalist Development* (London: Zed, 1998), 31–54.

10. For Malthus's eclipse, see Boner, *Hungry Generations*, 128; and Adrian Desmond and James Moore, *Darwin* (London: Michael Joseph, 1991), 485. The shift to a mineral economy is treated in E. A. Wrigley, *Continuity, Chance and Change: The Character of the Industrial Revolution* (Cambridge: Cambridge University Press, 1988); and E. A. Wrigley, *Energy and the English Industrial Revolution* (Cambridge: Cambridge University Press, 2010).

11. For the early economic commentators on Malthus, see Kenneth Smith, *The Malthusian Controversy* (London: Routledge, 1951), 47–206; their works are helpfully collected in ten volumes as Chuhei Sugiyama and Andrew Pyle, eds., *Malthus and the Population Controversy* (Bristol: Thoemmes Press, 1994).

12. On public moralists, see Stefan Collini, *Public Moralists: Political Thought and Intellectual Life in Britain, 1850–1930* (Oxford: Oxford University Press, 1993). For sales and the impact of Mill's *Principles*, see Donald Winch, *Wealth and Life: Essays on the Intellectual History of Political Economy in Britain, 1848–1914* (Cambridge: Cambridge University Press, 2009), 7 and 5. The putative eclipse by Marshall is mentioned in Roger Backhouse, *The Penguin History of Economics* (Harmondsworth: Penguin, 2002), 154. John Stuart Mill, *Autobiography*, ed. J. M. Robson (Harmondsworth: Penguin, 1989), 94. John Stuart Mill, "The *Quarterly Review* on Political Economy" (1825), in J. M. Robson, ed., *The Collected Works of John Stuart Mill*, vols. 4–5, *Essays on Economics and Society* (repr., Indianapolis, IN: Liberty Fund, 2006), 23–44 at 27, 26, 34–35, and 30.

13. Mill, *Autobiography,* 187 for *Principles;* and 94n for his arrest; J. M. Robson, ed., *The Collected Works of John Stuart Mill,* vols. 2 and 3, *Principles of Political Economy* (repr., Indianapolis, IN: Liberty Fund, 2006), 2:154, 2:345, 2:352, and 2:370; John Stuart Mill, "Chapters on Socialism" (1879), in Robson, ed., *Essays on Economy and Society,* 5:705–753 at 729. See Gregory Claeys, *Mill and Paternalism* (Cambridge: Cambridge University Press, 2013) for a treatment that emphasizes the entwinement of Mill's ideas with an engagement with Malthus.

14. William Stanley Jevons, *Papers and Correspondence,* 7 vols. (London: Macmillan, 1972–1977), 3:119 (Mill) and 1:203 (Gladstone).

15. See Winch, *Wealth and Life,* 149–176. Jevons's key works tying economics and climate are: "The Solar Period and the Price of Corn (1875), "The Periodicity of Commercial Crises and Its Physical Explanation" (1878/1882), and "Commercial Crises and Sun Spots" (1878–1879), all reprinted in *Investigations in Currency and Finance,* 2nd ed. (London: Macmillan, 1909).

16. Winch, *Wealth and Life,* 169; William Stanley Jevons, *The Coal Question; An Inquiry Concerning the Progress of the Nation and the Probable Exhaustion of our Coal Mines* (London: Macmillan, 1865), 148, 149, 150, and 154.

17. For Marshall's role in the emergence of economics from political economy, see Winch, *Wealth and Life,* 237–294; Collini, *Public Moralists;* Stefan Collini, Donald Winch, and John Burrow, *That Noble Science of Politics: A Study in Nineteenth-Century Intellectual History* (Cambridge: Cambridge University Press, 1983), 309–363; and Peter Groenewegen, *A Soaring Eagle: Alfred Marshall, 1842–1924* (Aldershot: Edward Elgar, 1995). John K. Whitaker, ed., *The Correspondence of Alfred Marshall, Economist,* 3 vols. (Cambridge: Cambridge University Press, 1996), 2:29 and 3:62–63.

18. Alfred Marshall, *Principles of Economics,* ed. C. W. Guillebaud, 9th ed. (Bristol: Overstone Press Reprint, 1997), 178, 179, and 180. For dodging the demographic bullet, see 166–167 and compare with Alfred Marshall, *Collected Essays, 1872–1917,* ed. Peter Groenewegen, 2 vols. (Bristol: Overstone Press, 1997), 2:557. For Bermondsey, see Groenewegen, *Soaring Eagle,* 450. For degeneration in the cities, see Marshall, *Principles,* 248; and Alfred Marshall, "The Pressure of Population on the Means of Subsistence" (1885), which first appeared in the *Malthusian,* a journal to which we will return at the end of the chapter, and which is reprinted in *Collected Essays,* 1:283–288, quotes at 286 and 287. Mill, *Principles,* 3:756. For Marshall and Garden Cities, see Groenewegen, *Soaring Eagle,* 452, and compare with Ebenezer Howard, *Garden Cities of To-Morrow* (1902; repr., Cambridge: MIT Press, 1965), 48.

19. William Godwin, *On Population* (London: Longman, Hurst, Rees, Orme and Brown, 1820); Robert Owen, *A New View of Society and Other Writings,* ed. Gregory Claeys (London: Penguin, 1991), where Malthus is discussed at 86–87.

20. Thomas Carlyle, "Signs of the Times" (1829), in *Selected Writings,* ed. Alan Shelston (Harmondsworth: Penguin, 1971), 61–85 at 64; Carlyle, "Chartism" (1839), in *Selected Writings,* 151–232 at 229; Thomas Carlyle, *Sartor*

Resartus (1833–34), ed. Kerry McSweeney and Peter Sabor (Oxford: Oxford University Press, 1987), 172 and 174.

21. All quotations in this paragraph are from John Ruskin, *Unto This Last and Other Writings,* ed. Clive Wilmer (London: Penguin, 1997), 207–209 and 222–226.

22. All quotations in this paragraph are from Ronald Meek, ed., *Marx and Engels on Malthus* (London: Lawrence and Wishart, 1953), 60, 61–62, 78, and 109 (Engels), and 83, 88, 124, and 108 (Marx). For Marx and Engels's veiled indebtedness to Malthus, see John M. Sherwood, "Engels, Marx, Malthus and the Machine," *American Historical Review* 90 (1985): 837–865.

23. Pierre-Joseph Proudhon, *The Malthusians,* trans. Benjamin Tucker (London: International, 1886), 4, 6, 12, and 11. See also Yves Charbit, *Economic, Social and Demographic Thought in the XIXth Century: The Population Debate from Malthus to Marx* (Dordrecht: Springer, 2009), 93–119.

24. For George's sales and the claim about being the most widely read economics book, see Richard W England, "Ricardo, Gold and Rails: Discovering the Origins of Progress and Poverty," *American Journal of Economics and Sociology* 69 (2010): 1279–1293 at 1289n1 and 1279. Quotes are from Henry George, *Poverty and Progress,* in *The Writings of Henry George* (New York: Doubleday, 1898), 98 and 99.

25. George Bernard Shaw is quoted from his essay "Economic" in Shaw, ed., *Fabian Essays in Socialism* (London: Fabian Society, 1920 edition), 21, 26, 27, and 29. For the fissures of Fabianism about Malthus and population, see Piers J Hale, "Labor and the Human Relationship with Nature: The Naturalization of Politics in the Work of Thomas Henry Huxley, Herbert George Wells and William Morris," *Journal of the History of Biology* 36 (2003): 249–284; Piers J Hale, "Of Mice and Men: Evolution and the Socialist Utopia: H. G. Wells, William Morris and George Bernard Shaw," *Journal of the History of Biology* 43 (2010): 17–66; and Mike Hawkins, *Social Darwinism in European and American Thought, 1860–1945: Nature as Model and Nature as Threat* (Cambridge: Cambridge University Press, 1997), 159–167.

26. Edward Bellamy, *Looking Backward, 2000–1887,* ed. Cecelia Tichi (London: Penguin, 1982), 39 (hunger), 188–193 (small population). For Bellamy and environmental utopianism, see William B. Meyer, "Edward Bellamy and the Weather of Utopia," *Geographical Review* 94 (2004): 43–54. Bellamy's *New Nation* essay "To a Discipline of Malthus" was reprinted as Edward Bellamy, *Talks on Nationalism* (repr., Freeport, NY: Books for Libraries Press, 1969), 118–122, quote at 121–122.

27. Andrew Berry, ed., *Infinite Tropics: An Alfred Russel Wallace Anthology* (London: Verso, 2003), 68–69; Charles Darwin, *Autobiographies,* ed. Michael Neve and Sharon Messenger (Harmondsworth: Penguin, 2002), 72. Wallace's Ternate paper is reprinted in Berry, ed., *Infinite Tropics,* 52–62; see especially 53–54 for Wallace's deployment of Malthusian terms. The paper in which Darwin and Wallace jointly announced the core ideas of evolution by natural selection also specifically styles its argument as "the doctrine of Malthus applied in most cases with tenfold force" (see Charles Darwin and

Alfred Russel Wallace, "On the Tendency of Species to Form Varieties, and on the Perpetuation of Varieties and Species by Natural Means of Selection" [1858], in John van Whye, ed., *Charles Darwin: Shorter Publications, 1829–1883* [Cambridge: Cambridge University Press, 2009], 282–96, quote at 284). For the Darwin industry on the Darwin-Malthus connection, see Sandra Herbert, "Darwin, Malthus and Selection," *Journal of the History of Biology* 1 (1971): 209–217; Peter Bowler, "Malthus, Darwin and the Concept of Struggle," *Journal of the History of Ideas* 37 (1976): 631–50; and Robert M. Young, "Malthus and the Evolutionists: The Common Context of Biological and Social Theory," *Past and Present* 43 (1969): 109–145.

28. For Darwin and the Martineau circle, see Desmond and Moore, *Darwin*, 216–218; and Adrian Desmond, *The Politics of Evolution: Morphology, Medicine and Reform in Radical London* (Chicago: University of Chicago Press, 1989), 398–414. For Malthus as contributor, not catalyst, see Herbert, "Darwin," 217. Malthus in the *Origin* is quoted from Jim Endersby, ed., *The Origin of Species* (Cambridge: Cambridge University Press, 2009), 58. R. C. Stauffer, ed., *Charles Darwin's Natural Selection: Being the Second Part of his Big Species Book written from 1856 to 1858* (Cambridge: Cambridge University Press, 1975), 176. Charles Darwin, *The Descent of Man and Selection in Relation to Sex,* ed. John Bonner and Robert May (Princeton: Princeton University Press, 1981), 131n51 and 134. For Malthus and Victorian anthropology more generally, see George Stocking, *Victorian Anthropology* (New York: Macmillan, 1987), 220–222; and Catherine Gallagher, *The Body Economic: Life, Death and Sensation in Political Economy and the Victorian Novel* (Princeton: Princeton University Press, 2006), 156–184.

29. Darwin, *Descent*, 137–138 and 136; Wallace, "The Origin of Human Races and the Antiquity of Man Deduced from the Theory of 'Natural Selection,'" in Berry, ed., *Infinite Tropics*, 189.

30. Darwin quote from Berry, *Infinite Tropics*, 321–322, from where also comes Wallace and Land Nationalisation (321–322), the impact of Owen (309) and of Bellamy (315–317, quote at 317). For Wallace's "Human Selection," see Charles H Smith, ed., *Alfred Russel Wallace: An Anthology of his Shorter Writings* (Oxford: Oxford University Press, 1991), 56 and 58–59. Material on Wallace's attitudes to Irish and English urban poverty is in Smith, ed., *Wallace*, 145–147, and on resource depletion at 125–126. All of these topics in Wallace's thought are addressed in Charles H. Smith and George Beccaloni, eds., *Natural Selection & Beyond: The Intellectual Legacy of Alfred Russel Wallace* (Oxford: Oxford University Press, 2008).

31. Details of Spencer's life from David Wiltshire, *The Social and Political Thought of Herbert Spencer* (Oxford: Oxford University Press, 1978), 20 and 54. Herbert Spencer, "A Theory of Population, deduced from the General Law of Animal Fertility," *Westminster Review* 57 (1852): 468–501, quote at 472. Patrick Geddes and J. Arthur Thomson, *The Evolution of Sex*, rev. ed. (London: Walter Scott, 1901), 298–315, about which see Chris Renwick, "The Practice of Spencerian Science: Patrick Geddes's Biosocial Program, 1876–1889," *ISIS* 100 (2009): 36–57. Peter Kropotkin, *Mutual Aid: A Factor in*

Evolution (repr., Mineola, NY: Dover, 2006), 60 and 2. Daniel Todes, *Darwin without Malthus: The Struggle for Existence in Russian Evolutionary Thought* (New York: Oxford University Press, 1989), Tolstoy quote at 43.

32. For social Darwinism as scientific Malthusianism, see Gregory Claeys, "The 'Survival of the Fittest' and the Origins of Social Darwinism," *Journal of the History of Ideas* 61 (2000): 223–240 at 228. Huxley from the slums, and his quote from the Wilberforce debate are taken from Adrian Desmond, *Huxley: From Devil's Disciple to Evolution's High Priest* (London: Penguin, 1998), xviii and 279. On the death of Marian, see Desmond, *Huxley,* 558ff. Thomas Huxley, *Collected Essays,* vol. 9, *Evolution and Ethics and Other Essays* (London: Macmillan, 1898), 7 and 4; Thomas Huxley, "The Struggle for Existence: A Programme," *Nineteenth Century* 132 (1888): 161–180, quotes at 168–169.

33. For all these examples, see Hawkins, *Social Darwinism,* 132 (badge), 135 (Haeckel), and 109 (Sumner). For Malthus and the American Civil War, see Dennis Hodgson, "Malthus's Essay on Population and the American Debate over Slavery," *Comparative Studies in Society and History* 51 (2009): 742–770.

34. *Oxford English Dictionary,* sub "Malthusian, adj and n," and compare with Rosanna Ledbetter, *A History of the Malthusian League, 1877–1927* (Columbus: Ohio State University Press, 1976), xiv–xv. Malthus's reference to improper arts is from Patricia James, ed., *An Essay on the Principle of Population* (Cambridge: Cambridge University Press, 1989), 2:97.

35. On the Malthusian League, see Ledbetter, *History;* F. D'Arcy, "The Malthusian League and the Resistance to Birth Control Propaganda in Late Victorian England," *Population Studies* 31 (1977): 429–448; F. H. Amphlett Micklewright, "The Rise and Decline of English Neo-Malthusianism," *Population Studies* 15 (1961): 32–51; Richard Soloway, *Birth Control and the Population Question in England, 1877–1930* (Chapel Hill: University of North Carolina Press, 1982); and Richard Soloway, *Demography and Degeneration: Eugenics and the Declining Birthrate in Twentieth- Century Britain* (Chapel Hill: University of North Carolina Press, 1990). The seven principles are in Ledbetter, *History,* 65, as is Drydale's comment (115) and figures for pamphlet distribution (68) and the global spread of leagues (172).

36. Desmond and Moore, *Darwin,* 628; Desmond, *Huxley,* 529. For Standring, see Ledbetter, *History,* 72–73, which also discusses the responses to the Malthusian League of Henry George (89–92); the Fabians (101–102); H. G. Wells (213–214); and Bertrand Russell and Ramsay MacDonald (113–114). For Besant, see Annie Besant, "The Law of Population and Its Relation to Socialism," *Our Corner* (June 1886): 324–332, quotes at 325, 330, and 331.

37. Sigmund Freud, "Sexuality in the Aetiology of the Neuroses," in James Strachey and Anna Freud, eds., *The Standard Edition of the Complete Psychological Works of Sigmund Freud,* vol. 3, *1893–1899* (repr., London: Hogarth Press, 1962), 261–285, quotes at 282, 281, 276, 277, and 278.

38. Shaw's list cited in Huzel, *Popularization of Malthus,* 105. Michel Foucault, "What Is an Author?," in James Faubion, ed., *The Essential Works of Foucault,*

vol. 1, *Aesthetics, Method and Epistemology* (London: Penguin, 1998), 205–222; and Michel Foucault, *Security, Territory, Population: Lectures at the Collège de France, 1977–1978,* ed. Michel Senellart (London: Palgrave, 2007), 55–86. George, *Progress and Poverty,* 102. For subconscious Malthusianism in the nineteenth century, see Gallagher, *Body Economic.* H. G. Wells, *Anticipations and Other Papers* (London: T. Fisher Unwin, 1924), quotes at 249 and 265.

7. Malthus and the Dismal Age

1. John Carey, *The Intellectuals and the Masses: Pride and Prejudice among the Literary Intelligentsia, 1880–1939* (London: Faber and Faber, 1992), 119.
2. For the professionalization of economics, see Donald Winch, *Wealth and Life: Essays on the Intellectual History of Political Economy in Britain, 1848–1914* (Cambridge: Cambridge University Press, 2009), 332–366. Toynbee quotes are taken from Arnold Toynbee, *Lectures on the Industrial Revolution of the 18th Century in England,* sixth impression (London: Longmans, Green and Co. 1902), 108, 112, and 113. For the broader historiography of the Industrial Revolution, see D. C. Coleman, *Myth, History and the Industrial Revolution* (London: Hambledon, 1992). For Bonar's life, see T. A. B. Corley, "Bonar, James (1852–1941)," *Oxford Dictionary of National Biography* (Oxford: Oxford University Press, 2004), www.oxforddnb.com/view/article/31951. James Bonar, *Malthus and His Work* (London: Macmillan, 1885).
3. See Richard Soloway, *Birth Control and the Population Question in England, 1877–1930* (Chapel Hill: University of North Carolina Press, 1982), quotes at 185 and 213. For the decline of the Malthusian League at this time, see Rosanna Ledbetter, *A History of the Malthusian League, 1877–1927* (Columbus: Ohio State University Press, 1976), 203–234.
4. For the decline in British birth rates, see Robert A. Woods, *The Demography of Victorian England and Wales* (Cambridge: Cambridge University Press, 2000), 391–397; for Germany, see Paul Weindling, *Health, Race and German Politics between National Unification and Nazism, 1870–1945* (Cambridge: Cambridge University Press, 1989), 189; and for France, see William H. Schneider, *Quantity and Quality: The Quest for Biological Regeneration in Twentieth-Century France* (Cambridge: Cambridge University Press, 1990), 15–16 and 38–39. Guy Chapman, *Culture and Survival* (London: Jonathan Cape, 1940), 212 and 243; Soloway, *Birth Control,* 160. The evolutionary step is cited in Paul Crook, *Darwinism, War and History* (Cambridge: Cambridge University Press, 1994), 161.
5. Richard Overy, *The Morbid Age: Britain and the Crisis of Civilization, 1919–1939* (London: Allen Lane, 2009), from where Mumford is cited (32); Carey, *Intellectuals;* and John Burrow, *The Crisis of Reason: European Thought, 1848–1914* (New Haven: Yale University Press, 2000).
6. For the debates about degeneration, see Daniel Pick, *Faces of Degeneration: A European Disorder, 1848–1914* (Cambridge: Cambridge University Press,

1989); Allan Chase, *The Legacy of Malthus: The Social Costs of the New Scientific Racism* (New York: Knopf, 1977), 82 and 75.

7. Thomas Robert Malthus, *An Essay on the Principle of Population* in E. A. Wrigley and David Souden, eds., *Works of Thomas Robert Malthus* (London: Pickering and Chatto, 1986), 63. For Galton on Malthusianism and Malthus, see Richard Soloway, *Demography and Degeneration: Eugenics and the Declining Birthrate in Twentieth-Century Britain* (Chapel Hill: University of North Carolina Press, 1990), 92–93, and compare with Nicholas Wright Gillham, *Sir Francis Galton: From African Exploration to the Birth of Eugenics* (New York: Oxford University Press, 2001), 168–169. Chase, *Legacy of Malthus*, 82–83.

8. Malthusian orthodoxy in France is discerned in Joshua Cole, *The Power of Large Numbers: Population, Politics and Gender in Nineteenth-Century France* (Ithaca, NY: Cornell University Press, 2000), 184. For French neo-Malthusiansism, see Schneider, *Quantity and Quality*, 33–34, who also cites the 1920 bill (120) and offers the concluding judgment of this paragraph (175).

9. For Italian emigration and Mussolini's 1927 speech, see Carl Ipsen, *Dictating Demography: The Problem of Population in Fascist Italy* (Cambridge: Cambridge University Press, 1996), 42 and 68 respectively. For Mussolini removing praise of Malthus in 1931, see Ispen, *Dictating Demography*, 205, while Gini's speech is cited in Matthew Connelly, *Fatal Mis-Conception: The Struggle to Control World Population* (Cambridge: Harvard University Press, 2008), 78. Casti Connubii can be read in English translation at: www.vatican .va/holy_father/pius_xi/encyclicals/documents/hf_p-xi_enc_31121930_casti -connubii_en.html, with the Lateran Treaty mentioned in paragraph 126 and the tempting of the flock in paragraph 3. *The Catholic Encyclopaedia*'s entry on "Theories of Population" can be found at: www.newadvent.org/cathen /12276a.htm, the citation being from the final paragraph of a section of "Criticisms of the Malthusian Theory."

10. For Soviet pro-natalism, see Connelly, *Fatal Mis-Conception*, 79–80, who also discusses Stoddart and Grant at 43 and 55. For other studies of American Eugenics, see Chase, *Legacy of Malthus;* and Daniel Kevles, *In the Name of Eugenics: Genetics and the Uses of Human Heredity* (New York: Knopf, 1985).

11. Marchant is discussed in Soloway, *Birth Control*, 161, and Elderton in Soloway, *Demography and Degeneration*, 90. For Lloyd George, see Overy, *Morbid Age*, 98. William Barry is cited from Soloway, *Birth Control*, 98 and 101; see also on this topic Flann Campbell, "Birth Control and the Christian Churches," *Population Studies* 14 (1960): 131–147.

12. Pessimistic demography is from Soloway, *Demography and Degeneration*, 232, as are the implications of the 1931 census figures, the *Observer* editorial (233), the material from Enid Charles (236, 237, 270), the hysterical headlines (241), and the BBC lectures (242). For Blacker, see Overy, *Morbid Age*, 133; the theme of babies or cars in this era is discussed more thoroughly in Angus MacLaren, *Reproduction by Design: Sex, Robots, Trees and Test-Tube Babies in Interwar Britain* (Chicago: University of Chicago Press,

2012), 37–56. For Beveridge, see José Harris, *William Beveridge: A Biography* (Oxford: Clarendon Press, 1977), 342–343.

13. Aldous Huxley, *Brave New World* (London: Vintage Classics, 2007), 43, on which see Nicholas Murray, *Aldous Huxley: An English Intellectual* (London: Little, Brown, 2002), 244–255. The Malthusian uterus is discussed in Soloway, *Demography and Degeneration*, 263. For the Hidden Huxley, see David Bradshaw, ed., *The Hidden Huxley* (London: Faber and Faber, 1994), 152 (sterilization); 156–157 (despoliation); and 228 (cars rather than children). For Julian as one of the five best brains, see C. Kenneth Waters and Albert Van Helden, eds., *Julian Huxley: Biologist and Statesman of Science* (College Station: Texas A&M Press, 1992), 241 and 230 for "some talented and others morons." For the 1922 turning point, see Julian Huxley, *Memories 1* (repr., Harmondsworth: Penguin, 1972), 143; and for Julian's praise of Malthus. see Julian Huxley, *Essays of a Humanist* (repr., Harmondsworth: Penguin, 1966), 237 and 242.

14. Murray, *Huxley,* 54–67; Huxley, *Memories 1,* 108–109; Robert Skidelsky, *John Maynard Keynes: The Economist as Saviour, 1920–1937* (London: Macmillan, 1992), 416; John Toye, *Keynes on Population* (Oxford: Oxford University Press, 2000), 205; Donald Winch, *Riches and Poverty: An Intellectual History of Political Economy, 1750–1834* (Cambridge: Cambridge University Press, 1996), 26–27. Keynes was by no means the only important economist to discuss Malthus in this era: see also Lujo Bretano, "The Doctrine of Malthus and the Increase of Population during the Last Decades," *Economic Journal* 20 (1910): 371–393; and Stephen P. Barrows, "The Law of Population and the Austrian School: How Austrian Economists Interacted with Thomas Robert Malthus," *American Journal of Economics and Sociology* 69 (2010): 1178–1205.

15. Keynes's 1912 and 1914 thoughts are reprinted in Toye, *Keynes,* 37–43 and 53–71, quotes at 38, 42, 43, and 66.

16. John Maynard Keynes, *The Collected Writings of John Maynard Keynes,* vol. 2, *The Economic Consequences of the Peace* (1919) (London: Macmillan, 1971), 5, 6, 7, 15, and 8–9.

17. William Beveridge, "Population and Unemployment," *Economic Journal* 33 (1923): 447–475, quotes at 448, 447, 452, 459, and 473. For Beveridge as "winning" the argument, see Toye, *Keynes,* 178. John Maynard Keynes, "A Reply to Sir William Beveridge," *Economic Journal* 33 (1923): 476–486, quote at 485.

18. John Maynard Keynes, "Thomas Robert Malthus: The First of the Cambridge Economists" (1933), in *The Collected Writings of John Maynard Keynes,* vol. 10, *Essays in Biography* (London: Macmillan, 1972), 71–103, quotes at 84, 88, 107, 98, 101, 99, and 107. Keynes's celebrated judgment of the relative merits of Ricardo and Malthus was rehearsed again in John Maynard Keynes, *The General Theory of Employment, Interest and Money* (London: Macmillan, 1936), 32.

19. Keynes, *General Theory,* 362, 25, 380, and 381. Keynes believed the sources of war could be eradicated within a century if the population issue

was addressed: see John Maynard Keynes, "Economic Possibilities for our Grandchildren" (1930), in S. P. Rosenbaum, ed., *A Bloomsbury Group Reader* (Oxford: Blackwells, 1993), 126–135 at 130. The final quotation is taken from John Maynard Keynes, "Some Economic Consequences of a Declining Population," in *The Collected Writings of John Maynard Keynes,* vol. 14, *The General Theory and After, Part 2* (1937) (London: Macmillan, 1973), 124–133 at 131–132.

20. Keynes cited from Toye, *Keynes,* 65, 63, 65, and 64. Keynes's fellow Bloomsberry, Bertrand Russell, had drawn much the same divide in *Freedom and Organisation, 1814–1914* (London: George Allen and Unwin, 1934 [1936 impression]), 102, arguing that a declining birth rate may have "destroyed the importance of his [Malthus's] theory so far as the white races are concerned," but "in Asia it remains important."

21. See S. Ambirajan, "Malthusian Population Theory and Indian Famine Policy in the Nineteenth Century," *Population Studies* 30 (1976): 5–14, from where Lytton is cited (7) as is the 1877 report (6). Mike Davis, *Late Victorian Holocausts: El Niño Famines and the Making of the Third World* (London: Verso, 2002), discusses Lytton (28–32); calorific intakes (38); a proto Third World (289); and Malthusia (306). See also John C. Caldwell, "Malthus and the Less Developed World: The Pivotal Role of India," *Population and Development Review* 24 (1998): 675–696, esp. 683–685. Amartya Sen, *Poverty and Famines: An Essay on Entitlement and Deprivation* (Oxford: Oxford University Press, 1981). For what we know of Malthus's teaching in Haileybury, see J. M. Pullen, "Notes from Malthus: The Inverarity Manuscript," *History of Political Economy* 13 (1981): 794–811.

22. Randolph Churchill, *Winston S. Churchill,* vol. 1, *Youth, 1874–1900* (London: Heinemann, 1966), 334. Winston Churchill, *My Early Life: A Roving Commission* (London: Thornton Butterworth, 1930), 123 and 126. Churchill's quote about the unmoved philosopher is cited from Madhusree Mukerjee, *Churchill's Secret War: The British Empire and the Ravaging of India during World War II* (New York: Basic, 2010), 204.

23. For Churchill and Eugenics, see Gillham, *Galton,* 345–346; his advocacy of sterilization is cited from Mike Hawkins, *Social Darwinism in European and American Thought, 1860–1945: Nature as Model and Nature as Threat* (Cambridge: Cambridge University Press, 1997), 233n28. For his *News of the World* article, see Soloway, *Demography and Degeneration,* 245.

24. Sen, *Poverty and Famines,* 75. Other information and quotation in this paragraph are from Mukerjee, *Churchill's Secret War,* 131, 143, 215, 203, 200, 197, and 271.

25. The Malthusian War map of 1914 is mentioned in Soloway, *Birth Control,* 165. The sociobiological explanation of war is from Crook, *Darwinism,* 130. For the Manchurian War as Malthusian, see the evidence cited in Connelly, *Fatal Mis-Conception,* 79; and Schneider, *Quantity and Quality,* 175.

26. Weindling, *Health, Race and German Politics,* 189 (birth rates), 189; (starvation in World War I); and 241–80 (on debates about stock). Oswald Spengler, *The Decline of the West: Abridged Edition* (Oxford: Oxford University

Press, 1991), 251–252; Yvonne Sherratt, *Hitler's Philosophers* (New Haven: Yale University Press, 2013), chap. 1.

27. For Haushofer introducing Hitler to Malthus's work, see Werner Maser, *Hitler's Mein Kampf: An Analysis* (London: Faber and Faber, 1970), 122; and for his reading habits, see Timothy Ryback, *Hitler's Private Library: The Books That Shaped His Life* (New York: Knopf, 2008). Hitler's Malthusian notes are reproduced and translated in Werner Masur, *Hitler's Letters and Notes* (London: Heinemann, 1974), 262–265. Adolf Hitler, *Mein Kampf*, trans. James Murphy (London: Hurst and Blackett, 1939), 122. Masur, *Hitler's Mein Kampf*, 124.

28. This paragraph is based on information in Götz Aly and Karl Heinz Roth, *The Nazi Census: Identification and Control in the Third Reich* (Philadelphia: Temple University Press, 2004), 2 (for total registration and Zahn's comment); 96 (useless eaters); 87–88 (for Arlt); and 98 (for Brandt's calculations). The 1940 paper on Jewry is cited from Götz Aly, *"Final Solution": Nazi Population Policy and the Murder of the European Jews* (London: Edward Arnold, 1999), 114–115. For the East as "elbow room" and its forced remodeling as a landscape, see David Blackbourn, *The Conquest of Nature: Water, Landscape and the Making of Modern Germany* (London: Pimlico, 2007), 238–296, quote at 273.

29. Chase, *Legacy of Malthus*, 84.

8. Malthus the Transatlantic Celebrity

1. Michael H. Hart, *The 100: A Ranking of the Most Influential Persons in History*, rev. ed. (New York: Simon Schuster, 1992), 395–398.

2. John McNeill, *Something New under the Sun: An Environmental History of the Twentieth Century* (London: Penguin, 2000), 9. For data explosion, see Björn-Ola Linnér, *The Return of Malthus: Environmentalism and Post-War Population-Resource Crises* (Isle of Harris: White Horse Press, 2003), 146.

3. "Malthus: A Realist Proved Right," *Times* (London), 11 February 1966, 13; "Bangladesh Bears out Malthus's Prophecy," *Times* (London), 5 November 1974, 7; "The Extraordinary Prospect of a Brave New World," *Times* (London), 24 October 1975, 16; "Malthus Refuted," *Times* (London), 8 March 1978, 1. Figures for population-based stories in the United States and sample headlines are found in Donald T. Critchlow, *Intended Consequences: Birth Control, Abortion, and the Federal Government in Modern America* (New York: Oxford University Press, 1999), 247n7. Figures for news releases from Population Reference Bureau in Linner, *Return of Malthus*, 155.

4. V. S. Naipaul, *The Overcrowded Barracoon* (Harmondsworth: Penguin, 1972), 277; foreword to Anthony Burgess, *The Wanting Seed* (repr., London: Hamilyn, 1983), unpaginated; *2001: A Space Odyssey* cited in Linner, *Return of Malthus*, 171; Isaac Asimov, *The Stars in Their Courses* (St Albans: Panther, 1975), 199, and compare with his comments in *Earth: Our Crowded Spaceship* (London: Abelard-Schuman, 1974) and *Our Angry Earth* (New York: Tom Doherty, 1991). Others in science fiction made similar connections: Robert Heinlein, in

Stranger in a Strange Land, full edition (1961; London: New English Library, 1991), 54, in a vein closely aped from *Brave New World,* alluded to contraception by discussing "Malthusian lozenges," while William F. Nolan and George Clayton Johnson's *Logan's Run* (London: Gollancz, 1969), which achieved fame as a film in 1976, was predicated on a society where, with overpopulation a fact, all had to be executed on reaching twenty-one years old. Malthusian futuristic scenarios were also ventured in Harry Harrison, *Make Room! Make Room!* (Penguin: Harmondsworth, 1967); and Larry Niven and Jerry Pournelle, *The Mote in God's Eye* (London: Weidenfeld and Nicolson, 1975).

5. J. E. Meade, "Population Explosion, the Standard of Living and Social Conflict," *Economic Journal* 77 (1967): 233–255, quote at 233; Amartya Sen, *Poverty and Famines: An Essay on Entitlement and Deprivation* (Oxford: Oxford University Press, 1981), 174–175 and *Development as Freedom* (Oxford: Oxford University Press, 1999), 204–226. See also Sen's essay "Population: Delusion and Reality," in Michael Cromartie, ed., *The Nine Lives of Population Control* (Grand Rapids, MI: William Eerdmans, 1995), 101–127. Gary S. Becker, *A Treatise on the Family,* enlarged ed. (Cambridge: Harvard University Press, 1991), 2, 19, and 137; Gary S. Becker, *The Economics of Life: From Baseball to Affirmative Action: How Real World Issues Affect our Every Day Life* (New York: McGraw-Hill, 1997), 287–294. For Myrdal's concern about population decline, see Gunnar and Alva Myrdal's 1934 *Crisis in the Population Question,* while his Malthusian concern about Asia is in *Asian Drama: An Inquiry into the Poverty of Nations* (New York: Pantheon, 1968), 1480–1495, and the quote is from 1530. F. A. Hayek, *The Fatal Conceit: The Errors of Socialism* (London: Routledge, 1988), 122. Other distinguished economists who engaged with Malthus include W. W. Rostow, *The Stages of Economic Growth: A Non-Communist Manifesto* (Cambridge: Cambridge University Press, 1960), 80–81; and *The Great Population Spike and After: Reflections on the 21st Century* (New York: Oxford University Press, 1998); and J. K. Galbraith, *The Affluent Society,* 3rd ed. (Penguin: Harmondsworth, 1979), 49.

6. C. P. Snow, *The State of Siege* (New York: Charles Scribner's Sons, 1969), 19, 39–40, and 43. For Snow's context, see Stefan Collini, *Absent Minds: Intellectuals in Britain* (Oxford: Oxford University Press, 2006), 451–472. Bertrand Russell, "Population Pressure and War," in Stuart Mudd, ed., *The Population Crisis and the Use of World Resources* (The Hague: W Junk, 1964), 1–5 at 1. For Sartre, see Linner, *Return of Malthus,* 156, who also mentions Van Der Post (43). Odum's Malthusianism is discussed in Thomas Robertson, *The Malthusian Moment: Global Population Growth and the Birth of American Environmentalism* (New Brunswick, NJ: Rutgers University Press, 2012), 53; see also Robert MacArthur and Edward Wilson, *The Theory of Island Biogeography* (Princeton: Princeton University Press, 1967). André Maurois, "The Good Life," in Fairfield Osborn, ed., *Our Crowded Planet: Essays on the Pressures of Population* (London: George Allen and Unwin, 1963), 175–179; E. P. Thompson, *The Making of the English Working*

Class (London: Victor Gollancz, 1963); David Harvey, "Population, Resources and the Ideology of Science," *Economic Geography* 50 (1974): 256–277; Michel Foucault, *Security, Territory, Population: Lectures at the Collège de France, 1977–1978,* ed. Michel Senellart (London: Palgrave, 2007), 55–86; Michel Foucault, *The History of Sexuality: An Introduction* (Harmondsworth: Penguin, 1979), 105.

7. Thomas Robert Malthus, *An Essay on the Principle of Population* ed. Michael Fogerty (London: Dent, 1958), 1:vi; Thomas Robert Malthus, *Population: The First Essay,* ed. Kenneth E. Boulding (Ann Arbor: University of Michigan Press, 1959), v; Thomas Robert Malthus, *An Essay on the Principle of Population,* ed. A. G. N. Flew (Harmondsworth: Penguin, 1970); Thomas Robert Malthus, *An Essay on the Principle of Population: Text, Background, Contemporary Opinion, Critical Essays,* ed. Philip Appleman (New York: Norton, 1976).

8. The exact question of why there was an explosion of interest in Malthus has been canvassed in Robertson, *Malthusian Moment;* Ronald W. Greene, *Malthusian Worlds: U.S. Leadership and the Governing of the Population Crisis* (Boulder, CO: Westview Press, 1999); Linner, *Return of Malthus;* and Derek S. Hoff, *The State and the Stork: The Population Debate and Policy Making in US History* (Chicago: University of Chicago Press, 2012). I am indebted to these studies in what follows.

9. For early American responses to Malthus, see Hoff, *State and Stork;* James Russell Gibson, *Americans versus Malthus: The Population Debate in the Early Republic, 1790–1840* (New York: Garland, 1989). On the civil war, see Dennis Hodgson, "Malthus's *Essay on Population* and the American Debate over Slavery," *Comparative Studies in Society and History* 51 (2009): 742–770. The frontier hypothesis and its culture are discussed in Stephen Kern, *The Culture of Time and Space, 1880–1918* (Cambridge: Harvard University Press, 2003). For Roosevelt and conservation, see the texts in David Stradling, ed., *Conservation in the Progressive Era: Classic Texts* (Seattle: University of Washington Press, 2004). Pearl, East, and Thompson are discussed in Robertson, *Malthusian Moment,* chap. 1; quote from Raymond Pearl, *The Biology of Population Growth* (New York: Knopf, 1925), 1. Robertson, *Malthusian Moment,* 20, notes East reading Malthus, while East himself is cited from Edward M. East, *Mankind at the Crossroads* (New York: Charles Scribner's Sons, 1925), 7 and 299. For "population–national security theory," see John Perkins, *Geopolitics and the Green Revolution: Wheat, Genes, and the Cold War* (New York: Oxford University Press, 1997), 119.

10. Robertson, *Malthusian Moment,* 36, in which *Time* is also cited, as is the *Economist* headline (242n1). The *New York Times* is cited from Kolson Schlosser, "Malthus at Mid-Century: Neo-Malthusianism as Bio-Political Governance in the Post World War II United States," *Cultural Geographies* 16 (2009): 465–484 at 471.

11. For the translation and serialization of *The Road to Survival,* see Pierre Desrochers and Christine Hoffbauer, "The Post War Intellectual Roots of the Population Bomb: Fairfield Osborn's 'Our Plundered Planet' and William

Vogt's 'Road to Survival' in Retrospect," *Electronic Journal of Sustainable Development* 1 (2009): 73–97 at 75; and Linner, *Return of Malthus,* 36–37. William Vogt, *Road to Survival* (London: Victor Gollancz, 1949), 32, unpaginated preface to the English edition, 71, 72, 31, 275, and 285.

12. Desrochers and Hoffbauer, "Post War Intellectual Roots," 75 and 77; Fairfield Osborn, *Our Plundered Planet* (New York: Pyramid Books, 1968), 9, 43, 44, and 158.

13. See Greene, *Malthusian Worlds,* 124 for Hugh Moore's pamphlet; Karl Sax, *Standing Room Only: The World's Exploding Population* (Boston: Beacon Press, 1960), xviii (see 189–192 for Catholics and Communists); and Philip Appleman, *The Silent Explosion* (Boston: Beacon Press, 1965), vii, 3, and 8.

14. Aldous Huxley, *Brave New World Revisited* (repr., London: Grafton, 1983), 19, and 24. His endorsement of *Our Plundered Planet* is on the back cover of the 1968 reprint. For the *New Yorker* interview, see Nicholas Murray, *Aldous Huxley: An English Intellectual* (London: Little, Brown, 2002), 370. Julian Huxley, *Memories 2* (Harmondsworth: Penguin, 1978), 30, 54, and 134; Julian Huxley, *Essays of a Humanist* (repr., Harmondsworth: Penguin, 1966), 243. For Julian Huxley at UNESCO, see Richard Symonds and Michael Carter, *The United Nations and the Population Question, 1945–1970* (New York: McGraw-Hill, 1973), 53–55.

15. For Truman, see Perkins, *Geopolitics,* 144–145; and Nick Cullather, *The Hungry World: America's Cold War Battle against Poverty in Asia* (Cambridge: Harvard University Press, 2010), 43–71, who styles this a blueprint at 45. Borlaug is cited from Cullather, *Hungry World,* 245, while the Draper Report is discussed in Peter J. Donaldson, *Nature against Us: The United States and the World Population Crisis, 1965–1980* (Chapel Hill: University of North Carolina Press, 1990), 23. Hoff, *State and Stork,* 146, dubs this the "Magna Carta." Johnson's State of the Union address is cited in Greene, *Malthusian Worlds,* 85 and 79. Robertson, *Malthusian Moment,* 101, notes the *New York Times* article.

16. My reading of the Indian famine of 1966–1967 is taken from Cullather, *Hungry World,* whence come the quotations about the Kremlin's pawns (136), Johnson's race (222), Imagineering (230), and an invented brush with Malthus (231). For the Great Chinese famine, see Frank Dikötter, *Mao's Great Famine: The History of China's Most Devastating Catastrophe, 1958–1962* (New York: Walker, 2010) from where comes the information about Mao's new war (174); how he lost that war (188); and the estimation of total fatalities (325). For the attack on Malthus and Ma Yinchu, see Judith Shapiro, *Mao's War against Nature: Politics and the Environment in Revolutionary China* (Cambridge: Cambridge University Press, 2001), 21–48, whence Mao is cited (31), and the family name issue comes (43).

17. On Earth Day, see McNeill, *Something New,* 539; and Adam Rome, *The Genius of Earth Day: How a 1970 Teach-In Unexpectedly Made the First Green Generation* (New York: Hill and Wang, 2013). The "Stop at Two" balloons were reported in the *New York Times* on 23 April, for which see Bill

McKibben, ed., *American Earth: Environmental Writing since Thoreau* (New York: Library of America, 2008), 485, which also reprints Mills's graduation speech (quote from 469). For the "Earthrise" image as iconic, see Denis Cosgrove, *Apollo's Eye: A Cartographic Genealogy of the Earth in the Western Imagination* (Baltimore: Johns Hopkins University Press, 2001). For sterilizing people via water, see Critchlow, *Intended Consequences,* 155–156.

18. For Ehrlich's vasectomy, see John Tierney, "Betting in the Planet," first published 2 December 1990 in the *New York Times,* and accessed at www.ny times.com/1990/12/02/magazine/betting-on-the-planet.html?pagewanted=all &src=pm. For the publication history and impact of *The Population Bomb,* see Paul R. Ehrlich and Anne H. Ehrlich, "The Population Bomb revisited," *Electronic Journal of Sustainable Development* 1 (2009): 5–13; and Paul R. Ehrlich, "Population, Environment, War and Racism: Adventures of a Public Scholar" *Antipode* 40 (2008): 383–388. The book being the most influential on population since Malthus is a claim made by Hoff, *State and Stork,* 165. Sales figures for the book are from Desrochers and Hoffbauer, "Post War Intellectual Roots," 73. For Ehrlich's rock star appeal, see Robertson, *Malthusian Moment,* 162. The quotes are taken from Paul Ehrlich, *The Population Bomb,* rev. ed. (New York: Ballantine, 1971), xi, 1, and 2. The discussion of Ehrlich's willingness to be termed a neo-Malthusian and the reasons why Malthus himself never appeared in his text are from an e-mail exchange between Ehrlich and the present author, 24–25 May 2012. For later works mentioning Malthus, see Paul Ehrlich and Richard Harriman, *How to Be a Survivor: A Plan to Save Spaceship Earth* (New York: Ballantine, 1971), 39; and Paul Ehrlich and Anne Ehrlich, *The Population Explosion* (London: Hutchinson, 1990), 6 and 168.

19. See Barry Commoner, *The Closing Circle: Confronting the Environmental Crisis* (London: Jonathan Cape, 1972), 125–139; see also Michael Egan, *Barry Commoner and the Science of Survival: The Remaking of American Environmentalism* (Cambridge: MIT Press, 2007). The key writings in ecological economics of Boulding and Daly are conveniently reprinted in Herman Daly and Kenneth Townsend, eds., *Valuing the Earth: Economics, Ecology, Ethics* (Cambridge: MIT Press, 1993). For the *Limits to Growth* as a Malthusian ghost in the machine, see Greene, *Malthusian Worlds,* 190. For the *Limits*'s litany, see Donella Meadows, Dennis Meadows, Jørgen Randers and William Behrens, *The Limits to Growth* (London: Earth Island, 1972), 171.

20. For Borgstrom as Cassandra or alarm clock, see Linner, *Return of Malthus,* 62 and 83, who also notes his translation of Malthus into Swedish (173) and the translations of *Hungry Planet* (156). Direct quotes are from Georg Borgstrom, *The Hungry Planet: The Modern World at the Edge of Famine* (New York: Macmillan, 1965), xiv, 305, and 454; and Georg Borgstrom, *Too Many: A Study of the Earth's Biological Limitations* (New York: Macmillan, 1969), 277.

21. Garrett Hardin, ed., *Population, Evolution, and Birth Control: A Collage of Controversial Ideas* (San Francisco: Freeman, 1964). Garrett Hardin, "The

Tragedy of the Commons" *Science* 162 (1968): 1243–1248; Garrett Hardin, *Exploring New Ethics for Survival: The Voyage of Spaceship Beagle* (New York: Viking, 1972), 7, and 223–224; Garrett Hardin, "Interstellar Migration and the Population Problem," *Journal of Heredity* 50 (1959): 68–70. For other neo-Malthusian science fiction, see Paul Ehrlich's pamphlet *Eco-Catastrophe!* (San Francisco: City Lights, 1969) and the material collected by the Zero Population Growth pressure group: Rob Sauer, ed., *Voyages: Scenarios for a Ship Called Earth* (New York: Ballantine, 1971), which features a foreword by Stephanie Mills, whose graduation speech we have already encountered.

22. William and Paul Paddock, *Time of Famines: America and the World Food Crisis* (Boston: Little, Brown, 1975), 7–9, 39, and 205ff. For the Draper Report on triage, see Donaldson, *Nature against Us,* 23. The Wilderness Act is cited from McKibben, *American Earth,* 342–343. For the introduction of the right to abortion, see Critchlow, *Intended Consequences,* 3; and for the Gruening hearings, see Greene, *Malthusian Worlds,* 85ff. Johnson is cited from Robertson, *Malthusian Moment,* 1, who also cites Nixon (85) and Carter (201). For Nixon's act, see David Stradling, ed., *The Environmental Movement, 1968–1972* (Seattle: University of Washington Press, 2012), 65.

23. *Malthus and America: A Report about Food and People* (Washington, DC: U.S. Government Printing Office, 1974), 9, 15, 4, 5, 1, and 2. For food shortages in 1974/1975, see Linner, *Return of Malthus,* 188.

24. For Notestein, see Daniel Callahan, ed., *The American Population Debate* (New York: Doubleday, 1971), 33 and 31, from where is also drawn Wattenberg's "nonsense explosion" (96–109). For Maddox, see Stradling, *Environmental Movement,* 131.

25. Earl Parker Hanson, *New Worlds Emerging* (London: Victor Gollancz, 1950), x–xi, 12, and 369; John Boyd Orr, *The White Man's Dilemma,* rev. ed. (London: George Allen and Unwin, 1964), foreword and 47. See also for Boyd Orr, Ruth Jachertz and Alexander Nützendahl, "Coping with Hunger? Visions of a Global Food System, 1930–1960" *Journal of Global History* 6 (2011): 99–119.

26. Ester Boserup, *My Professional Life and Publications, 1929–1998* (Copenhagen: Museum Tusculanum Press, 1999), 15 and 17–18. Ester Boserup, *The Conditions of Agricultural Growth: The Economics of Agrarian Change under Population Pressure* (London: George Allen and Unwin, 1965), 11. Thomas Robert Malthus, *An Essay on the Principle of Population* in E. A. Wrigley and David Souden, eds., *The Works of Thomas Robert Malthus* (London: Pickering and Chatto, 1986), 125.

27. Buckminster Fuller, *Operating Manual for Spaceship Earth* (1969; Baden: Lars Müller, 2008), 47, from where also comes fossil fuels as self-starter (128–130) and population explosion as myth (136). For "more with lessing," see R. Buckminster Fuller, *Utopia or Oblivion: The Prospects for Humanity* (Harmondsworth: Penguin, 1970), 269, which also discusses his optimistic models of world futures at 182–188. A more informed critique of Malthu-

sian computer models was offered in H. S. D Cole et al., *Models of Doom: A Critique of the Limits to Growth* (New York: Universe, 1973).

28. Julian Simon, *A Life against the Grain: The Autobiography of an Unconventional Economist* (New Brunswick: Transactions, 2002), 238; Julian Simon, *The Ultimate Resource* (Princeton: Princeton University Press, 1981), 158 and 9. Note that Simon's posthumous autobiographical *Life* lifts large excerpts from *The Ultimate Resource*.

29. Julian Simon, *The Economics of Population Growth* (Princeton: Princeton University Press, 1977), 4 and 6; Simon, *Ultimate Resource*, 177, 42, 218, and 49–50.

30. Simon, *Ultimate Resource*, 10.

31. For Simon's fame, see Paul Aligica, "Julian Simon and the 'Limits to Growth' Neo-Malthusianism," *Electronic Journal of Sustainable Development* 1 (2009): 49–60 at 49. For Reagan's 1971 speech, see Stradling, *Environmental Movement*, 114–118; and for his administration on population growth as neutral, see Dennis Hodgson, "Orthodoxy and Revisionism in American Demography," *Population and Development Review* 14 (1986): 541–569 at 560. For Buckley taking the same journey as regards population, see Robertson, *Malthusian Moment*, 163. A DVD of the William Buckley interview of Julian Simon is still available today, having been released in 2010 by Southern Educational Communications Association. The text is available in Julian Simon and William F. Buckley Jr., "Answer to Malthus? Julian Simon Interviewed by William Buckley," *Population and Development Review* 8 (1982): 205–218, quote at 213.

32. For the saga leading to the publication of Simon's essay, see Simon, *Life*, 266–267. Julian Simon, "Resources, Population, Environment: An Oversupply of False Bad News," *Science* 208 (1980): 1431–1437, quotes at 1432, 1433, and 1434.

33. For the publication bomb, see Simon, *Life*, 266. The brickbats feature on the dust jacket to Julian Simon, *Population Matters: People, Resources, Environment and Immigration* (New Brunswick: Transaction, 1990). Steve Singer et al., "Bad News: Is It True?," *Science* 210 (1980): 1296–1308, with the response of Holdren, Ehrlich, Ehrlich and Harte at 1296, 1298, 1301. Simon's response was at 1305, 1306, and 1308. For Ehrlich's private response to Simon's *Science* essay, see Tierney, "Betting," 1.

34. Paul R. Ehrlich, "Environmental Disruption: Implications for the Social Sciences," *Social Science Quarterly* 62 (1981): 7–22, quoted from 7 and 12, sparked the response in Julian Simon, "Environmental Disruption or Environmental Improvement," *Social Science Quarterly* 62 (1981): 30–43, quote from 30, with the offer of a bet at 39. Ehrlich responded to Simon in "An Economist in Wonderland," *Social Science Quarterly* 62 (1981): 45–49, with the "moronic" tag at 48 and the acceptance of a wager at 46. The further exchanges to agree terms for the bet are detailed in Julian Simon, "Paul Ehrlich Saying It is So Doesn't Make It So," *Social Science Quarterly* 63 (1982): 381–385; Paul Ehrlich, "That's Right—You Should Check It for Yourself,"

Social Science Quarterly 63 (1982): 385–387; and Simon, *Population Matters*, 374–375. The final quote in the paragraph is from Tierney, "Betting," 1.

35. The Hardin-Simon debate is reprinted in Simon, *Population Matters*, 381–404, quotes at 396 and 397.

36. Garrett Hardin, *Living within Limits: Ecology, Economics, and Population Taboos* (New York: Oxford University Press, 1993), 305; Garrett Hardin, *The Ostrich Factor: Our Population Myopia* (New York: Oxford University Press, 1998), 102–103. For being overoptimistic, see Donella Meadows, Jorgen Randers, and Dennis Meadows, *Limits to Growth: The 30 Year Update* (White River Junction, VT: Chelsea Green, 2004), xvi; and Ehrlich and Ehrlich, "Population Bomb Revisited," 8.

37. For Earth Day 1990, see McNeill, *Something New under the Sun*, 539. For Simon's and Ehrlich's contrasting fortunes on that day, see Tierney, "Betting," 4. The Ehrlichs' account of the bet and of proposed successor bets is in Paul Ehrlich and Anne Ehrlich, *The Betrayal of Science and Reason* (Washington, DC: Island Press, 1996), 100–104. Paul Ehrlich's immediate reaction is quoted from Tierney, "Betting," 5. For scholarly analysis of the bet, see Katherine Keil, Victor Matheson, and Kevin Golembiewski, "Luck or Skill? An Examination of the Ehrlich-Simon Bet," *Ecological Economics* 69 (2010): 1365–1367; and Philip Lawn, "On the Ehrlich-Simon Bet: Both Were Unskilled and Simon Was Lucky," *Ecological Economics* 69 (2010): 2045–2046.

9. Malthus Today

1. G. B. Hill and L. F. Powell, eds., *Boswell's Life of Johnson* (Oxford: Oxford University Press, 1934–50), 1:463.

2. Geoffrey McNicoll, "Malthus for the Twenty-First Century," *Population and Development Review* 24 (1998): 309–316, at 309. I am indebted to Simon Winder at Penguin for information about sales figures on the Penguin Classics edition of the *Essay*. Bill McKibben, *Maybe One: A Personal and Environmental Argument for Very Small Families* (London: Anchor, 1998), 80.

3. John F. May, *World Population Policies: Their Origin, Evolution and Impact* (Dordrecht: Springer, 2012), 14 and 108; Fred Pearce, *Peoplequake: Mass Migration, Ageing Nations and the Coming Population Crash* (London: Eden Project, 2010), 293. For declining spending on family planning, see Hania Zlotnik, "Does Population Matter for Climate Change?," in José Guzmán et al., eds., *Population Dynamics and Climate Change* (New York: United Nations Population Fund, 2009), 31–44 at 33–34.

4. McNicoll, "Malthus," 315; McKibben, *Maybe One*, 81, 11, and 95; Jane Lubchenco, "Entering the Century of the Environment: A New Social Contract for Science," *Science* 279 (1998): 491–497 at 495–496 and 493–494; Anne Pebley, "Demography and the Environment," *Demography* 35 (1998): 377–389, at 377 and 386.

5. David Attenborough, "This Heaving Planet," *New Statesman*, 27 April 2011 can be found at www.newstatesman.com/environment/2011/04/human-population-essay-food (quote from p. 3 of the online edition). Paul Demeny

and Geoffrey McNicoll, "The Political Demography of the World System, 2000–2050," *Population and Development Review* 32 (2006): 254–287 at 255 for 99 percent of growth in developing nations. For the Malthusian train crash, see George D. Moffett, *Critical Masses: The Global Population Challenge* (Harmondsworth: Penguin, 1994), 68; a similar formulation is offered in James A. Brander, "Viewpoint: Sustainability: Malthus Revisited?" *Canadian Journal of Economics* 40 (2007): 1–38 at 19. For demographic hot spots, see May, *World Population Policies*, 38–39; and Paul Demeny, "Population Policy Dilemmas in Europe at the Dawn of the Twenty-First Century," *Population and Development Review* 29 (2003): 1–28 at 9.

6. For European intrinsic growth rates, see Demeny, "Population Policy Dilemmas," 3, which also discusses the Russian example (7). Putin is cited from Peace, *Peoplequake*, 124, which is also the source for the "demographic black hole" (115) and "civilizations melting away" (123). For Europe's future as a theme park, see Demeny and McNicoll, "Political Demography," 272–273; and Vaclav Smil, *Global Catastrophes and Trends: The Next Fifty Years* (Cambridge: MIT Press, 2008), 102.

7. Demeny and McNicoll, "Political Demography," 280; Joel Cohen, "Human Population Grows Up," in Laurie Mazur, ed., *A Pivotal Moment: Population, Justice & The Environmental Challenge* (Washington, DC: Island Press, 2010), 27–37 at 27.

8. McKibben, *Maybe One,* 97 and 98. For population momentum, see May, *World Population Policies,* 14 and 28. For the water and land needed to feed this momentum, see J. R. McNeill, "Population and the Natural Environment: Trends and Challenges," *Population and Development Review* 32 (2006): 183–201 at 186–187.

9. Paul Ehrlich and John Holdren, "Impact of Population Growth," *Science* 171 (1971): 1212–1217; Bert Metz et al., *Climate Change 2007: Mitigation of Climate Change* (Cambridge: Cambridge University Press, 2007), 107. For the IPCC underplaying population, see Brian O'Neill, "Climate Change and Population Growth," in Laurie Mazur, ed., *A Pivotal Moment: Population, Justice & the Environmental Challenge* (Washington, D.C.: Island Press, 2010), 81–94 at 91, whence also comes the information about urbanization (83–84) and the impact of stabilizing population at 8 billion (91–92). See also Brian O'Neill, F. Landis MacKellar, and Wolfgang Lutz, *Population and Climate Change* (Cambridge: Cambridge University Press, 2001). For 7 percent making 50 percent of greenhouse gas, see Pearce, *Peoplequake,* 242, but for the greater proportional impact of population growth on other issues, see Paul Harrison, *The Third Revolution: Population, Environment and a Sustainable World* (Harmondsworth: Penguin, 1992), 242.

10. Joel Cohen, *How Many People Can the Earth Support?* (New York: Norton, 1999), 386; Bjørn Lomborg, *The Skeptical Environmentalist: Measuring the Real State of the World* (Cambridge: Cambridge University Press, 2001), vii, 34, and 60. Robert Bradley Jr., "President Obama's Malthusian New Deal; Recovery Not," *Forbes Magazine,* 28 May 2012, which can be found at: www .forbes.com/sites/robertbradley/2012/05/28/president-obamas-malthusian

-new-deal-recovery-not/. Robert Zubrin, *Merchants of Despair: Radical Environmentalists, Criminal Pseudo-Scientists and the Fatal Cult of Antihumanism* (New York: Encounter, 2012), 5, the start of a chapter entitled "Thomas Malthus: The Most Dismal Scientist."

11. Goldstone's connections with the U.S. government are taken from his author blurb in Jack A. Goldstone, "Flash Points and Tipping Points: Security Implications of Global Population Changes," *Environmental Change and Security Programme* 13 (2008–2009), 2–9. Jack Goldstone, "The New Population Bomb: The Four Megatrends That Will Change the World," *Foreign Affairs* 89 (2010): 31–43, quotes at 31 and 32.

12. Jessica Matthews, "Redefining Security," *Foreign Affairs* 68 (1989): 162–177. Richard Cincotta, Robert Engelman and Daniele Anastasion, *The Security Demographic: Population and Civil Conflict after the Cold War* (Washington D.C.: Population Action International, 2003). See also the essays in Jack A. Goldstone, Eric Kaufmann, and Monica Duffy Toft, *Political Demography: How Population Changes are Reshaping International Security and National Politics* (New York: Oxford University Press, 2012), which arrived too late to be used in this study but which does again discuss both Malthus and new Malthusian checks in our own age. A significant proportion of the contributors to the discourse of security demographics have advisory affiliations with the U.S. government and assorted lobby groups.

13. Cincotta, *Security Demographic*, 13. Valerie Hudson and Andrea den Boer, *Bare Branches: The Security Implications of Asia's Surplus Male Population* (Cambridge: MIT Press, 2004). For the positive spin on aging populations, see Ben Wattenberg, *Fewer: How the New Demography of Depopulation will Shape our Future* (Lanham, MD: Ivan R Dee, 2005); and for concerns, see Pearce, *Peoplequake*; and May, *World Population Policies*, 181.

14. Demeny, "Population Policy Dilemmas," 12 and 20.

15. Thomas Homer-Dixon, *The Upside of Down: Catastrophe, Creativity and the Renewal of Civilisation* (London: Souvenir Press, 2006), 75. For Malthustans, see Betsy Hartmann, "Will the Circle Be Unbroken? A Critique of the Project on Environment, Population and Security," in Nancy Lee Peluso and Michael Watts, eds., *Violent Environments* (Ithaca, NY: Cornell University Press, 2001), 39–62 at 53. Cincotta, *Security Demographic*, 13 and 73–74.

16. For the Malthusian slant, see Brander, "Viewpoint," 26. Jared Diamond, *Collapse: How Societies Choose to Fail or Survive* (London: Penguin, 2005), 526 (Ehrlich), 311, 312–313, 6 and 494–496. For Warren Christopher, see Betsy Hartmann, "Population, Environment and Security: A New Trinity," *Environment and Urbanization* 10 (1998): 113–127 at 123. For other readings of Rwanda, see Christopher Taylor, "Rwandan Genocide: Toward an Explanation in Which History and Culture Matter," in Patricia A. McAnany and Norman Yoffee, eds., *Questioning Collapse: Human Resilience, Ecological Vulnerability, and the Aftermath of Empire* (Cambridge: Cambridge University Press, 2010), 239–268. This collection more generally scrutinizes the worth of Diamond's collapse thesis. For the idea of a "demographic dividend," see

Nancy Birdsall, Allan C. Kelley, and Steven Sinding, eds., *Population Matters: Demographic Change, Economic Growth and Poverty in the Developing World* (Oxford: Oxford University Press, 2001). For critique of Malthusian readings of contemporary immigration, see Ian Angus and Simon Butler, *Too Many People? Population, Immigration and Environmental Crisis* (Chicago: Haymarket, 2011).

17. Vaclav Smil, *Feeding the World: A Challenge for the Twenty-First Century* (Cambridge: MIT Press, 2000); Julian Cribb, *The Coming Famine: The Global Food Crisis and What We Can Do to Avoid It* (Berkeley: University of California Press, 2010); Gordon Conway, *One Billion Hungry: Can We Feed the World?* (Ithaca, NY: Cornell University Press, 2012). For the Malthus lecture, see www.prb.org/EventsTraining/Malthus%20Lectures.aspx.

18. For varied estimates of the number of countries seeing food riots, see Pearce, *Peoplequake*, 250; Cribb, *Coming Famine*, 4; and Cullen Hendrix, "Markets vs Malthus: Food Security and the Global Economy," *Peterson Institute for International Economics Policy Brief* (2001), 1. Niall Ferguson, "Don't Count out Malthus," *Los Angeles Times*, 30 July 2007. Michael Schuman, "A Future of Price Spikes," *Time*, 14 July 2011. For Stiglitz, see Justin Lahart, Patrick Barta, and Andrew Batson, "New Limits to Growth Revive Malthusian Fears," *Wall Street Journal*, 24 March 2008; Paul Krugman, "We Are Wrong to Overlook the Food Crisis," speech to Momoagri (Mouvement Pour Une Organisation Mondiale de L'Agriculture), 20 April 2009, which can be found at: www.momagri.org/UK/points-of-view/For-Paul-Krugman-We-Are-Wrong -to-Overlook-the-Food-Crisis_479.html.

19. Pearce, *Peoplequake*, 252, sees the problem as consumption. The free-market reading of the price spike as caused by WTO rules is from Hendrix, "Markets vs Malthus," 3. For landgrabbing, see Fred Pearce, *The Landgrabbers: The New Fight over Who Owns the Earth* (London: Eden Project, 2012), 343 for specter; and ix for estimates of the hectares of land involved.

20. Simon Dalby, *Security and Environmental Change* (Cambridge: Polity Press, 2009), 15.

21. Estimates of increased malnourishment due to climate change and of the increased mortality it will cause come from Martin Parry et al., *Climate Change 2007: Impacts, Adaptation and Vulnerability* (Cambridge: Cambridge University Press, 2007), chaps. 5 and 8. For estimates of environmental refugees, see Cecilia Tacoli, "Crisis or Adaptation? Migration and Climate Change in a Context of High Mobility," in José Guzmán et al., eds., *Population Dynamics and Climate Change* (New York: United Nations Population Fund, 2009), 104–118 at 104.

22. Thomas Homer-Dixon, "On the Threshold: Environmental Changes as Causes of Acute Conflict," *International Security* 16 (1991): 76–116 at 104 and 100.

23. For Clinton's comment, see Hartmann, "Population, Environment and Security," 121. For Kaplan's importance, see Dalby, *Security*, 25–26. Robert Kaplan, "The Coming Anarchy: How Scarcity, Crime, Overpopulation, Tribalism, and Disease Are Rapidly Destroying the Social Fabric of Our Planet," *Atlantic*

Monthly, February 1994, which can be found at: www.theatlantic.com/mag
azine/archive/1994/02/the-coming-anarchy/304670/ (quotes from the online
version at 1 and 3). For copies being sent to all U.S. embassies, see Nancy Lee
Peluso and Michael Watts, "Violent Environments," in Nancy Lee Peluso and
Michael Watts, eds., *Violent Environments* (Ithaca, NY: Cornell University
Press, 2001), 3–38 at 4. For Kaplan's continued engagement with Malthus as
a scholar once mocked but now "getting more respect" as an anatomist of
modern woes, see Robert D. Kaplan, *The Revenge of Geography: What the
Map Tells us about Coming Conflicts and the Battle against Fate* (New York:
Random House, 2012), 119–120.

24. See Henrik Urdal, "People vs Malthus: Population Pressure, Environmental
Degradation and Armed Conflict Revisited," *Journal of Peace Research* 42
(2005): 417–434; and Clionadh Raleigh and Henrik Urdal, "Climate
Change, Demography, Environmental Degradation and Armed Conflict,"
Environmental Change and Security Programme 13 (2008–9): 27–33 for
statistical refutations of the Homer-Dixon argument. The "greening of hate"
is from Hartmann, "Population, Environment and Security," 120. For the
National Defence Strategy, see Jennifer Dabbs Sciubba, "Population in Defence Policy Planning," *Environmental Change and Security Programme* 13
(2008–9): 19–26 at 26 and see also Jennifer Dabbs Sciubba, *The Future
Faces of War: Population and National Security* (Santa Barbara, CA: Prae-
ger Press, 2011).

25. John Maynard Keynes, "Robert Malthus: A Centenary Allocution," in *The
Collected Writings of John Maynard Keynes,* vol. 10, *Essays in Biography*
(London: Macmillan, 1972), 104–108 at 108.

26. The Economist, *Megachange: The World in 2050* (London: Profile,
2012), 20.

27. John Gray, *Straw Dogs: Thoughts on Humans and Other Animals* (London:
Granta, 2002), 10, 181, and 180. See also John Gray, *Gray's Anatomy: Selected Writings* (London: Penguin, 2009), 14 and 221.

28. Beddington's speech is quoted from the online version, which can be accessed
at: www.govnet.co.uk/news/govnet/professor-sir-john-beddingtons-speech-at
-sduk-09. A formalized version of his argument was offered in John Beddington, "Food, Energy, Water and the Climate: A Perfect Storm of Global Events?,"
which can be accessed at: www.bis.gov.uk/assets/goscience/docs/p/perfect
-storm-paper.pdf.

29. Jeffrey Sachs, *The End of Poverty: How We Can Make It Happen in our
Lifetime* (London: Penguin, 2005), 358, 349, and 347. Al Gore, *The Earth in
Balance: Forging a New Common Purpose* (London: Earthscan, 2007), 127
and 295–360; cf. Al Gore, *The Future* (London: W. H. Allen, 2013), 144 and
150. Jeffrey Sachs, "Are Malthus's Predicted 1798 Food Shortages Coming
True?," *Scientific American,* 25 August 2008, which can be found at: www
.scientificamerican.com/article.cfm?id=are-malthus-predicted-1798-food
-shortages. Jeffrey Sachs, *Common Wealth: Economics for a Crowded Planet*
(London: Penguin, 2008).

30. Sachs, "Malthus's Predicted Shortages."

Epilogue

1. Information about the "Day of the Seven Billion" can be found on Wikipedia at: http://en.wikipedia.org/wiki/Day_of_Seven_Billion. Lara Hoffmans, "7 Billion Reasons Malthus Was Wrong," *Forbes*, 31 October 2011, which can be found at: www.forbes.com/sites/larahoffmans/2011/10/31/7-billion-reasons -malthus-was-wrong/. Edward Hadas, "7 Billion Reasons Why Malthus Was Wrong," *Reuters, Edition UK*, 2 November 2011, which can be found at: http://blogs.reuters.com/edward-hadas/2011/11/02/7-billion-reasons-why -malthus-was-wrong/. The claims that Malthus asserted that women have as many children as possible and that he argued without reasons come from the *Reuters* article. For Malthus underestimating human inventiveness, see Paul Vallely, "Population Panic Is the Rich World's Folly," *Independent*, 30 October 2011, which can be found at: www.independent.co.uk/voices/commen-tators/paul-vallely-population-panic-is-the-rich-worlds-folly-2377759.html ?origin=internalSearch. Malthus was also invoked at this moment in Clive Cookson, "Welcome, Number Seven Billion," *Financial Times*, 19 September 2011.

2. David Usborne, "Return of the Dustbowl," *Independent*, 11 August 2012; Geoffrey Lean, "No Rain Dance Can End This Blight," *Daily Telegraph*, 27 July 2012, which argues for a new age of scarcity.

3. Daniel Knowles, "If the Birth Rate Falls Again, We're in Serious Trouble," *Daily Telegraph*, 12 April 2012.

4. Frank Kermode, *Forms of Attention: Botticelli and Hamlet* (Chicago: University of Chicago Press, 1985); Danny Dorling, *Population 10 Billion: The Coming Demographic Crisis and How to Survive It* (London: Constable, 2013), 112.

Acknowledgments

Having worked previously on prolific writers in the form of Samuel Johnson and the scholar-geographers of the long eighteenth century, it is a relief to work on Malthus who, like myself, was frequently dilatory with his writing and was simultaneously encumbered and enabled by his academic responsibilities. *Malthus* was first conceived and sketched while I was in receipt of a Philip Leverhulme Prize courtesy of the Leverhulme Trust, spending time back in that most congenial of scholarly environments, St John's College, Oxford. The Philip Leverhulme award gave me the time and confidence to build a big project of this ilk. Much of the writing of the book took place during the academic year 2011–2012 thanks to the award of a British Academy/Leverhulme Trust Senior Research Fellowship, without which I doubt this book would ever have been completed. I also owe an enormous debt of gratitude to colleagues at the School of Geographical Sciences at the University of Bristol, both for allowing me to take this Fellowship and for the shared culture of scholarship that pervades. As the audit culture of U.K. academic life increasingly positions the writing of a monograph as outré, an indulgence, or both, it is a great pleasure to work surrounded by people who still see the value of scholarly inquiry.

I am indebted to the following for help at various stages in this project: Simon Cook, for answering queries about Malthus in the work of Alfred Marshall; Paul Ehrlich, for comments on his views on Malthus; Ron Greene, for his selflessness in the Republic of Letters in making available his *Malthusian Worlds* when I could not find an affordable copy in the United Kingdom; Ron Johnston for various prompts and pointers about Malthus's appearances in the modern media; Kelvyn Jones, for advice on modern demographic statistics; Jack Langton, for pointing me in the direction of Samuel Bamford and much else besides; David Livingstone, for constant support in this and other projects; Jose Romanillos, for Nietzsche's Malthusian comments; Yvonne Sherratt, for telling me Malthus would make a good story; Frances Willmoth, for advice on Malthus in the archives at

Jesus College, Cambridge; Simon Winder, for helping me with Malthus's sales figures as a Penguin Classic; Charles Withers, for Malthus in the Murray archive (which will be for another offshoot!) and for constant support; and Tony Wrigley for answering my queries about the emergence of his interest in Malthus. Others who have bolstered me in Malthusian and other projects through the years in which this book was conceived and written include: Jonathan Clark, Felix Driver, Howard Erskine-Hill, Bill Koelsch, Fredrik Jonsson, Karen O'Brien, Miles Ogborn, Richard Powell, and Paul Stock. Peter Robinson at Rogers, Coleridge and White has been a wonderfully supportive agent who believed in this project from the off and provided helpful comments on early drafts. Likewise John Kulka at Harvard saw the value of this project immediately, helped add clarity to the book's ambitions, and helped to weed my prose of at least some of its excesses. Also at Harvard, Heather Hughes has been admirably efficient to work with, as have the copyediting team at Westchester Publishing Services. Finally, this book is for my family.

Index